Edward Shils

THE CONSTITUTION

OF SOCIETY

THE HERITAGE OF SOCIOLOGY

A Series Edited by Morris Janowitz

Edward Shils

THE CONSTITUTION
OF SOCIETY

With a new Introduction by the author

THE UNIVERSITY OF CHICAGO PRESS

CHICAGO AND LONDON

The University of Chicago Press, Chicago 60637
The University of Chicago Press, Ltd., London

89 88 87 86 85 84 83 82   1 2 3 4 5

LIBRARY OF CONGRESS CATALOGING IN PUBLICATION DATA

Shils, Edward Albert, 1911–
    The constitution of society.

    (The Heritage of sociology)
    Essays reprinted from the author's previous
works: The intellectuals and the powers, and other
essays, Center and periphery, and The calling of
sociology and other essays on the pursuit of
learning.
    Contents: The integration of society—Society
and societies—The theory of mass society—
[etc.]
    1. Intellectuals—Addresses, essays, lectures.
2. Sociology—Addresses, essays, lectures.
3. Sociology of knowledge—Addresses, essays,
lectures.   I. Title.   II. Series.
HM213.S49   301   81-16413
ISBN 0-226-75327-1   AACR2

Contents

Introduction

THE ESSAYS in the first three sections of this book are
fragmentary parts of what appears to me to be a coherent general
view of the fundamental constitution of societies as wholes and
of the way in which the higher functions of the mind enter into
that constitution. The essay which makes up the fourth part of
the book may be regarded as a contribution to the historiography
of sociology; it is at the same time, however, one part of the
larger effort represented in the first three sections to understand
in individuals that state of consciousness which includes awareness of a self residing in them, including them, and transcending
them. The first three sections of the book are concerned with the
constitution of society through the formation of an image of the
society in the minds of its members; they deal with the consequences of that formation for the effectiveness of authority
and the maintenance of order in society. The last section is concerned with the intellectual effort to form such an image of
society by deliberate and methodical procedures.

All of these essays have been written within the past quarter of a century. The ideas contained in them were gradually
forming in my mind over the preceding quarter of a century.
These ideas have taken their direction in the course of my association with the University of Chicago which runs now to fifty
years and particularly of my association with Robert Park, Frank
Knight, and Harold Lasswell during the 1930s. For a good part
of the time which has elapsed since that decade, I have been
repeatedly returning to the problems raised in my mind by re-

reading and pondering on the works of Hobbes, Tönnies, and Max Weber in the presence of the ideas of the eminent social scientists whom I had the good fortune to know in Chicago. The education which I have thus been able to acquire has been put to work on the observations which I have made in the course of studying various aspects of Western, Asian, and African societies. These observations have in their turn had a marked influence on what I have developed from the distinguished figures who gave me my point of departure. This collection of essays contains some of the results of these intellectual interactions.

In introducing the eleven essays in this book, I shall try to show the way in which the theme of each particular essay represents a resolution or a differentiating clarification of unresolved or unperceived obscurities of my thought up to the time when I began to work on that essay. It might have been better for this particular purpose to have arranged the essays in the exact chronological order in which they were written. To have done so would, however, have broken the thematic intention of the collection.

It might also have been desirable to place each essay or set of essays into the setting of the body of sociological analysis as a whole and into the particular moment in the history of sociology in which it arose. I did not undertake to do that because, in the kind of sociology which I have done, I have not taken my point of departure from the latest position attained in the literature. I have learned much of what I know about sociology by wide reading, often too random, by research on particular topics, by constantly studying some of the classics of sociology, the writings of Max Weber in particular, and by recurrent reflection on the coherence and disorders of the Roman empire.

In all these activities, which have sometimes brought me into new territories, I have been preoccupied with the same dimly apprehended task which even now is difficult to formulate. That task has been to discern the effective constitution of large societies. Some writers have dealt with the role of markets in joining into an approximately bounded order individuals who do not know of each other's existence; other writers have dealt with the function of authority, exercised through law, and power, exercised by the probability of the use of coercion, in the establishment of a differentiated order within a bounded territory. I have no great quarrel with either of these classes of writers. Their contentions are correct up to a point, but both presuppose the existence of a society constituted by attachments to and images of symbolized persons, institutions, and territory. These attachments are not subjective states of mind. The individuals who possess them form not an aggregate of separate entities that can be added up but rather a determinate pattern or structure of interconnected individual minds that infuse actions. This interindividual structure of individual minds is what these writers presuppose. Those who contend that the market is the formative constituent of society presuppose effective authority; those who contend that authority and power together are the main constituents presuppose that there is a bounded territory over the residents of which those who exercise authority and power claim to hold sway. The market could not work to the extent that it does in the constitution of a society without this constituent element of beliefs; authority and power could not work without it. This primary interindividual structure of beliefs, cognitive and normative, along with the attachments to remote objects of belief which are not known through the direct experience of most of the members of society and are known only through symbolization, is the subject matter of these essays.

The essays are arranged according to the following scheme. The first group deals with various elements of the constitution of societies which are too large in number of members and in territory for any single individual, even the most experienced, to know directly more than a small fraction of the persons which the society includes as members and of the territory on which the society exists. In these essays the constitutional pattern which I call center and periphery is adumbrated.

The second group of essays deals with properties that are attributed to the center, which is the focal point of the interindividual consensus of beliefs, and with the consequences for the shape of society arising from those attributed properties. The third group of essays deals with the custodians, transmitters, and interpreters of beliefs which enter into the constitution of society. The essay which makes up the final section returns to the theme of the first section, namely, the cognitive self-image of society, dealing with the deliberate, organized effort to construct such an image through the cultivation of sociology as an academic discipline.

I

Before the Second World War, I was suspicious of those criticisms of modern Western societies which proclaimed the "disintegration" of these societies and which recommended the reestablishment of community—*Gemeinschaft*. I was especially distrustful of the argument that a society had to have a comprehensive, all-answering "ideology" in which all the members of the society shared. At the same time, I thought that some sort of very general legitimatory beliefs were necessary for a society, if the authority which was indispensable to its stability was to be effective and if society was not to become a war of each against all. The legitimacy of institutions, if it was to permit authorities to function more or less effectively, had to be widely acknowledged. This agreement or consensus of beliefs about the major organs of society did not, it seemed to me, preclude a considerable degree of disagreement about how scarce things should be distributed. That is why I was a consensual pluralist. My early interest in religious toleration in England in the seventeenth century and my interest in academic freedom in the nineteenth and twentieth centuries were equally accompanied by the conviction that neither religious freedom nor intellectual freedom could be maintained unless the beneficiaries of toleration and freedom accepted the rules imposed by their own traditions and by their membership in a loosely consensual society. At the same time, if the custodians of consensus aimed at the inclusion of all the members of society and all their actions, there would be no room for independence, corporate and individual, and no room either for shortcomings, waywardness, or creativity.

In 1945 and 1946 Morris Janowitz and I, drawing on our observations during the Second World War, wrote an essay on "The Cohesion and Disintegration of the *Wehrmacht* in World War II."[1] In this paper the limits of the power of the center and the significance of subcenters in the maintenance of an immense corporate body—in this instance the *Wehrmacht*—were touched upon. The central values held by German soldiers and attributed by them to German society, and the attitude of the soldiers to the authority of senior officers far from the front, were not disregarded by us. We certainly did not think that the German armed forces were nothing more than an arithmetic sum of primary groups. Commands from senior officers, distributed by intermediaries, and attachment to the *Wehrmacht* as a whole and to German society, mediated by attachment to junior officers and non-commissioned officers, were sustained, according to our argument, by attachments, within the immediate combat units, to particular soldiers, brave and loyal, who were also more "political" than the others and who were the spine of the *Wehrmacht*. As long as the spine was strong, the army was cohesive.

In the decade following the war, continuing my earlier interests in consensual pluralism—although I did not call it that—I was concerned to delineate the place of personal primary groups in the minimal cohesion of the larger society. I wished to define more clearly the properties of primary groups constituted by personal attachments and to understand why the properties of primary groups could not—as Charles Cooley had thought possible—be extended to become the dominant features of a whole society. This led me to an intensive study of personal primary groups as the sites of affectional and primordial attachments and of political sects as the sites of ideologies. I did not want to dissolve the larger society into primary groups. I was confident that no society could long be maintained by ideology and it was

1. *Public Opinion Quarterly* 12, no. 2 (Summer 1948): 280–315. It has been reprinted many times, most recently in *Center and Periphery* (Chicago: University of Chicago Press, 1975), pp. 344–83, and Morris Janowitz, *Military Conflict: Essays in the Institutional Analysis of War and Peace* (Beverly Hills: Sage Publishers, 1975), pp. 177–220.

equally clear to me that it could not be reduced to a marketlike equilibrium of interests or to a product of coercion. The limits of the market and coercion as alternative or complementary accounts of the constitution of society seemed to me so obvious that I did not bother to refute them. The alternatives which were being currently offered—namely, love and ideology—also accounted for limited zones of the actual conduct of large societies. It was important if I was to reject the efficacy and durability of intense and comprehensive ideologies that I should not fly to the opposite extreme. I wished to show the limits of both love and ideology in providing the intensity of attachment and the cognitive content of a loose consensus of a vast number of individuals who had no contact with each other and who were not voluntarily recruited, as they were in religious and political sects. A good part of my thought during the period from 1945 until 1955 was an attempt to find the respective jurisdictions of belief in charismatic qualities and things on the one hand, and attachments to persons on the other, or between "ideological" and "personal primary groups." This was a reformulation and a deepening of my earlier interest in consensual pluralism.

By the end of the first postwar decade I thought to find the balance in "civility," which was a relatively unintense attachment to society as a whole and a transcendence of the individual's spheres of personal and primordial attachment. Civility towards the larger society, towards society as a whole, did not demand a monopoly of the individual's loyalty or of his capacity for attachments. I did not inquire into the cognitive content of civility; that was an omission which I did not notice at the time.

This was where things stood for me until my return from India in 1956. None of the essays in this book was written before that date. Much of my writing on this topic during the years between 1946 and 1955—two manuscripts of substantial length, one on "Consensus and Liberty" and the other on "Love, Belief, and Civility," in which I put down those ideas as they then stood, have remained unpublished. I did, however, publish one paper on "The Meaning of the Coronation" and another on "Personal, Primordial, Sacred, and Civil Ties" in which I laid out the general outlines of my views as they then stood.[2] I also wrote in 1954 and 1955 a small book called *The Torment of Secrecy: The Background and Consequences of American Security Policies*[3] in which I dealt with the damage done to consensual pluralism by ideological demands for complete consensus, while at the same time arguing for the indispensability of consensus as a precondition of pluralism.

II

The first three essays in this volume were all written between ten and twenty years after my return from India. "The Integration of Society," the first essay in the book, was one of the last to be written; it was written in about 1973. It is a series of reflections on the papers presented in a seminar which I conducted at the Department of Anthropology at University College, London, in 1970. The seminar had many excellent members who had done a considerable amount of fieldwork in West Africa and in the West Indies. "The Integration of Society" was my contribution to the solution of the task of seeing to what extent the new states of West Africa and the West Indies could also be regarded as coterminous with societies. The problem there was the ascertainment of the extent to which and the ways in which societies were taking shape from the constituent tribal and local societies that found themselves within boundaries left behind by the former colonial rulers. This essay contains more than I thought on the matter in the decade between 1945 and 1955 since in the meantime I had been studying India and the societies of black Africa and had also hit upon the scheme of analysis of societies in terms of centers and peripheries. Nevertheless it represents an effort to deal with the task of defining the objects

2. *The Sociological Review*, n.s., 1, no. 2 (December 1956): 63–81, reprinted in *Center and Periphery*, pp. 135–52; *British Journal of Sociology* 8, no. 2 (June 1957): 130–45, reprinted in *Center and Periphery*, pp. 111–26.

3. London: Heinemann, 1956.

and the structure of consensus which had engaged my mind since before the war.

"Society and Societies" (Chapter 2 below) likewise represents an effort to deal with my old task in the light of my later reflections and observations in the decade after 1955. It too was much influenced by my studies in India from 1955 onward and by my African studies that began several years later and that were more extensive than intensive. Like all the other essays which I wrote after 1955, this one too was naturally influenced by the ideas about center and periphery that I began to elaborate after my studies in India.

III

"The Theory of Mass Society" (Chapter 3 below) was written in 1961. Its initial impulse came from my wish to respond to the critics of mass society. I do not hesitate to say that I found much of this literature rather odious because it came from snobbish radicals, some of them with aristocratic pretensions mixed with a hypocritical egalitarianism of Marxist inspiration. It would carry us a little too far afield if I were to go into an analysis of the Frankfurt School, the disingenuousness and crude prejudices of which I have dealt with in several papers.[4]

The proposition that the working classes have been incorporated into their respective societies in the West to a greater extent than was the case before the twentieth century seemed to me to rest on sound evidence. The "alienation" of the working classes was and still is real but it has diminished in the present century. What there is of it is for the most part quite compatible with a moderate amount of civility.

4. "Authoritarianism, 'Right and Left,'" in Richard Christie and Maria Jahoda, eds., *Continuities in Social Research II: Studies in the Scope and Method of "The Authoritarian Personality"* (Glencoe, Ill.: The Free Press, 1954), pp. 24–29, and "Daydreams and Nightmares," which was first published in *Sewanee Review* 65, no. 4 (October-December 1957): 586–608, and reprinted in *The Intellectuals and the Powers* (Chicago: University of Chicago Press, 1972), pp. 248–64.

Modern Western societies are still hierarchical in the distribution of income and wealth. Human beings work increasingly in large organizations; political parties although democratically competitive with each other are mass parties in which bosses, their underlings, and party bureaucrats play an important part; trade unions grow in power but they too are large organizations with high degrees of concentration of power over their members. Nevertheless, there has seemed to be a greater interest in and attachment to society as a whole as manifested in patriotism and civility in the working classes. There is also probably more civility in the upper classes than there had been before the present century and certainly more than there had been before the French Revolution of 1789. There has been a more widespread acceptance of the allocative institutions of society and less resistance to them. The small scale of revolutionary parties has seemed to me to be further evidence of the incorporation into society of the classes which the critics of "mass society" have alleged were wholly alienated and manipulated, seduced into "false consciousness" and coerced into submission by the upper classes. The "mass society," so contemned by intellectuals with superior airs and ingenious but false theories, turns out on examination a more consensual—still very far from a wholly consensual—society than it was alleged to be. The main thesis of my essay on mass society was formulated partly in terms of my newly developed views about the smaller distance between center and periphery. This is a complex phenomenon which needs much more analysis.

IV

"Center and Periphery" (Chapter 4 below) is the next stage in the development of the ideas which are partially presented in this book. This phase, one in which the charismatic takes a more prominent position, overlaps with the one which preceded it and builds upon it. The dominant theme of this phase first appeared in printed form in the paper on "The Meaning of the Coronation" that I wrote with Michael Young in the early summer of 1953. This was the first time that I hit upon the idea that consensual beliefs focus on central institutions; they comprise beliefs about charismatic qualities and the moral virtues associated with them that are attributed to that distant center. The ideas took on sharper definition as I thought about the results of my studies in India, although I must admit that they did not occur to me explicitly in the course of my work there. The relations between the center and periphery first occurred to me when I was analyzing the intellectual relations between "metropolis" and "province."[5] I was trying to put into order the numerous observations I had made of the guiding norms of modern Indian intellectual life, and when I first thought about it, it was as the relationship between British intellectual culture and modern Indian intellectual culture during the first decade of Indian independence as a sovereign state. The relationship which I discerned paralleled the relationship between metropolis and province in British academic life which I had observed not many years earlier. Almost as soon as I reformulated it in the light of these new observations, it became clear to me that the pattern of the relationship between intellectual metropolis and province, internationally and nationally, was only an instance of a more general class of relationships.[6] The more general pattern, it now became evident, was applicable to political relations within and between societies, as well as to the movement of religious and moral beliefs within and between societies and between civilizations.[7] It was appli-

5. My reflections on "metropolis" and "province" began in Manchester in 1953 and were first presented in a paper on British intellectuals before and after the Second World War at a seminar of the Committee on Social Thought at the University of Chicago in the winter of 1954. (It was received with complete incomprehension by a learned audience.) A revised version of the paper was published in *Encounter* 4, no. 4 (19) (April 1955): 1–22; reprinted in *The Intellectuals and the Powers*, pp. 135–53.

6. My first publication on this subject was written in 1956 or 1957. It was "Metropolis and Province in the Intellectual Community," in V. M. Dandekar and N. V. Sovani, eds., *Changing India: Essays in Honour of D. G. Gadgil* (Bombay and London: Asia Publishing House, 1961), pp. 275–94; reprinted in *The Intellectuals and the Powers*, pp. 355–71.

7. The more general account of center and periphery was set forth in

cable to the movement of patterns of manners and to the movement of technological and scientific knowledge.

The tendency towards the attribution of charismatic qualities to the center took on a new aspect for me in the course of the delivery of a paper to the American Sociological Society in Washington in the summer of 1957. I was speaking about the insistence of the politicians and higher civil servants of the new states of Asia and Africa that they alone were capable of promoting the economic development of their countries through more or less socialistic measures. In the midst of my address, it occurred to me that one of the reasons why these politicians and administrators thought that they were the only ones who had the necessary qualifications and that the ordinary people of their societies were only the raw material of national "redemption," lay in their attribution of charismatic qualities to themselves. These notions could develop from their traditional beliefs about caste, sultanate, kingship, and chieftainship and from a more recent tradition that the possession of scientific or quasi-scientific knowledge enables its possessor to participate in a higher realm of being. Their place at the center, ancestrally and in the present, endowed them, they thought, with "extraordinary" powers. The parallel between charisma in the religious sphere and the concentration of charisma in the sphere of governmental economic policy came into my mind in the course of my spoken discourse. It had not been in my paper.[8]

---

the autumn of 1958 for presentation at the Christmas meeting of that year of the American Association for the Advancement of Science; it was first published in Donald Roy, ed., *Trends in Social Science* (New York: The Philosophical Library, 1959), pp. 64–84. It appeared in considerably revised form in *The Logic of Knowledge: Essays in Honor of Michael Polanyi* (London: Routledge and Kegan Paul, 1961), pp. 117–30.

8. The paper originally set out to deal with attitudes towards economic efficiency in Asia and Africa. I widened the topic to include economizing behavior as well as efficiency. I began by thinking of the antithesis between traditionality and rationalization. The belief by the elites of these countries in their own charismatic powers, and their disparaging attitudes towards the uneducated persons and laborers, seemed

I had studied Max Weber's views about charismatic authority over and over again since the 1930s but their potentialities for extension had not come to me until about twenty-five years later when I was dealing with substantive topics which were superficially far from those to which Max Weber had applied them. On the one hand, everything that I was saying after my "discovery" seemed to be obviously "contained" in Weber's writings; on the other hand, I had not, in my earlier studies, seen what appeared to be so obvious until I came to deal with social stratification, a topic that Max Weber had not interpreted in those terms.

The three papers "Charisma," "Charisma, Order, and Status," and "Deference" (Chapters 5, 6, and 7 below) were all written in the first half of the 1960s. They are all variations on Max Weber's theme of the "routinization of charisma" which I reformulated into the dispersion and attenuation of charisma. (More recently, I have thought it desirable to add a temporal category which refers to the transiency and duration of charisma.) In the light of this reconstitution of the charismatic phenomenon, I was able to see that one component of consensus was the common attribution of charismatic qualities to the center of society; the center itself might be highly concentrated or it might be, in the extreme and impossible case of a wholly and genuinely populistic, democratic society, so dispersed as to be coterminous with the society itself. I had dealt with populism from the early 1950s onward[9] but I did not, in those years, describe it as an attribution of charismatic qualities to the mass of the population; I did not then see the implications of the statement *vox populi, vox dei.*

---

to go beyond traditionality. The revision of my prepared paper was later published under the title of "The Concentration and Dispersion of Charisma: Their Bearing on Economic Policy in Underdeveloped Countries," in *World Politics* 11, no. 2 (October 1958): 1–19; it has been reprinted in *Center and Periphery*, pp. 405–21.

9. First in "Populism and the Rule of Law," in *The University of Chicago Law School Conference on Jurisprudence and Politics* (April 1954): 91–107, and later in *The Torment of Secrecy*, pp. 98–104.

In the essay on "Deference" I took up an old theme that I thought had been neglected in the empirical literature on social stratification; it was one that I had first dealt with in my paper written with Herbert Goldhamer on "Types of Power and Status"[10] in about 1938. It is an elusive subject which is difficult to deal with empirically and I thought that the ad hoc resolution of the difficulty by a simple conceptual amalgam like "socioeconomic status"—accepted by several generations of sociologists with little reflection—had disregarded the fact that unlike distributions of wealth, income, and occupations, which were what German sociologists used to call "objective criteria" of social stratification, deference was a matter of cognitive beliefs and evaluations. The granting of deference, to the extent that it was granted, was in accordance with the extent to which the person being assessed was believed to possess certain properties. These properties, such as occupation, political power, ethnic quality, individual achievement, and lineage, correctly or incorrectly perceived, were each separately and all together assessed in the light of proximity to the center of society and to the charismatic quality believed to reside there. I arrived at the view that the granting of deference was a variant form of the attribution of charismatic quality; in this I was supported by the empirical research on the social status of occupation done by Paul Hatt and Albert Reiss when they worked at the National Opinion Research Center and by the many investigations which have been carried out since then on this topic in the United States and in other countries.

V

My interest in intellectuals must have had a close affinity with my interest in the kind of consensus of which a large society was capable and in the idea of a transcendent sacred order. Nonetheless, it took many years for me to begin to perceive some of these affinities and to make them explicit. Although my interest in intellectuals goes back further than any of my other interests,

10. *American Journal of Sociology* 45, no. 2 (September 1939) : 171-82; reprinted in *Center and Periphery*, pp. 239–48.

it appears in retrospect to have been pursued along a number of separate paths which converged only after many years.

From the early 1930s onward I was convinced that the formal properties of revolutionary thinking were different from those of the thought of moderate, liberal, and conservative intellectuals. I am not sure that my notions on this subject were not affected by Karl Mannheim's discussion of a closely related problem in *Ideologie und Utopie* which I read early in 1933. But when, a little later, I attempted to put together my thoughts on the revolutionary outlook for presentation in Robert Park's seminar, I did not have Mannheim in mind, although I had read his book only about a year earlier. My analysis was based on a comparison of the programs of communist parties with those of socialist and liberal parties and a fairly intensive study of communist, socialist, and liberal newspapers and journals.

When later in the 1930s, I gathered material on "nativists" and sympathizers with Nazism in Chicago, I was struck by the similarity of patterns of thought of the *soi-disant* "left" and the "right-wing" fanatics who were so opposed to each other. Both thought that "the system" was being deliberately and conspiratorially manipulated by a group which kept itself hidden from the public eye but that they alone had perceived. In "Authoritarianism 'Left' and 'Right,' " written in 1953, and in *The Torment of Secrecy*, written in 1954, I had pointed to many affinities between these two apparently diametrically opposed political outlooks. The common element was the ideological orientation. I continued to work on the elaboration of this idea. In the autumn of 1955, I wrote an essay entitled "The End of Ideology?"[11] in which I used the term in the specific sense that I later elaborated much more fully in the essays I wrote for Bernsdorf's *Wörterbuch der Soziologie*[12] and the *International Encyclopedia of the Social Sciences*[13] at the very beginning of the 1960s (the latter appears below as Chapter 9, "Ideology"). When I first published "Ideology and Civility," in 1958, even excellent and

11.   *Encounter* 5, no. 5 (24) (November 1955) : 52–62.
12.   2d ed. (Stuttgart: Enke Verlag, 1969), pp. 441–44.
13.   New York: Macmillan and The Free Press, 1968, vol. 7, pp. 66–75.

well-intentioned scholars failed to understand what I was getting at, just as the conception of ideology contained in "The End of Ideology?" had been generally misunderstood. A vulgar sort of Marxism had already infected the air in the United States and Great Britain so that all culture and all belief were thought of as "ideology." "Ideology" was understood as a set of ideas or a generalized outlook on the world which is possessed by all but the revolutionary working class and which pervasively falsifies or distorts the truth in the service of an unacknowledged interest in wealth, income, and power; this was the more or less Marxist view which I rejected root and branch. Marxists have also used the word "ideology" to refer to the revolutionary outlook of an idealized working class; this ideology is Marxism. It is comprehensive, systematic, alienated from the "world" as it is; it sees the world as a unity and emphasizes the interdependence of "theory" and "practice." This is a narrower sense and although I think that it is a false account of the outlook of the working classes, it does correspond to my conception of an ideology. My difference with Marxism in this matter lies in my observation that ideology in this sense is espoused only by sectarians, from whatever class they come; it is certainly not espoused by most of the working class in any country.

The term "ideology" has also been used, without a Marxian overtone of disparagement, of the views of the middle and upper classes and of nonrevolutionary intellectuals; or, with an overtone of approval, with reference to the revolutionary members of the working class. It has been used by social scientists who have wished to point out that all societies have a culture, that culture entails belief, that the beliefs are not randomly scattered and that no individual in any society is free from sharing to some extent in this more or less coherent set of beliefs. These patterns of interconnected beliefs, too, were called ideology. I have no objection to this view of ideology although I think that it overstates the coherence of the culture of any large society. In any case, it refers to something rather different from what I had in mind when I discussed ideology and it disclosed a confusion in the thought of the social scientists who failed to see the difference.

The other line of my interest in intellectuals did not at first have any obvious connection with my interest in ideology. In any case, I myself did not see the connection, although when I did make it later, it seemed very self-evident. My interest was first expressed in my studies of literary history, of how literary men gained their livelihood and of the attitude of literary men of the eighteenth and nineteenth centuries towards their own society and towards reforming and revolutionary movements.

My study of the works of Georges Sorel while I was an undergraduate opened my mind in a number of different directions. Through the study of Sorel's numerous books and booklets, Sombart's *Proletarischer Sozialismus*, and Henry de Man's *The Psychology of Socialism*, I gained a better understanding of the antinomian utopianism of some intellectuals and of their comprehensive rejection of modern society on the grounds of its materialistic disregard for the realm of transcendent things. This led me to seek the sources of the antinomianism of intellectuals in their own intellectual traditions and in the nature of intellectual activities. At the same time, I began to look into the varieties of the political attitudes of intellectuals, to distinguish the liberals and conservatives from those who accepted more of the existing revolutionary, traditionalistic, and bohemian traditions. At that time, I certainly did not see these things as phenomena which could be better illuminated by analysis in terms of the relationship between center and periphery or of the intellectuals' relationship to the realm of the charismatic.

The plan I drew up as an undergraduate for a book on Sorel was never realized and my earliest intention to write about the politics of intellectuals in that book was suspended. In the winter of 1947, I went to Manchester to deliver a lecture on intellectuals and politics before the Manchester Literary and Philosophical Society. That was my first public venture on the subject; my analysis was not sympathetically received and least of all by Michael Polanyi. I would add that it gave me special pleasure to find that by 1960 when he delivered the Eddington Memorial lecture at Cambridge under the title of *Beyond Nihilism*, he had accepted most of the position which I had taken in 1947 and which he had then so roundly denounced. Similar things have occurred to me on a number of occasions.

Beginning in the summer of 1949, I began to teach and write about intellectuals. My first writing on the subject was an introduction to a republication of T. E. Hulme's English translation of Sorel's *Réflexions sur la violence*.[14] That same summer I gave a seminar on intellectuals at the University of Chicago. I did this again in 1952 and wrote a very sketchy first draft of a book on intellectuals; this manuscript contained a chapter on intellectuals in countries without political sovereignty, i.e., without an indigenous political center. Of course, I did not, at that time, put it into terms of center and periphery or of the relations of intellectuals to the earthly or secular and the sacred or charismatic orders. This took place much later. In the beginning of the 1950s, my interest in intellectuals in countries without indigenous political sovereignty was still very concrete. It grew out of my conversations with South Asian, West Indian, and African students in the University of London.

In 1955 and 1956, I carried out a study of modern Indian intellectuals. In some respects this was a turning point in my life because it brought me into contact with the substance of a civilization which I had hitherto known only from books. In other respects, however, it was only an accentuation and sharpening of lines of thought already vaguely conceived. From 1950 onwards, I wrote a series of papers on intellectuals and began a sequence of revisions and elaborations of the manuscript which I had first written in 1952. It grew excessively so that when it was last revised for the fourth or fifth time in the early 1970s, it was about 1,500 pages in length. I still hope to come back to it, to reduce it and to release it from its present seclusion.

The paper "The Intellectuals and the Powers" (Chapter 8 below) was written as a programmatic declaration for the first issue of *Comparative Studies in Society and History*.[15] It was

14. Georges Sorel, *Reflections on Violence* (Glencoe, Ill., The Free Press, 1950), pp. 11–25.

15. *Comparative Studies in Society and History* 1, no. 1 (October 1958) : 5–22; reprinted in *The Intellectuals and the Powers*, pp. 3–22.

written earlier than *The Intellectuals between Tradition and Modernity: The Indian Situation*[16] but around the same time as the papers on "Ideology and Civility" and "The Intellectuals in the Political Development of the New States."[17] In neither of these later publications did I deal explicitly with the fascination which the earthly center exercises upon intellectuals and the simultaneous tendency which many of them have to judge it negatively in the light of the central norms of a transcendent order. I did not go as far as I went in the "Intellectuals and the Powers" which was written in the interim between them.

At this stage, the antinomian attitudes of intellectuals were the main focus of my attention: I was just beginning inchoately to see their connection with an attachment to an ideal or charismatic order. I was of course very aware of their influence on the formation of intellectual traditions and hence on subsequent generations of intellectuals, but I tended to accept at its face value the complaint made by many intellectuals that they were disregarded in their own society. I still did not give enough emphasis to the influence which intellectuals were beginning to exercise over their nonintellectual contemporaries and I did not incorporate into my more general views what I knew of the role of religious intellectuals in ancient Judaism, India, China, and in Western societies. Although I was in principle aware of the lines of affinity between ideological beliefs and those current in the consensual region of a society—the former being accentuations and intensifications of some of the latter—I was not attentive enough to these connections. For similar reasons, I was not mindful enough of the role of intellectuals in the formation of the consensus which their own antinomian influence was simultaneously undermining. I did not begin to bring together these various conjoint lines of analysis until the 1970s.

Although one of the heroes of American radical intellectuals

<hr/>

16. The Hague: Mouton, 1961.
17. *Sewanee Review* 66, no. 3 (July-September 1958): 450–80, and *World Politics* 12, no. 3 (April 1960): 329–68. Both have been reprinted in *The Intellectuals and the Powers*, pp. 42–70; 386–423.

of the 1950s and early 1960s, C. Wright Mills, had called the intellectuals, especially academic intellectuals, "the powerless people," his own experience and the history of the United States —to say nothing of other countries—belied that notion. However much intellectuals, above all in the United States, entertained the fantasy that they were "insulted and injured" in their own country, where allegedly no one cared for literature or fundamental science or disinterested scholarship, they have in fact acquired a great deal of influence in most Western societies in the past half-century. The United States could never have become the country which it is without the system of free and compulsory education in which the pupils learned from books about the geographical and social shape of the society of which they could have no firsthand knowledge. It could not have become what it is without the journalism which daily brought detailed knowledge of the rest of the country to the adult population. It could not have become the country which it is without the theorists and intellectual agitators of social reform and governmental regulation and provision, which have to a great extent been inspired by intellectuals, humble and exalted. In addition to these activities which helped to form the consensual substratum of American society, academic and publicistic intellectuals have for nearly a half-century affected the direction of governmental policies and aroused and guided powerful blocs of opinion in accordance with the ideas of collectivistic liberalism. That is a considerable achievement and one which is rather different from the collective self-image which American intellectuals have had of themselves and of their role in American society.

These were some of the ideas which were in my mind as I began to write "Intellectuals and the Center of Society in the United States" (Chapter 10 below) which I originally wrote for a *Festschrift* for my friend Talcott Parsons.[18] I tried to trace this influence in more detail in a paper delivered in Baltimore in 1976

18. Part of this paper was printed in Bernard Barber and Alex Inkeles, eds., *Stability and Social Change* (Boston: Little, Brown, 1971), pp. 211–43. It was printed in full in *The Intellectuals and the Powers*, pp. 154–95.

on the occasion of the centenary of the faculty of history of The Johns Hopkins University.[19]

VI

One constitutive element in the existence of any society is the perception, correct or incorrect, of that society by most of its members. This awareness is registered in the use by its members of the name of the society; the name, however important in itself for arousing the individual's identification of himself as a member of the society, is only a small part of that "collective self-consciousness" which enters into the constitution of a society. In the minds of most of the members of a society, this consciousness of their own society is vague and undifferentiated. In the minds of some—more curious, more experienced, more intelligent—persons, the consciousness of their own society is more clearly differentiated and defined. Ancient historians like Thucydides who wrote about their contemporary societies, travelers and historian-anthropologists like Herodotus who wrote about foreign societies in contrast with their own, were the forerunners of the sociology which is an intellectually constructed form of collective self-consciousness. A few stirrings could be seen before the eighteenth century, and it became a far more definite movement in the nineteenth century. It was an effort at "collective self-understanding" and it was also an effort at the infusion of that collective self-understanding, made detailed and precise, into practical affairs. It was intended by its early proponents to be widely shared, to lead to the illumination of public opinion and to the consequent correction and precision of the knowledge of society possessed by politicians and civil servants. Sociology was intended as a supplement to the knowledge needed for the exercise of authority in society, some of the leaders of which wanted it to be a "rational society." The writers who favored this outcome thought primarily of the diffusion of the results of socio-

---

19. See "Liberalism and Learning," in *The Calling of Sociology* (Chicago: University of Chicago Press, 1980), pp. 289–355.

logical study into public possession. I myself was also interested in understanding the actual conduct of sociological study as part of the process of the "self-discovery of society."

This subject has interested me for many years. I had read a good deal of the work of the German academic social scientists who had formed the *Verein für Sozialpolitik* and who made many contributions to its proceedings. Robert Park himself had been fascinated by the "social survey movement" but I think that, despite his great sensitivity to the role of the mind and its products in society, he had been interested in the social survey movement mainly as a precursor of the methodical empirical sociology which he was interested in promoting. Karl Mannheim, in several essays and in his inaugural lecture at Frankfurt am Main, had dealt with the distinctive features of American sociology and German sociology in relation to their respective societies.[20] I myself had written on a number of occasions on the relationship between sociology and its environing society, most elaborately in the epilogue to the collection which Talcott Parsons and I edited as *Theories of Society*.[21] In this essay, I began my inquiry into "social science as public opinion"; I referred to the process of sociological discovery as part of the process of becoming aware of the shape and dimensions of society which is an essential cognitive component of consensus and, hence, of the constitution of society.

In "Tradition, Ecology, and Institution in the History of Sociology" (Chapter 11 below) I do not deal with this sharing of sociological knowledge with those who live in the society. I deal rather with the growth of cognitive sensibility about society, rationalized and organized through teaching, research, publica-

20. "German Sociology: 1918–1933," *Politica* 1, no. 1 (February 1934): 12–33, reprinted in Karl Mannheim, *Essays in Sociology and Social Psychology* (London: Routledge and Kegan Paul, 1953), pp. 209–28. Review of Stuart A. Rice, ed., *Methods in Social Science: A Source Book, American Journal of Sociology* 38, no. 2 (September 1932): 273–82; reprinted in Mannheim, *Essays in Sociology and Social Psychology*, pp. 185–94.

21. This essay has been republished in revised form in *The Calling of Sociology*, pp. 3–92.

tion, and institutional propagation. In my view, sociology is the intellectual activity that discerns the significance of the cognitive component in the constitution of society and is itself a part of that cognitive component. For good or for ill, the results of this academically and otherwise institutionally organized cognitive activity are absorbed into the patterns of practical action in society.

VII

As I said at the beginning of this introduction, these essays are fragments. Perhaps it is not entirely correct to call them fragments because fragments are pieces which result when a whole has been broken into pieces. The whole from which these pieces are fragments does not exist as a finished work. It is a whole which had lain in a latent state, successive strata of which have been brought to the surface as I have been occupied with particular parts of it. As the strata emerged, pieces which had appeared separately reached out, almost by themselves, to establish a connection with the other pieces which had also emerged separately. Abstract though much of the analysis has been, it has never been deductive. Practically every essay in this volume has had a relatively concrete point of departure, a point of departure in interviews, in concentrated historical reading, and in responses to contemporary situations in Western societies, especially that of the United States, and in Africa and South Asia.

Where does the unity, which I have insisted is there, come from? Does it lie in the unfolding of a fundamental pattern inherent in reality, a pattern which could not be elicited until I had traversed a long distance through many peregrinations, doubling back and crossing the same fields from different angles? That is what I think it is.

Sometimes I think that it is the unfolding of a prejudice— not a prejudice in the sense of disliking others, without any experience of any of them. It is likely that some critics will say that it is the clouded unfolding of a political prejudice. I doubt very much that this is so. I have definite political beliefs but they have developed hand in hand with my sociological understanding. My preferences for certain political arrangements did not lead to my sociological views; up to a point it has been the other way around.

The concreteness of my points of departure in interviews and in the study of contemporary and historical situations gives me some assurance that my picture of how society is constituted is not arbitrary. It is vague—of that no one can be more aware than I am. It is sometimes focused on a level deeper than that of immediately perceivable events, and that is a handicap on its acceptability to contemporary social science. That does not worry me. In the forty years since I began to move in my present intellectual direction, I have found an increasing number of fellow travelers who have been moving on the same road and in the same direction. Some of this might be a result of my writings, some of it is more likely a result of the truthful unfolding of sound tendencies in the intellectual traditions which I share with many social scientists scattered throughout Western countries.

Why should it be otherwise than it has been? The unfolding of an intellectual tradition and the confluence of unfolding intellectual traditions are not just "subjective" intellectual experiences. The tradition unfolds and the traditions flow into each other as they confront a reality which has a deeper existence than the immediate "hard data" which are the rightful concern of many of the best social scientists of the age. The traditions which I have received have not come about by accident; they have not been lightly espoused. They have been formed by strenuous intellectual confrontation with the experiences of societies, past and present. They are not arbitrarily formed *Weltanschauungen*, unthinkingly received. They have grown through study and criticism, and I like many others have been their beneficiaries.

This being so, it is fitting that I should close this introduction by acknowledging my indebtedness to many powerful, wonderfully studious intelligences, some of whom I have known personally, others from the distance crossed by their written works. Among the former, I mention first my elders, Robert Park, Frank Knight, and Harold Lasswell at the University of Chicago, Talcott Parsons at Harvard, Audrey Richards, Karl Popper, and Siegfried Nadel at the London School of Economics, Michael Polanyi at Manchester, and Michael Postan and Eric Ashby at Cambridge; perhaps more than any others, Arnaldo Momigliano, whose presence transcends any particular place; among my coevals and juniors, Lloyd Fallers, S. N. Eisenstadt, Morris Janowitz, Joseph Epstein, Harry Johnson, and Jack Goody, variously in Chicago, Cambridge, London, and Jerusalem.

Of those I have not known, their number is countless but Max Weber should be mentioned far more than any other. After him, of writers who lived in the twentieth century, I mention Werner Sombart, Roberto Michels, Henry de Man, M. I. Rostovzeff, Anders Nygren, Martin Nilsson, Rudolf Otto, Maurice Halbwachs. I shall not go back past the beginning of the present century.

It might be asked, why so many creditors for so small a loan? I leave it for my readers to decide on the magnitude of the loans which I have taken and the use to which I have put my borrowings.

Edward Shils

I. The Constitution of Society

1

THE INTEGRATION OF SOCIETY

I

It has long been thought that a good society is one without conflict. Within any society, those persons who "have a stake in society" and who are solicitous about the maintenance of their own superiority in wealth, authority, and status seldom look with equanimity on conflict, rebellion, or even disobedience. Rulers have almost always wished their realms to be free of conflict; they attempt to prevent or to suppress those who could initiate active conflict against them. The rebels and revolutionaries who act against the power of the incumbent authorities, even though they believe that they can attain their ends only through engagement in conflict, insist that the society which they would install would be without conflict. The "innocent bystander," the "women and children," the apolitical ordinary man are all portrayed as the parties injured by the conflicts of others. The arts, civilization, social order are all damaged by conflict.

The benefits of conflict, aside from its value as an instrument to gain the particular objectives sought through the activity which "the other side" resists, are not generally appreciated. Even the "warrior" as an ideal does not initiate conflict; he responds heroically to those who initiate it or who seek otherwise to realize wicked ends. The ideal society is one in which there is no conflict—or at best, very little conflict. Conflict is generally regarded as something made necessary by ill-will, misfortune, injustice, undesirable scarcity, or historical inevitability. In contrast with this, a unified society, one in which conflict has been eliminated, is generally thought to be a good thing. Utopias are conflictless.

The society without conflict, the highly integrated society, has not only been the reverently cultivated ideal. It has also been the object of governmental policies. No imperial or city state of classical antiquity or of the orient was ever wholly indifferent to the integration of the society which lived under its authority. The Reformation settlement which declared that the religion of the ruler should also be the religion of his subjects was one sign of the desire of rulers not merely to gain the submission of their subjects but also to integrate them into a single society through the uniformity of beliefs. When nationality became an object of passionate devotion and when its realization and protection became a criterion for defining the boundaries and legitimacy of states and societies, rulers found what was to them an almost ideal basis for the integration of the societies over which they held dominion. In the late nineteenth and early twentieth centuries, the rulers of most advanced countries tried to integrate their societies through nationally comprehensive legislation and by the penetration of their authority into every part of their society, through the expansion of administration and policy up to the limits of their boundaries, through the extension of railways, highways, post and telegraph into a nationally coherent network, through public education on a national scale, and through the press and news reporting agencies.

Rulers have generally denied the existence of major conflicts in their societies. The governments of modern Europe and America have aimed at societies with minimal internal conflict, and where the conflict is accepted as inevitable they have attempted to restrain and discipline it. They have frowned on groups which instigate conflict. Internal peace and order have been the objects of their desire. Efforts were made to diminish the incentive for workers to join organizations which took up an actively conflicting attitude; the organizations themselves were impeded and constricted, and sometimes they were actually suppressed. The promotion of solidarity became an object of policy; the avoidance of conflict by repressive measures and by compromise has always been a technique of government.

There has not been unanimity regarding conflict. Some thinkers resignedly, others triumphantly, have pointed out that conflicts are of the very texture of society, even of the life of the species. The conflicts of races, the conflicts of classes have been asserted to be endemic to society. Within societies, conflict has been regarded as inevitable and necessary for justice and progress. Comtian positivism and Marxism both believed in the desirability and the ultimate realization of a wholly conflictless society in the future—the former in the positive stage, the latter under communism. They also regarded the refusal to submit to authority and the conflict of classes as characteristic of modern Western societies. Marxism regarded engagement in conflict as an obligation imposed by history in the course of its evolution toward justice. A hagiography of heroes of class struggle and revolution has been formed, but it does not derogate from the acceptance of the ideal of conflictlessness. Indeed, it is present-day Soviet policy to pretend that there is no conflict within the Soviet Union. Occasionally "laggards," "misfits," and "misguided persons" must be taken into custody, but the official pretence is that there are no inherent conflicts in Soviet society. The wickedness of bourgeois society is attested by the existence of the conflict of classes.

Interest in the integration of society is sometimes regarded by social scientists of Marxist sympathies as "reactionary." To them the hypothesis that some measure of integration exists does not correspond to their image of modern Western society; moreover, it also seems to them to deny the ethical validity of the conflicting actions of the lower classes and of outcaste ethnic groups. They really have had little ground for complaint.

Sociological theory influenced by Durkheim, Simmel, and Tönnies has given prominence to the "anomic," individualistic, and conflicting aspects of modern society. This tradition has become very firmly fixed in sociological analysis, and the elements of integration have nearly disappeared from view. Neither empirical sociology nor sociological theory have paid much attention to the integration of modern Western society. They have inveterately alleged that these modern societies were on the verge of disintegration. Nonetheless, they have not approved of this. Sociologists have estimated the extent of conflict in modern liberal industrial societies in accordance with a standard constructed from the image of a society practically free of conflict. Indeed, Durkheim gave much attention to the promulgation of a code of civic morality which would reduce conflict and produce an integrated society.

Despite the postulated integrated society which was contrasted with the conflictful society of modern times, modern sociologists have not devoted much attention to the study of the integration of society as a whole. This is a genuine problem. Its study is necessary for the better understanding of nearly every aspect of society. It is necessary if we are to understand political and social movements or social stratification and the development of intellectual and religious culture. It is, moreover, a practical problem.

II

In the period since the Second World War, in consequence of the formation of new sovereign states in succession to the former colonial empires of Great Britain, France, Belgium, and the Netherlands, the problem of the integration of whole societies has become an urgent practical concern through much of Asia and Africa. Colonial governments had for most of their careers sought to do little other than to maintain internal peace and to maintain their own authority. After independence, the new indigenous governments attempted to do more. They have attempted to "develop" their societies by increasing the productivity of agriculture and by promoting the growth of industry. They have attempted to bring self-sufficient peasant agriculture into a national economy; they have attempted to arouse their populations into a sense of the urgency of national development. In the course of these efforts, they have been made more aware that their societies are riddled with traditional divisions into castes, linguistic and ethnic groups, tribes and nationalities, religious communities, and locally bounded societies which are distrustful of and in conflict wtih each other and resistant to the central governmental authority of their newly sovereign states. They have believed themselves to be repeatedly in danger of disintegration— and their beliefs have not always been unrealistic.

The increased opportunities for gain by individuals, families, and communities through central governmental action have in fact brought to the fore rivalries and animosities previously dormant or even nonexistent. The expectations raised by the coming of independence and the plainly visible existence of national governments—which made many promises but could not carry them out—have exacerbated conflicts which had been, at most, only latent under the colonial regimes. Demands for the redrawing of the internal boundaries to permit greater autonomy for various tribes and "nationalities" within the new state, demands for greater shares in the benefits made available from the national revenues, and the resultant resistance of those who were not strong enough to withstand the claims of their rivals have repeatedly precipitated crises of integration. When these crises were resolved by concessions, the result was to give a public impression of the weakness of the central government or its collusion with a sectional interest and to aggravate the demands made by those who regarded themselves as injured by the concessions made to other claimants. The centrifugal forces in the new states of Asia and Africa have helped to weaken and discredit the civilian governments and have contributed to their replacement in many states by governments formed or dominated by the armed forces. The largest state in Black Africa underwent a long civil war.

The crisis of national integration has not been confined to the new states of Asia and Africa. In the longer established states of the West, after nearly a century and in some cases many centuries during which the acceptance of membership in the national society seemed intellectually and practically not to be an issue, similar centrifugal tendencies have become manifest. In Canada the French Canadians, in France the Bretons, in Switzerland the Jurassiens, in Spain the Catalans, and even in Great Britain the Welsh and the Scots have demanded greater autonomy and a corresponding loosening of the bonds of a long unquestioned national integration. In Northern Ireland, certain parts of the society have demanded their severance from the United Kingdom and their incorporation into the Republic of Eire. In the United States, the black population has demanded integration into a society into which they have regarded themselves as not sufficiently integrated, and some parts of that black population have also demanded greater autonomy and even withdrawal from the national, predominantly white society. Nor have the communist countries of Europe been immune from the problems of integration. In Yugoslavia, the very name of the country has become problematical. In the Soviet Union, Ukrainian nationalism continues to be a problem for the Soviet government and the Communist party; the three Baltic societies have certainly not been fully integrated into Soviet society.

At the same time, the major Western European states are attempting integration into a transnational community. Alliances of governments, mainly for military purposes, are very old, but the formation of a more closely integrated union has been hitherto a concern for political philosophers like Leibniz and Saint-Pierre. Now, however, arrangements are underway which aim to amalgamate the various Western European societies into a closer approximation to a single society.

III

In all these events and in discussions about them the "integration" of society is constantly at issue. The term is seldom defined. It is used because it refers to a particular condition of society which many persons regard as an ideal and the diminution or disappearance of which they would regret. The integration of a whole society has never been systematically analyzed. For one thing, the tradition of modern sociology has not found a place for it in its picture of modern society which has been envisaged as predominantly, if not exclusively, the scene of *anomie*, of anarchic and utilitarian individualism and of the conflicts of groups. Part and parcel of this neglect has been the neglect in modern sociology of the "macro-sociological" approach. By the macro-sociological approach, I mean the treatment of the whole society with special regard to what makes it a whole society.

To examine the integration of a society entails the examination of those minimal activities, beliefs, relationships and institutions, which must be present in an aggregation of human beings for them to form a society and to be more than simply a statistical aggregate of families, lineages, organizations, etc.

Human beings in families, lineages, organizations, etc., always live in societies, that is, inclusive, more or less bounded collectivities which are genetically self-reproducing and usually internally ordered. At one extreme, the society might be only a lineage or several linked lineages, and membership in a particular lineage will then be identical with membership in that society. At this point, lineage and society are identical in personnel and in self-denomination. Most of recorded human history is the history of societies with numerous lineages in which each of the lineages is less than the society. What is specific or characteristic of the society as a society no longer resides in lineage. The integrative structures which define the character of these "translineage" societies as societies do indeed include lineages but they are not exhausted by them. Lineages are only one class of structures which affect the integration of society. The integration of society is a condition which exists outside and across them as it does with respect to religious communities and institutions, social classes, economic and political organizations, which seek ends derived from membership in classes, political parties, etc. To the extent that these together constitute a society, the description of society is more than the enumerative description of all these distinguishable parts such as families, tribes, villages, farms, factories, firms, churches, governmental institutions, schools, etc., all occurring within a more or less bounded territory and within a given time period and therefore reasonably classified as being parts of a particular society. We are concerned not with enumeration and classification but with the bonds or structures which form these parts into a society. Integration is the structural sum of the parts; it is what makes the whole of society more than the arithmetic sum of its parts.

We are concerned, then, with the structures and processes through which the ensemble of the diverse parts of a society—activities, beliefs, relations and institutions—are held together, to the extent that they are held together. The integration of society is a number of different components and conditions, linked with each other in manifold and complex ways. Self-denomination, territorial boundaries, density and scale of interaction, orientation toward and linkage with a center, the system of allocation of valued things such as income, wealth, deference, etc., community of culture, and normative solidarity are the main elements which constitute the integration of society. Each of these might be present in different degrees of strength or effectiveness.

I am not ready at this point to say much about how these various elements vary in relationship to each other, although that is an urgent task. Nor can I at this point enter upon the main types of integration into which societies may be classified, although this too is a most urgent task. I do not even attempt here to provide designations for the various types or states of integration of societies. This too is a task at least as urgent as these others, because wtihout some progress toward its realization, we are left with that pair of vague terms: integration and disintegration. These two terms have been used to designate multitudes of quite distinct arrangements which represent quite different modes and states of integration. All I can attempt here is to make more vivid and apprehensible what is meant when we speak of a society and to explore the elements of the integration of societies.

To engage in the study of the integration of society is not the same as saying that all societies are equally highly integrated. Although a society requires a certain minimal integration just to be a society, that is not very much. The possession of that small degree of integration through the presence of one element or the other does not carry with it any necessity for further degrees and kinds of integration. Nor does the statement that to be a society requires a certain minimal degree of integration imply that even this low degree, once it exists, is guaranteed perpetual and unceasing survival.

Societies can cease to exist. This does not mean that every one of the institutions which they include ceases to exist. Rather the contrary. The human beings of a society which is ceasing to be a society do not cease to be members of families and local communities or churches or political parties, through which they were linked with the dying society. A society which ceases to be a society might appear for a time to be in a state of *bellum omnium contra omnes*, but no society is really ever in such a condition. Humans could not live in such a state for any substantial period. They cannot live without a society around them, and by this I do not mean that they need affection, collaboration, biological—lineage and erotic—ties, etc. They do need these but they also need to be members of a society in the sense of an inclusive collectivity with boundaries and the other features of society. If the society in which they have lived hitherto disintegrates, then they will form other societies once more. The cataclysmic breakup or the death of a society is a very rare phenomenon, although it does happen under certain circumstances. The gradual formation of a plurality of societies from a single society is a more common occurrence.

IV

It might be useful to open our discussion of integration by examining the most dramatic form of disintegration of societies, namely, secession.

In a little over a century, running from the American Civil War to the ultimately, if not independently, successful effort of East Bengal to free itself from Pakistan, and the fanatical effort to detach Ulster from the United Kingdom, the world has seen many instances of the organized effort of inhabitants of one part of a society to become independent of some dominant or central part of that society, and to become a society which is significantly separate from other societies. Ordinarily, these efforts are directed to escaping from the rulers who force membership in the established society on them. Secession may involve a comprehensive program, for example, the discontinuance of relationships of the exchange of goods and of the movement of persons with the dominant part of the society, the divestment of the culture and language which the rulers require of them or which they have to some extent shared previously with the dominant part of the society, or the cessation of the obligation to obey the laws of the central authority, and the replacement of the old by a new name. Separate territory as the locus of a separate society is basic to this program. Secession might not include all of these; it might involve only the establishment of an autonomous government, sovereign within a new set of boundaries.

The secession states of Central Europe and the Republic of Eire which came into existence after the First World War and the new states of Asia and Africa which came into existence after the Second World War were the results of the more comprehensive type of program. The secession of the Balkan societies from the larger Ottoman society and the secession of the Latin American societies from Spain and Portugal in the nineteenth century fell between the maximal and the minimal programs of secession. The separation of Norway from Sweden was minimal. The maximal program required self-contained, self-governing societies practicing their own culture within a bounded territory which belongs to themselves alone. Territoriality, that is, the possession of a bounded territory which is distinctive of the society, has become nowadays an element in the collective self-image of the members of a society. The boundaries also set the limit of the locus of interaction and the exercise of authority. The existence within the boundaries of a system of ownership, division of labor, and exchange brings with it a system of allocation of rewards which is integrative in itself and which has both integrative and disintegrative consequences for the society as a whole. The name of a society evokes territorial associations primarily; the name of a profession or of a religious body does not do so primarily, although an adjective of territorial reference is certainly common.

Populations living in contiguous territories as well as those living in remotely separated territories have both been integrated into societies but the former are more susceptible to integration than the latter. Where the populations of two territories assembled into a single society are remotely separated by large intervening spaces of land or sea, their integration is more tenuous than when their territories are contiguous. Ecological processes of integration such as the movement of persons, the selection of partners in marriage, and exchange within boundaries of continuous territory are among the chief elements of the integration of society. A society which transcends the limits of lineage in the recruitment and interaction of its members entails an image of bounded space, internally continuous and externally disjunctive, which is regarded as appropriate to a real or imagined collectivity. Territorial discontinuity places an obstacle to this kind of integration.

Yet continuity of territory is clearly not at all a sufficient determinant of the stability or irrefragibility of integration. This we see from the fact of the recurrent pressure for disintegration of societies located on continuous territories, for example, the agitation for autonomy in French Canada or Catalonia and the disintegration of the Hapsburg and the Ottoman empires. Yet secessions are more likely to be successful when they are undertaken by groups living on separated territory which is spatially separated from that which they seek to leave, by intervening stretches of land or sea, or which has had a distinctive and separate name and history.

The separation of southern Ireland from the United Kingdom and the creation of the Republic of Eire and the separation of India, Pakistan, and Ceylon from the British Empire were both successful secessions. There were major differences. Southern Ireland was more integrated ecologically, economically, and demographically into British society than were India, Pakistan or Ceylon. There was a nearly completely shared common language; there was much more overlapping of religious belief and of religious institutions. They were separated from each other by a relatively small body of water with no other societies intervening between them. India, Pakistan, and Ceylon did not possess similar features vis-à-vis the United Kingdom. They were very far away, with large bodies of water and many countries intervening between themselves and the United Kingdom; only a small part of each of their societies shared a common language with the United Kingdom. There was little interchange of populations, little common religious belief and religious institutions. Nonetheless, a decisive disintegration of the larger inclusive society occurred in both cases because significant members of each of the seceding societies thought that populations with a common culture should live within their own bounded, autocephalously ruled territories and thus constitute a distinctive autonomous society. Despite the community of the English language, Irish secessionists often stressed that that community did damage to the "true" language of Ireland. Despite the fact that both were Christian countries, the secessionists stressed the differences between Roman Catholics and Protestants within Christianity. The important thing is that boundary around a population bearing a common culture and disitnctive name is thought to be indispensable to the formation of an autonomous society. Natural, geological, or geographical barriers might aid in this territorial definition but they are not decisive.

Bohemia, Moravia, and Slovakia were territorially continuous with the ruling center, and they were integrated into Austro-Hungarian society in a way which resembled the integration of Ireland into British society more than it resembled the integration of India, Pakistan, and Ceylon into British society. They were in an active demographic and economic interchange. They shared many religious beliefs and institutions. Their linguistic situation, however, was somewhat like that of Ceylon, Pakistan, and India vis-à-vis Great Britain in the sense that only small parts of the population of each of the peripheral countries shared the language of the center. Despite the more favorable ecological factors which would have appeared to be more conducive to integration, Austro-Hungarian society disintegrated. Geographical contiguity and ecological interaction is no barrier to the formation of an image of a smaller but bounded, distinctive, and appropriate territory as the right place to live for a population hitherto incorporated into a large society within the larger inclusively bounded territory.

V

The resistance to secession is evidence of the integrative power or propensity which is resident in a society. Secession from a society existing on a continuous territory is rarely peaceful, and that is so because of the unwillingness of the one part to allow the other part to break the society by secession. This does not bespeak love for the seceding party; it does bespeak, on the part of those who resist secession, an attachment to the society as a whole and to the image of a society of a determinate territorial shape.

Secessions are seldom matters of agreement—the separation of Norway from Sweden and of Iceland from Denmark were exceptional. The struggle for independence of the various colonial societies after the Second World War ended in agreements, but the agreements in certain critical cases followed long periods of violent conflict and acrimonious contention. In crucial areas such as India, the Netherlands East Indies, Kenya, the Gold Coast, and Algeria, agreement came after prolonged agitation and resistance with violence being committed by both sides. When the contention came to an end, many other colonial territories benefited from the decision. These latter territories were the beneficiaries of a general emancipation.

The central part of the society almost always attempts to prevent secession. The separation of Singapore from Malaysia was not a secession. Singapore was expelled from the rest of Malaysia. The government of Malaysia thought that the retention of Singapore within the federation would endanger the existence of the Malaysian society or, more importantly, place it under Singaporean dominion. It was the equivalent of exiling a part of the society of the federation—like the expulsion or exiling of a class or an ethnic group, e.g., aristocrats or Jews. In this case, it entailed the excision of a territory as well. Such phenomena are very rare, but the Malaysian union with Singapore had been more an alliance of separate societies than an effective union into a single society. The rulers of Malaysia thought that Singapore was an element alien and hostile to the Malaysian society of the mainland. It was not that Singapore could not be integrated, but rather it was thought that it would dominate Malaysian society if integration continued. Efforts to prevent secession, wherever they have occurred, have been invariable in the new states of Asia and Africa, even though the centers were weak and had no long-established tradition of dominance. In Indonesia, Sumatra and Celebes both tried to gain independence from what they thought to be Javanese dominion. The powers at the center resisted successfully. Burma has been an almost unceasing battlefield in which the armed forces of the government of Burma have been attempting to impose membership in Burmese society on the hill tribes, Kachins, Chins, etc., who have wished not to be members of that society—or, at least, not to be members of Burmese society to the extent that the rulers at the center wished them to be. In Pakistan, the central government fought a very relentless war against those who wished to separate East Bengal from the rest of Pakistan. In India, the Naga people of the former North-East Frontier Area (NEFA) conducted a long civil war to gain their independence of India; on a reduced scale, the effort seems to continue. The government of India will not allow them to leave; it might allow some loosening or attenuation of integration but it will not allow the decisive territorial separation. In Iraq, the Kurds have sought to leave but the dominant powers in the society have not permitted them to do so. In the Sudan, there was for a long time a chronic struggle between the southern Sudanese, seeking to free themselves from the control of the government of Sudan, and the government forces, which did not relent in their efforts to overcome their resistance. The effort to secede has now more or less come to an end with the southern Sudanese remaining in Sudanese society although less integrally than the government of the Sudan had desired. Still, there, too, the established government was successful in preventing secession. The Somalis in Ethiopia have likewise sought to separate themselves from the society in which they regard themselves as unjustly forced into membership, but they have not been allowed to do so. In Kenya, the Somalis in the north also tried to get away but they were not allowed to do so. In West Africa, the Nigerian civil war, which ran for several years, was the most spectacular instance of a secessionist movement because it lasted so long and involved such relatively large military forces on both sides. What was impressive was the extent to which the government in Lagos was able to obtain sufficient support within the country to sustain its tenacious refusal to allow the not-at-all liked Ibo to go their own way.

The Nigerian case is one of the most instructive of recent years. Nigeria has repeatedly been affected by drastic disintegrative processes of which the sanguinary expulsion of the Ibos from the north was the most dramatic. Yet when secession finally came close to realisation, a mighty effort was made to prevent it. An "integrative force" was generated around the conception of an "appropriate" Nigerian territory. The self-denomination had become effective enough to cause some of those who bore it to abhor the prospect of amputation and to attempt to avoid it. It should be pointed out in passing that the military coups d'état, although they had disintegrative consequences, were not themselves intended to disintegrate Nigeria; they were rather attempts to integrate Nigerian society more stringently by the use of violence. The integration was to be made tighter; a unitary state was to replace the federation. The integration of Nigeria was not explicitly challenged by secession until the leaders of the Eastern Region decided to strike out for independence.

It has been said that the ruling groups of what remained of Nigeria only wanted the proceeds of foreign exchange from the oil resources of the Eastern Region. But, if this was their sole motive for preventing the secession, and if their membership in Nigerian society was only a publicly acceptable disguise for some anticipated benefits from the exploitation of natural resources, why did they not by the same token attempt to conquer the Cameroons to gain possession of the bauxite deposits there? These too would have produced foreign exchange. After all, since some political leaders in Nigeria once regarded the Cameroons as part of Nigeria, a case could have been made out for "reuniting" the "artificially separated" peoples of Nigeria and the Cameroons. Furthermore. even if the main reason for keeping the Eastern Region within Nigeria were taken to be its natural resources, it would still be necessary to account for the fact that "Nigeria" as such, and not the officials or the officials' families, etc., was being thought of as the proper beneficiary of the exploitation of the natural resources of the Eastern Region.

An act of secession is the most pronounced form of collective refusal to continue membership in a society. It is the result of a decision not to live under the political authority of that society, but it is more than that. A revolution is after all also a refusal to live under the given political authority of a society, but it is also indicative of an expectation of continued membership in that society even though the institutions of authority and particularly their incumbents would be drastically changed if the revolution were successful. The civil wars which arise out of revolutions, for example, the Russian and the Spanish civil wars, are indicative of the complexities of the integration of society. In the most brutal and destructive manner, both parties to a civil war show an unbreakable attachment to the society which is being fought over. Each side wishes to be or remain the dominant part of the society which they are rending.

Secession goes further than revolution. Like revolution, secession is intended to bring about changes in certain essential features of the society, not necessarily all features, but those which are thought by the seceding party to be essential to being "separate." The features which secession emphasizes are territorial separateness, separate self-regulatory institutions, and a distinctive name. Secession would create an ostensibly new and separate, distinctive society, although it would not necessarily change the internal order of the new society very much from what it was when it was a subordinate part of the society in which it was hitherto included.

A revolutionary civil war is different from a secessionist civil war, not only in the intention of its participants to remain within rather than withdrawing from the society, but also in the intention to retain its territorial boundaries. In a revolutionary civil war, each contender seeks to dominate the entire territory; in a secessionist civil war only one of the contending parties seeks to dominate the entire territory hitherto occupied by the society. In the revolutionary civil war, there is "agreement" between the conflicting parties regarding the territory which "belongs" to the society; in the secessionist civil war, there is "disagreement" about the territory "belonging" to the society. Whatever their differences, civil wars of secession and revolutionary civil wars are identical with respect to the profound disintegration which each brings into that society in which it is fought. In both of these types of civil war, the center of society is damaged. Several centers come into existence, each operating over mutually exclusive territories with fluctuating boundaries. The ecological integration of the society, whatever it was previously, is reduced by the diminution of exchange and of movement of goods and persons across the boundaries of the two societies ruled by the conflicting centers. Of course, there is nothing like an equivalent degree of integration within each of the societies. Integrative institutions such as families and schools continue to operate, even if they do so in a deformed manner; some measure of ecological integration exists within each of the societies, hampered and restricted by the fluctuations of boundaries and the destruction or diversion of the technological apparatus necessary for ecological integration, especially the apparatus of transportation and communication.

A civil war of secession is not the only way in which a society disintegrates to the point of ceasing to be a society. The disintegration of ancient Roman society as it existed in imperial times into the relatively separated societies of Europe at the beginning of modern times was a very long and generally very gradual process. There was a loosely integrated Roman society in the early centuries of the Christian era; there was much less of the same sort of integration a millenium and a half later. From having one or two major centers, the number of centers multiplied considerably. The higher culture, although retaining a certain amount of what had been once common, became more differentiated territorially; national languages and literatures proliferated and acquired a density, prominence, and prestige which the largely unwritten subordinate local cultures of Roman imperial times had never possessed. Self-denominations multiplied as the interior boundaries which divided Europe into national states became more significant and more clearly and emphatically defined. Of course the European societies of the eighteenth century were certainly not wholly sealed off from each other, and within each of them there were many subsidiary, partially self-contained societies. Nonetheless something like what became the various European national societies by the end of the nineteenth century was already in existence. The society of Roman imperial times had been replaced by numerous national societies—not just numerous states—but it took a very long time.

There are instances too of two new societies being disjunctively formed from one older society, not by secession but by forcibly imposed separation. The "two Germanies" of the post-Second World War period are such creations. The German society which was a result of the overcoming of the *Kleinstaaterei* by the formation of the Reich in 1871, had constantly aroused the concern of those who thought a society should be integrated. That was the reason why Max Weber contended for the direct election of the president and why that proposal was accepted in the Weimar constitution. Throughout the 1920s there was regional rivalry and a recurrent worry about integration. The National Socialist regime put these worries at rest by suppressing all opposition and prospective and potential opposition, by exiling, imprisoning, and killing large numbers of persons who might impair the "common culture," by abolishing the rights of the constituted states, and by many other practices. The lines along which, after the war, the Federal German Republic and the German Democratic Republic were formed did not, however, correspond to the lines of cleavage and disintegration which prevailed in the Weimar society or in German society just before the end of the National Socialist regime. The boundaries of the two postwar societies were the boundaries of the zones of occupation of the Soviet armed forces on the one side and the western allies on the other. Nonetheless, two distinctive societies have developed within a quarter of a century. Each has many disintegrative features which are suppressed by the threat and actuality of coercion in the eastern society, and which are magnified and accentuated by publicity in the western society. Nonetheless, each has the properties of a self-subsistent society.

The transformation of a society to such an extent that its character at the beginning of a period is very dissimilar to its character at the end of a period of a century or longer without the inordinate intervention of foreign military force or other drastic forms of disintegration, is not uncommon. It is probably even the common situation of societies, especially modern societies. Still, this is very different from the cessation of existence of a society. At no point in British or American history of the past century has there been a violent or profound disintegration. Disintegrative and integrative features of the society have coexisted, and many, perhaps all, institutions and strata have undergone constant changes, but the marks of continuity over a century testify to the absence of disintegrations strong enough to precipitate a disjunction.

VI

We speak of the continuity of a society and mean by that that a society has endured through time—that it has not become so disintegrated that it has been disjunctively broken. Yet even where such a disjunctive disintegration has occurred, as in the French Revolution or the Russian Revolution, the incompleteness of the disintegration is evident. One sign of this is the stability of the name of the society. The possession of a name is not simply a means of referring to something independently existent; it is part of the constitution of what it refers to. The use of a common name for their society by its members is not only a sign that many of the other necessities for the existence of a society exist; it helps to provide one of those necessities. The use of the same name through time is evidence that even profoundly disintegrative cleavages do not bring a society to an end. The use of a name, of a self-denomination, is a way of filling the space within the boundaries of the territory. It is an expression of a perception by the individual that his being part of society does not inevitably entail any particular action. To be a member of a society is a state of being; it is a quality, and that is what a name represents. Being a member of a society entails many more things, for example, the performance of roles in a division of labor, the performance of actions prescribed by law and custom, the pursuit of prescribed or permitted ends. Nonetheless, bearing and applying the name of the society to oneself and to others recognized as being members of that society is a necessary condition for the existence of the society, which is made up of actions such as those just mentioned.

Efforts might be made to form societies, but without a common self-denomination, societies will not be formed by the populations who live in the territory which bears the name. Steps toward the transcendence of parochiality in postcolonial Africa such as the proclamation of the series of United Arab Republics, the union of Ghana and Guinea, of Guinea and Mali, etc., have come to nothing. They could not form societies out of territories separated by stretches of intervening territory, which were not to be included in these societies. These measures could not form societies out of peoples who had no common name for themselves. The governmentally promulgated societies of Africa and the Middle East have not attained any integration; they had no commonly used names. They had no common center on which to focus their attention. They did not have an effective center to begin to create the institutions from which a common culture could be formed. There was not sufficient attachment to the territory of all the different and separate societies living on them to support resistance to disintegration. There was no institutional arrangement to which the partners to the union had enough of an attachment to cause them to attempt to coerce others—and their own fellow countrymen—and to prevent the union from lapsing. When the Eastern Region of Nigeria—calling itself Biafra—attempted to separate itself from the rest of Nigeria, it was attempting to break away from an ongoing society to which enough persons were strongly attached and which had enough of an institutional structure to be able to resist the Eastern effort to withdraw. There was nothing of this in the proclaimed unions of Egypt and Syria, and of others like them.

Societies, once they have transcended the primordial, have, despite all their conflicts and all their pockets of isolation, a powerful drive toward integration within a "casing" larger than lineage and locality. Some parts of these transprimordial societies have a strong impulsion to seek the center of the outer casing. This impulsion is unequally distributed in any society. It is usually much stronger at and near the center of the encasing society than it is at its periphery, where the primordially fixed casing is more intact. The incumbents of the center find it difficult to renounce any part of their society once they have found their way to it. Even where the "larger society" is relatively new and is not affirmed by allegedly long-standing traditions, those who have to some extent left the primordial behind and have come into some ecological, authoritative, or cultural contact with a center of a larger, more inclusive society are especially fertile for the growth of this impulsion toward a center. The incumbents of the center are ordinarily more "national" or more "patriotic" than the population at the periphery. They are especially so when it is a matter of the possible loss of territory by secession from within or conquest from without. (This is not invariably the case; some peripheral section of the society might at a given time be much more intensive and affective than the center in its self-denomination. There are occasions when those at the center might be less nationalistic than those in the peripheral sectors of the society.)

Secessions of the sort we are discussing are secessions from territorially bounded collectivities with recognizable and demanding centers and with a fairly distinctive self-denomination referring to all those living within the territorial boundaries. There are also more loosely integrated societies in which the larger bounded territory is an object of self-denomination, while primordial elements such as lineage and locality provide the boundaries of intermarriage, commensality, and worship and of ecological and genetic self-subsistence. Then there are collectivities like castes, possessing boundaries and centers which are very significant to their members and which define the boundaries of intermarriage, commensality, and worship. These collectivities are not, however, societies because they are part of ecological systems of division of labor and allocation which encase them into a wider system than that defined by the boundaries and centers to which they attribute primary significance. Furthermore, they also orient themselves toward the remoter center of the encasing society.

VII

There is an intricate affinity between territoriality and the qualities which are thought to be constitutive of membership in most large-scale, modern societies. The relationship appears to be unproblematic for those who think they possess these qualities and at the same time have a territory of their own. Nor is it problematic for those collectivities which possess such qualities but not the bounded territory; they simply demand the latter so that they can live separately from and independently of other societies. Almost always they demand the territory on which they are already living. Individual exiles, however attached they are to the idea of a society on the territory from which they have been exiled, do not form a society; they no longer live on the territory to which they "belong." If they hold themselves aloof for many generations from their host society, they can begin to form a partial society. Ordinarily, they return to their original societies or they or their descendants become fused into the inclusive host society.

The Jews in the time of the Diaspora were exiles who formed collectivities with many of the features of whole societies. They were genetically self-subsistent, they were self-denominative, they had boundaries and centers which together defined the areas of intermarriage, worship, and commensality, but they did not live on "their own" territory. Ecologically they were not self-subsistent; in division of labor and allocation they were parts of a larger society. The Jews of the Diaspora formed many such distinctive partial societies within distinctive whole societies. They never formed a whole society any more than an Indian caste could form a whole society, but their failures to do so were different in character.

By and large, residing in a given territory is an attribute which, many presume, confers or imposes some significant qualities on its residents. Territory becomes significant with the increased significance of a center which lies outside the boundaries of lineage and where the division of labor also exceeds the lineage boundaries.

Each act of participation in an integrative structure or arrangement leaves a precipitate in an image. Each performance of an action in a particular context arouses a disposition to name the self as part of that context. Actions by members of a workshop, of a kinship group, of a school, etc., all leave behind not only a factual memory of what occurred there but also a self-characterization as a member of that group. The particular images which are aroused by these actions are merged into a name. But there are self-designations which do not arise from particular actions in particular and clearly specifiable contexts. Residence in a city or a region or a larger territory such as a country, and participation in a system of division of labor and allocation on a scale which the eye cannot encompass, are not ordinarily so precisely representable in the mind as interaction in face-to-face situations. Nonetheless, human beings do come to perceive their membership in these translocal collectivities, and they designate themselves accordingly with a territorial name. Human beings in modern differentiated societies have many designations, but those territorial names which they bear as members of that society are among the most salient. The name need not have originally been a territorial name, but in the course of time it becomes territorial. It loses its original lineage or tribal reference.

Every society has a name, to its members and to those outside. A name alone could not constitute a society but it contributes to the constitution of the society. There might be aversion for the name among some of those who bear it, but they bear it nonetheless and they know that they bear it.

Why should residence on a territory be sufficiently significant to enter into an individual's shorthand description of himself, his description of others, and their description of him? Why should he give a territorial designation to the society of which he is a member? Why should he characterize other societies than his own by their territorial location? Is it merely a convenience or does it indicate that to experience what is thought to be a common location is crucial in the perception of the self and the other?

A first approach to answering these questions is to say that individuals take their self-denomination from the name of their state and that the state takes the name of the territory because the territory is that over which the state exercises sovereignty. In a sense, a state is described by its territory, and so in a sense are its citizens. Yet the matter is not so unproblematic. The selection of territoriality as one of the main criteria to define membership in society requires further exploration.

Of course, a territory is an indispensable convenience. Human beings are corporeal entities and they cannot do other than have a position in space. Still, why should not spatial location, if it is no more than an inevitable convenience, be neutral? Yet it is not neutral. Spatial self-denominations and solidarities seem to be ineluctible. It seems likely that spatial location, like lineage, possesses a primordial significance. In a very vaguely perceived way, human beings regard themselves as being constituted in part by the section of the earth's surface on which they live. The symbolization of the significance of territory by the construction of territorial deities has been transformed into a much more secular belief. Whatever else spatial location is thought to impart to the quality of a human being, it also provides a marker for the construction of an outer boundary. Geographical boundaries mark the property of rulers—the land and the resources and human beings over which they dispose—but they are also the boundaries of self-subsistent societies. Many human beings want them quite apart from any utility which they might have; they keep them to define the limits of their solidarity—not, of course, that they are very solidary most of the time—with all those who live within the territory. What goes on within the boundaries is the society.

VIII

Once patterns of selections of partners in marriage cease to be strictly regulated by rules of endogamy and exogamy with respect to lineage, they tend to be circumscribed by the boundaries of neighborhood, ethnic and religious communities, within a larger territorial circumscription. Partners in marriage come together from within the boundaries more frequently than they come together by moving across the outer territorial boundaries of the society. It is obvious that the coming together of spouses in the formation of a family is not random even within those boundaries. They come together much more frequently from smaller areas of narrower radius within the larger bounded area. They also are circumscribed in range of social status, religious adherence, and ethnic ties. Moreover, there could scarcely be a homogeneously, all-embracing familial linkage in any society located in a territory occupied by a population of more than, let us say, several thousand members. Lineage cannot provide the boundaries of a populous society; but societies do provide the boundaries of lineages.

Within a whole, larger society, the degree of inter-kinship group integration is bound to be slight; it will be differentiated by localities, status, ethnic and religious groups. In very small societies, a lineage and its society can be coterminous. They cannot be coterminous in larger societies and above all in societies containing a plurality of ethnic, religious, and status groups. Nonetheless, even in such large, pluralistic societies, kinship contributes to the integration of society; it also has opposite effects by strengthening the interior boundaries and the sense of identity of the constituent groups and strata.

Internal migration, emigration, and immigration are likewise significant in defining the external boundaries of a society and its internal integration. A territory without immigration or emigration and with equal movement in all directions within its boundaries would result in a situation in which all sub-areas contained populations similar in composition with respect to the provenience of their members. Of course no such societies exist. Nonetheless, there are demographic boundaries which coincide with the boundaries of the economy, the state, and the outer limits of the selection of mates in marriage. But again, as in the economy, some sectors and areas are less integrated within the boundaries than others; there is also extension beyond these outer boundaries. Migrations and marriages do occur across the outer boundaries of societies. Such occurrences are part of the larger body of instances of the limits to the self-subsistence of societies; such occurrences do not, however, undo the reality of the self-subsistent character of societies. On the other side, lineage, the selection of partners in marriage, and procreation do not, except at the margin of small-scale societies, constitute or define the boundaries of society. Their radius is too narrow. But by their preponderant occurrence within the wider boundaries of society, they confirm these boundaries.

IX

A society is integrated if its various parts are indirectly and directly in interaction with each other beyond the ties of lineage, intermarriage, and procreation through a planned or unplanned division of labor and through the network of exchange of goods and services. It is integrated if it has a pattern of distribution of rewards which is seen as spanning the "entire society"—the population residing within the significantly delineated territory. It is integrated if those living on the territory are at one time or another under a common authority which is exercised in accordance with a conception of legitimacy attributed to it by many persons living in the territory who regard it as the rightful authority over that territory. It is integrated if those who live in its territory have a common culture. Finally, it is integrated on the ground that they possess "qualities" conferred simply by regularly living on the bounded territory which defines the outer limits of the society. They are "affectively," even if not conflictlessly, attached to each other on the basis of their common possession of those qualities—whether they are in direct interaction with each other or act toward each other only indirectly and at a distance.

A society is not, however, formed from individual human beings simply by their coexistence within a bounded territory or by the sense of identity which they each experience in consequence of the perception of that common location. There is much else that makes a society from those located and self-denominated persons.

A society is partly constituted by its economy. This constitution works in a variety of ways. First of all, the location of the activities by which a society obtains its food, shelter, garments, weapons, tools, and needed services helps to define its significant boundaries. If most of what is consumed or used is produced by self-sufficient agricultural units or within an area of relatively small radius, the territorial self-denomination will be formed correspondingly. This in turn influences the scope of inclusiveness of the allocative system and affects awareness of the center. Where the extraction and transformation of the products of nature—mineral, vegetable, and animal—the division of labor, the specialization of individual roles and of regions and localities in the extraction, cultivation, and transformation of natural objects, and in their distribution and exchange, are organized so as to extend over a much larger area, the society will be correspondingly larger. To the extent that the economy is more than a composite or aggregate of autonomous and self-sufficient households, the division of labor and exchange among the various productive units bring larger numbers of persons, distributed over larger areas into a corresponding integrated structure. Every ecologically integrated structure has some correspondence—precipitating and defining—on the cognitive plane; it leaves some trace in the self-denomination. The degree of integration of the economy influences awareness of the center and affects the solidarity of the society. Increased economic integration does not necessarily increase solidarity even though it integrates the society ecologically and heightens awareness of the center and intensifies its self-denomination.

As in most of the categories of the integration of societies, the integration of the economy is not a matter of sharply disjunctive outer boundaries or of internal homogeneity. Even the most autarchic econo-mies consume some goods produced outside their boundaries and produce some goods which are consumed outside those boundaries. Similarly, the dispersion of exchange is not equal in all directions within the boundaries within the economy. Some areas are more integrated with each other, others less so.

X

Wherever societies have existed, there have been inequalities in the allocation of wealth, income, and status, in consequence of differences in economic roles and in aptitude in the performance of those roles, and in consequence of kinship connections, relationship to authority, etc. In one sense, allocation could be said simply to be a statistical artifact. Even if it were only an artifact resulting from ecological and economic processes, the image of the distribution becomes part of a vague map of the society as a whole which many members of the society carry in their minds and in the light of which they orient certain of their actions and beliefs. Their perception of the distribution and of their position in it "places" them in their society. That "self-placement" carries with it certain beliefs about rights and obligations with respect to other parts of the society. They see themselves as different, often very significantly different, from others who occupy different positions in the distributions. This self-image of themselves as incumbents of "positions" in the distribution of wealth, income, and status joins their self-image as members of the society.

This does not mean that they necessarily like or approve of their roles, shares, and positions in the distributions which are characteristic of society. They can, while being integrated ecologically, and allocatively, dislike what they do and what happens to them. They might submit; they might complain, they might struggle actively within rules or up to the limit of their coercive power over others to change their position or share, or even to change the structure of roles and the criteria by which roles and rewards are allocated or appropriated.

Refusal to cooperate, and action to prevent the structure from operating can only be of limited duration. The violent refusal to cooperate and the violent effort to overcome the resistance of those whose demands for allocative shares are incompatible with their own can be of only limited duration. The conflict is destined to end with the reestablishment of an allocative system and a division of roles, either similar to or different from that previously obtaining. A set of distributions or allocations, whatever its determinants, exists in every society, and it becomes part of the "macrosocial" map carried in the minds of its members. It helps to define for them what that society is, its boundaries and its internal properties.

The cognitive map of the distributions postulates a prior image of the society, and this in turn postulates the ecological—economic and demographic—integration of society and its corresponding denomination. Ecological—economic and demographic—and allocative integration are compatible with conflict. Indeed, all conflict arises from and continues within the ecologically and allocatively integrated structure of society. Class conflict is inconceivable without some ecological integration, a division of labor, a system of appropriation of the means of production and of their products in a system of stratification. It is indeed because the members of the society are integrated into these institutional arrangements that they quarrel with each other over their respective roles, positions, and shares within them. The conflict between the haves and have-nots presupposes the perception and function of the center.

The perception of stratification is inevitably, and often grudgingly, a confirmation of the existence of the society, and it focuses attention on the center of society as well as on its periphery. The stratification system is perceived as connected with a center of society. It not only focuses attention on the distribution of valued things—material objects, deference, wealth, and the power which it confers, and the education and culture which these make possible and which are assimilated with them—throughout the society; it also contributes to its definition. Awareness of a "system" of distribution or stratification gives additional prominence to the center. The stratification system operates in part through the deliberate decisions of those at the center, to hold and acquire what they believe they are entitled to hold and acquire and by their already superior share of what there is to hold and acquire. The shape of the stratification system is in part a function of the prior allocation of resources, rights, privileges, etc., in which the center plays a major part through the exercise of authority and its power of coercion. The center is formed in part by its superior share of those valued objects. The resultant allocations then contribute to the sharpening of the outlines of the center by conferring superior shares. The center might as a result of this be hated and fought against, but these very actions, to say nothing of others less hostile, are an acknowledgment that those who perform them are "in the same boat," i.e., in the same society as those who are at the center.

Those who occupy any position in the stratification system are allocatively integrated into society. Their taking cognizance of their position integrates them cognitively into their society. Their perceived position in the distribution is evidence to them of that membership, even if it is an aspect of membership which they do not like.

XI

Secessionists wish to cease being members of the society which they dislike. But they acknowledge that they are members of it until their secession is successful. They also know that membership is not simply a matter of liking to be members, of an affirmative attitude toward its rules and laws, or of an appreciation of its culture. Breaking its laws or being in revolt against it does not cause the society to cease to exist. Individuals scattered through society can dislike being members of that society, they can disparage and refuse to accept its culture, but they remain members of it nonetheless—nominatively, ecologically, and even authoritatively and culturally. However different they conceive or "feel" themselves to be from the other sectors of the society from which they wish to remove themselves, they are members of their society in many important respects. However much they wish to escape from it or however profoundly they wish to change it, they are integrated into their society. They can withdraw into agricultural self-sufficiency, they can emigrate, or they can commit suicide. That is the only way they can break their ties to their society, and even the first way is partial and limited unless they can bring themselves to foreswear the use of roads, to raise or make everything they need, and to purchase or barter nothing from their neighbors. It was easier in past periods of history when the center was not so pronounced and when the periphery was not so densely linked with the center.

Separatism and territorial peripherality have often gone together. There are good reasons for this. Societies have a territorial center; location at the center is more conducive to attachment to the center. The attaching power of territory tends to become more attenuated with greater peripherality. It has frequently happened that those sectors of a society which are at the boundary have been detached from another society or deprived of their independence as a society by military force. Such incompletely assimilated societies have tended to retain, through mechansms of transmission, their own traditions and hence some sense of their past distinctiveness and separateness. They retain some of the properties of self-subsistence, the distinctive possession of which disposes toward the aspiration to form a society. Their spatially peripheral position and their lesser ecological integration have usually resulted in a sparser and more fragmentary participation in the central "national" culture.

The fact of being at the periphery and being relatively concentratedly and undilutedly in occupation of the peripheral or boundary area has a logistical significance quite apart from its appearance in the image of the collective self. If those who live at the periphery are ill at ease in their society, if they feel aggrieved over injustice or are convinced of the injustice or the injuriousness of the laws which the rest of the society would impose on them, they have available to them an imaginable possibility of collective withdrawal from the authority of the rest of the society. They can try to break their ties with their society and "set up on their own." Those who live concentratedly at the edge of a territory can organize themselves within the boundaries of the space at the edge so that they have the ecological possibility of forming a more or less self-contained society. They can do this if their population includes persons who can perform the indispensable variety of roles in the division of labor which a society needs for its self-maintenance and self-reproduction.

Secession—even attempted secession—is not a feasible alternative to most groups which are not culturally integrated into their societies and which are dissatisfied with their roles, positions, and powers. They cannot evade or withdraw from their ecological and allocative integration into the inclusive society, however much they might hate it. The most they can do is to emigrate to form a new society elsewhere or to form a relatively autonomous culture within the exisitng society, if it does not demand a very intensive or closely articulated integration of its members.

Their situation is illuminated by an examination of the situation of groups which, while living within the territory of their society, do not live at its peripheries and do not possess a concentrated and undiluted occupation of a large space delimited within its outer boundaries. Neither the Negroes in American society since their large-scale northward migration, nor the Roman Catholics in Germany in the time of the *Kulturkampf,* nor the working classes in modern industrial societies, nor the middle classes and Protestants in the ancien régime in France had separatist possibilities because of their territorial dispersion and dilution and because of their ecological and allocative integration. An ethnic group or nationality living in a marginal area of a territory and already forming a protosociety can realistically envisage secession. A class or ethnic group which is constituted by its past in a division of labor cannot do so; neither can a religious or national group if it is not concentrated in a marginal area.

Emigration to other societies is open to them, but in a populous and settled world they will have to fit into some other society. They can emigrate as some of the Dissenters did in the seventeenth century, but they cannot stay where they are while freeing themselves from their environing society. They are enmeshed in an ongoing division of labor which annuls self-sufficiency and from which they cannot withdraw collectively to establish a new society if they do not possess the resources or facilities needed for the performance of the new roles they will have to perform.

Unlike the separatists, the aggrieved who cannot escape cannot encourage their disposition to rename themselves so as to dissociate themselves from their society. Some very few might argue and even act violently for separation, renaming, and complete separation from the central authoritative and cultural systems, but however prominent they become, they have little chance of success. Not only are they bound by their articulation into a division of labor which is the negation of self-sufficiency; they are also bound into their society by beliefs which they cannot expunge from their minds, and are thus denied the means of escape available to a concentrated, spatially peripheral ethnic group or nationality. They are members of a society, whether they like it or not.

An ethnic group at the territorial periphery of an ecologically, allocatively, and culturally loosely integrated society can be a protosociety in a way in which a social class, or even an ethnic group which is articulated as a social or occupational stratum into a functional division of labor, cannot be. The former has the differentiated set of roles and the resources for its self-maintenance and reproduction in a way in which the latter has not.

XII

We began by discussing a society as a bounded, self-subsistent collectivity for which certain members have a name which distinguishes that society from others in their own cultural imagery. We then turned from the cultural sphere—from the symbolic representation of the society in the minds of some of its members—to the ecological, space-occupying features of society, to society as a physical and biological phenomenon in its dealing with physical nature and its dependence on the physical and biological properties of its members and its environment. The manipulation of objects drawn from the environment directly or indirectly, the biological self-reproduction of the society, the physical movement of members of the society from one part of the bounded area to other parts of the area, and the division of labor in the manipulation and exchange of products are all physical events occurring in the physical and biological spheres. They could, in abstraction, be considered as occurring in the animal kingdom, although in fact any realistic consideration would immediately have to take into account the symbolic significance which is attributed to them by the human beings who enact them and the cultural beliefs and values which enter into them and regulate them. To take one example: the exchanges between those engaged in a division of labor assume a certain standard of value by which the equivalences of different material objects and services are decided; there are beliefs about how much one thing is worth in terms of other things, about what the producer is entitled to receive for what he produces. Then there are beliefs about the criteria on the basis of which it is decided who is entitled to possess the products and the means of production. To take another example: the lineage of biological self-reproduction is not simply a fact of biological history; much significance is attributed to membership in a lineage by its members and those who are outside it. To take still another example: many of these various beliefs and evaluations are cast into the form of rules which regulate the actions of those who engage in them, and some of these rules are enforceable in case of breaches. There are institutions which enforce the rules through the exercise of authority, and there are beliefs about the rightfulness of this exercise of authority. In brief, even in the ecological and biological sphere, beliefs about what is right and proper and what is wrong and improper are pervasive, and the physical and biological events are hedged about, controlled, and even instigated in part by these beliefs.

With this we enter into another realm of the integration of society, a realm where beliefs about the right ends of action and about the standards for the assessment and regulation of the pursuit of the ends become more tangible. These are mainly beliefs and standards which refer to allocation and the exercise of authority generally and as it affects allocation in particular.

XIII

Societies are characterized by the exercise of authority over the population residing within a bounded territory. It is exercised by an authority which claims—and is accorded by most of those over whom it is exercised and for most of the time and in the most crucial situations—the right to exercise that authority whatever the grounds for the claims and attribution of legitimacy of that authority. Territorial validity is one—but only one—of those grounds. The location of ruler and ruled in the bounded territory is one of the grounds for according obedience and for demanding it. The exercise of this territorially bounded and legitimated authority is one of the decisive features of the integrative system of a society.

The performance of acts of authority is in itself an integrative action. It is integrative in itself insofar as it is successful; obedience to a command is the articulation of the obeying person's action with the commanding person's action; it is very often obedience to an "agent" of the center of the society. The issuance of a command, once obeyed, is an integration of the action of a class of persons with the action of the commanding person. It is an integration around the center of the society even though no single authoritative action is an action which integrates the entire society. It is an integration of center and periphery; it is a linkage of various sectors of the periphery with each other and the center. The performance by an authority of a service for its subjects is likewise an integration of center and periphery; it too is an articulation of actions commanded and performed.

Authoritative actions come in bundles. They are performed through institutions, particularly political and governmental institutions, which perform numerous authoritative actions. Religious—ecclesiastical—institutions perform such actions; so, in a belief-forming way, do cultural institutions. All of these types of institutions perform them directly from the center or indirectly through affiliated and subsidiary institutions. They perform them also through institutions such as lineages and families insofar as the lineage is not more or less coterminous with the society. In varying degrees societies become organized around the institutions which perform these numerous authoritative actions within them.

The center of society does not monopolize authority in society, and it is not by any means the sole integrating power in society. There are, furthermore, societies in which the central authority is relatively inactive and uninfluential, and to that extent it contributes little to such integration as those societies possess. (I do not refer here only to governmental or political authority.) But where it is imposing enough in scale, frequency, and vitality or seriousness of its actions, it integrates the society directly by its action and indirectly, over a stretch of time extending into the future, by the image of the society which it precipitates. The image amalgamates the numerous performers of these authoritative actions and the numerous institutions of which the performers are members and on behalf of which they exercise authority, into an image of a dominant and single center of society.

Where the center possesses these properties arising from presumedly effective action, it sharpens the outlines of the self-denomination of those who reside at the nearer periphery, and it diffuses the images more vaguely into the remoter periphery. The exercise of power, legitimate authority, and visible influence with the intention that it should reach up to the boundaries of society tends to establish the identity in name of the center and the periphery. The inhabitants of the periphery acquire a more salient image of themselves as members of their society when the center is prominent and presumedly effective. Self-denomination is a partial resultant of the power of the center. At the same time, self-denomination enables the central authority to be effective, and thus it lays the basis for the future effectiveness of the center.

The importance of governmental law-making and coercive power in the allocation and the resultant stratification adds to the prominence of the governmental center. At the same time it reinforces the association in imagery of the political center and the center of wealth and deference. The prominence conferred by the exercise of authority is reinforced and accentuated by the association with superior positions in the distributions of wealth, income, and deference. The legitimacy enjoyed by the central authority legitimates the distributions of wealth, income, and status, which also claim and to some considerable extent are accorded their own legitimacy. Sometimes, where the latter is weak, it is shored up by the legitimacy of political authority. The cultural—religious and secular intellectual—centers are in a state of partially autonomous interdependence with the centers of power, authority, wealth, and deference.

The occasional presence of civil servants, judges and magistrates, tax collectors, policemen, postal officials, priests, and teachers, each performing some integrative action in various areas of the territory of the society, draws, in virtue of those actions, the persons, localities, and groups so affected into the society. The actions of these agents of the center are integrative as such for the duration of their performance. Together they add up to an unevenly dense network of integration. But in addition to the actions themselves and the immediate more or less obedient responses they call forth, a precipitate of awareness of the center and of a reinforced self-denomination is left behind.

The civil servants, judges, and magistrates might appear only a few times a year for short periods and not many persons might see them, the policeman might be seen a little more frequently, the priest and the teacher might appear still more frequently and regularly before variously small or large sections of the population. They integrate by their commands and by their representation of the center of the society. But their powers of integration are limited. Their commands are not always obeyed, and, when they are obeyed, it is often resentfully. In every society there are persons who disobey laws. Many do so for their own advantage, others because authority as such is repugnant to them, and others do so on grounds of principle. In most societies there have been organized and concerted efforts to overpower the existing centers, particularly the political and governmental centers. In modern liberal societies there are publicly organized centers of criticism of the existing centers and publicly organized efforts to concert disagreement and to remove from office the actual encumbents. Much of this latter activity operates within laws and conventions so that unintegratedness works within limits of integration.

Unlike ecological integration, from which it is difficult to escape, integration by authority is limited in its power to integrate the society. Indeed, the more integrated a society is ecologically, the more acute is the conflict between those in authority and those over whom authority seeks to exercise its powers. The integration by any particular incumbents of the positions from which authority is exercised always confronts limits at various levels. The legitimacy of particular institutions might be contested but the mode by which it is sought to change or abolish those institutions might be fixed by a framework of integrating rules which are shared by the parties to the conflict. This conflict does not necessarily entail disobedience to existing laws and commands because the dissidents might obey the laws and commands while seeking to change the laws and to replace the incumbents of the political center.

The strains on and breaches of the integration of society by authority are often focused on the process of allocation. Those who cannot escape from the ecological integration of society seek to change the existing allocative results of that integration. They may seek to change the shape of the distribution or they may seek to modify their position within it by rising higher in those distributions.

The successes and failures of integration by authority are not exclusively attributable to the limited coercive and commanding power of those in positions of authority. The successes and failures are connected with the cultural sphere, which is the sphere of beliefs and standards, and with the cognitive images of the society, which are expressed in self-denomination.

XIV

The culture of a society is never completely uniformly shared by all the members of that society. The culture of a society comprises the language or languages of its members, their cognitive images of the society in which they live, their images of that society's institutions, especially its authoritative institutions; it includes their moral beliefs. It includes beliefs about the structure of that society, about its territorial features, about the value of the groups which make it up; it includes beliefs about the history of all these things.[1] It includes beliefs about the universe and

---

1. Ernest Renan wrote that a nation requires, in addition to language, common interests, religious affinity, and military necessity, two things: "L'une est la possession en commun d'un riche legs de souvenirs; l'autre est le consentement actuel, le désir de vivre ensemble, la volonté de continuer à faire valoir l'héritage qu'on a reçu indivis. . . . Le culte des ancêtres nous ont faits ce que nous sommes. Un passé héroïque, des grands hommes, de la gloire . . . voilà le capital social sur lequel on assied une idée nationale. Avoir des gloires communes dans le passé, une volonté commune dans le présent; avoir fait de grandes choses ensemble, vouloir en faire encore, voilà les conditions pour être un peuple." From "Qu'est-ce qu'une nation?" *Discours et conférences* (1887), *Oeuvres complètes*. Paris: Calmann-Lévy, n.d. vol. 1, pp. 903–4.

its meaning, about man's nature, the powers which rule the universe and which determine man's destiny. It includes of course the works in which all these beliefs are contained. To all these substantive contents of the beliefs which constitute the culture obtaining in the society must be added the belief that the culture is common—or diverse—and the resultant sense of affinity with those who share that culture—and the sense of difference from those who do not share it.

Language has integrative consequences through the substance of its vocabulary, which makes available a common set of objects in the world and the names for them. Having this common set of objects with the same names makes for sense of being alike of those who use these names. Where there is a common language, it integrates the society directly as does a command by permitting the formation of a structure formed by conversation or by the reading of written texts originating in the society. The use of a language not only permits acts of communion about particular objects, such as sacred objects or central objects; it is also an act of communion in itself. The facts of speaking to each other, of being more or less understood and replying more or less intelligibly, form to that extent an integrative structure of society. The result is not, it is true, an integration which penetrates into every sphere of activity, but it is a structure in which the participants' actions are—at a very general level—coherently articulated with each other.

The culture—common or separated—has among its objects the other integrative phenomena. The awareness that others use the same name as oneself fosters a sense of affinity with those who share that name. The perception that others live in the same territory, the image formed of that territory, the perception of others participating in the same ecological order—movement and biological ties—in the same system of division of labor, in the same allocative system, and in the same system of authority, all these generate a sense of affinity. The sense of affinity with those bearing the same name and involved in the same integrative processes is not all-conquering. It does not impose a consensus of beliefs about the principles of allocation or about the legitimacy of authority or the rightness and beneficence of the acts of authority. It does, however, heighten the sense of "partness" and under some conditions makes for readiness to act "on behalf of" the society; it sometimes makes for a greater receptiveness toward cultural beliefs and objects which can be attributed to the common culture.

The receptiveness which makes for a community of culture is fostered by the fact of living under the same authoritative institutions as others in the same territory over which the authoritative central institutions are sovereign. Effectively exercised authority is a phenomenon which arouses the disposition to attribute charismatic qualities; some of the charismatic quality is attributed derivatively to those over whom it is exercised and who form a community with those who exercise it. The result is a shared or dispersed charisma which is acknowledged by those who share it.

In a society which is not highly integrated ecologically or authoritatively, where a common name is not salient, and where the center is not prominent, the dispersion will be less than it is where these constituents of integration are more effectively present. In a society in which authority is not effective or visibly continuous and intense, in other words, a society with a relatively weak authority, the charisma of authority does not flow far outward. A belief in the common possession of charisma brings the center and the periphery closer to each other in mutual evaluation and self-evaluation and in responsiveness to each other's desires. This makes for a higher degree of cultural integration. In a society in which the ruled subjects are believed, in the common culture, to be devoid of charisma, the center is thought to concentrate charisma within itself. There center and periphery do not enter into that partial fusion which is a characteristic of culturally more integrated societies. The same is true of societies in which the periphery—as regards authority and position in the various distributions—is thought to possess more charisma than the center. Again the result is in the direction of unintegratedness between center and periphery. There the periphery becomes a counter-center.

It is difficult for societies to become highly integrated culturally, even though they might have some elements of a widely shared common culture such as a common language, a common religion, and universal compulsory education. In most societies there is much cultural heterogeneity, even where certain elements of a common culture are widely shared. For one thing, there are wide disparities in the level of educational acquisition; there are correspondingly wide disparities in the substance of the culture possessed by the strata which are characterized by similar positions in the distribution of wealth and income. Nearly every country includes a plurality of religious beliefs, even though the beliefs fall within the same family of beliefs; it also includes a variety of ethnic communities with their respective and different cultures. Many societies, even the most integrated ecologically and authoritatively, have been constituted from the partial amalgamation through immigration, conquest, and dynastic union of rather distinct societies with cultures of their own.

The existence of a measure of common culture has integrative effects like those of the ecological integration of society. It renders the center more visible and thereby makes the boundaries of the society more evident. But it does not necessarily make for wholly consensual integration around a common authority. The spread of literacy and of acquaintance with the Bible increased sectarian animosity against the church and against the state with which it was associated. The spread of education in modern societies has likewise produced an increased sense of nationality and therewith of identity with the society living within the boundaries of the territory ruled by the sovereign authority. It has also increased the amount of conflict regarding the rightfulness of the action of the center.

This increase in the participation in conflict of groups which had previously been more indifferent to each other's existence—as is the case in many newly independent countries in Asia and Africa—must not obscure from us the increased integration which has in fact occurred. The same is true of modern Western societies in which conflicts regarding the distribution of wealth, income, and deference are more open and more institutionally conducted; patriotism and public spirit have also been increased by the community of culture and by the common authority. All of these things exist alongside each other; they are indeed interdependent.

Culture is created. Creativity establishes, and is believed to be connected with, a cultural center to which attention and deference are accorded. Those who receive and share that culture are attentive to those who produce or reproduce that culture. Literacy, universal and compulsory education, and the interest in the media of mass communication bring certain bits of this culture into a very wide circulation. The common culture is a mixture of serious and frivolous culture. The serious culture is focused on the center; much of the frivolous culture is as well—in a sacrilegious way. The center of the authoritative institutional system seeks the legitimating service provided by the creative center of cultural production and reproduction. It has always received a certain amount of that service, and a relationship of mutual support between the cultural and the authoritative centers of society is established. This establishment of a mutual support renders the integrative action of each more powerful by that fact. The capacity of the authoritative center to integrate by command is thereby enhanced; the capacity of the cultural center to integrate through the heightening of the attachment to symbols espoused by or allegedly embodied in the center is also enhanced by this mutual support.

The authoritative institutional center is associated with the common culture by the dependence of the reproduction and transmission—but not the creation—of the common culture on institutional arrangements in which the authoritative center has a weighty part. Schools above all, universities, priesthoods, theaters, museums have often been organized, supported, or controlled and supervised by government; where they are not so sponsored and supported, they have been supported by churches or by wealthy persons. The common culture which comes through these institutions is thus associated with the center of authority and power in the minds of those who receive that culture. The institutions of reproduction and transmission of the common culture carry with them a strong infusion of the imagery and normative beliefs of the central institutional system.

The mutual support of the cultural center and the other more earthly centers is not complete or constant. The cultural center is often preoccupied with a transcendent realm from which the earthly realm and its centers can be judged. The judgments are often mixed; both approbation and disapprobation of the earthly center are characteristic of the cultural centers. The cultural center sometimes becomes a counter-center and in that capacity places an obstacle before the integration of society by the authoritative center.

XV

The integration of a society is the outcome of a number of independent processes or factors. They do not all operate in the same direction. Each of them, furthermore, has contradictory results: they both increase and diminish integration. But even if there were not contradictions within and among the various processes, each has its inherent limits. Self-denomination has its limits; human beings are not only one thing, and if the society is differentiated, as it is bound to be in ecological integration, very few or no human beings can conceive of themselves only as members of their larger society. Quite apart from the fact that they would be wrong to do so, it is beyond their powers to do so. Human beings have too many roles, and even though they often are not correct in their self-perception, the roles are too different from each other for them to be able wholly to overlook all those differences. A similar limitation is to be found in ecological integration. There cannot be a wholly national market without regional and local conformations and without transnational connections. Parallel and derivative limitations exist with regard to the other processes in the integration of society.

Integration is thus not an indefinitely extensible condition of society. Human beings have limited capacities for integration, and the collectivities they form likewise have limited capacities. The increase in the integration of society occurs at the expense of the internal integration of parts of the society and some of the most important limits to the integration of society are thrown up by the exertions of the communities, corporate bodies, and social strata to maintain an internal integrity which would be lost by a fuller integration into society. They are reluctant to renounce what degree of internal integration they possess, with so much entailed in the way of culture, social attachments, and vested interests in status and power.

It is impossible for any society to be fully integrated. It is also impossible for it to be completely unintegrated. Such integration as a society possesses at any given time is not an equal integration of all its members at the same time. Even without the heterogeneity of cultures and their traditions which are drawn into any large society which has grown through conquest and immigration, there are always unequal degrees of heteronomy of the constituent institutions of society. All institutions acquire and seek some measure of autonomy, vis-à-vis the centers of power which would dominate them. Their autonomy consists in their unintegratedness into the order sought by the central authority of the society.

There are variations in degrees of authoritative and cultural integration corresponding generally to positions in the stratification of the society. Ecologically, too, as the distance from the center increases, there is a diminution in the effectiveness of integration of all types. Those parts of the society which are in more attenuated intercourse with the center are likely to be less integrated culturally into the center and more recalcitrant toward efforts to bring them under the authority of the center.

The degree of directness of integration likewise varies among societies and from one part of society to another. Some parts are integrated to the center of society through a "link." Leaders of groups which are integrated are often more integrated than are their followers who might be integrated primarily to them and then through them to the center. Ordinary soldiers in military units are usually less attached to the center; they have assimilated less of the culture of the center and are less under its direct command than are their officers, who constitute something like a spine which holds the ordinary members of the institution "in place" in the military society. The system of "indirect rule" in the government of colonies was exactly this sort of indirect integration. Similarly the father and mother of a family are more directly integrated into the center through authority, stratification, and culture than are their children. The parents guide their offspring into certain attitudes toward the authority and culture of the center; these attitudes might not take root if they were not sustained by parental authority. The children are guided into preparation for entry into certain positions in the division of labor and into the stratification of the society; they are guided toward certain occupations and expectations of a certain style of life. They are not drawn there by their own direct contact with the stratification system. The same may be said for their reception of the common cultural system; their language is received from their parents, and it is only in the course of time that the children begin to receive their culture directly through the central institutions of the common culture. Ecclesiastical institutions—apart from independent congregations—exemplify similar forms of indirect integration through links with the center. The indirectness of the integration of a society presents numerous opportunities for breaches and imperfections to occur.

These structures of integration and unintegratedness existing simultaneously in intricate patterns are by no means entirely stable. Integration is an intermittent phenomenon. Sometimes it is high in the relations of one sector of society to the center, at other times it might be suspended or loosened; at still other times in the same sector and within a relatively limited time period, integration might be modified into some degree of conflict, with some measure of integration persisting in that as well as in other spheres. Similarly, between points of time, parts of society which have been relatively closely integrated to the center can cease to be so, while others which have been relatively unintegrated might become more integrated. And then they might revert to the prior situation, but there is no inevitability in this.

So it goes. Integration is not homogeneous over the entire society. It is never more than partial. It is not constant or continuous. It is frequently shifting from one part of the society to others. In some respects, various parts of the society might be well integrated, others less so; on other issues, the integratedness might have quite a different structure. Perhaps most important of all is the fact that within the spheres of authoritative and cultural integration, integration and conflict might exist simultaneously in the conduct of the same person. Conflict and disagreement might be intense between two parties to a dispute, but at the same time they conduct their contention and mutual criticism in accordance with rules and standards which they both accept. This indeed is the most significant kind of integration, but it is also one of the most difficult to discern and describe.

XVI

Conflict would seem by definition to be incompatible with integration. In principle, parties to a conflict reject the claims of their antagonists. They refuse to accept the authority of their antagonists, and in rhetoric they often refuse to acknowledge the legitimacy of the authority. So it appears. In reality, however, conflict and integration are incompatible only with respect to the particular actions and intentions constitutive of the conflict, and the particular ends sought by each of the parties to the conflict. When we look beyond these, we see that the conflicting parties are not antagonistic with respect to every end they seek and every action in which they engage.[2] Above all, they might be in agreement regarding

2. This was long ago pointed out by Georg Simmel in *Über soziale Differenzierung* and *Soziologie* and has since been observed with a slightly different nomenclature by a number of recent writers.

the means which each may use in the pursuit of their respective ends, and they might equally respect a higher authority than either of them claims, for example, the authority of laws enacted by a parliamentary body or the authority of the interpretation of the law found by a judicial body.

The parties to a conflict remain, moreover, parts of a single society by virtue of their acknowledgment of a common name, by their participation in certain common institutions of division of labor and allocation from which they cannot extricate themselves except by secession, emigration, or anchoritic or cenobitic withdrawal. They have to accommodate themselves to much of their ecological and even structural integration because they have such small resources that they cannot withdraw and because they have such limited powers to coerce the other party past a certain point. Pessimism about resources, powers, and support are important conditions of the actual integration of societies. Those who think that they cannot resist, yield. They yield not because they share a moral consensus which legitimates the authority of the center but because they have no power or support which would enable them to resist.

All these acts of submission are reinforced by the interlocking of internal moral restraints—which are evidence of some measure of cultural integration—and the unforthcomingness of desired and necessary allies who are, moreover, similarly constrained. Submission is also supported by the uncertainty of the magnitude of resources which might be available to the antagonist if the conflict persists or is aggravated. Uncertainty regarding the availability of allies is a secondary or derivative factor in integration; it operates because those who are not themselves bound by integration are constrained to act as if they are, because they anticipate that others are in fact so bound and will not come to their support.

Two subordinate or peripheral groups in severe conflict with each other are kept in restraint by the anticipation that the center can call on the rest of the society which does not share their conflict. The rest of the society will impose restraint because, in accordance with the rules or standards of the center which they share, they will disapprove of the conduct of the conflict beyond certain limits and will support a coerced restraint upon the antagonists. This is true in contemplated secessions, putsches, and other violent actions against the center or against another peripheral group. Temporary withdrawal of a service in a division of labor can coerce, but there are limits to the magnitude and duration of the withdrawal. Withdrawal and refusal to submit to the center can be effective only if it can count on the support of a large and significant enough part of the society and can be effective quickly enough for the resources of the initiating party not to become exhausted and for the dislocation of the division of labor not to be so injuriously experienced by the supporters as to cause them to withdraw their support.

XVII

The integration of society is thus an extremely incomplete affair. It is labile, shifting, intermittent. Yet it exists. It has an extraordinary tenacity in society even though it is labile, shifting, and intermittent. When, however, we look at almost any society of the past or the present, conflict comes prominently before us. There are various reasons why this is so. Conflicts are much more spectacular than harmonious collaboration and submission. Crime is more dramatic than law-abidingness. Violence is more dramatic than peace. Violence, resistance, crime, strikes, secessionist movements are all regarded by those who are not their agents as untoward, improper, and regrettable. Rulers naturally deplore disobedience; moralistic historians and philosophers also have often deplored it and thus granted it prominence in their writing. The growth in modern times of theorists, chroniclers, and proponents of revolutions and other violent actions has added to the prominence of conflict. But the major reason why conflict is evident is that it is disruptive of the order which is otherwise taken for granted.

Conflict is universal. There are no societies without it. Conflicts are endemic, but they are, like integration, shifting and discontinuous. They spread and contract; sectors of society in conflict become pacific, and conflicts emerge in sectors previously pacific. The motility of conflict corresponds more or less inversely to the motility of integration by authority. The inversion is not complete because there are large areas in society which are neither in conflict nor in consensual or authoritative integration. There are societies in which groups live to themselves. These are societies with a relatively low ecological integration. Even in societies with a relatively high degree of ecological integration, however, pluralism and privacy—where these are allowed by authority and common culture to exist—provide islands which are free both from conflict with other parts of society and from integration into society.

It is evident that it is not given to human beings to live in completely integrated societies. Fortunately so! It is also evident that it is—no less fortunately—not the fate of human beings to live in societies with incessant and all-embracing conflicts. A completely national culture focused exclusively on a single national center is improbable. The complete consensus which is required for complete cultural and authoritative integration is not attainable. Scarcity, ambition, human contrariness, divergent traditions, conflicting loyalties, and the great unevennesses of ecological integration all stand in the way of anything closely approximating a stable, continuous, inclusive, all-embracing cultural and authoritative integration.

Nonetheless, societies do exist, and that necessarily entails integration of varying sorts. Mankind cannot live in the state of nature portrayed by Hobbes. Secessionist and autonomist movements are not uncommon, but they are movements which testify to the reality of society by their efforts to reduce or obliterate the hold which actually existing societies have on those who adhere to those movements. The societies from which secession or autonomy are sought remain societies even though they are badly frayed at their peripheries. Class conflicts exist, but they exist within societies which survive, the class conflicts notwithstanding. Revolutions occur and violence and wars, but the societies withstand them because not all of the integrative structure of society is ever destroyed in these cataclysms. Political democracies exist even though their very existence postulates conflict—conducted through conflicting political parties working through representative institutions and the organs of public opinion. Societies have constitutions and legal systems which postulate conflicts of interest and aspiration and which are intended to contain these conflicts within a frame of integration. Constitutions and legal institutions exist to regulate and adjudicate these conflicts, to settle them in accordance with rules of substance and procedure, and to a considerable extent they do perform these intended functions.

Integration is not the same as traditionality, but a society integrated around its center, however narrow or broad its radius is, is to some extent anchored by what is given from its immediate past. The proto-societies or constituent societies which are amalgamated into a newly formed sovereign state maintain an identity with their own past and an attachment to what they have received. In such societies the center might be more "progressive" than the periphery which it attempts to bring along with it. But in all societies, a fairly high degree of integration entails a moderation of the role of change.

It is through integration that societies maintain their characteristic identity through time. Particular governments and regimes or governmental systems survive for extended periods; national names and identities exist through long periods, and the cultural or belief systems associated with them likewise have long endurance. Stratification systems exist for extended periods, and the changes they undergo show striking continuities at the same time as striking changes. Some measure of integration is present at all times covering and embracing much of the society at any one time, even where the center has lost for a time its attraction and controlling power and even in the course of a civil war.

No society is ever, even at best, a tidy affair. Even the most integrated society ever known is riddled with cleavages and antagonistic actions. Many societies have pockets and enclaves of isloated groups and communities which have their own culture, their own internal system of biological self-reproduction. Some of these have their own separate economies which are not articulated with the economy of the larger society which surrounds them. They have systems of authority which are largely autonomous vis-à-vis the system of authority of their larger society. They are little concerned with the center of the society at the periphery of which they live. Yet completely isolated enclaves are very rare because the power of the center, even of a very inefficacious center, is usually sufficiently great and sufficiently expansive to reach into these relatively highly isolated communities in one way or another.

When we say that such and such a thing is a society, we mean that it contains some minimal integration. Just where the threshold falls is, in our present state of knowledge and analytical understanding, an open question.

XVIII

Integration in its variable forms ranging from complete integration to complete unintegratedness is also a characteristic of all the collectivities which are embraced within society. Families, neighborhoods, platoons and whole armies, universities, friendships, are all internally integrated to various degrees and in various ways. The extent and ways in which these and other formations like them are internally integrated affects the integration of society. The effects may be either positive or negative. The mechanisms of integration of these lesser collectivities are in some respects similar to those which operate in the larger society. But there are also significant differences, and the most significant is that all these lesser collectivities exist within society. Every society exists within a setting of other societies, but all these societies do not yet form a whole society embracing all of mankind. Every one of these lesser collectivities is, as long as it does not form a whole society, enveloped, loosely or tightly, in a larger society. This envelopment is of at least two sorts: one is envelopment by the institutions and culture which constitute or which emanate from the center; the other is envelopment by other institutions and cultures at more or less the same distance from the center. For example, a given family is enveloped in the state, church, division of labor, and stratification system; it is also enveloped in a neighborhood of other biologically unrelated families and a lineage of other biologically related families. Every single institution of a society is linked with other institutions of its own kind and of other kinds, but its linkage to the center directly and through these other institutions is my concern here. Families are linked to each other through intermarriage and kinship, but, as regards the larger society, it is not this type of linkage which constitutes them as parts of the same society. Universities are linked with each other by their common culture and the movement of students and teachers from one to the other, but it is not these particular linkages which determine their membership in the larger society. It is only when their relations with each other are affected by the relation of each with the center that they fall into the field of our present concern. To cite an example: the statistics of the movements of teachers and students from one university to another become interesting to me insofar as those movements are related to the hierarchy of prestige of universities, their reputations as centers for learning about "serious" things, their relations to earthly and transcendent powers. Similarly with respect to families and lineages. Their affections and antipathies are of course interesting in themselves, but here their relations are interesting to me insofar as these relations contain within themselves elements of their relations to the standards and rules which are part of the moral center of society. Thus when families consider and act toward each other in terms of their "respectability" or as being part of "society," then the integration of society is immediately involved. It is primarily this linkage to the center which makes an institution into a part of society. The indirect structures of integration are important, but their importance must be appreciated in the light of the fact that it is largely through their relations to the center, its derivatives, and its antitheses, that various parts of a society form a society and are so regarded by its members and by outsiders to that society. They are linked together as a society through their participation in ecological and other arrangements which are as extensive as the society, and through their orientation toward the center— through, for example, culture, religion, and law. They perceive these relations with other groups in society through their relationship to the center, i.e., the extent to which they act in accordance with the standards which are characteristic of it, and the extent to which they perform roles in the division of labor which bind them to those of the center or those close to it. The members of the diverse social strata act toward each other in the light of their perception, consensual or dissensual, of their respective relations, proximate or remote, to the center. The members of different ethnic groups respond to each other in accordance with their assessment of their respective distances from the center and their acceptance or rejection of the center.

If the various aggregates of human beings residing within a larger territory—however different they are from other aggregates in the same territory, however self-contained or self-sufficient they are with regard to each other—believe in, acknowledge, or respond to the existence of a center, give themselves its name, and act within a division of labor which lies in the territory which possesses that center, then they form a society. They are members of a society insofar as they believe that there is a center which reaches out to cast a perimeter around them and which thereby gives them a name. The existence of a central institutional system, however rudimentary, necessarily carries with it an intimation of territorial delimitation, even though that delimitation is not always as precise as the legally promulgated boundaries which are recognized by neighboring societies and by laws and conventions.

There are of course the marginal cases of nomadic peoples, but they do not wander randomly and their boundaries have some minimal territorial reference even though it is a shifting one. To carry out their roles as members of a society, they require some relationship in space. The spatial location of its members defines the space of a society; the space of a society defines its members. The radius of the power and attraction of the center and its incumbents throw up territorial boundaries; in addition, those who occupy the center are inherently impelled to set boundaries because these exclude other, external centers from intrusion and also because these boundaries help to define those whose obedience and deference they wish to elicit. The center has a tendency to seek integration around itself. It generates stratification and it entails authority. Both of these products of the center erect obstacles to the integration which it seeks.

Every human collectivity receives and generates a culture, that is, a set of beliefs and images and an idiom for expressing them; these beliefs and images include standards and rules which transcend the existing society and its center in power or validity and seriousness. Much of the content of the culture of any group consists in references to itself; much of the culture of any society also consists in references to the central institutional system. It refers among other things to the legitimacy of the incumbents of the center and to the legitimacy of the center as such. The legitimacy of the earthly center lies in its conformity with the transcendent center, which need not have any spatial or temporal location but often does in the tradition of a particular society. The center has its culture and it tends to promote the adoption of that culture through its power to patronize and control the agents of culture. There is a tendency for the incumbents of the central institutional system and the agents of the central cultural system to come together; the one needs the other even though—as often happens, especially in larger and more complicated societies—they might be in conflict with each other for ascendancy. The incumbents of the earthly center seek to establish the conformity of their center with the requirements of the transcendent center. The agents of the central cultural system, values, and beliefs regard themselves as the agents of the transcendent center. At the same time, they are preoccupied with the earthly center. That is why these two sectors of the center desire each other and are nonetheless in tension with each other.

The culture which is espoused by the center and which we call the central cultural or value system, however aided and supported it might be by the authoritative center, is never its creation. Culture grows from sources which greatly transcend the powers of the authority-exercising institutions of the center.

The central cultural system is moreover not exhaustive of the larger culture obtaining in any society. The culture is received from and generated by many sources, and although those in affinity with the central institutional system contribute markedly to this larger culture, they do not monopolize it or its lesser and peripheral subcenters of generation. Yet the lesser culture shows its "ecological" integration with the central culture by its deference to it, its defensiveness vis-à-vis it, and its assimilation of certain elements from it. The opposite is also true; the central culture absorbs elements from the lesser and peripheral cultures and therewith gives them a new status.

The complete integration of the culture of society is probably as impossible as the complete integration of society. Quite apart from the always latent discrepancies between the agents of the earthly and the transcendent centers, the differentiation and stratification of society makes for heterogeneity in the culture and conflicts in standards of what is good and right and especially in the interpretation of these standards. The ecological integration of society as well as the existence of a stratification encompassing the whole territory of the society bring the center into common focus and thus help to create some elements of a common culture. But they also generate conflict, and—whether this conflict is about material objects or ideal goods—they hinder the integration of the society into a comprehensively common culture.

Nonetheless, no society is culturally chaotic. It possesses some order, the order of some measure of common culture. Like much of the conflict in society, culture heterogeneity occurs within a matrix of consensus about some significant matters. This general and underlying consensus need not embrace all sectors of the society and it need not embrace equally those which do share it. It is possible that there can be disagreements on the most fundamental questions of culture, but the existence of bitter cultural or intellectual conflict is no evidence that there is not also agreement on very important matters. This is one of the features of cultural integration; even far-reaching cultural integration— or consensus—is compatible with the most bitter and rancorous conflict. This seems to represent an interesting difference in patterns of consensus and conflict between the cultural and the authoritative spheres of the integration of society.

XIX

Although the integration of society has been neglected in the social sciences, it has not been neglected by rulers or by social and political philosophers, especially those who dare to allow their imagination to play on the ideal society. Rulers have always had a practical interest in the integration of their societies: they have invariably desired them to have more integration than they actually possessed, although their levels of aspiration have varied. No rulers have ever sought more thoroughgoing integration in every regard than the rulers of the modern totalitarian states. Liberal and humane rulers too have sought integration but often only in the minimal sense of an open national market, freedom of movement and occupational choice, and in consensus about the fundamental rules of political contention. The acceptance of the principles of the rule of law, the separation of powers, the freedom of belief, association, and representation of beliefs and interests was indicative of the restrained demand for integration of the ruling circles of liberal societies. Nonetheless, they too were concerned about rents in the integration. Today, too, when the demand for integration in a welfare state is much greater than it was in the nineteenth century, the principles of the rule of law, the separation of powers, the freedom of belief, association, and representation of belief and interests are still widely accepted—even though not infrequently infringed on.

The problems of the integration of society are most acutely felt by the rulers of the new states of Asia and Africa. Generally the rulers of well-established modern states may accept as given the uniform self-denomination of their citizens and a fairly open national market—or a planned simulacrum thereof. This has been lacking in the new states and it has made the situation much more difficult. Alongside this lack or in consequence of it, the rulers confront a population which is not yet formed into a society but which consists of a number of proto-societies with their own relatively disjunctive cultures. It is not by accident that there is such a preoccupation with the integration of society in the new states of Asia and Africa. Sometimes they seem to demand an impossible degree of integration.

Social and political philosophers too have been preoccupied with the integration of society. Their preoccupation has led them in the direction of the total integration of society, although in more recent years few have had the temerity to delineate such a society as a desideratum, as their forebears did. Instead, they only imply the desirability of such a total integration by contrast with what they think they see around them as the total unintegratedness of contemporary Western societies. On the other side there are a few negative utopias of a totally integrated society. What I have written here is no more than a very tentative effort to develop a more qualified, albeit excessively abstract, view of this phenomenon which, however elusive, is basic to our being.

2

SOCIETY AND SOCIETIES
THE MACROSOCIOLOGICAL VIEW

I

When we speak of American society or British society or Arab or African societies, we certainly do not have in mind anything like a voluntary association such as a cooperative society or a debating society or a society for the protection of ancient monuments. Nor do we have in mind the "society" of the wealthy, the beautiful, the powerful, and the well dressed whom we used to see in *The Tatler* and whom we still see in the newspapers and magazines of many parts of the world. (The preemption of the word "society" for a part of the society was significant in revealing the nature of the society.) We think of something "deeper," more permanent, more rooted in the constitutive properties of man's being; we think of something less particular in its ends, less contrived in its genesis, less calculating in its conduct, or less trivial and less frivolous. But depth, fundamentality, persistence, and seriousness are found among families, neighborhoods, villages—in all those modes of the organization of life which I call "primordial communities." These would, however, be recognized as societies only under special circumstances. The most special circumstance is self-sufficiency—self-government or self-regulation, self-reproduction, cultural self-generation.

In other words, a social system is a society if it is predominantly not part of a larger society. A kinship group, a lineage, or a tribe is not part of a larger society if its marriages take place within itself, if it has a territory which it regards as its own, if its new members are recruited

Previously published in a slightly different form in *American Sociology I*, edited by Talcott Parsons (New York: Basic Books, 1968), pp. 287–303. © 1968 by Basic Books, Inc. Used with permission of the publisher.

primarily from those born to persons already acknowledged to be members, if it has its own system of government, if it has a name of its own, and if it has a history of its own, that is, a history which many or most of its adult members think is an historical account of their links with "their own past," and finally if it has a culture of its own, which includes these self-symbolizing elements. Under these conditions of self-containment, a primordial community is a society. But there is practically no part of the world left where this still occurs.

Now a cooperative society has some of these charateristics of self-containment. It has a name of its own; to some extent it has a system of government of its own, and it might even have a history of its own; but it lacks certain other very important features. It has no territory which is exclusively its own, its members are not recruited by birth from among those who are already members, and its system of government must act within laws promulgated by a more powerful government which prevails over the territory within which the cooperative society is located.

What is singular to the phenomenon which we wish to distinguish is that it is a kind of social system which has a genetic history and territory of its own, and which has parts but is itself not a part of a more embracing system of authority exercised over that territory but located and resident outside it.

The definition of a society when applied to a modern society presupposes the existence of families, neighborhoods and cities, churches and sects, states and provinces, schools and universities, firms, farms, industrial plants, and cooperative societies, all interpenetrating each other and performing and exchanging services with each other within a common, bounded territory and possessing a common, all-inclusive system of authority which makes and enforces rules and suppresses or adjudicates conflicts. It is just as applicable to nonmodern, primarily agricultural societies with less differentiated institutional systems. In such societies too the concept of society presupposes the existence of kinship and territorial units, religious beliefs and organization, economic organization, etc. The main point is that these are all units or subsystems of a larger whole. They themselves are not self-contained, but the larger whole is more self-contained than its parts.

But what is contained within them? We have already said that the more differentiated among them contain not only families and lineages but also associations, unions, firms and farms, schools and universities, armies, churches and sects, parties, and numerous other corporate bodies or organizations, and these too have boundaries which define the membership over which their respective corporate authorities—parents, managers, presidents, etc.—exercise some measure of control. There are also sytems organized formally and informally around a territorial focus—neighborhoods, villages, districts, cities, regions, etc.—and these too have some of the features of societies. Then there are those unorganized aggregates of human beings within societies—social classes or strata, occupations and professions, religions, and linguistic groups—which have a culture more common to those who possess a certain status or occupy certain positions than to those who do not. Why are all or any of these not societies? We have already answered that question but we will now reformulate the answer somewhat differently. Each of them exercises such authority as it does exercise within the framework of, or in subordination to, a common authority which is outside itself and which is the authority of the whole society, within which all are included.

Of course, self-containedness or self-sufficiency is a relative matter. No social system which we call a society is wholly self-contained or self-sufficient. Few societies which we recognize to be societies recruit their populations solely by natural increase. Most larger societies have no single history but rather an amalgam of histories of the various peoples who have been incorporated into the society through conquest or immigration. Some societies do not have clearly delineated boundaries of their territories, and in the past the proportion of those with clearly dilineated boundaries was smaller than it is nowadays. No society nowadays has a culture which is exclusively its own. Even the best and most firmly established societies of North America or of Western Europe do not have cultures which are exclusively theirs. The United States shares its language and literature with Great Britain, Mexico with Spain. France shares its language with parts of Belgium and Switzerland and with the educated classes of francophone Africa, and it shares its culture with much of the world. No society which conducts anything approximating a modern scientific enterprise is scientifically self-sufficient: even the countries which are most advanced scientifically have drawn many of the basic ideas of their science from other countries, not only in the past but in the present as well.

On the economic side, too, there is no society which is economically completely self-maintaining and self-sufficient. All societies import goods from other countries and export to other countries. They are involved in complex relationships, in contracts which they usually observe and which they sometimes breach—to their disadvantage (but not always).

Sovereignty with respect to other sovereign states is one of the properties of a society nowadays, and something like sovereignty has always been a feature of societies even in ages and in cultures in which the conception of sovereignty had not become as clear-cut as it is today. And today when the conception of sovereignty is relatively clearly defined, the United Nations constitutes an infringement on it. It is not, it is true, a very powerful infringement, but it is an infringement nonetheless, not really because of any coercively enforcible authority possessed by the United Nations but through the opinions which its organs enunciate and echo. The important thing about sovereignty is that it is an acknowledgment by outsiders that the country which possesses it is entitled to be a self-contained entity, a self-propelling, self-generating entity.

Thus we see that complete self-sufficiency is not an absolute prerequisite for a social system to be defined as a society. To be a society, a social system must have its "center of gravity" within itself, i.e., it must have its own system of authority within its own boundaries. It must also have its own culture. Part of its culture it will necessarily share with other societies from which it derives and with which it has intercourse—but part of this culture will be particular to itself. Some of this particular culture will be about itself. It will consist of beliefs about the history and nature of the society, its relationship to certain ideal or transcendent entities or values, its origin and destiny. It will include beliefs about the rightfulness of its existence as a society and about what qualifies its members to belong to the society. It will, of course, include works of art, literature, and thought—many of which will reflect on the just-mentioned topics. There is a tendency for societies to be "national" societies, i.e., societies within "national states."

Modern "national" societies—societies which claim that they embody a quality of nationality, with their own national culture, their own more self-contained than "un-self-contained" economic system, their own systems of government, with their own genetic self-reproduction and their own sovereignty over a bounded territory—these national societies are the most self-contained of all the social systems which we know through the course of human history.

II

Thus we see that a society is not just a collection of individual, corporate bodies, and primordial and cultural collectivities interacting and exchanging with each other and being attached to each other on various grounds. All of these collectivities form a society by virtue of their existence under a common authority, which exercises its authority over a bounded territory and which maintains and imposes a more or less common culture. These are the things which constitute the composite of relatively specialized primordial, corporate, and cultural collectivities of a society.

Every component part bears the impress of the fact that it is a part of a society, of that society and no other. It is one of the numerous tasks of sociology, and of that particular branch of sociology which has come to be called macrosociology, to elucidate the mechanisms or processes by which this collection or aggregate of primordial, corporate, and cultural groups functions as a society.

The main factors which establish and maintain a society are a central authority, consensus, and territorial boundedness. Central authority forms a society not just through the actual influence and power which it exercises over any particular actions in any particular circumstances, although such acts of influence and power are important as such. Particular acts of authority also leave behind a residue among those over whom they are performed. The residue is: (1) a central focus of attention; (2) a sense of identity with others who share the experience of being under this authority—all those who share the territory over which the authority is exercised; and (3) the belief in the legitimacy of that authority to act as it does. These three residual effects of subordination to a common authority make those so subordinated into members of their society by affecting their imagery and beliefs. Ecological interdependence and the coercive power of authority do not constitute but they help to engender the culture which is essential to the existence of a society.

These three residual effects enter into the culture, that is, into the beliefs of the members of the society and the symbols of membership in the society. Membership in a society does not, as such, generate the culture of the society. The culture of a society is the product of the creative and imaginative powers of creative individuals—religious prophets and saints, scientists, great writers and lesser ones, artists, journalists, philosophers, elders, and sages—whose vision of the world and of the realm of the ideal recommends itself to their contemporaries and their descendants. The culture is the product of the need of ordinary, less creative persons to have an image of their world which gives meaning to the major events of existence and which explains why things happen and why some things are better than other things. The main culture and the variant cultures of a society are in certain measure self-generating. They are generated by the genii of the cultural sphere. They are never wholly and seldom even largely creations of the existing central authorities of any society. But their diffusion owes a great deal to the alliance of the cultural genii and the custodians of the central institutional system.

The three residual effects which I have mentioned above become assimilated into the culture of the various constituent parts of the society. They do so because the creators of culture often refer directly, in their religious promulgations or in their philosophic discourses or in their literary and artistic creations, to the facts and emblems of the central authority. The central authority is on their minds, and they cannot avert their minds from it. They do so because the might and majesty of central authority have overtones which enter constitutively into the preoccupations of creative persons. Furthermore, the three residual effects of central authority are matters of belief and, as such, are themselves parts of culture. They are therewith bound to enter and to fuse in various ways with the products or contents of the self-generating religious, literary, artistic, scientific, scholarly, and reflective or philosophical culture.

In consequence of these processes, therefore, every society acquires alongside the central system of authority—which is, as we shall see, by no means exclusively governmental or political or military—a central cultural system. The central cultural system consists of those beliefs and expressive symbols which are concerned with the central institutional system and with "things" which transcend the central institutional system and which reflect on it. The central cultural system has its own institutional system—churches, sects, schools, universities, libraries, museums, etc. The elites or those who rule these cultural institutions enter into various and frequent relations with the central institutional system and become parts of it. The educational system is that part of the central power-institutional and cultural-institutional complex which inculcates considerable parts of the central cultural system into other sectors of the society. It contributes thereby to the formation, diffusion, and maintenance of the common culture.

The central cultural system in most societies for much of their duration includes many cultural productions which have an affirmative attitude toward the central institutional system. Where the central cultural system becomes predominantly alienated from, or has never been unitary with, the central institutional system, the latter loses or fails to acquire some of its legitimacy and therewith its capacity to exercise its authority peacefully and effectively. Severe conflict results and pronounced changes are in store. It is difficult for a society to function effectively and for order to be maintained when the authoritative and the cultural centers are at odds with each other.

III

Thus far we have been speaking about what constitutes the center of a society. But every society, seen macrosociologically, may be interpreted as a center and a periphery. The center consists of those institutions (and roles) which exercise authority—whether it be economic, governmental, political, military—and of those which create and diffuse cultural symbols —religious, literary, etc.—through churches, schools, publishing houses, etc. The periphery consists of those strata or sectors of the society which are the recipients of commands and of beliefs which they do not themselves create or cause to be diffused, and of those who are lower in the distribution or allocation of rewards, dignities, facilities, etc.

The periphery is very differentiated: it may be said to cover a large area around the center. Some sectors of the society are more peripheral than others. The less powerful, the less rewarded, the less creative, the less possessed of the culture which emanates from the center, and the less continuously reached by the power of the central institutional system any stratum or section of society, the more peripheral it may be said to be.

The center commands attention as well as demanding obedience. It has an attractive power which enters into imaginations and often preoccupies them. It both seeks to do so—although in varying degrees in different kinds of regimes—and it does so simply by its existence.

It should be added in passing that all territorially extensive societies tend to have a spatial center as well, which is, or is thought to be, the seat of the central institutional and cultural systems. To this center or centers, much of the population looks for guidance, instruction, and commands concerning conduct, style, and belief. The center of a given society might also be in some respects the center of other societies—for example, Paris has been for several centuries the cultural and artistic center not only of France but of much of Europe and of French-speaking Africa.

We have, up to this point, been speaking of society in general—almost as if all societies are the same. But societies are not the same. Just as families and family systems differ from each other from epoch to epoch and from society or region to society or region, or as universities and university systems differ, so societies too differ. From the point of view of our macrosociological interest, they differ with respect to the relationship between center and periphery.

In some societies, there is a more intense relationship between center and periphery than in others. Whereas in some societies, where there is a major center there are also minor centers, the existence of which diminishes the centrality of the major center, in the societies of the type of which we wish to take note at this point, there is a center which excludes all other centers and seeks to preempt their functions. To put it somewhat differently, the periphery in the type of society under consideration is under more intense, more continuous impingement from the center. In such societies, there is also a great distance in power and in dignity between center and periphery—the two might seldom come close to each other, but there is a constant outward flow from a center the incumbents of which seek to saturate the periphery by their commands and their beliefs. This structure is that which has been aspired to by the totalitarian societies of the twentieth century. There the elites have tried to make the mass of the population, down to the smallest and most outlying rural areas, believe what they themselves believe on every subject; they have also tried to make the conduct of the mass conform completely with models and prescriptions emanating from the center. The center dominates and saturates the periphery—at least it aspires to do so and to some extent it succeeds. The society becomes more integrated—from the center outward—in belief and in action.

This is one type of a pattern of unilateral relations between a center and a distant periphery. Another is one which has been much more frequent in world history. It too is characterized by a great distance between center and periphery; but in this second type of society, much of the periphery, for most of the time and in most spheres of action and belief, lies outside the radius of effectiveness of the center. The outermost fringes of the periphery remain very remote and, except for the occasional and ill-administered collection of taxes and tribute and the occasional imposition of certain services, the periphery is left alone. These remote zones of the periphery, which might include most of the population of the society, have their own relatively autonomous centers. Indeed, in many significant respects this pattern stands at the margin of our conception of what a society is. There is a minimum of common culture, and the issue of legitimacy arises only intermittently because of the very discontinuous actions and demands of government. Such societies usually have had little public political life; such as there was of public and all that there was of the secret political life was carried on within the center itself or very close to the outer circles of the center.

This was the pattern of the great bureaucratic-imperial societies, which, despite the fluctuating aspirations of their rulers for a higher degree of integration, were on the whole very minimally integrated societies. The pattern of the bureaucratic-imperial societies, which resembled the totalitarian societies of the present century as regards the difference in dignity between center and periphery, stands at the opposite pole from the totalitarian societies with respect to the amount of domination and saturation of the periphery aspired to and attained by the center.

There is an intermediate pattern of great distance between center and periphery. In this, the distance is filled by a series of graded levels of authority, each of which possesses a certain measure of self-sufficiency while acknowledging the preeminence of the great center. Feudal systems —and federal systems to a lesser extent—are instances of this pattern of a major center and a plurality of subcenters. A manor was a small quasi-society, a partial society. Its partial character arose from the derivation of the power of the lord of the manor from his superior in the hierarchy of nobility and from the dependence of his culture and the culture he sought to impose upon his subjects on the culture of the kingdom and the religious institution which was associated with it.

Then there are societies in which center and periphery do not stand far apart. These are of two main sorts. Certain of the so-called traditional or tribal African societies in some respects resembled the Greek *polis* in the sense that nearly everyone was known to nearly everyone else, and everyone was ritually or primordially in affinity or both. In such societies, to the extent that the rulers and the ruled were not the same persons, the two strata were characterized by the strong sense of affinity which bound them together. They were "closer" to each other.

This proximity of rulers and ruled, this sense of common identity or affinity of elites and masses, is found in modern "mass societies." These are far more complex and differentiated than the other societies which show a similar proximity. The proximity which the modern mass societies exhibit is therefore not manifested in situations of face-to-face contact between those who occupy the center and those who occupy the periphery. The sense of approximate equality works rather through representative institutions and ultimately through attitudes of affinity, beliefs in the common existence of certain crucial properties which inhere in all or most of the members of the society and which are thought to be approximately equally distributed. The most important of these are the simple and indefinable fact of humanity and the plain and obvious fact of membership in the civil community which is manifest in long residence there.

IV

This is one of the major differences between modern advanced societies and those which are found in earlier epochs of European history and in the Orient. Whereas in practically all large societies prior to modern mass society and in most small societies which have outgrown their basis in lineage, charisma has been thought to inhere in the center, in modern mass society charisma is thought to be dispersed more widely. The common culture in modern mass society includes the belief that human beings as such, by virtue of their membership in the national community and their residence on the shared and bounded territory, possess a charismatic quality which was previously thought to be the possession of the elites of the central institutional and cultural systems. (The elites were thought to be "society"; the others were "dangerous" classes, i.e., dangerous to society.)

What is this charismatic quality? It is a quality which an individual or a class or a lineage or a cluster of roles possesses. It is a quality possessed by virtue of being "connected" or being "infused" with a "metaphysical essence." This metaphysical essence is a construction of the human mind, which senses that some things in life are of fundamental importance, so important indeed that they call forth reverence or respect or deference. Their fundamental importance is constituted by their "ultimate" character, ultimate in the sense of being irreducibly right, good, or powerful.

Throughout most of human history, the ultimate has been symbolized as divinity; and even now, in an age when at least the educated classes are perhaps less religious in any traditional sense than they have ever been before, this conception of the ultimate is still most frequently defined in terms which bear marks of a religious imagery. But regardless of whether this metaphysical essence is formulated in traditional religious terms or in terms of modern political theories regarding the "rights of man" or the "sovereignty of the people," the fact remains that the population of the periphery has changed its status vis-à-vis the center. It has acquired some of the fundamental qualities which were once thought to be a monopoly of the center and which were thought to be accessible only through the mediation of the center—as in the performance of religious rites by priests or in the granting of titles, ranks, and privileges by earthly rulers.

It would take us too far afield to attempt an explanation of this change. It must suffice to say that economic advancement through the greater productivity of the economy, which has given a higher standard of living to the lower strata, changes in political institutions, which have given more power to the poor, the unfolding of ideas, which has given more power and dignity to those on the periphery, and a more widespread diffusion of education, which has given a more equal participation in the realm of the ideal—some of these changes deriving ultimately from religious beliefs— have all contributed greatly.

V

One major consequence of this change in the culture of modern societies, which began in the West, has been decolonization—the growth of nationalist movements in colonial territories and the establishment of many new states in Asia and Africa.

Asia before the imposition of European imperial rule consisted of societies which were of the type which we have characterized by a great distance between center and periphery. Where they were feudal or bureaucratic-imperial regimes, there was only intermittent contact and a very feeble sense of affinity of rulers and ruled in these countries. The periphery was not saturated by the center; the center had little sense of affinity with the periphery.

In such a condition of loose integration, the intrusion of a new foreign ruling class, although resented bitterly by the former rulers, at first made little difference in the periphery. Foreign rule and the gradual and partial incorporation of the colonial societies into the economy, polity, and culture of the Western societies brought about very important changes in the colonially dominated societies. The creation of a small educated class, urbanization, a somewhat increased rationalization of agriculture, and some small measure of industrialization set loose some of the same tendencies which had been in operation earlier and on a larger scale in Western Europe and America. Here and there in the colonial territories, scattered individuals and organizations began to desire a society more like that which had developed in the West. It is true that to some extent this desire was shaped by the content of Western education and Western political thought. This cultural influence was, however, only part of the larger story.

Fundamental attitudes began to change. A society in which there was a closer affinity between the center and the periphery began to be desired by the more creative indigenous members of these societies. For those who wanted such a closing of the distance between center and periphery, between elite and mass, the fact that the elite was ethnically alien stood as an obstacle. The fact that the center was only a center of political and economic authority, and that it was not also a center of cultural values, made the sense of insuperable alienation of the periphery from the center all the more acute.

The growth of national sentiment was the growth of a belief that a society should be constituted by those who share the basic property of long residence in a definite territory. Had the British or the Dutch settled in India or Indonesia as conquerors had in the past, rather than serving as the transient agents of remote, territorially disjunctive areas of the earth's surface, the nationalist movements would have gathered only a smaller momentum. But the foreign elites never became parts of the societies in which they ruled; they remained parts of other societies. They could not therefore be included into the incipient emergent demand for a self-contained civil society with a center of its own—a cultural and authoritative center of its own.

Simultaneously with these developments, the changes in the structure of the metropolitan societies rendered more intelligible and more acceptable the idea that societies should be self-contained, that center and periphery should be in closer affinity, and that the culture of the center should saturate the periphery. It was evident that the culture of the center in the colonial countries could not saturate the periphery. (Indeed, the colonial political authorities by and large had studiously avoided efforts at such saturation.) These two concurrent movements, both in the same direction, created a public opinion in the metropolitan countries which was favorable to colonial emancipation. It was, of course, stronger in the United Kingdom than it was in France and the Netherlands—proportionately to the greater advancement of the former to the condition of a modern mass society. Portugal, which belongs in its domestic structure to a hybrid of bureaucratic oligarchy and totalitarianism, is the least sympathetic with the strivings of colonial populations to form self-sufficient, i.e., self-governing, societies.

Since independence, none of the formerly colonial societies has succeeded in forming itself into a modern mass society, civil in its politics. India has come closest because it was the society in colonial times which was the most modernized in the sense of possessing a substantial indigenous political elite, a large intellectual class, a considerable middle class, and the beginnings of an urban proletariat. It was in these sectors of Indian society that the stirring for a self-sufficient society, in which membership and rights were defined by long residence on Indian territory, began. It was at bottom a changed conception of who is a member of society that was at work; on top of this was the further belief that the boundaries of the territory to be ruled defined the qualifications of those who were to rule it. If a population was to form a society, its rulers were to be evidence of its self-sufficiency. To form a society, it had to have a center peopled by persons who stood in primordial—ethnic or territorial—affinity with its population.

For the present at least, the properties which made India susceptible to the acceptance of foreign rule are hindering its progress toward the condition of a modern society. The belief that charisma resides in hereditary rulers, in landowners, in ethnic groups and lineages and castes, obstructs India's path toward the civility of a modern mass society. Poverty is one of the root causes of this, together with a deeply rooted central cultural system which for centuries has existed in separation from its central institutional system.

Mutatis mutandis, the same applies to many other new states of Asia and Africa. They have not yet become societies in a modern sense, because they do not yet have effective centers, and that is why the valiant efforts of some of their politicians and many of their civil servants to bring them forward economically have thus far not been very successful.

VI

All human collectivities have a tendency toward closure into self-containment. They seek through their authorities to establish and maintain a certain identity, to define their boundaries, and to protect their integrity. They try to maintain their numbers and to prevent the slipping away of members. In very many of these microsocial collectivities this tendency is weak because their members join them for restricted and special purposes, and they do not allow the claims of the collectivity to become too strong. Furthermore, in large-scale societies of an openly pluralistic sort, individuals are members of many collectivities, and there are competing and conflicting claims for time, loyalty, and obedience which cannot all be gratified simultaneously. Yielding to the claims of one collectivity practically always involves refusing the claims of others.

There are certain types of collectivities, however, in which the tendencies toward closure are stronger than in others. Primordial collectivities such as families, tribes, and villages are of this sort. Where human beings define their membership and perceive other members with respect to certain primordial properties or characteristics, such as common biological characteristics (e.g., origin from a common parentage or ancestry) or a common territorial location (e.g., a large estate or a village), there will be a greater need for closure and a greater responsiveness to the demands of closure. Even these, however, cannot become completely closed: ecological exigencies, the pressure of external power, and the force of individual affections and wants break through the boundaries which the process of closure would establish.

One of the major features of historical development or evolution has been the erosion of some of the primordial grounds of closure. Kinship and tribe have diminished in their relative significance. Locality has likewise diminished. These diminutions have not, however, yielded entirely. In the case of locality, which is a specific variant of territoriality, the category has remained but its reference has changed. Territoriality has shifted from locality to a larger territory, larger than what any average individual could know immediately and from his own experience. This shift to a larger territoriality has been fostered by ecological changes caused by the growth of larger markets and improvements in the technology of transportation and communication. Education has helped to reveal the existence of a larger territory. The increased activity and the greater efficiency of governments have made men more aware of the larger territory in which they live.

This increased awareness of the larger territory has run hand in hand with the diminution of the purely biological criterion of affinity among human beings. It has in part been replaced by the territorial criterion of affinity—which as locality had hitherto been associated with the biological criterion.

As long as governments were weak and inefficient and as long as they could not imagine complete dominion over their subjects—even when they were thought to be absolute rulers—societies were bound to have numerous minor centers around which some measure of closure occurred. The major center in societies such as the bureaucratic empires and feudal systems was too unimposing. It could not gain the ascendancy over the imaginations of its subjects because it could not exercise its authority permeatively or effectively.

When, however, the sense of affinity changed its reference and when governments became more active and powerful, the major center of society began to win over the lesser centers. It has never been able completely to abolish the lesser centers—even in societies in which the rulers have been totalitarian in their aspirations. Nonetheless, a shift has occurred toward the predominance of the major center. This shift has inevitably changed the range of what was enclosed by the tendency toward closure. Now the major center reached out to groups, individuals, and strata who lived in the larger territory. Citizenship began to replace kinship and membership in the village and tribe. The biological-primordial criteria have not been obliterated. Not only does the family survive, but ethnicity has come forward—replacing wider kinship and lineage.

Ethnicity is a construction of the imagination, and when a wider territoriality became the major criterion for discerning one's fellow man, ethnicity was sublimated and transformed into nationality. Even where nationality has divested itself of ethnicity—or race—there is still much that is mythological in the conception of nationality, since it is a construction of the imagination.

Mythological or not, nationality now forms an essential component—a cultural component—in modern societies. In some of these societies—in those in Asia and Africa which have not yet become societies in the modern sense and which are still confronted by weakness at the center and considerable strength among lineage, ethnic, and local subcenters—nationality has not yet become well established throughout much of the population. For this reason, the center remains weak. If, however, the administrative machinery and the machinery of order are strengthened or remain strong, and if the economies become national or market economies, the major center will impose itself on the periphery and will come to dominate the minds of those who dwell there. The center will, in doing so, begin to become the center not only of the institutional system but of the cultural system as well. In this way, the new states might succeed in becoming the modern—i. e., integrated—societies which some members of their elites at present wish them to be.

Integrated societies in which the authoritative institutional and cultural systems are well established can become civil societies with a wide diffusion of the virtues required for the effective practice of citizenship. They can become so where closure around the center is accompanied by the approximation of center and periphery. This is the path which has been followed over the past century and a half in Western Europe, the United States, and Australia, and to a lesser extent by Japan and Canada. In these countries, the mutual interchange between center and periphery, and the heightened sense of affinity which attends this interchange, have brought larger proportions of the population into the center and obliterated to some extent the boundary which has in the past separated center from periphery.

This is not, however, the only alternative; but the possibility of others cannot be entered into in a short exposition which has already covered so many complex problems.

3

THE THEORY OF MASS SOCIETY

A specter is now haunting sociologists. It is the specter of "mass society." This phantasm is not of the sociologist's own making. The conception of mass society which had its origin in the Roman historians' idea of the tumultuous populace and its greatest literary expression in *Coriolanus* is largely a product of the nineteenth century. In this epoch, it is a product of the reaction against the French revolutions which run from 1789, through 1830 and 1848, to 1871. Jakob Burckhardt and Friedrich Nietzsche, fearful of the inflammability of the mob in the presence of a heated demagogue—that demagogue was Louis Napoleon—came to envisage modern society, particularly modern democratic society, as tending toward an inert and formless mass, lying in brutish torpor most of the time and occasionally aroused to plebiscitary acclamation by a "great simplifier." Tocqueville's critique of the absolutist *ancien régime* presenting an image of a society which has lost its framework of feudal liberty through the destruction of the autonomous corporations and estates on which it rested, is a cornerstone of the construction. The arid zone between the absolute prince and the mass of the population was field for passion and manipulation.

This notion of the mob received a certain amount of subsequent embroidery through the work of LeBon and Sighele. A deeper supplementation, which was not drawn at the time, lay in the work of the German sociologists. They distinguished between *Gemeinschaft* and *Gesellschaft*; the latter, characterized by the evaporation of moral bonds, the shriveling

Previously published in a slightly different form in *Diogenes*, no. 39 (1962), pp. 45-66.

of kinship and traditional institutions and beliefs, and the isolation of the individual from his fellows, was alleged to correspond to modern Western society.

The synthesis of these elements took place in the quasi-Marxist assessments of the regime of National Socialist Germany. The disintegrative influence of capitalism and urban life had left man alone and helpless. To protect himself, he fled into the arms of the all-absorbing totalitarian party. Thus the *coup d'état* of Louis Napoleon of December 1851, and the *Machtergreifung* of March 1933 became the prototypical events of modern society, and the society of the Weimar Republic was declared to be the characteristic pattern of modern society in preparation for its natural culmination.

This is the intellectual background from which the conception of mass society has grown. It has gained new strength from the developments in the technology of communication, which were called "mass communications" before their association with mass society occurred. Yet the accident of similar designation has facilitated the fusion of the criticism of the intellectual and cultural content of press, radio, and television with the apprehension about the standardless and defenseless masses.

The result is the following image of mass society: a territorially extensive society, with a large population, highly urbanized and industrialized. Power is highly concentrated in this society, and much of the power takes the form of manipulation of the mass through the media of mass communication. Civic spirit is low, local loyalties are few, primordial solidarity is virtually nonexistent. There is no individuality, only a restless and frustrated egoism. It is like the state of nature described by Thomas Hobbes, except that public disorder is restrained through the manipulation of the elite and the apathetic idiocy of the mass. The latter is broken only when, in a state of crisis, the masses rally around some demagogue.

I think that this is an untruthful picture of Western society of recent decades. It is a gross distortion of certain features of the large-scale liberal-democratic societies of the West. It is taken from a standpoint which postulates, as the right ordering of life, an entirely consensual, perfectly integrated, small-scale society, permeated by a set of common theological beliefs which give meaning to every aspect of life. Empirically, this view is blind to the whole range of phenomena indicated in this paper; theoretically, it fails to see that no society could go on reproducing itself and maintaining even a coerced order if it corresponded to the description given by the critics of "mass society." Yet the conception of mass society has the merit of having responded, however erroneously, to a characteristic feature of this recent phase of modern society; namely, the entry of the mass of the population into greater proximity to the center of society. Although I think that most of the analysis contained in the prevailing conception of this form of twentieth-century Western society is incorrect, it has the virtue of having perceived a certain historical uniqueness and of having given it a name.

The name does not appeal to me. I use it with much misgiving because it has cognitive and ethical overtones which are repugnant to me. Yet, since it has the merit of having focused attention on a historically and sociologically very significant phase of modern society, and since it is the resultant analysis which I wish to correct, I shall go on using the term, while trying not to be a captive of the problems and categories which it carries with it. Furthermore, there is no other term which has a comparable evocative power.

I

The term "mass society" points generally and unsteadily at something genuinely novel in the history of human society. It refers to a new order of society which acquired visibility between the two world wars, and actually came noisily and ponderously into our presence after the end of the second. In the United States and Canada as well as Great Britain, France, Germany, Northern Italy, the Low and Northern European countries, Australia, and Japan, this new society has become tangibly established. Less evenly and more partially, some of its features have begun to appear in Eastern and Central Europe, and they have here and there begun to show incipient and premonitory signs of existence in Asian and African countries.

The novelty of the "mass society" lies in the relationship of the mass of the population to the center of the society. The relationship is a closer integration into the central institutional and value systems of the society.

An aggregate of individual human beings living over a territory constitutes a society by virtue of its integration into a system in which the parts are interdependent. The types of societies with which we are concerned here are those in which the integration occurs not through kinship but through the exercise and acceptance of authority in the major subsystems of the society, in the policy, the economy, and the status and cultural orders, that is, in educational and religious institutions and their associated norms and beliefs. Integration occurs in two directions—vertically and horizontally. A society is vertically integrated in a hierarchy of power and authority and a status order; it is horizontally integrated by the unity of the elites of the various sectors of life or subsystems of the society.

The absolutist societies of the European ancien régime, and indeed the great monarchies of the Orient and of Western antiquity, were characterized by a fluctuating degree of horizontal integration of the elites at each level of the society. There was some affinity and cooperation between the governmental, political, religious, military, and intellectual elites. Vertically, however, these societies were often very poorly integrated. Villages, estates, regions lived their own lives, connected with the center through the payment of taxes, the provision of obligatory labor services, the performance of religious rites in which the central authority had an acknowledged place, and the occasional recourse to a more or less unitary judiciary. These connections were, on the whole, highly intermittent. The major continuous integration from the center was through the church, where, as in Europe, such existed, or through common religious beliefs where there was no formal ecclesiastical body, countrywide in the comprehensiveness of its coverage. The central institutions of government, education, and religion did not reach very far into the life of the mass. The cultural, economic, and administrative autonomy of territorially restricted areas was great, and the center intruded into local life only occasionally. The symbols of the center to which there was a widespread, highly continuous, and common attachment were practically nonexistent. The very meager coverage of the educational system meant that the culture possessed by the educated classes was scarcely shared at all by the vast majority of the population; and, correspondingly, the conception of the world and the standards of judgment of the various strata of society must have had little in common. To a limited extent, this feebleness of the vertical integration from the center was probably offset by the closer contacts between the "big house" and the tenants and laborers on the large estates. Even within this short local radius, however, the amount of vertical integration, although fairly strong as regards authority, must have been slight as regards values, because of the very steep hierarchy of status and the profound differences in culture among the various strata.

At the lower levels, the regimes of the great states were scarcely integrated at all horizontally. Villages and estates, over the country as a whole, were scarcely in contact with each other either directly through exchange or sympathy or even through their links with the center.

Indeed, it might be said that, except at the level of the highest political, ecclesiastical, administrative, military, and cultural elites, there really was scarcely a society covering a large territory. The mass was a part of this society largely in the ecological sense; it was hardly part of its moral order, or even, for that matter, of its system of authority except on narrow occasions.

When we turn our attention to advanced modern societies, the situation is quite otherwise. Government is more continuously and effectively in contact with much of the population through the variety and comprehensiveness of its legislation, through the continuity and intensity of administration, through nearly universal public education until well into adolesence. The capital of a country and its major urban centers are no longer centers only to the notabilities of the society, but for the ordinary people as well. The economy of a mass society is much more integrated both horizontally and vertically than has ever been the case in past epochs of history and outside the advanced industrial societies. Whether by a nationwide market economy, dominated by large nation-wide corporations and by central government regulation, or by a socialistically planned economy, scarcely any part of the economic order of the society lives in isolation from its rulers or competitors. The higher level of educational attainment, the higher degree of literacy, and the greater availablity of cultural products like books, periodicals, records, television, and radio programs, spread the culture which was once confined to a narrow circle at the center over a far greater radius. These, and the much greater "politicization" of the population, bring about a historically unique measure of community of culture.

The intensity of vertical integration differs among societies. Federations are less intensely integrated vertically than unitary regimes; regimes with strong local government are less integrated than regimes like France, where local government is largely in the hands of a centrally appointed official; regimes which allow private and parochial schools are less integrated than those which require that everyone receive his education at a state educational institution. The fundamental distinction among societies with a fairly high degree of integration is that between pluralistic and totalitarian regimes. The lattter are much more completely integrated vertically.

Their intense vertical integration is reinforced, furthermore, by their almost equally intense horizontal integration. Their horizontal integration is expressed in the unitary structure of their elites. Their elites are in their functions differentiated. Only a very small and very simple society could have an elite in which the same persons performed practically all elite tasks. Differentiation of roles and specialization to the roles of the persons who fill them are an unavoidable and monumental fact of any advanced civilization, however much overlap there is among roles and however much passage there might be among them.

II

The mass society is a new phenomenon, but the elements from which it has arisen are not new. The *polis* was its seed; it was nurtured and developed in the Roman idea of a common citizenship extending over a vast territory. The growth of the sense of nationality, from an occasional expression prior to the French Revolution to an expanding reality in the social life of the nineteenth century and the early twentieth century, was the form taken by this deepening sense of affinity among the members of diverse strata and regions of modern countries. When the proponents and agents of the modern idea of the nation put forward the view that life on a contiguous, continuous, and common territory, beyond the boundaries of kinship, caste, and religious belief, united the human beings living in that territory into a single collectivity, and when they made language the evidence of that membership, they committed themselves, not often wittingly, to the mass society. The primordial root of territorial location persists; like other primordial things, it can only become attenuated, but can never disappear. Language, and all that is contained in language and transmitted by it, becomes the link through which the members of the "mass" society are bound to each other and to the center. The sharing of a language is the sharing of the essential quality which confers membership in society.

The sense of the primordial, and attachment to it, have been transformed and dispersed in mass society. Common existence on a contiguous territory has passed ahead of biological kinship, which obviously has insuperable limitations as a criterion with respect to which union over a large territory is possible. At the most, kinship is capable of extension into ethnicity, and in this transmutation it has great vitality. The criterion of territoriality is capable of greater extension. The rise to prominence of the criterion of territoriality is one of the main features of the modern sense of nationality, which is in its turn a precondition for the emergence of mass society. The fact that a man lives in our own territory, however extensive, now confers on him rights to our consideration which earlier societies did not know on this scale. The vital thing is that the territory which possesses this capacity to establish communion has become so greatly extended.

This shift in the balance at the cost of primordiality has been part of a wider sublimation of the sacred from the primordial to the dispositional. In early modern times, it was a disposition of belief—even of specific theological belief—which those most involved in authority thought was necessary for the formation of union over a bounded territory. The dominion of this category of assessment of one's fellow man has been lightened to the advantage of a more general inclination to view another human being in accordance with a conception of him as a bearer of less specific dispositions—either entirely personal or more or less civil. The civil disposition is nothing more than the acknowledgment of the legitimacy of the authority—definitely located in persons or offices or diffuse in the form of the legitimacy of the social order—which prevails over a territory.

This change has made possible a consensus, fundamental and broad, which includes as fellow men all those living on a bounded territory acknowledging by their presence the legitimacy of the order and the authorities who prevail there. The inclusion of the entire population in the society or a pronounced tendency toward that inclusion is what makes the mass society.

III

When we say that this new order of mass society is a consensual society, this does not mean, however, that it is completely consensual, a fabric of seamless harmony. The competition and conflict of corporate bodies resting on diverse class, ethnic, professional, and regional identifications and attachments are vigorous and outspoken in this new order of society. So are the unorganized antagonisms of individuals and families of these diverse classes, ethnic, professional, and regional sectors. Inequalities exist in mass society, and they call forth at least as much resentment, if not more, than they ever did. Indeed, there is perhaps more awareness of the diversity of situation and the conflict of sectional aspirations in this society than in most societies of the past.

What is specific to this modern mass society, with all its conflicts, is the establishment of consensually legitimate institutions within which much of this conflict takes place and which impose limits on this conflict. Parliaments, the system of representation of interests through pressure groups, systems of negotiation between employers and employees, are the novel ways of permitting and confining the conflict of interests and ideals characteristic of modern mass societies. These institutions, the very constitution of the mass society, can exist because a widespread consensus, particularly a consensus of the most active members of the society, legitimates them, and, more fundamentally, because a more general and more amorphous consensus of the less active often imposes a restraint on the more active when they might otherwise infringe on the constitution. This consensus grows in part from an attachment to the center, to the central institutional system and value order of the society. It is also a product of a newly emergent—at least on such a vast scale—feeling of unity with one's fellow men, particularly within the territorial boundaries of the modern societies.

Hence, despite all internal conflicts, there are, within the mass society, bridging and confining those conflicts, more of a sense of attachment to the society as a whole, more sense of affinity with one's fellows, more openness to understanding, and more reaching out of understanding among men, than in any earlier society of our Western history or in any of the great Oriental societies of the past. The mass society is not the most peaceful or "orderly" society that has ever existed; but it is the most consensual.

The maintenance of public peace through apathy and coercion in a structure of extremely discontinuous interaction is a rather different thing from its maintenance through consensus in a structure of a more continuous interaction between center and periphery and among various peripheral sectors. The greater activity of the periphery of the society, both in conflict and in consensus—especially in the latter—is what makes this a mass society. The historical uniqueness of the modern society, notably in its latter-day phases, is the incorporation of the mass into the moral order of its society. The mass of the population is no longer merely an object which the elite takes into account as a reservoir of military and labor power or as a source of public disorder. Nor does it any longer consist of a set of relatively discrete local societies occasionally in contact with the center under the impulsion of coercion and interest.

The center of society—the central institutions governed by the elites and the central value systems which guide and legitimate these institutions—has extended its boundaries. A center still exists and must always exist; and this entails an inevitable unevenness of the participation in the consensus formed around the center. It is, however, now an unevenness which slopes less steeply, so that most of the population—the "mass"—stand in a closer moral affinity and in a more frequent, even though mediated, interaction with the center than has been the case in either premodern societies or the earlier phases of modern society. The greater proximity to the center of society consists in a greater attachment to that center—to the institutions which constitute it and the values which are embodied in it. There is, accordingly, a greater feeling within the mass of being continuous with the center, of being part of it, and of its being a part of the same substance of which one is oneself formed.

This consensus, however, has not been unilaterally formed, and it is not sustained merely by the affirmation at the periphery of what emanates from the center, in which the mass has come to share the standards and beliefs of the elites. It consists also in the greater attachment of the center to the peripheral sectors of the society. The elites have changed as well as the masses. One feature of the mass society is that, at least to some extent and in various ways, the elites have come to share many of the objects of attention and fundamental standards which originate, or at least have their main support, in the mass. Of course, elite and mass are not identical in their outlooks or tastes, but the mass means more to elites now than it did in other great societies. It has come to life in the minds of its rulers more vividly than ever before. This change has been brought about in part by the increased political, and then the increased purchasing, power of the mass; but, ultimately and profoundly, it is a product of the change in moral attitudes which has underlain the enhancement of the dignity of ordinary people. The enhanced dignity of the mass—the belief that, in one way or another, *vox populi, vox dei*—is the source of the mass society. Both elites and the masses have received this into their judgment of themselves and the world; and, although they believe in much else and believe in this quite unequally, the maxim which locates the sacred in the mass of the popuation is the shaping force of the most recent developments in society.

The sacredness of authority diminished with the dispersal of the sacred into the mass of the population. It is still an object of awe. Charisma is still attributed to it. The awe-inspiring, charismatic quality of authority can never be completely eradicated. Even in mass society, the charisma of the elite is alive, and not solely as a survival from an earlier epoch. It is simply given in the nature of power. The unique feature of the mass society is, however, the dispersion of charismatic quality more widely throughout the society, so that everyone who is a member of the society, because he is a member, comes to possess some of it.

This diminution in the status of authority is part of the same process which loosens the hold of traditional beliefs, especially those promulgated and espoused by hierarchical institutions. A society entirely without tradition is inconceivable. Traditions continue to exert their influence; but they are less overtly acknowledged, somewhat more ambiguous, and more open to divergent interpretations.

The diminished weight of primordiality, the greater concentration on the disposition of those residing at the moment on the bounded territory means that the mass society is the society of the living, contemporaneous mass. It is almost as if society possessed a quantum of charisma, which, if it be attributed to the living, leaves little over for attribution to the ancestors. Since, however, no society can ever cut itself off from its past as a source of its own legitimacy, any more than its sensitivity to the primordial can ever evaporate completely, the traditional inheritance is adapted to the necessities of mass society by the diverse interpretations of rights which correspond to the vital heterogeneity of interests within the mass society itself.

The attenuation of traditional belief and of attachment to the past is accentuated by the less authoritative relationship of adults to children—

which in itself is an outcome of the same moral shift which has enabled modern society to become a mass society. The dispersal of the charisma which confers dignity may be observed in the attitudes toward women, youth, and ethnic groups which have hitherto been in a disadvantageous position. It is noticeable within families, in the rights of children, and within corporate bodies like factories, universities, and churches, in the rights of subordinates.

IV

This dispersion of charisma from the center outward has manifested itself in a greater stress on individual dignity and individual rights in all generations, strata in both sexes, and in the whole variety of ethnic groups and peoples. This extension does not always reach equally into all spheres of life; and it does not equally embrace all sectors of the population. Inequalities remain, partly from tradition, partly from functional necessity, and partly from the fact that the movement toward equality is not the only fundamental impulse that moves men and women. Sadism, pride, interest, awe before the creative, still persist and limit the spread of equality.

Nonetheless, this consensus, which leans toward the interpretation of every living human being as sharing in the uniting essence which defines the society, has produced a wide distribution of civility. Civility is the virtue of the citizen, not the virtue of the hero or of the private man. It is the acceptance of the tasks of the management of public affairs in collaboration with others and with regard to the interests, individual, sectional, and collective, of the entire society. The sense of responsibility for and to the whole, and a general acceptance of the rules which are valid within it, are integral to civility. Civil politics are the politics of effective compromise within an institutional system accepted as of inherent legitimacy. The idea of civility is not a modern creation; but it is in the mass society that it has found a more widely diffused, if still a deeply imperfect, realization. The very idea of a citizenry practically coterminous with the adult population living within far-flung territorial boundaries is a product of this extension of the "center," i.e., of the belief that charisma belongs in the mass as well as in the elite.

The moral equalitarianism which is such a unique trait of the West, in real practice and not just as the dream of philosophers, is another manifestation of this expansion of the center.[1] The moral equality which has a tangible reality in mass societies is the equality which is a function of the sharing in membership in a community, by the sharing of the language in which the essence of the society is expressed. Those who share in this membership, as it is evinced by their share in the language, come to be regarded as sharing in the charismatic essence of the society and therewith may legitimately claim an irreducible dignity.

V

The mass society lifted the lid on impulse, hitherto held down by the hierarchy of authority, tradition, and ancestry. The believed perception of charisma of the social order in one's ordinary, individual fellow man has taken form in a redirection of sensitivity to disposition, to qualities lying within the individual. The civil disposition is only one such disposition. There is also the personal disposition which has been increasingly discovered in mass society. It is discovered in oneself and in society.

The personal dispositions, those qualities of rationality and impulsiveness, amiability and surliness, kindliness and harshness, lovingness and hatefulness, form the constitution of the individual. Felt by himself, acknowledged by himself, coped with by himself, they are formed into his individuality.The perception and appreciation of individuality in others moves in unison with its development in the self.

Personal individuality and the sacredness of the individual in the civil order are not identical. Indeed, they are almost polar opposites; the latter is in a certain sense a denial of the former. It transcends personal individuality and suspends it. Nonetheless, they both have grown from

1. In a society touched by moral equalitarianism, the possibility of a populistic inequalitarianism, in which some become "more equal than others," is by no means remote. In American society, and possibly in Australian, which have gone farther in this direction than any other countries, and where populism is not merely a doctrine of the intellectuals but a belief and practice of the populace and its politicians, there is always some danger that a strong gust of populistic sentiment can distract the civil order. Such was the situation during the years from 1947 to 1954, when the late Senator McCarthy stirred and was carried by a whirlwind of an extreme populism. But it never spread into the entire society; and, in the end, it broke on the rocks of Republican respectability. It remains a latent possibility, inherent in the ethos of mass society.

the lightening of pressure of the primordial and from the loosening of the rigor of a sacred order based on common belief, on a shared communion with divinity.

Individuality, personal relationships, and love have not been discovered by mass society. They have been known in practically all cultures. It is, however, only in mass society that they have come to be regarded as part of the right order of life, and have come to be striven for and occasionally, however unstably, attained.

The mass society has gone further in the creation of a common culture than any previous society. Regional cultural variations have diminished as well as those of class and profession and even those of generation. Yet this more widely extended uniformity, which for sheer repressive force might be no smaller or greater than the repression of the more local sectional cultures of the past, has been dialectically connected with the emergence of a greater individuality. The value attributed to contemporaneity in mass society, the heavier stress on present enjoyment rather than on the obligation of respect toward tradition, involves necessarily an opening to experience. The diminished respect for the sacredness of authority has been accompanied by the shift of the center of gravity into the individual. Of course, as the critics of mass society often point out, this can result in a dull acceptance of what is readily available to the most visible models in the culture, and in fact it frequently does so, with the result that individuality in many instances is no better situated in mass society than it was in more hierarchical and traditional societies. Nonetheless, there has been a great change, not too different from that which Burckhardt perceived in the Renaissance. The individual organism has become a seeker after experience, a repository of experience, an imaginative elaborator of experience. To a greater extent than in the past, the experience of the ordinary person, at least in youth, is admitted to consciousness and comes to form part of the core of the individual's outlook. There has come about a greater openness to experience, an efflorescence of sensation and sensibility. There has been a transcendence of the primordially and authoritatively given, a movement outward toward experience, not only toward organic sensation, but toward the experience of other minds and personalities. It gives rise to and lives in personal attachment, it grows from the expansion of the emphatic capacities of the human being.

In a crude, often grotesque way, the mass society has seen the growth, over wide areas of society, of an appreciation of the value of the experience of personal relationships, of the intrinsic value of a personal attachment, nowhere more than in the vicissitudes of love and marriage in modern society, with all its conflict and dissolution. Perhaps too much is demanded of the frail and unstable capacities of the organism for personal attachment, but the sensitivity and the striving are there. The talk about "human relations" in private and public administration might be largely cant and unthinking cliché, but not entirely. This is the age in which man has begun to live, to breathe with less congestion, and to open his pores. The pleasures of eye and ear and taste and touch and conviviality have become values in larger sections of the population.

People make many choices in many spheres of life and do not have choices made for them simply by tradition, authority, and scarcity. They enjoy some degree of freedom of choice, and they exercise that freedom in more spheres than in societies which are not mass societies. The choices are often unwise, and manifest an unrefined taste. They are often ill considered. But they are choices and not the dumb acceptance of what is given.

Prior to the emergence of modern mass society, the mass of population lived in a primordial, traditional, hierarchical condition. All of these three properties of a society hamper the formation of individuality and restrict its movement once it is generated. The twin processes of civilization and industrialization have reduced some of these hindrances, and set loose the cognitive, appreciative, and moral potential of the mass of the population.

I would not wish to have the foregoing observations interpreted to imply that the individuality which has flowered in mass society has been an unqualified moral and aesthetic success, or that it is universally attained within the boundaries of mass society, or that there are not persons to whom it is not a value, or that in Germany the elite of the society—at least many of its members—did not go to the opposite extreme and enthusiastically and brutally deny the value of individual human existence. A significant proportion of the population in every society lives in a nearly vegetative routine, withdrawn and unresponsive except for occasional patches of harsh aggressive expansiveness. In the mass society of the present century, the proportion seems smaller, the period of sensitivity in the individual's course of life longer.

Personal relations, friendship and love, are beset by vicissitudes and frequently culminate in painful disruption; sensibility and curiosity are often perverse and injurious. Privacy is frequently affronted and transgressed and indiscriminately renounced. In certain sections of the population, the discovery of the possibility and pleasures of sensation has been carried to the far reaches of a negative withdrawal from society and to an often active rejection. In others, it releases an egoistic hedonism, an individual expansiveness, which leaves nothing available to the civil sphere and the consensus which it requires.

Some of these are as much the products of man's nature amidst the possibilities of mass society as are the heightened individuality, curiosity, and sensibility, the enhanced capacity for experience, conviviality, and affection which are its novel contributions. They are the price which is paid for entering into the opening of human potentialities on a massive scale.

VI

The mass society is a welfare society. As a function of a greater attachment to the whole society and the strengthening of the sense of affinity which cuts across class, ethnic, and kinship boundaries, there has grown the concern for the well-being of others. Christianity as a body of specific beliefs might have faded from men's minds—although probably not as much as the *laudator temporis acti* insists—but the sentiment embodied in the idea of Christian charity and Christian love has expanded and spread. These are now a part of the constitution of mass society—in the allegedly "secular state." Material help and emotional sympathy may be claimed without specific payment or counterperformance. Regardless of whether the economic regime is nominally socialistic or capitalistic, and whether the ruling political party regards itself as socialist or "bourgeois," it is commonly acknowledged that, at least at the lower levels of the social and economic scale, there need not be any commensurate relationship between specific performance and reward. In the corporate bodies which conduct the main industrial and commercial activities of the mass society, trade union principles and the practices of personnel management have eroded the standard that rewards must be precisely correlated to specific performances in a role.

This process, like the other processes which characterize mass society, has its limitations. It comes into conflict with the exigencies of operation of any large scale undertaking which requires impersonal administration in accordance with reasonably explicit and differentiated rules. A modicum of efficiency and of justice too require a measure of specificity in the standards which govern the allocation of opportunity for access to many occupational roles. Efficiency and justice require also a fixation of the rules governing rights and obligations in the society at large and within particular corporate bodies.

VII

Mass society is an industrial society. Without industry, that is, without the replacement of simple tools by complicated machines, mass society would be intellectually inconceivable and actually impossible. Modern industrial technique through its creation of an elaborate network of transportation and communication has rendered it possible for the various parts of mass society to have a frequency of contact with each other which was unknown to earlier, nonindustrial societies. The different social classes and regional sectors of a society can become more aware of each other's modes of life. This heightened mutual awareness, impossible without the modern technology of communication and transportation, has enlarged the internal population which dwells in the minds of man.

Modern industrial technique makes possible and requires the proliferation of the intellectual professions. It has produced the education which, numerous though its deficiencies might be, has, through reading and instruction, opened the mind to the varieties of experience of other human beings. It has liberated men from the burden of physically exhausting labor; it has given him a part of each day and week free from the discipline and strain of labor, and it has given him resources through which new experiences of sensation, expansion into conviviality, and interior elaboration have become realities.

Mass society has witnessed a reinterpretation of the value of a human being. Simply by virtue of his quality of membership in the society he acquires a minimal dignity.

The elevation of the *qualities* of humanity and of membership in a wider, territorially circumscribed community to a position in which they markedly determine the status and rights of individuals, groups, and classes, has led to a diminution of the importance of individual *achievement* as a determinant of status. The increased value of experience, of pleasurable experience, most easily obtainable in mass society through the cultivation of a style of life, has had a parallel effect. The quality of life has tended to replace—it can never entirely replace—occupational achievement and proficiency as a source of self-esteem and as a criterion for esteeming others.

This produces a grandiose historical paradox. Mass society, which has been made possible by technological and economic progress, which in turn has been impelled by the desire for achievement in the proficient performance of a role, contributes toward a situation in which occupational achievement has become less important in the claiming and acknowledgment of status.

A large-scale society requires large-scale bureaucratic administration. Its well-being depends on technological progress. Both of these depend on the wide distribution in the population of individuals capable of acting in the light of impersonal, universalistic standards, capable of performing specific and specialized tasks, capable of discipline. All of these are alien to the ethos of mass society, and the disjunction can only make for an incessant tension of the mass of the population, and in many personalities, in the face of the value orientations required by the type of society to which men are committed by the circumstances of their birth and their own desires.

VIII

The mass society is a large-scale society. It involves populations running into the millions and hundreds of millions, and it covers large territories. It is therefore inevitably a differentiated society, differentiated in function, outlook, and attachments. The complete homogeneity which the critics of mass society perceive is an impossibility. There is, of course, perhaps a greater homogeneity than in the much less loosely integrated societies of the past—this is given by the fact of the greater consensuality, the greater sense of unity, the speaking of a common language. There are, however, real, although probably indeterminable, limits to the homogeneity which any large-scale society can sustain. Similar limits are imposed on the consensuality of the society, even if it had not inherited such a variety of cultural traditions of class orientations and religious beliefs.

IX

The picture which I have given here will immediately strike any moderately informed person as widely at variance with the image of the mass society which has been set going by the creators and the patrons of that term. They have stressed alienation, belieflessness, atomization, amorality, conformism, rootless homogeneity, moral emptiness, face-lessness, egotism, the utter evaporation of any kind of loyalty—except occasionally the passionately zealous attachment to an ideological movement. They point to the indiscipline of youth and the neglect of the aged; they allege a frivolous hedonism and a joyless vulgarity. There is a little truth in these assertions but not very much. All of the phenomena referred to do exist in modern mass societies, but a great deal more exists. Some of the features to which the critics of "mass society" point are closely connected with these others which I have emphasized. The alienation so often mentioned is an extreme form of the disenchantment (*Entzauberung*) of authority; the unchecked egotism and frivolous hedonism are associated with the growth of individual sensibility; the indiscipline of youth is a product of the lightening of the force of the primordial and the diminished pressure of hierarchy. The narrowing of the scope of local autonomy is connected with the formation of a more integral society. The apathy which so many notice is brought to the forefront of attention as a result of the greatly extended opportunity for judgment and sharing in the exercise of decision which mass society offers. The vulgarity is one of the manifestations of the expansion of sensibility; it is an unrefined and unappealing expression of sensibility, which replaces the long prevailing torpor of much of the race.

The consensuality of mass society, the closer approximation of center and periphery, the greater moral equality of the various strata and sectors, the growth of sensibility and individuality are all, as I have said, imperfect. Their imperfection comes from the inherent impossibility for any large-scale society to attain perfection in those categories, or of any society to attain perfection in any category. The imperfections of mass society are in part a result of the distribution of moral qualities in human beings. In part they come from the nature of mass society as such and its inheritance from the past of mankind.

Mass society has arisen from an inequalitarian, pluralistic society, pluralistic out of the sepatateness of the classes, the isolation of localities from each other, and, in modern times, the principle of organization of society. It has arisen against a background of puritanical authority which, whatever its own practices, viewed with disapproval the pleasures of the mass of the population and of all that seemed to distract them from their twin obligations of labor and obedience. The proletariat of these past societies, except for a few skilled occupations, with elaborate traditions of their own, were a poor, besotted lot: the peasantry were clods, sometimes woodenly pious, sometimes simply woodenly dull. In so far as they had loyalties, they were strictly local. There is practically no history of civility in the lower classes of premodern societies, and it appears only fitfully, albeit impressively, among the highest level of the artisan stratum in the nineteenth century.

The emancipation of the hitherto disadvantaged classes from the burdensome moral traditions and the sheer poverty and heavy labor which confined the development of their emotional and moral potentialities let loose, together with the more positive striving for experience and pleasure, a hitherto suppressed antiauthoritatian aggressiveness. The transfer of a certain amount of libido from kinship, class, and ethnic groups to the larger community has not been a readily encompassable task. In many cases, the old loyalties have fallen away and the larger loyalty has not replaced them. It is quite possible that many human beings lack the capacity to sustain a loyalty to such remote symbols, and they are, in consequence, left suspended in apathy and dissatisfaction between narrower loyalties no longer effective—probably never very effective for many—and broader loyalties not yet effective—and perhaps never to become effective for all.

None of these conditions has been very conducive to the realization of a civil, cultivated, consensual, more egalitarian society, quite apart from ineluctable functional constraints.

X

Can it ever be fully realized? Can mass society move forward to the fulfillment of the possibilities which have been opened by technological progress and the moral transmutation arising from the shift in the locus of charisma?

There are very stringent limitations. There are limitations which the trend toward moral equality must encounter because the propensities which impel men to seek and acknowledge a measure of fundamental moral equality are neither deeper nor more enduring than those which demand and produce moral inequality. A large-scale society will necessarily be regionally differentiated, and this will entail differences in interests and loyalties. The natural differences in intellectual capacities and in temperament will inevitably make for differences in assimilation of the central value system. Occupational differences will sustain different streams of cultural tradition and different relationships to the authorities at the heart of the central institutional system. And naturally, the differences of age and the culture of the various generations will also be a source of fissure. These differences are all anchored in "objective" differences, ineluctably associated with the human lot in general or with the unavoidable conditions of any large-scale industrial society. They are objective differences on which the dispositions toward evaluative discrimination will always seize. Then too there is not only the need for communion. There is the need for separation and distance—collective as well as individual—which will create in any society lines of fissure in the surface of union and the sense of moral equality which attends it.

For the same reasons, the realization of a common culture is an impossibility. The growth of individuality too has its limits imposed in part by the other features of mass society and, in part, by the wide range of dispersion among human beings of the intensity of need for individuality.

Finally, the propensities which have been released and cultivated by the mass society are not harmonious with disciplined individuality. It also cannot evade a complex division of labor, with many occupational and professional roles, some of which are highly creative and others quite routine. Nor will an equality in status attend these occupational and income differences, and some of them will call for and nurture dispositions which are contrary to the diffusely equalitarian, consensual, hedonistic, affective, humanitarian tendencies inherent in mass society. The dispositions to primordial attachment will also persist—kinship, and its ethnic sublimation, locality, sexuality—and might be further transmuted in mass society, but they can never be eradicated. They will continue to be at war with the elements which constitute mass society and those required for a large-scale society. Thus there is likely always to be tension among these diverse sets of elements, which are so dependent on each other. Each will limit the expansion of the others and contend against them and will prevent the society from ever becoming wholly a mass society. But the tension will never be able to prevent these properties of the mass society from finding a grandiose expression.

The potentiality for the mass society has always lain within the human soul. It could only find its opportunity for realization in the peculiar conjuncture of spiritual, political, and technological events which are at the basis of modern society. It comes into realization in an age when the human race is for the first time in its history in considerable prospect of extinction at its own hands, and that as the result of skills which were essential to the ideals of the enlightenment and to the genesis of mass society. Yet, even if the race were to end, the philosophers of the enlightenment, or their heirs who would be born in a new beginning, would have to admit that their ideals had not been vainly espoused and that the race had not ended before many of their deepest ideals had been attained.

II. The Sacred in Society

4

CENTER AND PERIPHERY

I

Society has a center. There is a central zone in the structure of society. This central zone impinges in various ways on those who live within the ecological domain in which the society exists. Membership in the society, in more than the ecological sense of being located in a bounded territory and of adapting to an environment affected or made up by other persons located in the same territory, is constituted by relationship to this central zone.

The central zone is not, as such, a spatially located phenomenon. It almost always has a more or less definite location within the bounded territory in which the society lives. Its centrality has, however, nothing to do with geometry and little with geography.

The center, or the central zone, is a phenomenon of the realm of values and beliefs. It is the center of the order of symbols, of values and beliefs, which govern the society. It is the center because it is the ultimate and irreducible; and it is felt to be such by many who cannot give explicit articulation to its irreducibility. The central zone partakes of the nature of the sacred. In this sense, every society has an "official" religion, even when that society or its exponents and interpreters, conceive of it, more or less correctly, as a secular, pluralistic, and tolerant society. The principle of the Counterreformation—*Cuius regio, eius religio*—al-

Previously published in a slightly different form in *The Logic of Personal Knowledge: Essays in Honour of Michael Polanyi* (The Free Press of Glencoe, 1961). © by The Free Press of Glencoe, 1961. Used with permission of The Macmillan Company.

though its rigor has been loosened and its harshness mollified, retains a core of permanent truth.

The center is also a phenomenon of the realm of action. It is a structure of activities, of roles and persons, within the network of institutions. It is in these roles that the values and beliefs which are central are embodied and propounded.

II

The larger society appears, on a cursory inspection and by the methods of inquiry in current use, to consist of a number of interdependent subsystems—the economy, the status system, the polity, the kinship system, and the institutions which have in their special custody the cultivation of cultural values, e.g. the university system, the ecclesiastical system, etc. (I use "ecclesiastical" to include the religious institutions of societies which do not have a church in the Western sense of the term.) Each of these subsystems itself comprises a network of organizations which are connected, with varying degrees of affirmation, through a common authority, overlapping personnel, personal relationships, contracts, perceived identities of interest, a sense of affinity within a transcendent whole, and a territorial location possessing symbolic value. (These subsystems and their constituent bodies are not equally affirmative vis-à-vis each other. Moreover the degree of affirmation varies through time, and is quite compatible with a certain measure of alienation within each elite and among the elites.)

Each of these organizations has an authority, an elite, which might be either a single individual or a group of individuals, loosely or closely organized. Each of thes elites makes decisions, sometimes in consultation with other elites and sometimes, largely on its own initiative, with the intention of maintaining the organization, controlling the conduct of its members and fulfilling its goals. (These decisions are by no means always successful in the achievement of these ends, and the goals are seldom equally or fully shared by the elite and those whose actions are ordained by its decisions.)

The decisions made by the elites contain as major elements certain general standards of judgment and action, and certain concrete values, of which the system as a whole, the society, is one of the most preeminent. The values which are inherent in these standards, and which are espoused and more or less observed by those in authority, we shall call the *central value system* of the society. This central value system is the central zone of the society. It is central because of its intimate connection with what the society holds to be sacred; it is central because it is espoused by the ruling authorities of the society. These two kinds of centrality are vitally related. Each defines and supports the other.

The central value system is not the whole of the order of values and beliefs espoused and observed in the society. The value systems obtaining in any diversified society may be regarded as being distributed along a range. There are variants of the central value system running from hyperaffirmation of some of the components of the major, central value system to an extreme denial of some of these major elements in the central value system; the latter tends to, but is not inevitably associated with, an affirmation of certain elements denied or subordinated in the central value system. There are also elements of the order of values and beliefs which are as random with respect to the central value system as the value and beliefs of human beings can be. There is always a considerable amount of unintegratedness of values and beliefs, both within the realm of value of representative individuals and among individuals and sections of a society.

The central value system is constituted by the values which are pursued and affirmed by the elites of the constituent subsystems and of the organizations which are comprised in the subsystems. By their very possession of authority, they attribute to themselves an essential affinity with the sacred elements of their society, of which they regard themselves as the custodians. By the same token, many members of their society attribute to them that same kind of affinity. The elites of the economy affirm and usually observe certain values which should govern economic activity. The elites of the polity affirm and usually observe certain values which should govern political activity. The elites of the university system and the ecclesiastical system affirm and usually practice certain values which should govern intellectual and religious activities (including beliefs). On the whole, these values are the values embedded in current activity. The ideals which they affirm do not far transcend the reality which is ruled by those who espouse them.[1] The values of the different

1. This set of values corresponds to what Karl Mannheim called "ideologies," i.e., values and beliefs, which are congruent with or embodied in current reality (*seinskongruent*). I do not with to use the term "ideology" to describe these value orientations. One of the most important reasons is that in the past few

elites are clustered into an approximately consensual pattern.[2]

One of the major elements in any central value system is an affirmative attitude toward established authority. This is present in the central value systems of all societies, however much these might differ from each other in their appreciation of authority. There is something like a "floor," a minimum of appreciation of authority in every society, however liberal that society might be. Even the most libertarian and equalitarian societies which have ever existed possess at least this minimum appreciation of authority. Authority enjoys appreciation because it arouses sentiments of sacredness. Sacredness by its nature is authoritative. Those persons, offices, or symbols endowed with it, however indirectly and remotely, are therewith endowed with some measure of authoritativeness.

The appreciation of authority entails the appreciation of the institutions through which authority works and the rules which it enunciates. The central value system in all societies asserts and recommends the appreciation of these authoritative institutions.

Implicitly, the central value system rotates on a center more fundamental even than its espousal by and embodiment in authority. Authority is the agent of *order*, an order which may be largely embodied in authority or which might transcend authority and regulate it, or at least provide a standard by which existing authority itself is judged and even claims to judge itself. This order, which is implicit in the central value system, and in the light of which the cental value system legitimates itself, is endowed with dynamic potentialities. It contains, above all, the potentiality of critical judgment on the central value system and the central institutional system. To use Mannheim's terminology, while

___

decades the term "ideology" has been used to refer to intensely espoused value orientations which are extremely *seinstranszendent*, which transcend current reality by a wide margin, which are explicit, articulated, and hostile to the existing order. (For example, Bolshevist doctrine, National Socialist doctrine, Fascist doctrine, etc.) Mannheim called these "utopias." Mannheim's distinction was fundamental, and I accept it, our divergent nomenclature notwithstanding.

2. The degree of consensuality differs among societies and times. There are societies in which the predominant elite demands a complete consensus with its own more specific values and beliefs. Such is the case in modern totalitarian societies. Absolutist regimes in past epochs, which were rather indifferent about whether the mass of the population was party to a consensus, were quite insistent on consensus among the elites of their society.

going beyond Mannheim, every "ideology" has within it a "utopian" potentiality. To use my own terminology, every central value system contains within itself an ideological potentiality. The dynamic potentiality derives from the inevitable tendency of every concrete society to fall short of the order which is implicit in its central value system.

Closely connected with the appreciation of authority and the institutions in which it is exercised, is an appreciation of the *qualities* which qualify persons for the exercise of authority or which are characteristic of those who exercise authority. These qualities, which we shall call secondary values, can be ethnic, educational, familial, economic, professional; they may be ascribed to individuals by virtue of their relationships or they may be acquired through study and experience. But whatever they are, they enjoy the appreciation of the central value system simply because of their connection with the exercise of authority. (Despite their ultimately derivative nature, each of them is capable of possessing an autonomous status in the central zone, in the realm of the sacred; consequently, severe conflicts can be engendered.)

The central value system thus comprises secondary as well as primary values. It legitimates the existing distribution of roles and rewards to persons possessing the appropriate qualities which in various ways symbolize degrees of proximity to authority. It legitimates these distributions by praising the properties of those who occupy authoritative roles in the society, by stressing the legitimacy of their incumbency of those roles and the appropriateness of the rewards they receive. By implication, and explicitly as well, it legitimates the smaller rewards received by those who live at various distances from the circles in which authority is exercised.

The central institutional system may thus be described as the set of institutions which is legitimated by the central value system. Less circularly, however, it may be described as those institutions which, through the radiation of their authority, give some form to the life of a considerable section of the population of the society. The economic, political, ecclesiastical, and cultural institutions impinge compellingly at many points on the conduct of much of the population in any society through the actual exercise of authority and the potential exercise of coercion, through the provision of persuasive models of action, and through a partial control of the allocation of rewards. The kinship and family systems, although they have much smaller radii, are microcosms of the central institutional system and do much to buttress its efficiency.

III

The existence of a central value system rests, in a fundamental way, on the need which human beings have for incorporation into something which transcends and transfigures their concrete individual existence. They have a need to be in contact with symbols of an order which is larger in its dimensions than their own bodies and more central in the "ultimate" structure of reality than is their routine everyday life. Just as friendship exists because human beings must transcend their own self-limiting individuality in personal communion with another personality, so membership in a political society is a necessity of man's nature. This by no means implies that the satisfaction of the intermittently intense need to be a member of a transcendent body, be it a tribe or a nation or a political community, exhausts the functions of political community. A political community performs many functions and satisfies many needs which have little to do with the need for membership in a political community. There is need to belong to a polity just as there is a need for conviviality. Just as a person shrivels, contracts, and corrupts when separated from all other persons or from those persons who have entered into a formed and vital communion with him, so the man with political needs is crippled and numbed by his isolation from a polity or by his membership in a political order which cannot claim his loyalty.

The need for personal communion is a common quality among human beings who have reached a certain level of individuation. Those who lack the need and the capacity impress us by their incompleteness. The political need is not so widely spread or so highly developed in the mass of the population of any society as are the need and capacity for conviviality. Those who lack it impress by their "idiocy." Those who possess it add the possibility of civility to the capacity for conviviality which we think a fully developed human being must possess.

The political need is of course nurtured by tradition, but it cannot be accounted for by the adduction of tradition. The political need is a capacity like certain kinds of imagination, reasoning, perceptiveness, or sensitivity. It is neither instinctual nor learned. It is not simply the product of the displacement of personal affects onto public objects, although much political activity is impelled by such displacement. It is not learned by teaching or traditional transmission, though much political activity is guided by the reception of tradition. The pursuit of a political career and the performance of civil obligations gains much from the impulsion of tradition. Nonetheless, tradition is not the seed of this inclination to attach oneself to a political order.

The political need, which may be formed into a propensity towards civility, entails sensitivity to an order of being where "creative power" has its seat. This creative center which attracts the minds of those who are sensitive to it is manifested in authority operating over territory. Both authority and territory convey the idea of potency, of "authorship," of the capacity to do vital things, of a connection with events which are intrinsically important. Authority is thought, by those with the political or civil need, to possess this vital relationship to the center from which a right order emanates. Those who are closely and positively connected with authority, through its exercise or through personal ties, are thought, in consequence of this connection, to possess a vital relationship to the center, the locus of the sacred, the order which confers legitimacy. Land, which is a constituent of "territoriality," has similar properties, and those who exercise authority through control of land have always been felt to enjoy a special status in relation to the core of the central value system. Those who live within given territorial boundaries come to share in these properties and thus become the objects of political sentiments. Residence within certain territorial boundaries and rule by common authority are the properties which define membership in society and establish its obligations and claims. It is not entirely an accident that nationalism is connected with land reform. Land reform is part of a policy which seeks to disperse the special relationship to a higher order of being from a few persons, that is, the great landlords in whom it was previously thought to be concentrated, to the large mass of those who live upon the territory.

It must be stressed that the political need is not by any means equally distributed in any society, even the most democratic. There are human beings whose sensitivity to the ultimate is meager, although there is perhaps no human being from whom it is entirely absent. Nor does sensitivity to remote events which are expressive of the center always focus on their manifestations in the polity.

Apolitical scientists who seek the laws of nature but are indifferent, except on grounds of prudence, to the laws of society are one instance of this uneven development of sensitivity to ultimate things. Religious persons who are attached to transcendent symbols which are not embodied in civil polity or in ecclesiastical organization represent another variant. In addition to these, there are very many persons whose sensitivity is exhausted long before it reaches so far into the core of the central value system. Some have a need for such contact only in crises and on special, periodic occasions, at the moment of birth or marriage or death, or on holidays. Like the intermittent, occasional, and unintense religious sensibility, the political sensibility, too, can be intermittent and unintense. It might come into operation only on particular occasions, for example, at election time, or in periods of severe economic deprivation or during a war or after a military defeat. Beyond this there are some persons who are never stirred, who have practically no sensibility as far as events of the political order are concerned.

Finally, there are persons, not many in any society but often of great importance, who have a very intense and active connection with the center, with the symbols of the central value system, but whose connection is passionately negative.[3] Equally important are those who have a positive but no less intense and active connection with the symbols of the center, a connection so acute, so pure, and so vital that it cannot tolerate any falling short in daily observance such as characterizes the elites of the central institutional system. These are often the persons around whom a sharp opposition to the central value system and even more to the central institutional system is organized. From the ranks of these come prophets, revolutionaries, doctrinaire ideologists for whom nothing less than perfection is tolerable.

IV

The need for established and created order, the respect for creativity, and the need to be connected with the center do not exhaust the forces which engender central value systems. To fill out the list, we must consider the nature of authority itself. Authority has an expansive tendency. It has a tendency to expand the order which it represents toward the saturation of territorial space. The acceptance of the validity

3. T. S. Eliot has pointed out, in discussing Baudelaire, the profound difference between the atheist who feels strongly about the nature of the universe and who is vehemently antireligious and the person who is utterly indifferent to religion.

of that order entails a tendency toward its universalization within the society over which authority rules. Ruling indeed consists in the universalization—within the boundaries of society—of the rules inherent in the order. Rulers, just because of their possession of authority and the impulses which it generates, wish to be obeyed and to obtain assent to the order which they symbolically embody. The symbolization of order in offices of authority has a compelling effect on those who occupy those offices.

In consequence of this, rulers seek to establish a universal diffusion of the acceptance and observance of the values and beliefs of which they are the custodians through incumbency in those offices. They use their powers to punish those who deviate and to reward with their favor those who conform. Thus, the mere existence of authority in society imposes a central value system on that society. I would regret an easy misunderstanding to which the foregoing sentences might give rise. There is much empirical truth in the common observations that rulers "look after their own," that they are only interested in remaining in authority, in reinforcing their possession of authority and in enhancing their security of tenure through the establishment of a consensus built around their own values and beliefs. Nonetheless these observations seem to me to be too superficial. They fail to discern the dynamic property of authority as such, and particularly of authority over society.

Not all persons who come into positions of authority possess the same responsiveness to the inherently dynamic and expansive tendency in authority. Some are more attuned to it; others are more capable of resisting it. Tradition, furthermore, acts as a powerful brake upon expansiveness, as does the degree of differentiation of the structure of elites and of the society as a whole.

V

The central institutional system of modern societies, probably even in revolutionary crises, is the object of a substantial amount of consensus. The central value system which legitimates the central institutional system is widely shared, but the consensus is never perfect. There are differences within even the most consensual society about the appreciability of authority, the institutions within which it resides, the elites which exercise it, and the justice of its allocation of rewards.

Even those who share in the consensus do so with different degrees of intensity, whole-heartedness, and devotion. As we move from the center of society, the center in which authority is possessed, to the hinterland or the periphery, over which authority is exercised, attachment to the central value system becomes attenuated. The central institutional system is neither unitary nor homogeneous, and some levels have more majesty than others. The lower one goes in the hierarchy, or the further one moves territorially from the locus of authority, the less one appreciates authority. Likewise, the further one moves from those possessing the secondary traits associated with the exercise of authority into sectors of the population which do not equally possess those qualities, the less affirmative is the attitude towards the reigning authority, and the less intense is that affirmation which does exist.

Active rejection of the central value system is, of course, not the sole alternative to its affirmation. Much more widespread, in the course of history and in any particular society, is an intermittent, partial, and attenuated affirmation of the central value system.

For the most part, the mass of the population in premodern societies have been far removed from the immediate impact of the central value system. They have possessed their own value systems, which were occasionally and fragmentarily articulated with the central value system. These pockets of approximate independence have not, however, been completely incompatible with isolated occasions of articulation and of intermittent affirmation. Nor have these intermittent occasions of participation been incompatible with occasions of active rejection and antagonism to the central institutional system, to the elite which sits at its center, and to the central value system which that elite puts forward for its own legitimation.

The more territorially dispersed the institutional system, the less the likelihood of an intense affirmation of the central value system. The more inegalitarian the society, the less the likelihood of an intense affirmation of the central value system, especially where, as in most steeply hierarchial societies, there are large and discontinuous gaps between those at the top and those below them. Indeed, it might be said that the degree of affirmation inevitably shades off from the center of the exercise of authority and of the promulgation of values.

As long as societies were loosely coordinated, as long as authority lacked the means of intensive control, and as long as much of the economic life of the society was carried on outside any market or almost exclusively in local markets, the central value system invariably became attenuated in the outlying reaches. With the growth of the market, and the administrative and technological strengthening of authority, contact with the central value system increased.

When, as in modern society, a more unified economic system, political democracy, urbanization, and education have brought the different sections of the population into more frequent contact with each other and created even greater mutual awareness, the central value system has found a wider acceptance than in other periods of the history of society. At the same time these changes have also increased the extent, if not the intensity, of active "dissensus" or rejection of the central value system.

The same objects which previously engaged the attention and aroused the sentiments of a very restricted minority of the population have in modern societies become concerns of much broader strata of the population. At the same time that increased contact with authority has led to a generally deferential attitude, it has also run up against the tenacity of prior attachments and a reluctance to accept strange gods. Class conflict in the most advanced modern societies is probably more open and more continuous than in premodern societies, but it is also more domesticated and restricted by attachments to the central value system. Violent revolutions and bloody civil wars are much less characteristic of modern societies than of premodern societies. Revolutionary parties are feeble in modern societies which have moved toward widespread popular education, a greater equality of status, etc. The size of nominally revolutionary parties in France and Italy is a measure of the extent to which French and Italian societies have not become modernized in this sense. The inertness, from a revolutionary point of view, of the rank and file of these parties is partially indicative of the extent to which, despite their revolutionary doctrines, the working classes in these countries have become assimilated into the central value system of their respective societies.

The old gods have fallen, religious faith has become much more attenuated in the educated classes, and suspicion of authority is much more overt than it has ever been. Nonetheless in the modern societies of the West, the central value system has gone much more deeply into the heart of their members than it has ever succeeded in doing in any earlier society. The "masses" have responded to their contact with a striking measure of acceptance.

VI

The power of the ruling class derives from its incumbency of certain key positions in the central institutional system. Societies vary in the extent to which the ruling class is unitary or relatively segmental. Even where the ruling class is relatively segmental, there is, because of centralized control of appointment to the most crucial of the key positions or because of personal ties or because of overlapping personnel, some sense of affinity which, more or less, unites the different sectors of the elite.[4]

This sense of affinity rests ultimately on the high degree of proximity to the center which is shared by all these different sectors of the ruling class. They have, it is true, a common vested interest in their position. It is not, however, simply the product of a perception of a coalescent interest; it contains a substantial component of mutual regard arising from a feeling of a common relationship to the central value system.

The different sectors of the elite are never equal. One or two usually predominate, to varying degrees, over the others, even in situations where there is much mutual respect and a genuine sense of affinity. Regardless, however, of whether they are equal or unequal, unitary or segmental, there is usually a fairly large amount of consensus among the elites of the central institutional system. This consensus has its ultimate root in their common feeling for the transcendent order which they believe they embody or for which they think themselves responsible. This does not obtain equally for all elites. Some are much more concerned in an almost entirely "secular" or manipulative way with remaining in power. Nonetheless, even in a situation of great heterogeneity and much mutual antipathy, the different sectors of the elite tend to experience the "transforming" transcendental overtones which are generated by incum-

4. The segmentation or differentiation in the structure of elites is an important factor in limiting the expansiveness of authority among the elites. A differentiated structure of elites brings with it a division of powers, which can be totally overcome only by draconic measures. It can be done, as the Soviet Union has shown, but it is a perpetual source of strain, as recent Soviet developments have also shown.

bency in authoritative roles, or by proximity to "fundamentally important things."

VII

The mass of the population in all large societies stands at some distance from authority. This is true with respect both to the distribution of authority and to the distribution of the secondary qualities associated with the exercise of authority.

The functional and symbolic necessities of authority require some degree of concentration. Even the most genuinely democratic society, above a certain very small size, requires some concentration of authority for the performance of elaborate tasks. It goes without saying that nondemocratic societies have a high concentration of authority. Furthermore, whether the society is democratic or oligarchical, access to the key positions in the central institutional system tends to be confined to persons possessing a distinctive constellation of properties, such as age, education, and ethnic, regional, and class provenience, etc.

The section of the population which does not share in the exercise of authority and which is differentiated in secondary properties from the exercisers of authority, is usually more intermittent in its "possession" by the central value system. For one thing, the distribution of sensitivity to remote, central symbols is unequal, and there is a greater concentration of such sensitivity in the elites of the central institutional system. Furthermore, where there is a more marginal participation in the central institutional system, attachment to the central value system is more attenuated. Where the central institutional system becomes more comprehensive and inclusive so that a larger proportion of the life of the population comes within its scope, the tension between the center and the periphery, as well as the consensus, tends to increase.

The mass of the population in most premodern and non-Western societies have in a sense lived *outside* society and have not felt their remoteness from the center to be a perpetual injury to themselves. Their low position in the hierarchy of authority has been injurious to them, and the consequent alienation has been accentuated by their remoteness from the central value system. The alienation has not, however, been active or intense, because, for the most part, their convivial, spiritual, and moral center of gravity has lain closer to their own round of life. They have been far from full-fledged members of their societies and they have very seldom been citizens.

Among the most intensely sensitive or the more alertly intelligent, their distance from the center accompanied by their greater concern with the center, has led to an acute sense of being on "the outside," to a painful feeling of being excluded from the vital zone which surrounds the center of society (which is the vehicle of "the centre of the universe"). Alternatively these more sensitive and more intelligent persons have, as a result of their distinctiveness, often gained access to some layer of the center by becoming schoolteachers, priests, administrators. Thus they have entered into a more intimate and more affirmative relationship with the center. They have not in such instances, however, always overcome the grievance of exclusion from the most central zones of the central institutional and value systems. They have often continued to perceive themselves as outsiders, while continuing to be intensely attracted and influenced by the outlook and style of life of the center.

VIII

Modern large-scale society utilizes a technology which has raised the standard of living and which has integrated the population into a more unified economy. In correspondence with these changes, it has witnessed a more widespread participation in the central value system through education, and in the central institutional system through the franchise and mass communication. On this account, it is in a different position from all premodern societies.

In modern society, in consequence of its far greater involvement with the central institutional system, especially with the economy and the polity, the mass of the population is no longer largely without contact with the central value system. It has, to an unprecedented extent, come to feel the central value system to be its own value system. Its generally heightened sensitivity has responded to the greater visibility and accessibility of the central value system by partial incorporation. Indeed, although, compared with that of the elite, its contact is still relatively intermittent and unintense, the enhanced frequency and intensity of that contact are great universal-historical novelties. They are nothing less than the incorporation of the mass of the population into society. The "process of civilization" has become a reality in the modern world.[5]

To a greater extent than ever before in history the mass of the population in modern Western societies feel themselves to be part of their society in a way in which their ancestors never did. Just as they have become "alive" and hedonistic, more demanding of respect and pleasure, so, too, they have become more "civilized." They have come to be parts of the civil society with a feeling of attachment to that society and a feeling of moral responsibility for observing its rules and sharing in its authority. They have ceased to be primarily objects of authoritative decisions by others; they have become, to a much greater extent, acting and feeling subjects with wills of their own which they assert with self-confidence. Political apathy, frivolity, vulgarity, irrationality, and responsiveness to political demagogy are all concomitants of this phenomenon. Men have become citizens in larger proportions than ever before in the large states of history, and probably more, too, than in the Greek city states at the height of the glory of their aristocratic democracies.

The emergence of nationalism, not just the fanatical nationalism of politicians, intellectuals, and zealots, but a sense of nationality and an affirmative feeling for one's own country, is a very important aspect of this process of the incorporation of the mass of the population into the central institutional and value systems. The more passionate type of nationalism is an unpleasant and heroic manifestation of this deeper growth of civility.

IX

Nonetheless, this greater incorporation carries with it also an inherent

---

5. Cf. Norbert Elias, *Der Prozess der Zivilisation*, 2 vols. (Basel, 1937). The phenomenon of *das sinkende Kulturgut* was noticed by German writers on late medieval society, and a parallel phenomenon was observed by Max Weber in his studies of Indian society. He called it "brahmanization." This theme has been treated by Professor M. N. Srinivas in his studies of "sanskritization." This assimilation of elements of the value systems of higher classes and castes by lower strata which occurs in every society is not, however, identical either in quality or extent with the growth of the *sense of fundamental affinity* which characterizes modern society.

tension. Those who participate in the central institutional and value systems—who feel sufficiently closer to the center now than their forebears ever did—also feel their position as outsiders, their remoteness from the center, in a way in which their forebears probably did not feel it. The modern trade union movement, which has disappointed those whose revolutionary hopes were to be supported by the organized working classes, illustrates this development. The leaders of the trade unions have come to be part of the central institutional system and accordingly, at least in part, they fulfill the obligations which are inherent in the action within that system. At the same time, the unions' rank and file members also have come to share more widely and intensely in the central value system and to affirm more deeply and continuously than in the past the central institutional system. Nonetheless, the leaders, deriving from sections of the society which have felt themselves to be outside the prevailing society, still and necessarily carry traces of that position in their outlook; the rank and file, less involved in the central institutional system than the leadership, experience even more acutely their position as outsiders vis-à-vis the central value system. The more sensitive among them are the most difficult for the leaders of the unions to hold in check.

Parallel with this incorporation of the mass of the population into society—halting, spotty, and imperfect as this incorporation is—has gone a change in the attitudes of the ruling classes of the modern states of the West. (In Asia and Africa, the process is even more fragmentary, corresponding to the greater fragmentariness of the incorporation of the masses into those societies.) In the modern Western states, the ruling classes have come increasingly to acknowledge the dispersion, into the wider reaches of the society, of the charisma which informs the center. The qualities which account for the expansiveness of authority have come to be shared more widely by the population, far from the center in which the incumbents of the positions of authority reside. In the eyes of the elites of the modern states of the West, the mass of the population have somehow come to share in the vital connection with the "order" which inheres in the central value system and which was once thought to be in the special custody of the ruling classes.

The elites are, of course, more responsive to sectors of society which have voting powers and, therewith, legislative power, and which possess agitational and purchasing powers as well. These would make them simulate respect for the populace even where they did not feel it. Mixed with this simulated respect, however, is a genuine respect for the mass of the population as bearers of a true individuality, and a genuine, even if still limited, appreciation of their intrinsic worth as fellow members of the civil society and, in the deepest sense, as vessels of the charisma which lives at the center of society.[6]

X

There is a limit to consensus. However comprehensive the spread of consensus, it can never be all-embracing. A differentiated large-scale society will always be compelled by professional specialization, tradition, the normal distribution of human capacities, and an inevitable anti-nomianism to submit to inequalities in participation in the central value system. Some persons will always be a bit closer to the center; some will always be more distant from the center.

Nonetheless, the expansion of individuality attendant on the growth of individual freedom and opportunity, and the greater density of communications, have contributed greatly to narrowing the range of inequality. The peak at the center is no longer so high; the periphery is no longer so distant.

The individuality which has underlain the entry into the consensus around the central value system might in the end also be endangered by it. Liberty and privacy live on islands in a consensual sea. When the tide rises they may be engulfed. This is another instance of the dialectical relationships among consensus, indifference, and alienation, but further consideration must be left for another occasion.

6. The populism of the rulers of totalitarian and oligarchical societies is, in part, hypocrisy and, in part, acknowledgement of the existence of "outsider" feelings in these elites, who still believe in their hearts that the modern liberal Western states constitute the center of the world. But I would venture to state that there is more to it than that. These oligarchical and totalitarian elites also share in the fundamental expansion of sensibility and empathy which opens their imaginations to the charisma of the ordinary human beings who live outside the key positions of the central institutional system. These observations should not, however, obscure the fact that this widened sensibility coexists with a still very deeply rooted belief in the concentration of charisma in the authoritative center of society. The rulers' widened sensibility must still contend with their appreciation of the sacredness of the peaks of authority in the central institutional system.

5

CHARISMA

In all societies deference is accorded to authoritative roles, their incumbents, and the norms they promulgate in consideration of their capacity to create, maintain, and change the order of society. In all societies there is a propensity in most human beings, on occasion, to perceive, beyond immediate and particular events, the forces, principles, and powers which govern the immediate and the particular and which impose and necessitate an order which embraces them. Particularly serious attention and respect are given to what are thought to be those transcendent powers which are manifested in the orders of nature and society and in patterns of norms which intend the ordering of human action. Where institutions, roles, persons, norms, or symbols are perceived or believed to be connected or infused with these transcendent powers, we say that they are perceived as charismatic.

Charisma, then, is the quality which is imputed to persons, actions, roles institutions, symbols, and material objects because of their presumed connection with "ultimate," "fundamental," "vital," order-determining powers. This presumed connection with the ultimately "serious" elements in the universe and in human life is seen as a quality or a state of being, manifested in the bearing or demeanor and in the actions of individual persons; it is also seen as inhering in certain roles and collectivities. It can be perceived as existing in intense and concentrated form in particular institutions, roles, and individuals—or strata of individuals. It can also be perceived as existing in attenuated and dispersed form.

Previously published in a slightly different form in *The International Encyclopedia of the Social Sciences,* edited by David L. Sills, vol. 2, pp. 386-90. © 1968 by Crowell Collier and Macmillan, Inc. Used with permission of the publisher.

The propensity to seek contact with transcendent powers and to impute charismatic qualities varies in any society; it is extremely strong in some persons, feeble in others. It also varies during the life span of individuals and in the history of particular societies. Some societies are characterized by a greater frequency of intense and concentrated charisma; others, by a greater frequency of attenuated and dispersed charisma. Both types exist in varying admixtures in all societies.

Intense and Concentrated Charisma

The propensity to impute charisma is a potentiality of the moral, cognitive, and expressive orientations of human beings. The propensity to seek contact with transcendent powers and to impute charisma is rooted in the neural constitution of the human organism. The intensity with which it is experienced and the strength of its motivation are also influenced by situational exigencies and by the prevailing culture. It can be deliberately cultivated by isolation from the routine environment, by instruction and self-discipline. It can be so prized that individuals are encouraged to allow it to come forward in their sensitivity. A culture can foster the discernment of charismatic signs and properties by focusing attention, providing canons of interpretation, and recommending the appreciation of the possession of these signs and properties.

Whatever the sources of the propensity to impute charisma—neural, situational, cultural, or any combination of these—when this propensity is intense enough to seek to penetrate beyond the immediate present, beyond the particular and the concrete to the more general categories and patterns which underlie and generate the vicissitudes of human existence, it results in a subjective experience of possession of charismatic quality or in a sensitivity and responsiveness to the subjectively experienced charisma manifested in the bearing, words, and actions of other individuals and institutions. Those persons who possess an intense subjective feeling of their own charismatic quality, and who have it imputed to them by others, we will call charismatic persons. In the charismatic persons it is "directly" experienced; in the others it is experienced only in "mediated" form through intensely and concentratedly charismatic persons or institutions. The authority exercised by these individuals who "experience" charisma directly, over all others in the society who experience it only in mediated form, we will call charismatic authority.

The concept of charisma derives from the reference in II Corinthians which describes the forms in which the gifts of divine grace appear. It was taken up by Rudolf Sohm in his analysis of the transformation of the primitive Christian community into the Roman Catholic church;[1] the emphasis there was on a "charismatic institution." The conception of charisma underwent its most important extension and formulation in the writings of Max Weber.[2] He treated charisma as a property attributed to great innovating personalities who disrupt traditionally and rational-legally legitimated systems of authority and who establish or aspire to establish a system of authority claiming to be legitimated by the direct experience of divine grace. Weber also applied the concept to creative, expansive, innovating personalities who are regarded as "extraordinary" even though they neither claim to possess divine grace nor have it imputed to them.

According to Weber's usage, charismatic quality may be attributed to religious prophets and reformers, to dominating political leaders, to daring military heroes, and to sages who by example and command indicate a way of life to their disciples. In such personalities, the charismatic quality is believed to be manifested in extremes of passionate and intense action or of willed passivity, in extremes of exultant or serene possession. Charismatic quality is attributed to expansive personalities who establish ascendancy over other human beings by their commanding forcefulness or by an exemplary inner state which is expressed in a bearing of serenity.

The "extraordinariness" (*Ausseralltäglichkeit*) of these charismatic persons is not simply statistical infrequency; rather, it is the intense and concentrated form in which they possess or are thought to possess qualities which are only slightly present in routine actions. Routine actions are those which are governed mainly by motives of moderate, personal attachment, by considerations of convenience and advantage, and by

1. Rudolf Sohm, *Kirchenrecht*, 2 vols. (Leipzig: Duncker & Humblot, 1892–1923).
2. Max Weber, *Wirtschaft und Gesellschaft: Grundriss der verstehenden Soziologie*, 2 vols., 4th ed. (Tübingen: Mohr, 1956); see especially 2:832–73: "Die charismatische Herrschaft und ihre Umbildung." Weber, *The Theory of Social and Economic Organization*, ed. Talcott Parsons (Glencoe: Free Press, 1957); see especially pp. 358–63: "Charismatic Authority"; pp. 363–72: "The Routinization of Charisma"; and pp. 386–92: "The Transformation of Charisma in an Anti-authoritarian Direction."

anxiety to avoid failure in conforming to the immediate expectations and demands of peers and superiors. Routine actions are not simply repetitive actions; they are uninspired actions in which immediately prospective gratifications and the demands of immediate situations and of obligations to those who are close at hand play a greater part than does the link with transcendent things. If any charismatic attribution is present in the pattern of routine action, it is not dominant and certainly is not vividly perceived.

Such uninspired actions maintain social structures, and they also change them through numerous minor adjustments. They do not impel drastic changes. Charismatic persons, and those who are responsive to charismatic persons, aspire to larger transformations. They seek to break the structures of routine actions and to replace them with structures of inspired actions which are "infused" with those qualities or states of mind generated by immediate and intensive contact with the "ultimate"—with the powers which guide and determine human life.

The charismatic person is a creator of a new order as well as the breaker of routine order. Since charisma is constituted by the belief that its bearer is effectively in contact with what is most vital, most powerful, and most authoritative in the universe or in society, those to whom charisma is attributed are, by virtue of that fact, authoritative. Charismatic authority is antipathetic to those forms of authority which invoke recently and currently acknowledged criteria of legitimacy and which call forth the performance of the previously performed. Even where such authorities command or recommend new actions, they legitimate the commands or recommendations by subsuming them under existing norms recently and currently accepted as valid. The bearer and the adherents of charismatic authority, in contrast, tend to think of their norms as legitimated by a source remote in time or timeless, remote in space or spaceless. The legitimacy of the norms enunciated by charismatic authority lies outside the norms practiced in the existing society. Although it is contained in the culture of the existing society, the source or the criterion of the legitimacy of charismatic authority occupies a position within that culture which, under the dominance of routine, is incompatible with the expansive aspirations of any charismatically asserted authority. Since it asserts the value of action which derives its impetus immediately, intensively, and unalloyedly from direct contact with "ultimate" sources of legitimacy, charismatic authority is of necessity revolutionary.

Charismatic authority denies the value of action which is motivated by the desire for proximate ends sufficient unto themselves, by the wish to gratify personal affections, or by the hope of pecuniary advantage. Charismatically generated order is order which acknowledges and is generated by the creativity which seeks something new, by discovery which discerns something new, by inspiration from transcendent powers.

The actions of men in all ongoing societies are impelled by a variety of considerations. Personal affections, primordial attachments, anticipations of advantage and fears of loss, destructiveness, responsiveness to obligations or expectations of role performance in corporate bodies, unimaginative acceptance of given norms where no alternative seems visible or practicable, respect for concrete already-functioning authority —these, together with an intermittent flickering of charismatic responsiveness, form the complex of impulsions from which any society reproduces itself and moves onward. Such charismatic elements as ordinary societies contain exist either in a highly segregated form or in a diffuse half-life. Concentrated and intense charismatic authority transfigures the half-life into incandescence. It involves a tremendous heightening of charismatic sensitivity. That is why charismatic authority, really intensely imputed and experienced charisma, is disruptive of any routine social order.

Segregation and Discipline of Intense Charisma

All societies seek to make some provision for those persons whose actions are impelled by the possession of charismatic legitimacy. Within religious systems, the cenobitic or anchoritic monastic orders are institutional frameworks for the segregation and control of the charismatically endowed, i.e., those who are prone to experience a sense of direct contact with transcendent powers. This removes them from the scene of the routine and at the same time preserves and disciplines their charismatic quality within the legitimate order of the religious collectivity, in which a certain measure of attenuation and dispersal of charisma has been stabilized.

Universities, which must reproduce many established patterns of thought and evaluation and carry on traditions, face similar problems in dealing with young persons of highly charismatic intellectual and moral propensities. Through training and research, they attempt to discipline these charismatic propensities and to bring them to bear, at least at first, on the accepted problems and the accepted vision of the order of nature. The discovery of utterly new truths through intuition, unbridled by the accepted techniques of observation and interpretation, is rejected. Those who persist in practicing their intuition are either excluded or are constrained to submit to the prevailing discipline. This discipline involves learning and affirming what is already known and accepting the prevailing canons of assessment. Once this process of discipline has been accomplished, the acolyte is then freed to discern and create a new order through research.

In party politics, there is often apprehension among the party bosses about persons who are thought to be charismatic and who arouse the charismatic sensitivity of the mass of the party, because of the dangers which they represent to established interests within the party. But because of their wider appeal outside the party machine itself, which is concerned with routine practices, they will be tolerated and even sought in order to win the support of the charismatically sensitive for the party.

In armies, the charismatically heroic officers find a tolerated place among shock troopers and special units using unconventional methods of warfare in situations in which the routine procedures of military organization are thought to be inadequate. The military bureaucracy at higher staff levels does not find it easy to accommodate within its own circles the charismatically inclined soldier who tries to attain to new principles of warfare or who, as a hero, arouses the devotion of ordinary soldiers whose charismatic sensitivity is aroused by the danger of battle.

In bohemias, and in the circles of artists and literary men, aesthetically charismatic persons find the segregated environment congenial to disregard for the rules of routine social life and the creative transcendence of the traditional modes of artistic and literary expression. The authorities of the routine sectors of society are more inclined to tolerate these manifestations of aesthetic charisma as long as they do not intrude into the routine sectors. Nonetheless, because of the vagueness of the boundaries, friction is frequent.

By segregation, the custodians of the routine spheres of social life show both their apprehension of the disruptive nature of intense and concentrated charisma and their appreciation of a virtue requiring acknowledgment. Nonetheless, despite these efforts to contain those with intense charismatic propensities within situations where they can operate charismatically and to subject them to the discipline of institutionalization, the boundaries are sometimes infringed. A continuous reinforcement of the barriers against a free movement of charismatic persons is carried on by the custodians of routine order. They do not always succeed. Churches have been broken from within by charismatic prophets and have often suffered defeat, at least for a time, by a sectarian rival under charismatic leadership. States have been destroyed by charismatic revolutionaries, parties swept away from their traditional pattern by charismatic demagogues, constitutional orders supplanted by charismatic statesmen. Sciences have been revolutionized by unsuppressible charismatic intelligences; artistic genres have been transformed, against the resistance of orthodoxy, by the bearers of an original—charismatic—sensitivity.

Conditions of Intense and Concentrated Charisma

Crises which discredit routine institutions and the authorities who govern them arouse in the more charismatically disposed persons a more acute awareness of the insufficiency of an organization of life in which contact with the ultimate powers and standards of right and wrong has become attenuated by mediation and segregation and by absorption into routine. Their demand for the right order of things is intensified; their sensibility to the divergence between this right order and the actually existing state of affairs is heightened.

These crises, which reveal to the afflicted members of the society in which they occur the inadequacy of the inherited and prevailing institutional systems and discredit the elites which have hitherto dominated them, operate on charismatic propensities in a twofold manner. Those in whom the charismatic propensity is strongest—out of intelligence, moral sensibility, metaphysical inclination, etc.—will be the promulgators of the new vision of a better order; those in whom the charismatic propensities, although not strong enough to permit charismatic originality, are strong enough to respond to such a vision when concretely embodied—and mediated—in a charismatic person, are the most likely followers.

Crises which are failures of the inherited order enhance the need of the potential followers for protective contact with the ultimately right and powerful. The incapacity of the hitherto prevailing institutions to afford moral and metaphysical nurture and succor to those who feel the need for it, and to afford it under morally and cosmically right auspices, generates in these defenseless persons a state of mind which is fertile for the seed of the more intensely creative charismatic persons. The result is a collective effort to establish a charismatically legitimate society—or church, or party, etc.—which will possess a greater authenticity.

Often these efforts are unsuccessful. Most of the movements are broken, after a brief period of excitation, into dispirited fragments which sometimes survive in segregation. Less often, the movement is successful, and the result is a charismatic order or at least an order in which a charismatic overlay covers the more tenacious routines of the older institutional system. The routine relations between superiors and subordinates in families, armies, workshops, and farms tend to reassert themselves after an initial adaptation to the pressures of charismatic visions and convictions. Once the crisis which generated the more intense charismatic sensibility is somehow resolved—often as a result of the intervention of the charismatic inspiration—routine actions return to the forefront of social life.

With the increased effectiveness and consequent stability of institutions, the need for protective charisma which puts their members into direct, or in any case less mediated, contact with the sources of inspiration and purification is reduced. The selection of prospective leaders is again institutionalized, reducing the likelihood that intensely charismatic persons will be chosen. Thus, the process of the imputation of charisma is restored to its normal state.

Attenuated and Dispersed Charisma

The intensely charismatic element of the new order never evaporates entirely. It can exist in a state of attenuation and dispersion. The very effort of a charismatic elite to stabilize its position and to impose a charismatic order on the society or institution it controls entails deliberate dispersion. It entails spreading the particular charismatic sensitivity to persons who did not share it previously. This means a considerable extension of the circle of charisma: more persons have to become charismatic; existing institutions have to have charisma infused into them; new institutions have to be created. All this brings with it not only a deliberate dispersion from a smaller to a larger number of persons but also produces an attenuation which is less intentional but more unavoidable.

The inevitability of death and the need to provide for succession call for dispersion of charisma from a few persons and institutions to institutional offices, lineages, governing bodies, electoral procedures, or specified groups. The last of these, although not absolutely or proportionately numerous in their societies, are considerably larger than the original bearers of the imputed charisma, and their charismatic sensibility is, of course, much less intense.

Then there is the tenacity of routine to be considered. Life cannot go on without routine, which is constantly reasserting itself. Thus, the charismatic founders of a new society might have elevated a particular norm of conduct—e.g., equality or saintliness—to a dominant position, to the practical exclusion of all others. As time passes, personal and primordial attachments, considerations of expediency, and loyalties within particularistic corporate bodies become more prominent again. The norms of equality or of saintliness might still be respected, but not exclusively respected. This is what is meant by attenuation.

Not all dispersions are the result of the changes in the situation of a new elite in which charisma was both concentrated and intense. One of the greatest dispersions in history is that which has taken place in modern states, in which an attenuated charisma, more dispersed than in traditional aristocracies—where it was already more dispersed than in primitive tribes or absolute monarchies—is shared by the total adult citizenry.

The extraordinary charisma of which Max Weber spoke was the intense and concentrated form. Its normal form, however—attenuated and dispersed charisma—exists in all societies. In this form it is attributed in a context of routine actions to the rules, norms, offices, institutions, and strata of any society. Though normal charisma plays a reduced part in the ordinary life of society, it is nonetheless a real and effective force. Quite apart from its manifestations in the routines of life which are loosely governed by religious attachments, it enters into obedience to law and respect for corporate authority. Furthermore, it provides the chief criterion for granting deference in the system of stratification and pervades the main themes of the cultural inheritance and practice of every society. Thus, normal charisma is an active and effective phenomenon, essential to the maintenance of the routine order of society.

6

CHARISMA, ORDER, AND STATUS

In this paper I explore the ramifications of charismatic sensitivity, that is, the propensity to impute charismatic qualities to actions, persons, institutions, and cultural objects. My analysis takes its point of departure in Max Weber's analysis of charismatic authority. In trying to analyze charismatic authority more systematically than Weber was able to do, I have concluded that he was dealing with one particular variant of the charismatic propensity, which has more far-reaching, more permeative manifestations than his analysis has hitherto led us to believe.

Charisma According to Max Weber

Max Weber repeatedly emphasized that none of the three types of legitimate authority he set forth was ever found in its pure form. In his analysis of the structure of religious, monarchical, and feudal institutions, he dealt repeatedly with the coexistence of the charismatic and the other types of authority. In his analysis of modern parliamentary political— and to a lesser extent administrative and economic—institutions, he also dealt with a recurrent appearance of charismatic qualities imputed to a spectacular, extraordinary, disruptive exercise of authority by an individual.

Central to Weber's interpretation of society was the distinction between the "extraordinary," or the explosively novel, and the recurrent processes through which institutions reproduce themselves, by virtue of the effective empirical validity of the traditional and legal rules or norms, and by the

Previously published in a slightly different form in the *American Sociological Review,* vol. 30 (1965), pp. 199 ff.

acceptance by "siginficant" sectors of a society or its institutional sub-systems of the results of these norms or rules. He wished to distinguish innovators and creators from maintainers—in W. I. Thomas's old classification, "creative persons" from "philistines." It was in the pursuit of this central theme that he distinguished the "charismatically" legiti-mated authority of an individual innovator from the "traditionally" and "rational-legally" legitimated types of authority which keep a system moving in a stereotyped manner. The distinction between the extraordi-nary, the creative, the innovative, on the one side, and the ordinary, the routine, the recurrently reproduced, is not merely a distinction between infrequent and frequent actions, or between actions generated by "great" personalities and those which are the result of the anonymous adherence to roles and rules. It is supported implicitly in Weber's scheme of analysis by a distinction between an intense and immediate contact with what the actors involved believe to be ultimate values or events, and a more attenuated, more mediated contact with such values or events through the functioning of established institutions. Weber regarded the former as the locus of the charismatic, which he seems to have believed to be intrinsically alien to the latter. I do not think the matter is as clear-cut as Weber apparently thought. It seems to me that an attenuated, mediated, institutionalized charismatic propensity is present in the routine functioning of society. There is, in society, a widespread dispo-sition to attribute charismatic properties to ordinary secular roles, institutions, symbols, and strata or aggregates of persons. Charisma not only disrupts social order; it also maintains or conserves it.

Of course, Weber was not blind to particular instances of this con-serving, institutionalized manifestation of the charismatic propensity. He certainly attended to the ways in which ecclesiastical institutions retained a considerable component of the charismatic authority with which they were endowed by their prophetic founders. Nonetheless, it remains true that he saw the charismatic element as essentially alien to the other modes of authority by which churches are governed. Likewise, in his studies of political, bureaucratic, and administrative machines, he emphasized that charismatic personalities emerge and establish an ascendancy beyond that called for by a "rational-legal" definition of their roles. But these are only instances of coexistence; they testify to the irrepressibility of the need to attribute charismatic properties to individ-uals under certain conditions, and to the probability that certain kinds of personality—expansive and dominating, with strong and fundamental convictions—will emerge, under conditions of stress, in specific decision-making, power-exercising roles.

Weber's problem was to describe the mechanisms and to state the conditions of the emergence of charismatic leadership and its subsidence into a routine and occasionally dynamic coexistence with traditional and bureaucratic authority. My aim is to see the charismatic phenomenon in a more comprehensive perspective. I wish to examine the mechanisms of the charismatic phenomenon in secularized societies, to see it at work in the nonecclesiastical institutions that have conventionally been considered entirely free of the charismatic, except for the occasional disruptive or transforming intrusion of charismatic personalities. The problem then becomes the elucidation not only of the conditions under which the propensity to impute charismatic qualities is concentrated on individuals but also of the conditions under which it finds a more dispersed focus on institutions and strata and on the properties of roles.

The Redefinition of Charisma: Awe-Arousing Centrality

In this section I wish to render more explicit what is already implicit in the current usage of the concept of charisma, and in so doing I will disclose the unity of the religious and the secular conception of charisma.

Charisma in the narrower and original sense is the state or quality of being produced by receipt of the gifts of grace.[1] In Weber's usage, charisma is, in the first instance, a property of conduct and personality regarded by those who respond to it as a manifestation of endowment with, or possession by, some divine power. (Weber did not insist that the person really be "possessed" or "endowed"; only that he be thought to be possessed by or endowed with these qualities.) Weber did not restrict his usage of "charisma" to refer only to manifestations of divinity. He often used the term to refer to extraordinary individualities, i.e., powerful,

---

1. These are the gifts of grace conferred by the Spirit: "For to one is given by the Spirit the word of wisdom; to another the word of knowledge by the same Spirit; to another faith by the same Spirit; to another the gifts of healing by the same Spirit; to another the working of miracles; to another prophecy; to another the discerning of spirits, to another divers kinds of tongues, to another the interpretation of tongues; but all these worketh that one and the self-same Spirit, dividing to every man severally as he will." Corinthians 12:8–11. (See also Romans 12.)

ascendent, persistent, effectively expressive personalities who impose themselves on their environment by their exceptional courage, decisiveness, self-confidence, fluency, insight, energy, etc., and who do not necessarily believe that they are working under divine inspiration. He used the term to refer to politicians, scientists, soldiers, and other occupations the incumbents of which nowadays think of themselves as having, or are thought to have, nothing to do with religion, in the conventional sense, in the performance of their roles. Sometimes, indeed, he made the content of charisma quite psychological, using it to refer to a particular constellation of personality qualities. (In this latter sense charisma has come to be widely used in current high and middle-brow speech, in sociological and political analyses, and the superior ladies' magazines.) The common feature of these different manifestations, religious and psychological, was extraordinariness—an extraordinariness constituted by the high intensity with which certain *vital, crucial* qualities are manifested, in contrast with the low intensity with which they appear in the ordinary round of life.

The charismatic quality of an individual as perceived by others, or himself, lies in what is thought to be his connection with (including possession by or embodiment of) some very central feature of man's existence and the cosmos in which he lives. The centrality, coupled with intensity, makes it extraordinary. (Infrequency is only an incidental feature, although of course the combination of intensity of presence and centrality of significance is infrequent.) The centrality is constituted by its formative power in initiating, creating, governing, transforming, maintaining, or destroying what is vital in man's life. That central power has often, in the course of man's existence, been conceived of as God, the ruling power or creator of the universe, or some divine or other transcendent power controlling or markedly influencing human life and the cosmos within which it exists. The central power might be a fundamental principle or principles, a law or laws governing the universe, the underlying and driving force of the universe. It might be thought to reside in the ultimate principles of law which should govern man's conduct, arising from or derived from the nature of the universe and essential to human existence, discerned or elucidated by the exercise of man's most fundamental rational and expressive powers. Scientific discovery, ethical promulgation, artistic creativity, the exercise of political and organizational authority (*auctoritas, auctor,* authorship), and in fact all forms of genius, in the original sense of the word as permeation by the "spirit," are as much instances of the category of charismatic things as is religious prophecy.

This extended conception of a charismatic property (as perceived by one who is responsive to it, including the "charismatic person" himself) refers to a vital, "serious," ultimately symbolic event, of which divinity is one of many forms. Presumptive contact with the divine, possession by the divine, the possession of magical powers, are only modes of being charismatic. Contact with this class of vital, "serious" events may be attained through reflective wisdom or through disciplined scientific penetration, or artistic expression, or forceful and confident reality-transforming action. All these are also modes of contact with, or embodiment of, something very "serious" in Durkheim's sense, which is thought to be, and therewith becomes, central or fundamental to man's existence.

This contact through inspiration, embodiment, or perception, with the vital force which underlies man's existence, his coming-to-be and passing-away, is manifested in demeanor, words, and actions. The person who—through sensitivity, cultivated or disciplined by practice and experience, by rationally controlled observation and analysis, by intuitive penetration, or by artistic disclosure—reaches or is believed to have attained contact with that "vital layer" of reality is, by virtue of that contact, a charismatic person.

Most human beings, because their endowment is inferior or because they lack opportunities to develop the relevant capacities, do not attain that intensity of contact. But most of those who are unable to attain it themselves are, at least intermittently, responsive to its manifestations in the words, actions, and products of others who have done so. They are capable of such appreciation and occasionally feel a need for it. Through the culture they acquire and through their interaction with and perception of those more "closely connected" with the cosmically and socially central, their own weaker responsiveness is fortified and heightened.

All of these charismatic "connections" may be manifested intensely in the qualities, words, actions, and products of individual personalities. This was emphasized by Weber, and it has entered into contemporary sociology. But they may also become resident, in varying degrees of intensity, in institutions—in the qualities, norms, and beliefs to which members are expected to adhere or are expected to possess—and, in an attenuated form, in categories or strata of the members of a society.

Weber's chapter on the transformation of charisma touched on institutionalized forms of charismatic phenomena of lesser intensity, but he did not subject them to more elaborate consideration.[2] He discussed the transformation of genuine, i.e., intense, individually concentrated charisma into such patterns as "kinship charisma"[3] (*Gentilcharisma*), "hereditary charisma" (*Erbscharisma*), and "charisma of office" (*Amtscharisma*).[4] In his treatment, the institutionalization of charisma was confined to ecclesiastical, monarchical, and familial institutions, where the sacred and the primordial are massively or tangibly present. Even there, he tended to think of such charismatic patterns as lacking the genuinely charismatic element, and as greatly supported by considerations of "interest" in guaranteeing stable succession and continuing legitimacy. For the most part, he dealt with the "segregation" of charisma in the course of institutional establishment through its concentration into specific action, roles, or occasions, while it evaporated from the rest of the system, which was constituted by elements of action wholly alien to "genuine charisma."

He did not consider the more widely dispersed, unintense operation of the charismatic element in corporate bodies governed by the rational-legal type of authority.

In other words, Weber had a pronounced tendency to segregate the object of attributed charisma, to see it almost exclusively in the most concentrated and intense forms, and to disregard the possibility of its dispersed and attenuated existence. He tended, indeed, to deny the

2. He came closest to it in his discussion of the influence of the Lutheran idea of authority on the German attitude toward the state: "The fundamentally different attitude of the ordinary German toward the official and his office, toward the "transpersonal" authorities and their aura, is of course conditioned in part by the particular features of Lutheranism, but in its endowment of the earthly powers with the "official" charisma of "God-given authority" it corresponds to a very general type. The purely emotional metaphysics of the state which flourishes on this ground has had politically far-reaching consequences" (*Wirtschaft und Gesellschaft*, vol. 1, pp. 758–59).

3. Charismatic qualities may be manifested in primordial things (in blood or in locality) and in the roles defined by primordial properties (kinship roles or membership in a territorial community).

4. "The phenomenon of charisma of office—the belief in the specific endowment of a social institution with grace—is by no means confined to the churches and even less to primitive societies. In modern societies, too, it finds a politically important expression in the deepest attitudes toward the state of those who are subject to it" (*Wirtschaft und Gesellschaft*, vol. 1, p. 775).

possibility that charisma can become an integral element in the process of secular institutionalization. (This might well be part of Weber's more general tendency to see the modern world as *entzaubert*, as devoid of any belief in the possibility of genuine charisma.)

Weber's intent was to characterize the modern social and political order as one in which belief in transcendent values and their embodiment in individuals and institutions was being driven into a more and more restricted domain, as a result of the processes of rationalization and bureaucratization, which he so rightly underscored as characteristic of modern society. This historicist concern to delineate the unique features of "modern society" hindered his perception of the deeper and more permanent features of all societies.

The Need for Order

No one can doubt the grandeur of the historical-philosophical vision in Weber's view of the uniqueness of modern society, or that it represented vast progress in sociological analysis. Yet it is too disjunctive in its conception of the uniqueness of modern societies, and in a way not differentiated enough. It is too historicist.

A great fundamental identity exists in all societies, and one of the elements of this identity is the presence of the charismatic element. Even if religious belief had died, which it has not, the condition of man in the universe and the exigencies of social life still remain, and the problems to which religious belief has been the solution in most cultures still remain, demanding solution by those who confront them. The need for order and the fascination of disorder persist, and the charismatic propensity is a function of the need for order.

I do not know why this need for order exists. It is not simply a need for an instrumentally manageable environment, though that is part of it. It is more like the need for a rationally intelligible cognitive map, but it obviously is more than cognitive. There is a need for moral order—for things to be fit into a pattern which is just as well as predictable.

The generator or author of order arouses the charismatic responsiveness. Whether it be God's law or natural law or scientific law or positive law or the society as a whole, or even a particular corporate body or institution like an army, whatever embodies, expresses, or symbolizes the essence of an ordered cosmos or any significant sector thereof awakens the disposition of awe and reverence, the charismatic disposition. Men need an order within which they can locate themselves, an order providing coherence, continuity, and justice.

A Digression: Individual Variations in the Need for Order

The need for order is not equally great among all men. Many, of course, whose "antennae" are short, whose intelligence and imagination either are limited or have not been aroused by a cultural tradition which exhibits events of central significance, do not have the need to "know" the cosmos or society as a whole or to be in contact with its "vital" or "animating" principle. For such persons, who are many in the world, the need for affection, for self-maintenance, for justice, for self-transcendence, can be gratified largely in personal primary groups with spouse and offspring and kinsmen, or in working collectivities with colleagues and immediate subordinates. Much of the order they need, as well as the affection and rewards they desire, perhaps even most that is of value to them, is found in such circles of small radius. Their minds must be prodded by education and exhortation to seek the wider reaches of the cosmos and society, and in most instances, these do not have much impact. There is a constant falling away from attachment to the wider order. Only idiots—idiots in a sense halfway between the classical Greek usage and our present-day psychological usage—can, however, dispense entirely with cosmic and social order. Most people, occasionally, and intermittently, feel the need to see themselves in a deeper, wider frame of things. Birth, death, marriage, transitions from one ordered condition to another—even when they are orders of narrow radius—cause faint or dormant sensibilities to open. Their judgments of the justice of allocations within their narrow circles often invoke explicitly a standard connected with a more general rule, something more universal in scope and validity. Their judgments of worthy and unworthy tasks and accomplishments are judgments referring, however vaguely, to a scale of distance from or proximity to central things. Wars, national elections, large-scale disorders, bring men into confrontation with events of the larger world.

In no society can the problem of the larger order be avoided entirely. For one thing, some individuals, by virtue of high intelligence or moral sensitivity or preoccupation with power, need to locate themselves and connect themselves with a larger order that gives meaning to discrete and otherwise meaningless events. Then, too, the desire of men for power and for the expansion of the small orders they have created or generated lead to collisions that shake those who would dwell in peace within their narrow confines. The reverberations of the collisions of the larger orders shake the framework of the smaller. Even without natural catastrophes, the catastrophes of national markets, military vicissitudes, and the mismanagement of human affairs—indeed, the very existence of national economies alone—would force those, who by their spontaneous and normal sensitivity, would not reach out far enough to become aware of the events of the larger frame or to locate themselves in relation to them.

The major religions recommend themselves by providing such ordering patterns. They "explain" by reference to divine intention how the world came into existence and why it exists. They assess society in the light of this order and assert what it should be.

The fundamental discoveries of modern science in cosmology, astronomy, medicine, neurology, geology, genetics, are significant as disclosures of the basic order of the cosmos. Scientific order, like the order disclosed by theology, has its imperatives. Being in "regular relations" with the truths of science, doing things the "scientific way," having a "scientific attitude," are as much responses to the imperatives of the order disclosed by scientific research as pious God-fearingness is a response to the imperatives of the theologically disclosed religious order.

Metaphysics, the philosophy of history, political and moral philosophy, even sociology, seek to discern an order that is coherent, continuous, and just. More secularly, the constitution and the legal system, effective governmental institutions and the moral opinion in which they are embedded, provide such meaningful orders. It is within the context of such orders that the life of the individual and that of his society become meaningful to him. Perception of and "belief" in such orders permit events and actions to be sorted out and discriminated by reference to the "forces" thought to lie at their root. They calm the mind, or they become the objects of criticism. They gratify by putting the individual into the "right relationship" to what is important, or they leave him discontented by forcing him to be out of the "right relationship."

This "perception of the central" and the "seriousness" of mind it arouses is accompanied by the "attribution of sacredness" to the powers, transcendent or earthly, which men perceive as ruling their lives. Those in contact with them by being possessed by them or by being in cognitive or expressive contact with them, or who are charged with their earthly objectivation, become the objects of the attribution of charisma.

The Charisma of Ordering Power

The disposition to attribute charisma is intimately related to the need for order. The attribution of charismatic qualities occurs in the presence of order-creating, order-disclosing, order-discovering power as such; it is a response to great ordering power.

Order-destroying power, great capacity for violence, attracts too, and arouses the charismatic propensity. It does so because it promises in some instance, to provide a new and better order, one more harmonious with the more inclusive and deeper order of existence. Order-destroying power also arouses the charismatic propensity because of a profound ambivalence in men's relations to the central things. Order not only gives meaning; it also constricts and derogates.

The effectiveness or successful exercise of power on a large scale, on a macrosocial scale, evokes a legitimating attitude. Every legitimation of effective large-scale power contains a charismatic element. All effective rulers possess charismatic qualities, that is , have charismatic qualities attributed to them, unless it is known that they are *fainéants*, who have abdicated their responsibilities out of moral weakness or are otherwise incompetent. Even then, it is not easy to divest failed incumbents of the charismatic qualities attributed to them during their sovereignty (e.g., kings in exile, abdicated monarchs, ex-presidents, retired generals, the Duke of Windsor, King Carol, King Peter, and even the Comte de Paris, Don Carlos, or the Archduke Otto of Habsburg). What was attributed to the person in the role adheres to him in attenuated form after he has ceased to occupy it, or even when by his own weakness he diminishes the expected effectiveness of the role itself.

Why does great power as such arouse man's propensity to attribute intense, concentrated charismatic qualities to persons or attenuated and dispersed charisma to collectivities, roles, and classes of persons? Great power announces itself by its power over order; it discovers order, creates order, maintains it, or destroys it. Power is indeed the central, order-related event.

The highly imperative, the extremely powerful, in nature and in society, intervenes in man's life or is acknowledged to be capable of such intervention on a drastic, life-changing scale. Earthly power, as well as transcendent power, can protect or damage; it has the power to end life or to continue it; it has the power to create new forms of social life, to maintain and protect both the new and the old patterns. It is involved in processes, as vital as those at the disposal of priests and magicians.

The highest authorities of a society—presidents, kings, prime ministers, party secretaries, governors, judges, lawmakers—are the rulers of the fullest, most inclusive order of existence here on earth. Great earthly power has a manifold, obscure affinity with the powers believed to inhere in the transcendent order. Those who believe in divinely transcendent orders also believe that earthly powers, to enjoy legitimacy, must have some connection with transcendent powers, that rulers are necessarily involved in the essential order of things. Rulers themselves have claimed that their rule and the rules issuing from it are continuous with, i.e., legitimated by, something even more ultimate than themselves—the will of divinity[5]—through primordial contact with a charismatic person —hereditary kingship—through a cumulative insight, engendered by continuous tradition, into the nature of existence, into the ethical imperatives and the prudential considerations disclosed by long-enduring, continuous existence, or through the will of all the adults who constitute the community (popular sovereignty). Today, almost all the rulers of state-bound societies claim legitimation from the charismatically endowed citizens who form the electorate—although they do so with different degrees of reluctance.

The most fundamental laws of a country, its constitution, its most unchallengeable traditions and the institutions embodying or enunciating them, call forth awe in the minds of those in contact with them; they arouse the sense of *tremendum mysteriosum* which Rudolf Otto designated as the central property of the "idea of the holy." The ritual

---

5. Although much has been written about the divine right of kings, few efforts have been made to see this phenomenon as one instance of a general class. Alexander Ular's *Die Politik,* in the series Die Gesellschaft: Sammlung sozial-psychologischer Monographien (Frankfurt am Main, 1909), is one of the very few attempts to do so. More recent publications—*La regalità sacrà: Contributiti e tema dell' VIII congresso internazionale de storia delle religione, 1955,* by G. Widengren et al. (Leiden: J. Brill, 1959); Luc de Heusch, *Le pouvoir et le sacré,* Annales du Centre d'étude des religions 1 (Université libre de Bruxelles, Institut de sociologie, 1962)—do not go beyond conventional understanding of the phenomenon.

surrounding the highest office, even in republics, the awe before the place where the ruler sits—as the Presidential Office in the White House, or the Kremlin, or the Elysée—testify to the ways in which high "secular" authority draws to itself from those who exercise it and from those who are its objects, the disposition to attribute charisma.

Of course, a liberal, democratic, secular republic is a far cry from an absolute, caesaropapistic monarchy or a theocracy. A secular bureaucracy is different from a religious sect or church. The scope of the charismatic element in a system of authority resting on rational-legal legitimation is different from its scope in a system of authority resting on preponderantly and permeatively charismatic legitimation. The difference between the former and the latter is a difference in the locus and intensity of charisma in the two systems. In the rational-legal system, the charisma is not concentratedly imputed to the person occupying the central role or to the role itself, but is dispersed in a diminished but unequal intensity throughout the hierarchy of roles and rules. The charisma is felt to inhere in the major order-affecting system of roles. In the democratic order, there is both a legitimacy conferred on rulers by the acknowledgment of the charisma-bearing populace, and the legitimacy drawn simply from the charisma of very powerful—and effective—authority as such. In modern societies where belief in both the charisma of the populace and the charisma of the highest authority is a common phenomenon, the tensions of populism and constitutionalism are not uncommon.

Rational-legal legitimation is, of course, unique in some respects. It is manifested in a property of a role which derives from its position in a more or less logical cosmos or system of rules. Legitimacy dwells in the substance of the rule realized by the role, in the procedure of establishing the role, and in the procedure of appointing its incumbent. The role of the civil servant issuing a command to a subordinate, or of a judge rendering a judgment—leaving aside the coercive power available to each for enforcing the command or judgment—is perceived as legitimate, as Weber said, because it has been created and filled in a manner procedurally subsumable under a valid general principle or by another higher legitimate authority possessing, in accordance with that valid principle, the right to act authoritatively. The command or the judgment uttered might also be perceived as itself subsumable under or derived from a more general rule or a particular judgment with generalizable validity. In that image of the right to create and fill the role and promulgate the law, of which civil servants' and judges' declarations are particular applications, and in the commands and judgments themselves, there is an element deriving from the ultimate charismatic legitimation of government resting on the "will" of the charismatic populace.

But beyond this, the authority of the official and his rule has another charismatic source. That is the perception of a property derived from the "participation"—in the sense developed by Lévy-Bruhl and Przyluski—of the particular official role and its official incumbent in the inclusive corporate body, which is conceived of as being under a supreme authority. The particular command or judgment is conceived—very vaguely, perhaps ineffably—as a "part" or as an emanation of the cosmos of commands and judgments at the center of which is a supremely authoritative principle or a supremely authoritative role incorporating that principle. The particular incumbent of the role of civil servant, administrator, or judge is perceived as a manifestation of a larger center of *tremendous* power.

What the "subject" responds to is not just the specific declaration or order of the incumbent of the role—as the definition of rational-legal authority would have it—but the incumbent enveloped in the vague and powerful nimbus of the authority of the entire institution. It is a legitimacy constituted by sharing in the properties of the "organization as a whole" epitomized or symbolized in the powers concentrated (or thought to be concentrated) at the peak. This is "institutional" charisma; it is not a charisma deduced from the creativity of the charismatic individual. It is inherent in the massive organization of authority. The institutional charismatic legitimation of a command emanating from an incumbent of a role in a corporate body derives from membership in the body as such, apart from any allocated, specific powers.

The awareness of the grant of powers to the individual incumbent of the role, the knowledge that the rule or judgment he enunciates derives from a higher, more comprehensive rule, closer to the source of all rules—rational-legal legitimation in the narrow sense—fuses with the response to the official and his command or judgment as a participant in the powerful organization.

Institutional charisma permeates but does not by any means completely saturate the entire corporate structure. It is present in every act of obedience, even though it does not account for the whole act of obedience. To the individual "representative" of the organization "as a whole"—representative in the sense of being endowed with some of its properties—some of this charisma is attributed. (This is perhaps one of the reasons why contacts with the police and the courts are abhorrent to quite innocent persons who might seek their aid against infringements of the law—entirely apart from the residue of fear of dealing with wicked, arbitrary, exploitative, and immoral authorities.)

Thus, the mixture of the charismatically and the rational-legally legitimated types of authority involves not just the appearance of an occasional charismatic personality in the higher stratum of the corporate body, nor is it simply concentrated at the peak of a bureaucratic structure, which is as much as Weber seemed ready to acknowledge. The charisma of an institution or of a corporate body does not depend on its foundation by a charismatic person (although it might well be true that only charismatic persons can command the authority and resources to create a new and very powerful institution or corporate body). Corporate bodies—secular, economic, governmental, military, and political—come to possess charismatic qualities simply by virtue of the *tremendous* power concentrated in them.

Of course, earthly authority—political or governmental—has to contend with the attachments of various groups to their own patterns of life, their own desired ends, and their conceptions of what will affect those ends negatively or positively ("interests"). It has to contend with disobedience impelled by "interests," competing loyalties and sheer antinomianism. It has to contend with the fact that its charisma might not reach to all sectors of the population living within the boundaries over which it claims to be sovereign. Authority might be hated, partly because it is injurious to the realization of private or sectional aspirations. Likewise, authority may be sustained not only by its own charismatic legitimacy but by its contribution to the realization of ends desired by the members of particular sub-sectors of the society.

Charismatic Activities and the Allocation of Deference

But effective, massive power over the affairs of men is not sufficient in itself to satisfy the need for order, much as it contributes to its satisfaction and great though the charisma, i.e., the connection with vital things, which is attributed to it may be. Effective power, however great, does not automatically and completely legitimate itself simply by its effective existence. The social order it appears to create, maintain, or control must not only give the impression of being coherent and continuous; it must also appear to be integrated with a transcendent moral order. It must incorporate a standard of justice referring to an order beyond that already realized in existing institutions.

The "allocative problem," the problem of who is entitled to what, must be recurrently resolved. Here coercive power alone, even if it could be generated in sufficient magnitude, could not in and of itself provide a generally acceptable answer in any society. Even the mighty, whose power itself engenders a belief that those who possess it are entitled to do so, must reinforce that belief by invoking a standard which *justifies* their possession of power and rewards by their qualities and their performances. The demand for justice, or for the alleviation of injustice, both in the system as a whole and in particular relationships within a limited sector of the distribution, derives from the demand for a social order consonant with a transcendent moral standard. If the effective exercise of earthly power alone were the only locus of presumptive charisma, the problem of injustice in the actions of the powerful would never arise. If men were willing to regard it as just that rewards should be exclusively proportionate to the exercise of a society-wide, order-creating and -maintaining power, and to proximity to those who exercise it, the problem of a just order might not arise. That is, however, not the case; in too many instances the distribution of rewards proportionately to power arouses the criticism that it diverges from a distribution enjoined by an ultimate standard. "Accidents" of inheritance in societies in which primordial connections have lost their once self-evident charisma are illustrative of this divergence. Furthermore, there are other connections with the charismatic or transcendent order: scientific insight, theological reasoning, medical intervention, or physical heroism which faces and overcomes danger on behalf of order. The holders of the greatest power over the lives of others are not necessarily in harmony with the elites of the spheres in which these other order-connected activities are carried on. Each elite prizes and feels most immediately the particular sector or conception of the transcendent order to which it is attached and for which it claims responsibility.

Even though different sectors of the elite tend to be in consensus and to support each other, from the sense of affinity generated by their common centrality, their consensus cannot be complete. The very differences in their relations to the cosmic and social orders, the differences in the intensity of their contact with it, produce some degree of dissensus. This intra-elite dissensus spreads to other sectors of the society and finds particular reception among strata and groups already unwilling to acknowledge the claims of the powerful to supreme and exclusive embodiment of principles of cosmic and social order.

Still, dissensus notwithstanding, the center of society does impose itself. Its centrality is acknowledged widely. Evidence of this acknowledgment abounds. The acknowledgment takes form in spontaneous law-abidingness and in the deference system. The judgments constituting the deference system confirm the superiority of the center from which order is discerned, sustained, and controlled, and represent an assent to the unequal distribution of rewards and facilities.

In the results of sample surveys regarding the prestige or status of various occupations in the United States,[6] Supreme Court justices, state governors, physicians, federal legislators, cabinet members, nuclear physicists and other scientists, professors, and metropolitan mayors receive the most deference. Somewhat further down but still very high are lawyers and directors of large corporations. Some of these occupations—that of state governor, for instance—involve the exercise of great authority through commands which affect many persons; others, like scientists and professors, can command very few persons, and in their central activity, the authority they exercise has no coercive power associated with it. The case of the Supreme Court justice, who heads the list, is especially instructive, for he asserts the highest law, the Constitution, in the light of its most general principles. General conceptions of rational justice and the common good, transcendent principles by which individual articles of the Constitution are interpreted, are at the very center of transcendent order. (The recurrence of the terminology of natural law is itself expressive of this connection.) The justice of the Supreme Court is the link between the transcendent order and the earthly order. Scientists and scholars, seeking the general pattern of the universe, of man's nature and the objectivations of his creative powers,

6. The most important of these was conducted by the National Opinion Research Center, Chicago, and is reported in Albert Reiss et al., *Occupations and Social Status* (New York: The Free Press, 1961).

participate in the same order. Creative and expressive persons, to the extent that their objectivations become known, are likewise regarded as connected with this ultimate normative and symbolic stratum. Legislators, who create law in accordance with the higher law of the constitution, likewise participate in this connection between the higher, charismatic order and the earthly order, the maintenance of which is in their charge; they deeply affect the order of life of many people by their decisions. Lawyers, who interpret this law and who enter into authoritative positions in government, likewise receive high deference.

Below the peaks, the esteemed occupations entail, in some measure, an attenuated contact and collaboration with the central institutional and value systems, or they permit an attenuated measure of creativity in ordering things. Schoolteachers, welfare workers, the skilled manual trades, and small business managers are instances of these.

The occupations enjoying least esteem are farthest from the center of society and from the central value system formed around the expressive, moral, and cognitive activities directed toward the charismatic stratum of being. The unskilled, uncreative occupations whose incumbents order very little, handle brute matter as brute matter, express little that is vital, and do not penetrate intellectually into the nature of anything, rank very low. The occupations whose incumbents handle only the detritus of man's existence and do so only by manipulating it directly come lowest. Functionally, these occupations perform indispensable tasks, but they rank low because they do not approximate the charisma-affected orders.

To summarize, deference is an acknowledgment of, a response to, the presumptive charismatic connections of roles at the center of society and at the center of life.[7] The main recipients of deference are those who exercise authority in the central institutional system and those who occupy the main positions in the central value system of the society. In their occupations they perceive and enunciate the most general principles (laws, rules, judgments) in their most immediate manifestation of or connection with the ultimate or charismatic, or which maintain or protect the earthly order enjoined by these principles. The most powerful roles, even where they do not occupy themselves directly with the norms deriving from ultimate cosmic or moral order, arouse by the generality

7. Weber refers explicitly to charismatic proximity as a major criterion in his discussion of the status of various Japanese noble families (*Wirtschaft und Gesellschaft*, vol. 1, pp. 772-74).

and magnitude of their power, a sense of the charismatic. They thereby become the recipients of deference; so do the roles that directly protect vitality in consequence of their immediate connection with such central things as great physical power and cognitive penetration into and control over nature.

The wealthy and the highly remunerated are esteemed, not for the possession of great wealth or income as such, or the comfort they afford, but because wealth arises from—or permits—the exercise of authority, or is thought to be the reward for order-creating activities or the manifestation of creative, penetrative powers. Style of life is esteemed because it is a ritualized manifestation of what is the necessity and obligation of those at the charismatic center; it is part of a pattern appropriate to proximity to the center. Education is esteemed because it opens the way to contact with the norms and the cultural objectivations which constitute the central value system and because it facilitates entry to the central institutional roles in which authority is exercised and fosters contact with persons in such roles.

The properties that appear to be relevant to the assessment of the deference-worthiness of a role or an action are wealth, income, occupation, the power to order by command, prohibition and control over resources, style of life, standard of living, education, primordial connections, including kinship, with persons possessing these properties, and the power to protect or benefit the community or life itself. The distributions of these properties are distributions of primary or derivative distances from the charismatic. Those at the upper ends of the distributions are close to it; at the lower ends, they are remote from it. Personal and organismic qualities such as humor, generosity, gentleness, physical strength, and beauty are significant in the distribution of deference in face-to-face relationships, but they are not taken into account when the "objectively existent" status system, the "serious" status system, is considered. They are regarded as irrelevant, and, given man's charismatic propensity, they are irrelevant because they are not closely involved in the charismatic order. They have scarcely any connection with the ultimate determinants of cosmic order or the ultimate grounds of power and justice.

Some of the macrosocially relevant deference or status qualifications are primary: they are authority, creativity, penetration, and promulgation, as embodied in occupational role and education. These things are at the center of the institutional and cultural systems of any society.

Income and style of life are derivative. Kinship connection too is derivative in highly differentiated societies, and so, in large measure, is ethnicity. The primary and the derivative properties are intertwined in very complicated ways, and the latter often acquire a certain measure of autonomy as primary objects of judgment, striving and emulation.

The Plurality and Paradoxy of Charismatic Objects

In the foregoing I have given instances of the working of an attenuated and dispersed charisma in corporate bodies and in the stratification system. I have implied that there is a widespread but not all-inclusive consensus throughout much of the society in the assessment of those affected with charismatic properties. I have suggested, also, that dissensus is apt to arise between persons whose occupational roles are concerned with perceiving and promulgating order and those whose roles are concerned with its conduct and management. This notwithstanding, a considerable degree of consensus exists among the various sectors of the elite.

An endemic dissensus, however, coexists with the society-wide consensus. (A great deal of "idiocy" is also fostered by isolation, ignorance, and insensitivity.) The sources of this dissensus are many, and I cannot deal with all of them here. The most important arise from divergent conceptions of the locus and substance of charisma. I shall touch on a few of these.

Their immediate proximity to the sources of charisma, their awareness of their majesty, distorts the minds of those who live in such proximity. This distortion tends in the direction of an identification of the transcendent with the social orders, so that considerations of state and of individual and group advantage are made out to be in accord with the dictates of the transcendent order.

Then too, there is a differential sensibility to the respective orders. Some persons are by temperament, just as some are by their culture, more sensitive than others to the transcendent order or to particular transcendent orders, and are more attached to the transcendent. For the transcendentally more sensitive, the claim of the managers and beneficiaries of the social order to be the exhaustive theophany of the transcendent order is not reasonable. The social order seems relatively unimportant in comparison with the transcendent order and unequal to it in dignity. The pretensions of the custodians of the social order to be the sole and proper agents of the transcendent order seem so obviously implausible that they scarcely would need refutation but for the pragmatic strength of the "earthly powers."

These two sources of dissensus recur in the internal relationships of various sectors of the elite, but another pattern of dissensus affects the modal and lower sections of the distribution. Those who suffer the burdens of distance from the center, who are the victims of the unequal distributions of dignity and more tangible rewards, are inevitably somewhat hostile toward those who dominate the earthly order. All charisma calls forth not only awe and deference but also a sacrilegious, "atheistic" hostility. In a firm and stable order where the earthly elites are patently effective, these antinomian dispositions are held in check. Nonetheless, the impulse exists, and the critical attitude of the more transcendentally oriented sector of the elite strengthens it. It leads to some measure of refusing the pretensions and claims of the earthly elite.

Those near the lower ends of the distribution are, for example, impelled by their condition toward somewhat different criteria for esteeming occupational roles. They do not wholeheartedly acknowledge authority and creativity; they value wealth somewhat more as a criterion. Because their own occupational roles derogate them, they evaluate occupation less highly than some of the more accessible primary and derivative criteria such as education and style of life, which might be more easily acquired. And even with respect to a given deference-relevant property, they might seek to invert the prevailing standard of evaluation in ways that would enhance their own dignity.

There are, moreover, multiple interpretations of transcendental orders, flowing from different cultural traditions and different complexes of experience. There are divergent "interests," too, in the vulgar sense of the word—the desire to possess scarce things that are or might be possessed by others; the very desire is evidence of the weakness with which charisma is attributed to those who possess the desired things. These give rise to dissensus in opinion and conflicts among those who espouse the divergent interpretations.

The contents of the transcendent order can never be unequivocally specified; they are bound to be ambiguous and to give rise to and sustain divergent interpretations, especially among those who are very sensitive to transcendent things. Thus, out of considerations of the balance of ease and pain, from the desire for dignity as well as from more intellectual disagreements, the spread of consensus about the locus of the charismatic over an entire society encounters obstacles. But in addition to these endemic sources of dissensus about the locus and content of the charismatic, two others merit special mention. The oldest carriers of earthly charisma are the primordial collectivities, kinship and local territorial groups, and ethnic aggregates. Primordial qualities still function powerfully as charismatic qualities, and their conflict with the charismatic claims of ordering authority is a constant feature of historical societies. The problems of the new states as well as the Negroes' civil rights problems in the United States testify to the tenacity of the belief in the ultimate validity of primordial qualities.

The other variant form of the dispersion of charisma which restricts, and even sets up a counterstandard to the charismatic claims of, earthly authority, is the charisma of the nation or of the populace. The two, though somewhat different, have much in common. The proponents and beneficiaries of this dispersion attribute charismatic qualities to the sectors of the society that are peripheral with respect to their share in the exercise of authority and the embodiment of culture and in the distribution of wealth, income, and education. Where charisma is attributed to these strata, the distance between center and periphery is diminished, and their position in the hierarchy of deference is much elevated. The spread or range of the distribution of deference is narrowed as the periphery is brought closer to the peaks.

Through this dispersion of charisma into the periphery, the society moves toward a civil society. A widely dispersed charisma is an indispensable condition of civility, but it is not a sufficient ground for its existence. Civility entails not only the imputation of charisma to the mass of the population by itself; it also requires that the established and effective elite impute charisma to the mass as well, that the elite regard itself, despite all its differences as sharing some of the charisma that resides in it with the rest of its society. It requires, too, that the virtues implicit in this widespread and consensual dispersion of charisma should be practiced in and with respect to the central institutional system—government and law, above all.

The Motives and Mechanisms of the Dispersion of Charisma

There is a strong tendency toward a consensual "acknowledgment" of the charismatic quality of those in positions of highest authority. So far as authority is visible—this is part of its effectiveness—it does have a self-legitimating consequence. It arouses the attribution of charisma, and this is why an often uncomfortable alternation exists in references to the "upper classes," the speaker denying their superiority emphatically while acknowledging it implicitly as an "objective" fact that has nothing to do with his explicit individual evaluation, which is negative. The denial is made because the affirmation is already there, and both are genuine.

The mechanism of simultaneous affirmation and denial comes into play where the distance from the charisma-generating center is so great that its effectiveness is enfeebled, but not so enfeebled as to be without consequence. The consequence of distance from the charismatic center is a sense of inferiority. Those who are far from the locus of charisma experience that distance painfully.

The sense of being inferior is most painful for those who cannot divert their attention to their orders of narrow radius. The condition of inferiority is itself a strong impetus to deny the validity of the distribution in which they fare so badly. This usually entails a denial of the connection between the transcendent order and the moral standards it implies or asserts, and the social order in which they are relegated to a position so distant from the center. One of the major responses of the sensitive who are placed at the periphery is to invoke the charisma of the transcendent order and to insist on its disjunction from the prevailing social order and its authority—which, however, still compels a reluctant attribution of charisma, despite the intense and genuine efforts to deny it. This is the motive for disassociating the allegedly theophanous rulers from the transcendent order.

This account does not exhaust the subject. There are deeper causes. One is the capacity and impulsion of every human being toward individuality. Everyone has in some degree this capacity and impulse. It dies early in most human beings, partly because it is not strong itself and partly because it is crushed by primordial ties, and by primordial, corporate, cultural, and political authority. It needs cultivation if it is to flower in any but the most forceful. (Weber's observations about charismatic education, the nurturing of the charismatic capacity, apply as well to this property of man's spirit and are capable of a broader application than he himself made.) Where individuality, the perception of the self and the appreciation of its value, comes into substantial existence, it is accompanied by an increased sympathy, a greater readiness to perceive the minds of others and to appreciate them emphatically as entities with inherent qualities—not just as instances of a category. The consequent perception of other individualities contributes to the process of attributing charisma to them.

Another positive factor implicit in what I have said, which has led in modern times to the widening dispersion of charisma over the whole society and hence to the belief in the charisma of the people, is the growth of the national state, entailing a visible, tangible, coherent, and effective central authority. The sharing of this charisma which flows from the central authority, however small that share might be, with a multitude of others who live within a territory ruled by the central authority, has gradually and in conjunction with the factors already mentioned led to the direct attribution of charisma to all citizens of the national state.

Free, universal education works in the same direction. It brings the oncoming generation directly into contact with the central value system. It gives those who receive it a sense of sharing in what is central in the cosmos and in their own society. The mere acquisition of literacy has a similar impact. It changes a person's image of himself; he too gains, by virtue of education, contact with the transcendent and earthly orders, and with their central symbols.

The Permanent Tension regarding the Locus of Charismatic Qualities

The dispersion of charisma can never go so far as to engender a completely equalitarian society. Quite apart from the differences in the creative powers of individuals, and the unequal distribution of rewards and motives which impel men unequally to contact with charismatic things, there remains the basic and irrefragible fact of authority. In a large-scale society which has many demands and which therefore generates many tasks, authority is bound to be unequally distributed. Indeed the very dispersion of charisma, by enhancing the individual's conception of his own rights and values, increases his demands for performance on the part of elites. These performances cannot be carried out without a very considerable allocation of authority.

Authority, when it is massive and continuous, calls forth, by its mere existence, the attribution of charisma. It calls it forth from those who are not in authoritative roles and who attribute it to themselves, and even in the elites who also impute charisma to the rest of their society. It cannot do otherwise. It is too important, too *serious* a matter to do otherwise, even in secular societies. Authority is too crucial to the creation and maintenance of order to be able to void the sentiments that need and are evoked by order.

The consequence is that large modern societies, even more than the large societies of the past, are enmeshed in a perpetual strain of competing conceptions about the ultimate locus of charisma. The discerners and interpreters of the transcendent order, the agents of earthly order, and the populace which wishes to share in these higher orders and already regards itself as sharing in them sufficiently, are bound to be engaged in a contest with each other. The earthly elite is under pressure from the charisma of the transcendent order and from charisma embodied in the populace. It can never avoid its attribution of charisma to its own central position, but neither can it avoid contention, pressure, and criticism from the other bearers of charismatic qualities. And any improvement in the position of any one of the three contestants is bound to arouse and strengthen the affirmation of their own charisma in the other two, while at the same time laying it open to criticism and refusal.

With these concluding but not definitive observations, we come again to Weber's famous proposition about the revolutionary character of charisma. As in so much else that he said, much truth resides. But the truth of the matter is more complicated, the phenomenon is more protean, and the distance to be traversed for its understanding is still very great.

7

DEFERENCE

Into every action of one human being toward another there enters an element of appreciation or derogation of the "partner" toward whom the action is directed. It enters in varying degrees; some actions contain very little of it, some consist almost entirely of appreciation or derogation, in most actions the appreciative or derogatory elements are mingled with others, such as commanding, coercing, cooperating, purchasing, loving, etc.

Appreciation and derogation are responses to properties of the "partner," of the role which he is performing, of the categories into which he is classified or the relationships in which he stands to third persons or categories of persons—against the background of the actor's own image of himself with respect to these properties. This element of appreciation or derogation is different from those responses to the past or anticipated actions of the "partner" which are commands, acts of obedience, the provision of goods or services, the imposition of injuries such as the withholding or withdrawal of goods and services, and acts of love or hatred.

These acts of appreciation or derogation I shall designate as *deference*. The term "deference" shall refer both to positive or high deference and to negative or low deference or derogation. Ordinarily, when I say that one person defers to another, I shall mean that he is acknowledging that person's worth or dignity, but when I speak of a person's "deference-position," that might refer either to a high or low deference position.

Previously published in a slightly different form in *Social Stratification*, edited by John A. Jackson (Cambridge University Press, 1968), pp. 104–32.

What I call deference here is sometimes called "status" by other writers. There is nothing wrong with that designation, except that it has become associated with a conception of the phenomenon which I wish to modify. The term "deference," with its clear intimation of a person who defers, brings out the aspect which has in my view not been made sufficiently explicit in work on this subject in recent years.

Deference is closely related to such phenomena as prestige, honor, and respect (and obscurity and shame, dishonor and disrespect), fame (and infamy), glory (and ignominy), dignity (and indignity).

Acts of deference are performed in face-to-face relationships and in the relationship of actors who have no direct interactive relationship with each other but who are members of the same society. It can exist too in the relationships of individual actors or collectivities in different societies, although to the extent that this occurs the societies in question cease to be totally separate societies.

The granting of deference entails an attribution of superiority or inferiority, but it is not the same as an attribution of goodness or wickedness. It does, however, often have such overtones; occasionally there is a suggestion that the superiority requires goodness for its completeness. It is an attribution of merit or of demerit; it is an assessment which attributes worthiness or unworthiness which is quite distinct from an attribution of moral qualities. What this worthiness consists in is an obscure matter.

To be the recipient of deference from another actor, whether in some tangible or clearly perceivable and discrete form of action from other persons, or to possess it in an autonomous symbolic form which is regarded as an "objectification of deference" quite apart from the deferential actions of concrete actors, or to possess it by believing oneself to be entitled to it through the possession of the qualities which are conventionally accepted as the grounds on which deference is elicited or granted, is a widespread desire of human beings. It might even be said that the desire to be "worthy" is a "need" of human beings in the way in which affection, erotic gratification, and the satisfaction of organic needs such as nutriment and bodily warmth are "needs."

To grant or accord deference is also a "need" of human beings aroused or generated by the process of interaction and by the fact of living in a society which goes beyond the limited radius of face-to-face interaction. Just as they wish to be worthy and to have that worth acknowledged by the deference of other persons, so they also often have a need to live in a social world implanted with worthiness, to acknowledge the embodiments of that worth and to derogate those who are unworthy.

Deference of the sort which I discuss in this paper is a way of expressing an assessment of the self and of others with respect to "macrosocial" properties. By macrosocial properties, I refer to those characteristics which describe the role or position of persons in the larger (usually national) society in which they live. The act of symbolization of deference is an attribution of deference position or status in the total society. In acts of deference performed within face-to-face relationships or within limited corporate groups, the deference is often but not always accorded primarily with respect to status in the larger society. The deference accorded to a father as head of a family is not deference in my sense of the word when it does not make reference to the father's position in the society outside the family. The deference awarded to a superior or colleague within a corporate body is a mixture of deference with respect to intracorporate status and to "macrosocial" status. The deference accorded to a woman or to women as a category or to a man or to men as a category is at the margin of macrosocial deference. The deference accorded to age or youth is similarly marginal. Both age and sex are significant factors in the determination of the "life chances" of a person and therewith of the likelihood that that person will receive deference. They are, moreover, themselves the objects of deferential judgments. Yet the deference granted to age or to sex seems to be of a different order from that deference which is an appreciation of worthiness or a derogation of unworthiness in the imagined or actually experienced larger society.

The Bases of Deference

The disposition to defer and the performance of acts of deference are evoked by the perception, in the person or classes of persons perceived, of certain characteristics or properties of their roles or actions. These characteristics or properties I shall call deference-entitling properties or entitlements. While they do not by themselves and automatically arouse judgments of deference, they must be seen or believed to exist for deference to be granted. Deference entitlements include: occupational role and accomplishment, wealth (including type of wealth), income and the mode of its acquisition, style of life, level of educational attainment, political or corporate power, proximity to persons or roles exercising political or corporate power, kinship connections, ethnicity, performance on behalf of the community or society in relation to external communities or societies, and the possession of "objective acknowledgments" of deference such as titles or ranks.

It is on the basis of the perception of these entitlements that individuals and classes of more or less anonymous individuals who are believed to possess some constellation of these entitlements are granted deference; it is on the basis of the possession of these properties that they grant deference to themselves and claim it from others. It is on the basis of simultaneous assessments of their own and of others' deference entitlements that they regulate their conduct toward others and anticipate the deferential—or derogatory—responses of others.

Why should these properties be singled out as pertinent to deference? What is it about them which renders them deference-relevant? Why are they and not kindness, amiability, humor, manliness, femininity, and other temperamental qualities which are so much appreciated in life, regarded as deference-relevant?

The cognitive maps which human beings form of their world include a map of their society. This map locates the primary or corporate groups of which they are active members and the larger society which includes these groups, but with which they have little active contact. The map which delineates this society entails a sense of membership in that society and a sense of the vital character of that membership. Even though the individual revolts against that society, he cannot completely free himself from his sense of membership in it. The society is not just an ecological fact or an environment; it is thought to possess a vitality which is inherent in it and membership in it confers a certain vitality on those who belong to it. It is a significant cosmos from which members derive some of their significance to themselves and to others. This significance is a charismatic significance; i.e., it signifies the presence and operation of what is thought to be of ultimate and determiniative significance.

If we examine each of the deference-relevant properties with reference to this charismatic content, i.e., with reference to the extent to which it tends to have charisma attributed to it, we will see that each of these properties obtains its significance as an entitlement to deference primarily on these grounds.

Occupational role is ordinarily thought of as one of the most significant entitlements to deference. The most esteemed occupations in societies, for which there are survey or impressionistic data, are those which are in their internal structure and in their functions closest to the centers. The centers of society are those positions which exercise earthly power and which mediate man's relationship to the order of existence—spiritual forces, cosmic powers, values and norms—which legitimate or withhold legitimacy from the earthly powers or which dominate earthly existence. The highest "authorities" in society—governors, judges, prime ministers and presidents, and fundamental scientists—are those whose roles enable them to control society or to penetrate into the ultimate laws and forces which are thought to control the world and human life. Occupational roles are ranked in a sequence which appears approximately to correspond with the extent to which each role possesses these properties. The charismatic content of a given occupational role will vary with the centrality of the corporate body or sector in which it is carried on. The most authoritative role in a peripheral corporate body will carry less charisma than the same type of role in a more centrally located corporate body. The roles which exercise no authority and which are thought to have a minimum of contact with transcendent powers call forth least deference.

Of course, occupational roles and their incumbents are also deferred to on account of certain highly correlated deference-entitling properties such as the income which the practice of the occupation provides, the educational level of its practitioners, the ethnic qualities of its incumbents, etc. Conversely, occupational roles which are ill remunerated and the incumbents of which have little education and are of derogated ethnic stocks receive little deference on the grounds of these traits as well as on the grounds of the nature and functions of the occupational role itself. Nonetheless, occupational role is an independent entitlement to deference.

Beyond occupational role, accomplishment within the role is a deference entitlement both micro- and macrosocially. To be not only a judge but an outstanding judge, to be not only a scientist but an outstanding scientist constitutes a further deference entitlement. It does this not only because outstanding accomplishment renders its performer more "visible" and therewith more likely to be the recipient of deference but much more because accomplishment is the realization of the potentiality of creative action. Creativity is a feature of centrality; creative action makes the creator part of the center.

Wealth is deferred to—great wealth is greatly deferred to, and poverty is derogated—because it is powerful. But without association with charismatic occupation or with political power, wealth is not as much deferred to as when it enjoys those associations. Wealth which is manifested only by purchasing power is not as esteemed as wealth which embodies its power in the ownership and management of landed estates or in the directorship of great industrial corporations, employing many thousands of persons. Wealth is, in one important aspect, purchasing power, and as such it is like income; it is also the power to employ and the power to dismiss from employment. These powers over physiological existence and access to dignity are tremendous, but they are not peculiar to wealth and are quite compatible with the propertylessness of those who exercise these powers. Wealth also calls forth deference when it is associated with a certain style of life, for which it is indeed a condition.

Wealth alone calls forth a qualified deference. Until the wealthy acquire an appropriate style of life and associations, they do not gain "acceptance" by those whom they equal or exceed in wealth and who already have a high deference position. The contempt shown towards the *nouveau riche* is well known and it often takes a generation for wealth to acquire the appropriate education, religion, occupation, and style of life which are necessary for assimilation into a higher deference stratum. Wealth is therefore both a derivative and a conditional entitlement to deference. It is a derivative from occupation, from the exercise of power, over persons and over the soil; it is conditional to a "style of life." It is also conditional to income; it itself and alone is significant primarily as a potentiality of power. To gain the deference which sociologists often assert is the reward of wealth it must find completion in a wider complex of properties such as the actual exercise of power through an authoritative occupational role, through a "validating" style of life, etc.

It is pertinent to refer here to the anomaly experienced in the contemplation of very wealthy persons who do not *use* their wealth in the practice of an appropriate style of life, who exercise no power through its use, employing no one, exercising no control over the agricultural or industrial properties in which it is invested, and who practice no occupation. All they have is the potentiality which we know from the observation of other cases wealth possesses. They enjoy such deference as they receive—apart from what they might receive by virtue of their family name—because of the potentiality rather than the actuality of their exercise of power. Potentiality is less instigative of deference than actuality. As a result, they are the objects of an ambivalent judgment, deference granted for the potentiality of power which wealth confers, deference withheld for their failing to complete the potentiality of wealth by manifesting it in the fuller pattern which is incumbent on anyone who is high in any single distribution.

Income too is regarded as an entitlement to deference as a manifestation of power, but it is a limited and segmental power which is exercised in the specific buyer-seller relationship in the purchase of goods and services. Purchasing power, confined as it is to very specific exchange relationships, is not a very weighty entitlement to deference. Income alone possesses only potential deference entitlement. Nonetheless, a high income, like a large fortune, is regarded as a valid entitlement to deference when it is used to acquire what it can most legitimately be used for, namely the style of life to which it corresponds, or to acquire those other purchasable entitlements like educational opportunity, and associational membership. Income is therefore a *conditional* deference entitlement which acquires deference primarily when manifested in another category. In itself it possesses as little charisma as an immediate and specific but only potential power confers. Although all resources in particular distributive categories contain the potentiality of conversion into a position in another distributive category, they vary in their degree of specificity. Income can be used to purchase objects at relatively fixed rates, e.g. household furnishings, books, education, etc.; education is not equally specific in the response which it is thought to be entitled to call forth. Neither is political authority. In general we can say that the more diffuse a potentiality, the greater is its entitlement to deference.

A style of life is a deference entitlement because it is a pattern of conduct which is a voluntary participation in an order of values. A style of life is value-permeated; it demonstrates connection with a stratum of being in which true value resides. The conventional and long-standing deference given to the "leisure classes" was not given because idleness was a virtue or because work or occupation was a burden but because leisure permitted the cultivation and practice of a value-infused pattern of life. Like an authoritative occupation, it was a value-generating and value-infused existence. More than authoritative occupations, it belongs, despite its material embodiment, to the realm of culture. It included eating ("commensality") "in style," living in the midst of an appropriate décor, in an appropriate quarter ("a good address"), surrounded by servants who provide not just labor power but a ritual environment. Of course, "style of life" can be shriveled to hedonistic self-indulgence, "conspicuous consumption," or sheer idleness, all of which are capable of gaining ascendancy within the pattern. In its highest form, "style of life" was found in courts and palaces, in great country houses and *grand bourgeois* establishments. Style of life requires income as a condition but it is an entitlement to deference not as a direct function of wealth and income or simply as an indicator of wealth and income. It is facilitated by wealth and income, but it enhances them and transfigures them. It does so because it partakes of a charismatic quality which they contain only in the potentiality but not in their sheer and specific actuality.

The level of educational attainment possesses deference-entitling properties partly because it is often conditional to entry into authoritative, creative, and remunerative occupational roles but even more because it is an assimilation into an ideal realm. It is an assimilation into a pattern of values and beliefs which are part of the center of existence. The "possessor" of a large amount of education is often an incumbent of an authoritative occupation and as an actual or potential incumbent of such an occupation he receives deference; he also has the likelihood of a higher than average income and an appropriate style of life, and as such he receives deference also. The educated person is one who has received the culture of beliefs and appreciations which are central in the society. These beliefs may be scientific beliefs about the way in which the world works, they may be beliefs about the "essential" nature of the society, its history, its religion, its cultural traditions and objectivations. Education is also the acquisition of skills which prepare for participation in the center of the society through the exercise of authority, technological performance, the discovery and transmission of vital truths about the universe, man and society, in short for *creating* and *ordering*. Education is an autonomous, nonderivative entitlement to deference because it is integral to and testifies to its possessor's participation in the charismatic realm. The deference entitlement of education is also affected by the institutions and countries in which it is acquired. Some schools and universities and university systems are thought to be more central than others. Those educated in them acquire more of a charismatically infused culture.

The exercise of power, whether in an occupation or through the employment of purchasing power, is determinative of the life chances of the persons over whom it is exercised; therewith it shares in the charisma which is inherent in the control of life. It is difficult to separate power from occupational role because much or even most power is exercised in occupational roles, in corporate bodies, particularly if we include inherited, entrepreneurially initiated, appointed, and elected incumbency in roles in the state, church, armies, economic organizations, universities, etc. Authority exercised through occupational roles becomes more diffuse the higher its position within any corporate hierarchy, whether the hierarchy be religious, political, military, or whatever. Its diffuseness, which is another facet of its creating and ordering responsibility and capacity, is crucial to its deference entitlement.

There is undoubtedly some power which is not occupational in the locus of its exercise. It might be worthwhile, therefore, to employ a separate category for power as a deference entitlement for those persons whose charismatic ascendancy is not a function of an occupational role. Just as within occupations there are interindividual differences in creativity or productivity, so it is perfectly conceivable that this creativity can manifest itself avocationally and outside the corporate bodies within which such activities are ordinarily carried on. There are religious prophets who arise out of the laity, revolutionary politicians who are not incorporated into the established political order, intimates of rulers who have no formal political occupation and whose own occupations are not constitutively endowed with power. All of these are exercisers of power in a way which is independent of their occupational roles.

Where everyone in a society or at least all adults stand in at least one important respect in equal relationship to the exercise of authority in government through citizenship, deference is dispersed. A more democratic power and the attendant equalization of deference through citizenship do not abolish the inequality of power and thus the inequality of deference associated with the unequal distribution of authoritative occupational roles. It does, however, offset it and in some situations to a very considerable extent.

Relative proximity to persons in powerful roles is another deference entitlement. The proximity may be a fiduciary relationship between the incumbent of a very authoritative role and his "personal staff"; it may be a close personal relationship of friendship or affection; it may be little more than the acquaintanceship of frequent encounter; it may be the primordial tie of kinship. Whatever the content of the relationship, the important thing is that the magnitude of its entitlement to deference for a given person is assessed by (*a*) the deference position of the person to whom he stands in proximity and (*b*) the degree of proximity. To be the son or cousin or the intimate friend of a person of no significant status adds no status to those in that degree of proximity; indeed it makes for the insignificant status of those who stand in such proximity. Being a close friend or a frequently met colleague of a person of a high deference position confers more deference than would a slighter degree of friendship or a less intense collegial intercourse. The deference position of the person at the end of the chain is determined by the properties already referred to; the relationship is the channel through which a fundamentally charismatic quality is transmitted. Just as the member of a corporate body participates in the charisma of his organization, whether it be a university, a church, or a government, so membership in a personal relationship or in a primordial collectivity, e.g., family, is constituted by or results from a diffusion of the charisma of the central person or role of the collectivity. Those who stem from "famous" families, those who keep the company of important persons, who move in "important circles," share in the charismatic quality of those whose charisma gives fame to families and importance to circles. The three modes of linkage—primordial, personal, and collegial—are all different from each other and yet each has been regarded as a legitimate channel through which charisma and, consequently, the entitlement to deference can be shared.

Ethnicity is very much like the kinship tie—they are both primordial, being constituted by the significance attributed to a presumed genetic connection and the primordial unity arising therefrom. Unlike kinship connection as an entitlement to deference, ethnicity does not refer to a genetic link with a particular important person or persons. It is a link with a collectivity in which a vital, charismatic quality is diffused. It is thought to represent the possession of some quality inherent in the ethnic aggregate and shared by all its members. Indeed the possession of that "essential" quality, as manifested in certain external features such as color, hair form, physiognomy, and physique, constitutes membership in the aggregate. In societies which are ethnically homogeneous, the ethnic entitlement is neutral; in societies which are ethnically plural, the ethnic entitlement can only be neutralized by an overriding civility or sense of citizenship or by the disaggregation of the society to the point where it almost ceases to be a society.

Areal provenience, whether it be rural or urban, regional or local, provincial or metropolitan, can also be a deference entitlement in a variety of ways. In some respects, it can be derivative from occupational roles and the exercise of authority insofar as particular occupational roles and the exercise of authority tend to be more concentrated—although not necessarily in the same locations—to a greater extent in some areas than in others. It might also be derivative from the greater proximity to authority and eminence which is more likely in some areas than in others. But the soil and the city might be independent entitlements, one gaining ascendancy over the other in accordance with prevailing beliefs concerning the sanctity of the soil or the charisma of urban existence.

Religious adherence or affiliation is similar to ethnicity in that it is a deference entitlement referring to membership in a collectivity, but in this case the collectivity is constituted by the sharing of beliefs about sacred things and therewith by the sharing of the charisma of the church or sect. Whereas practically all societies are differentiated in occupational roles and in income and power or authority and are bound to be so by their nature as societies, ethnic and religious heterogeneity is not inevitable. But it is very widespread.

Indulgence conferred on the community or on society by protecting it from injury or by enhancing its position—power, wealth, deference—among communities or societies is regarded as an entitlement to deference for those who confer such indulgence. Successful military men, politicians and statesmen, diplomats, athletes in international competitions, literary men, and artists are deferred to within their own societies in proportion to their external deference or their enhancement of the power of their own society vis-à-vis other societies. The enhancement of the deference position and power of the society enhances the deference position of its members by virtue of their membership in it. It is the same here as in the case of proximity to importance or membership in primordial collectivities. There is a sense of some shared essential quality with those who "represent" the society. There is a deference stratification among societies. It includes the deference stratification of whole societies and an international deference system of individuals, which is, however, extremely fragmentary.

A title or emblem conferred by the major deference-bearing institutions of the society is an entitlement to deference—such are the criteria by which deference is allocated in societies. They are not all of equal importance in the formation of deference judgments, nor do their relative weights remain constant through time or among societies. Ethnicity, area, religion might vary considerably in their significance in accordance with the strength of the sense of civility and the extent and intensity of religious belief. Education might become more important when a larger proportion of the population seeks education and possesses different amounts and kinds of education. The more equal the distribution of any given deference entitlement, the less weight it has in differentiating the deference positions of the members of a society. This does not mean that it loses its significance in the determination of the allocation of deference, only that it ceases to differentiate the worth of individuals. In fact, while ceasing to differentiate, it might at the same time raise the deference position of most individuals throughout the society. But there is also a possibility that a particular criterion might become irrelevant, or at least diminish in relevance, to deference, losing its influence on the level of deference as it ceases to discriminate among individuals, groups, and strata.

If we can imagine a society, the technology of which has become so automated that a large part of the gainfully employed population ceases to be differentiated by occupation, we are confronted by a situation in which occupations, at least for a large part of the population, have lost their capacity to confer different deference positions on their practitioners. This does not mean that the entire gainfully employed population has become occupationally homogeneous, but for that section which has become homogeneous occupation will count for no more than race in an ethnically almost homogeneous society.

Deference Behavior

The phenomena of the stratification system are generally thought of as so massive in their impact on the rest of society that it is only natural that it too should be conceived of as having a substantial existence. Indeed, they are spoken of as if they possessed a continuous, almost physical tangibility which enables them to be apprehended by relatively gross methods of observation. In fact, many of these properties are very discontinuous or intermittent in their performance. When they are not actual, they fall into a condition of "latency." The different entitlements vary in the continuity and substantiality of their performance or manifestation. And what is true of entitlements to deference applies even more to deference behavior itself.

First of all, however, before considering deference behavior as such, I should like to consider the substantiality and continuity of the entitlements.

Occupational roles are, for example, performed for one-half or two-thirds of the waking life of the human being so employeed for most of the days of each week for most of the weeks of the year over a period of forty to fifty or more years, through youth, adulthood, and old age. A wealthy person usually has his wealth in the form of real property, chattels, or convertible paper, available to him whenever he wishes to call upon it and as long as he owns it. The receipt and expenditure of income is a less continuous property, not only because the amount of income received fluctuates or varies over the course of a decade or a lifetime but also because once expended it ceases to be available, and because when not being used it is not visible. Only the results of expended income are visible in the material or tangible components of a style of life. Income is recurrent, and it can be regularly recurrent as a disposable sum but not continuously, and it is not always substantially manifested.

The style of life of a person or a family is a pattern heterogeneous in its composition and pervasive in apparel, speech, domestic arrangements, physical, social, and cultural. Its material apparatus is grossly observable. Like occupational role, among the deference entitlements, it is performed, enacted, or lived in a larger proportion of waking time (and even sleeping time) than the other deference entitlements. Style of life is, with occupational role, the most substantial and continuous of the various deference entitlements. It is, with occupation, the most visible.

Level and type of educational attainment are a different kind of thing. They are like kinship by their conferring of membership in a category which entails no present action. (Indeed, kinship entails no action on the part of the actor in question. It is a past biological connection, a present genetic composition, and classification by self and other.) Level of educational attainment, insofar as it is a past qualification for present incumbency in a role, has ceased to exist except as a marker of a past accomplishment, like a medal awarded for heroism in a long past battle. Where it is interpreted as an approximate indication of present level of culture, it refers to very discontinuously performed actions. Insofar as it refers to the number of years in which studies were carried on, to the subjects studied and certifications which attest to amounts, etc., it refers to past events which provide a basis for present classification by self and other. Thus, while to an external analyst the level of educational attainment is a stable property of a person, it is not continuously operative in that person's action or interaction with others. It is a fluctuating and intermittent quality, sometimes of high salience, sometimes latent. It need not be so in all societies, in all strata, or in all individuals. In societies or strata which are highly "education-conscious," it will be more continuously salient as a categorial property than in those which are less "education-conscious." Persons of a given level of educational attainment will manifest it more substantially in their speech, thought, and conduct.

Power, which is so closely and often associated with the performance of occupational role, resembles it in this respect too, since it is often exercised or performed for significantly continuous periods, with sufficiently regular recurrence. (It is also like occupational role in the sense that it places its practitioner in a category which calls forth responses from self and other situations outside the occupational or power-exercising role.)

The foregoing observations were intended to render a little more explicit than is usually done the temporal discontinuity of entitlements, their intermittence and periodicity of performance and visibility. I have done this because these characteristics of entitlement affect their probability of being perceived and therewith of calling forth deference. I have also done it because I wish to call attention to what appear to me to be important, even if not readily evident, features of deference behavior.

The term *status,* when it is used to refer to deference position, ordinarily carries with it, as I suggested earlier, overtones of the stability, continuity, and pervasiveness which are possessed by sex and age. A person who has a given status tends to be thought of as having that status at every moment of his existence as long as that particular status is not replaced by another status. One of the reasons why I have chosen to use the term "deference position" in place of "status" is that it makes a little more prominent the fact that status is not a substantial property of the person arising automatically from the possession of certain entitlements but is in fact an element in a relationship between the person deferred to and the deferent person. Deference toward another person is an attitude which is manifested in behavior.

Acts of deference judgments are evaluative classifications of self and other. As classifications they transcend in their reference the things classified. A person who is evaluatively classified by an act of deference on the basis of his occupation is in that classification even when he is not performing his occupational role. The classificatory deference judgment, because it is a generalization, attains some measure of independence from the intermittence of entitlements. It has an intermittence of its own which is not necessarily synchronized with that of the entitlements.

Overt, concentrated acts of deference such as greetings and presentations are usually short-lived, i.e., they are performed for relatively short periods and then "disappear" until the next appropriate occasion. The appropriate occasions for the performance of concentrated acts of deference might be regular in their recurrence, e.g., annually or weekly or even daily, but except for a few "deference occupations" they are not performed with the high frequency and density over extended periods in the way in which occupational roles are performed. But does deference consist exclusively of the performance of concentrated deferential actions? Is there a "deference vacuum" when concentrated deferential actions are not being performed? Where does deference go when it is not being expressed in a grossly tangible action?

To answer this question, it is desirable to examine somewhat more closely the character of attenuated deferential actions. There are concentrated, exclusively deferential actions which are nothing but deferential actions just as there are exclusively power or style of life or occupational actions but in a way different from these others. Occupational actions are substantial; all effort within a given space and time is devoted to their performance. They can be seen clearly by actor and observer as occupational actions; the exercise of authority has many of these features, especially when it is exercised in an authoritative occupational role. Expenditures of money are of shorter duration but they too are clearly definable. The acts of consumption and conviviality which are comprised in a style of life are of longer duration, but they too are also clearly defined. On the other hand, level of educational attainment and kinship connection and ethnicity are not actual actions at all, they are classifications in which "objectively" the classified person is continuously present, although, once present in the class, he does nothing to manifest or affirm them.

But deferential actions—deferring to self and other, receiving deference from self and other—are actions. They result in and are performed with reference to classifications, but they are actions nonetheless. They are not, however, always massive actions of much duration. They occur mainly at the margin of other types of action. Deferential actions performed alone are usually very short-lived; they open a sequence of interaction and they close it. Between beginning and end, deferential actions are performed in fusion with nondeferential actions. Throughout the process of interaction they are attenuated in the substance of the relationship in which the performance of tasks appropriate to roles in corporate bodies, to civil roles, to personal relationships, etc., occurs. Deferential actions have always been largely components of other actions; they are parts of the pattern of speaking to a colleague, a superior or an inferior, about the business at hand in an authoritatively hierarchical corporate body, of speaking about or to a fellow citizen, of acting toward him over a distance (as in an election). In other words, deferential actions seldom appear solely as deferential actions and those which do are not regarded, especially in the United States, as a particularly important part of interaction in most situations. Nonetheless, deference is demanded and it is accepted in an attenuated form.

This then is the answer to the question as to where deference goes when it ceases to be concentrated: it survives in attenuation, in a pervasive, intangible form which enters into all sorts of relationships through tone of speech, demeanor, precedence in speaking, frequency and mode of contradiction, etc.

Deference can, however, become extinct. A person who fails to retain his entitlements in the course of time also loses the deference which his entitlements brought him. He might not lose it entirely; ex-prime ministers, professors emeriti, retired generals, long after they depart from their occupational roles continue to receive some deference, although it is probably, other things being equal, less than they received while active incumbents. Kings in exile, great families fallen on hard times, also lose much of their deference, and some, sinking away into peripheral obscurity, cease to be known and their deference becomes entirely local.

The salience of deference behavior is closely related to deference sensitivity. Indifference to deference is a marginal phenomenon, but individuals, classes, and societies differ in the degree to which they demand deference—whether concentrated or attenuated—or are relatively unperceptive regarding its appropriateness, its presence or its absence. A snob is a person whose demand for deference is great and for whom the deference position of those he associates with is their most relevant characteristic.

Deference and Equality

Modern Western societies and even societies outside the West seem to be moving in the direction of deference indifference and attenuation. The movement is very uneven among modern societies with the United States, Canada, and Australia in the lead, with other countries some distance behind but they too seem to be moving further along than they were a half century ago. The movement is also very uneven within societies, with marked differences between classes and generations.

The equalitarian tendencies of contemporary Western societies have not only witnessed the attenuation and retraction of deference, they have also seen it assimilated into the pattern of intercourse among equals. But can it be said that deference still exists in relations among equals? Is not equality a point where deference disappears? Concentrated and salient deference behavior was a feature of the relations between the great of the earth and their subordinates. There is, to be sure, no elaborate ritual of deference between equals in contemporary Western societies and particularly in American society, except that which still obtains between heads of states, between heads of churches, heads of universities on especially ceremonial occasions, etc.

Concentrated deference actions have by no means disappeared, but they have become less elaborate, and with their diminished elaboration they have been abbreviated. They have become less substantial and less separate from other actions. Ceremonial deference and formalized etiquette have diminished in magnitude and frequency.

The decline in the power of aristocracies and the diminution of the number of monarchies have been accompanied by a reduction in the amount or proportion of ceremonial deference in societies. Modes of spoken and written address have come to bespeak a more homogeneous distribution of deference throughout societies, and in doing so they have moved towards simpler, briefer forms. The movement is not, however, all one way; the strata which previously were treated with the minimum of deference or indeed with negative deference have now begun to receive an enhanced deference although in the simplified and shorter forms of a less ritualized society.

The inherited rituals of deference tended largely to be concerned with the relations of superiors and inferiors. As an equalitarian outlook became more prominent, the rituals of deference fell into the same discredit as relationships which they expressed. It is however an open question whether equality or approximate equality is antithetical to rituals of deference. What seems fairly certain is that the relationships of equals can and do at present contain considerable elements of attenuated deference and can indeed not dispense with them.

Nonetheless, it would be wrong to fail to acknowledge that contemporary societies are less oriented toward their centers with respect to deference than their ancestors of a century ago. It is not merely on account of the decline of aristocracy and monarchy. These are only instances of a more general phenomenon, namely the diminution of the ruling classes in the various countries. When elites were smaller, educational opportunity more restricted, and the kinship tie more respected than they are nowadays, the various sectors of the center—the political, administrative, ecclesiastical, cultural and military elites—and to some extent the economic elite—were closer to each other through common origins, common institutional experiences, a shared conviviality and the linkage of kinship than they are now when the obligations of kinship are less observed in recruitment to the elite, when specialization has gone further, and numbers have greatly increased. One of the consequences of this pluralization of the elites is that their models are less imposing. Each sector is taken for what it is, and, except for the very pinnacle of the head of state and the head of the government, the sense of difference in worth is felt to be less great than it once was.

The Distribution of Deference

It has long been characteristic of the study of deference and of the deference positions—status—which it helps to produce to ascribe to them a distribution similar in important respects to the distribution of entitlements such as occupational roles and power, income, wealth, styles of life, levels of educational attainment, etc. The entitlements are all relatively "substantial" things which are not matters of opinion but rather "objective," more or less quantifiable, conditions or attributes and as such capable of being ranged in a univalent and continuous distribution. Every individual has one occupation or another at any given period in time or for a specifiable duration; every individual has—if it could be measured—such and such an average amount of power over a specifiable time period. Every individual has some style of life, certain components of which at least are enduring and observable—and he either possesses them or does not possess them. There are of course cases of persons having two widely different kinds of occupational roles within the same limited time period ("moonlighting"), of persons having widely divergent incomes within a given period, but these and other anomalies can quite easily be resolved by specifiable procedures for the collection of data and for their statistical treatment and presentation.

Present-day sociological notions of deference—status, esteem, prestige, honor, etc—grew up in association with the "objective" conception of social stratification. The "objective" conception concerned itself with the relatively substantial entitlements, the "subjective" with the "opinion"-like elements. For reasons of convenience in research and also because common usage practiced a system of classification into "middle," "upper," "lower," etc., classes, research workers and theorists attempted to construct a composite index which would amalgamate the positions of each individual in a number of distributions (in particular, the distributions of occupational role and education) into some variant of the three class distribution. The resultant was called "social-economic status" or "socio-economic status." (The prevalence of the trichotomous classification and variations on it is probably of Aristotelian origin. There is no obvious reason why reflection on experience and observation alone should have resulted in three classes. This might well be a case where nature has copied art.)

It is quite possible that this pattern of thought, which emerged in the nineteenth century, was deeply influenced by the conception of social class of the nineteenth-century critics of the ancien régime and of the bourgeois social order which succeeded it. In the ancien régime the most powerful ranks were designated by legally guaranteed titles which entered into the consciousness of their bearers and those who associated with or considered them. These designations were not "material" or "objective." They did not belong to the "substructure" of society. They were therefore "subjective" but they were also unambiguous. They could be treated in the same way as "objective" characteristics. By extension, the same procedure could be applied to the other strata.

The "subjective" conception of social stratification appreciated the "opinion"-like character of deference, but for reasons of convenience in research procedure and because of the traditional mode of discourse concerning social stratification the "subjective factor" itself tended to be "substantialized," and it too was regarded as capable of being ranged in an univalent distribution. Sometimes as in the Edwards classification in the United States or in the Registrar-General's classification in the United Kingdom, this "subjective factor", impressionistically assessed by the research worker, was amalgamated with the "objective factors" in arriving at a single indicator of "status." Status was taken to mean a total status, which included both deference position and entitlements, constructed by an external observer, not a participant in the system. But this conception has not found acceptance because it is patently unsatisfactory. Deference position—or esteem, prestige, or status—does belong to a different order of events in comparison with events like occupational distribution, income and wealth distribution, etc. It belongs to the realm of values; it is the outcome of evaluative judgments regarding positions in the distributions of "objective" characteristics.

The improvement of techniques of fieldwork in community studies and sample surveys has rendered it possible to collect data, relatively systematically, about these evaluations and to assign to each person in a small community or to each occupation on a list a single position in a distribution. Research technique has served to obscure a fundamental conceptual error. As a result, since each person possessed a status (or deference position), they could be ranged in a single distribution. Such a distribution could occur, however, only under certain conditions. The conditions include (a) an evaluative consensus throughout the society regarding the criteria in accordance with which deference is allocated; (b) cognitive consensus throughout the society regarding the characteristics of each position in each distribution and regarding the shape of the distributions of entitlements; (c) consensus throughout the society regarding the weights to be assigned to the various categories of deference-entitling properties;[1] (d) equal attention to and equal differentiation by each member of the society of strata which are adjacent to his own and those which are remote from it;[2] (e) equal salience of deference judgments throughout the society; (f) univalence of all deference judgments.

Were these conditions to obtain, then the distribution of deference positions in such a society might well have the form which the distributions of "objective" entitlements possess. There are, however, numerous reasons why the distribution of deference positions or status does not have this form. Some of these reasons are as follows: (a) Some consensus concerning the criteria for the assessment of entitlements might well exist

1. Where these three conditions exist, there would also exist a consensus between the judgment which a person makes of his own deference-position and the judgments which others render about his position.
2. This also presupposes equal knowledge by all members of the society about all other members.

but like any consensus it is bound to be incomplete. Furthermore, criteria are so ambiguously apprehended that any existent consensus actually covers a wide variety of beliefs about the content of the criteria. (*b*) Cognitive consensus throughout the society regarding the properties of entitlements and the shape of their distributions is rather unlikely because of the widespread and unequal ignorance about such matters as the occupational roles, incomes, educational attainments of individuals and strata. (*c*) The weighting of the various criteria is not only ambiguous, it is likely to vary from stratum to stratum depending on the deference position of the various strata and their positions on the various distributions; it is likely that each stratum will give a heavier weight to that distribution on which it stands more highly or on which it has a greater chance of improving its position or protecting it from "invaders." (*d*) The perceptions of one's own stratum or of adjacent strata are usually much more differentiated and refined and involve more subsidiary criteria than is the case in their perceptions of remote strata. Thus even if they are compatible with each other, there is no identity of the differentiations made by the various strata. (*e*) Some persons are more sensitive to deference than are others and this difference in the salience of deference occurs among strata as well. Some persons think frequently in terms of deference position, others think less frequently in those terms. Accordingly, assessments of other human beings and the self may differ markedly within a given society, among individuals, strata, regions, and generations with respect to their tendency to respond deferentially rather than affectionately or matter-of-factly or instrumentally. The arrangement of the members of a society into a stratified distribution as if each of them had a determinate quantity of a homogeneous thing called deference (or status or prestige) does violence to the nature of deference and deference positions; it further obscures an already sufficiently opaque reality. The possibility of dissensus in each of the component judgments—cognitive and evaluative —which go to make up a deference judgment can, of course, be covered by the construction of measures which hide the dispersion of opinions. If all interindividual disagreements are confined to differences in ranking within a given stratum, the procedure would perhaps be acceptable. But if 80 percent of a population place certain persons in stratum I and if 20 percent place them in stratum II, is it meaningful to say that the persons so judged are in stratum I?

The dissensus which results in interindividually discordant rankings seriously challenges the validity of procedures which construct univalent deference distributions and then disjoin them into strata. This difficulty would exist even if there were agreement about the location of the boundary lines which allegedly separate one deference stratum from the other. But there is no certainty that there will be consensus on this matter, and the purpose of realistic understanding is not served by assuming that there is such consensus or by constructing measures which impose the appearance of such a consensus regarding the data.

The conventional procedure of constructing deference distributions has tended to assume a considerable degree of clarity and differentiatedness in the perception of the distribution of deference-entitling properties through the society. But as a matter of fact perceptions are vague and undifferentiated. Terminologies and classifications, particularly in relatively "class-unconscious" societies, are not standardized and terms like "poor," "working people," "lower classes," "ordinary people," etc., are used in senses which the user has not reflected upon and which do not have a definite referent. There is no reason—at least until further research has been done—to think that they are interchangeable with each other although sociologists do treat them as if they are.

If differentiation and specificity are slight in speaking about strata adjacent to one's own, they are even less developed in reference to remoter strata of which the judging person has no direct experience. This does not mean that deference judgments are not made about these remoter strata; it does mean that such judgments are made with scant knowledge of the extent to which these deference entitlements actually exist in the persons or strata so judged. The cognitive stratification map becomes vaguer with regard to those areas of the society far from the range of experience of the judging person. This too renders cognitive consensus impossible even if evaluative criteria were identical. What one judge looking at his own immediate stratification environment sees as highly differentiated, another who views it from a distance sees as homogeneous. Thus every sector of the stratification system is highly differentiated but only to those who are living in the midst of that sector. The question arises therefore whether a distribution of deference positions incorporates the perceptions and categorizations which are applied to one's own and adjacent strata or those which are applied to remote ones. Whichever alternative is followed, the factitious character of the distribution so constructed is evident.

Up to this point I have cast doubt on the conventional treatments of the distribution of deference positions by referring to the diverse sorts of dissensus among individuals, strata, regional cultures, etc. But I wrote as if each of these agents of judgment spoke with a single voice. There is some justification for this since there is a tendency in many societies to regard the deference system as something objective, as *sui generis*, as existing outside the judging persons and independently of their own evaluations and appreciations of persons and strata. This tendency to "objectivize" the distribution of deference is in part a product of the perception of the deference judgments of other persons in one's own society. But it also represents a tendency to believe in the "objectivity," the "givenness" of deference stratification which is a product of a tendency to believe that in addition to our own tastes and dispositions there is a realm of normative being which exists independently of those tastes and values.

But alongside of this tendency to believe in an "objective" order of worthiness, there is a widespread alienation from that order and the acceptance and alienation exist very often in the same persons. This ambivalence is very difficult to apprehend by present-day techniques of research, and it is even more difficult to deal with it systematically—at least for the present. It exists nonetheless, and it is apt to become stronger as society becomes more differentiated and as the "ruling class" in the sense of a set of persons intimately interrelated through kinship, common institutional experiences, and long personal frienships, filling most of the positions at the top of the various distributions, gives way before a less unitary and therefore less imposing elite.

There is nothing pathological about this ambivalence. Submission to the ascendancy of the center and to the standards which affirm it is painful because the indignity of inferiority is painful. The society which focuses on the center imposes such indignity on the periphery. The more highly integrated a society ecologically, the greater will be the strain on the periphery, and the less imposing the elite at the center, the more likely the emergence of the negative side of the ambivalence. The implications of this ambivalent attitude are far-reaching and they cannot be gone into here. Let it suffice to say the presently prevailing methods of describing deference distributions cannot accommodate these simple facts. Yet without these simple facts of ambivalence and alienation in the stratification system, how can class conflict and movements for reform by the reallocation of deference and its entitlements be dealt with? And what is one to make of the antiauthoritarianism and antinomianism which has been a fluctuatingly frequent phenomenon of modern societies? How does this fit into a picture which portrays deference positions as univalently and consensually distributed?

Finally, I should like to conclude these reflections on the problems of deference distribution with some observations on equality. In general, the prevailing techniques for representing deference distributions proceed with a fixed number of strata or by means of scales which rank occupations or persons on a continuum running from 0 to 100. Both procedures assume a constant distance between the extremes and between the intervals or strata. This does not, however, seem to accord with the realities of the movement of modern societies toward a higher degree of equality of deference than was to be found earlier.

The range of deference distribution probably varies among societies. Some are more equalitarian than others. In what does this equalitarianism consist apart from increased opportunities or life-chances for peripheral strata? Does it not consist in an appreciation of the greater worthiness of the peripheral strata—a judgment shared to some extent throughout their society? It is indeed a matter of opinion, but it is an opinion of profound significance for the stratification system. I cannot go into the causes of this development; I wish here only to call attention to its relevance to any realistic description of deference systems.

Deference Institutions and Deference Systems

Whereas most of the things valued by men become the explicit foci of elaborate institutional systems concerned with their production, acquisition, protection, maintenance, control, and allocation, the same cannot be asserted of deference. Unlike economic or military or political or ecclesiastical institutions, deference institutions are marginal to the valued objects which they seek to affect. There is a College of Heralds, there are chiefs of protocol in departments of foreign affairs, there are *Who's Who's* and *Social Registers,* authors and publishers of books on deportment and on modes of address, there are advisers to prime ministers and presidents on the award of honors, there is an *Almanach de Gotha*, a great many states have a system of honors and many have had a system of titles and orders. Armies award medals and universities award earned and honorary degrees. Armies have titles of rank as do universities. Civil services too have ranks and designations which denote differences and ranks of authority but which are also titles of deference. Some of those institutions have handbooks which specify orders of precedence. All of these institutional arrangements confer or confirm deference; they seek to express deference, to create and legitimate claims to deference, to specify who should receive it, and to entitle particular persons in a way which objectifies their claims to deference. Only a few of these institutions have sought explicitly to determine a "generalized" deference position, namely those which sought to control and guarantee membership in nobilities or aristocracies. Others awarded deference for rather specific qualifications and although in many of these cases the deference was generalized, in others it remained an indicator of a quite specific achievement and thereby attained scarcely any measure of generalization. But at best, they have touched only a small part of the societies in which they have functioned and although they intensify and strengthen the deference system they cannot be said to create it or to manage it.

The deference system of a society extends throughout the length and breadth of that society. Everybody falls within it, yet very few of those have their deference positions determined by the deference-conferring and deference-confirming institutions. The actually functioning deference system of a society envelops the deference institutions and takes them into account but it is not predominantly determined by them.

Most of the deferential behavior—the behavior which expresses deference—occurs in the face-to-face interaction of individuals and very few of those who receive some allocation of deference have any titles or medals. The deference which they receive is received from other persons who respond not to titles or honors of which they have heard or emblems which they see on the garments of the persons deferred to, but to the entitling properties which they believe are possessed by the person to whom deference is given. Titles and medals might be taken into account, and, even when the title is used in full and correctly, the use of the title in addressing the person deferred to is at most only a part of the deference expressed. The title is thought to stand for something more than itself: for kinship connections, acknowledgment by the sovereign, or occupational role, and these too are not ultimate; they are evocative of other characteristics, of positions on various distributions.

The deference granted is, as I have said earlier, expressed in overtones of speech and action. Much of it is expressed in relations of authority, and it appears together with commands and acts of obedience, with the giving of counsel and the taking of counsel, in the interplay of authorities and subjects, colleagues, and neighbors performing the actions called for by authority, collegiality, and neighborliness. It is far more subtle and richer than the prescriptions for the ritual manifestations of deference, and it is also often more impoverished. Being a duke or a professor or a colonel constitutes only one element—a quite considerable element—in the generalized deference which the incumbents of those ranks and the bearers of those titles receive. Those who associate with them and who defer to them respond to other things about them as well as to their ranks and titles. The excellence of their performance past and current, the power which they actually exercise or have exercised, the level of culture and their style of life, insofar as these can be perceived or imagined or are already known from previous experiences and from other sources, enter into the determination of the deference granted and expected.

Deference institutions are more important in some types of societies and in some strata than in others. In societies in which there is a sharp disjunction between center and periphery, they will have more influence than in societies in which the periphery has expanded inwardly and approximated the center.

Deference institutions are especially important at or near the center of society although ordinarily it is not the intention of those who manage them to confine their influence to that zone. But because deference is more intense in face-to-face relationships and direct interaction than it is in remote relationships, there is a tendency for deference systems to become dispersed in a particular way. Deference systems tend to become territorially dispersed into local systems which are more differentiated to those who participate in them than is the national system. I do not mean to say that the several systems ranging from local to national are in conflict with each other. Indeed, they can be quite consensual, and the local usually could not be constituted without reference to persons, roles, and symbols of the center. In the various zones and sectors of the periphery where the center is more remote, the imagery of the center still enters markedly into the deference system, and local differentiations are often simply refined applications of perceptions and evaluations which have the center as their point of reference. Thus, for example, local deference judgments will make more subtle internal distinctions about occupational role and authority, income, and style of life than would judgments made from a distant point either peripheral or central. Still, the distinctions will refer to distances from some standard which enjoys its highest fulfillment at the center. It seems unlikely that blindness to the center can ever be complete in any society.

Nevertheless, the various systems do to some extent have lives of their own. The local deference system is probably more continuously or more frequently in operation than the national system—although as national societies become more integrated and increasingly incorporate their local and regional societies, the national deference system becomes more frequently and more intensely active.

In all societies, the deference system is at its most intense and most continuous at the center. The high concentrations of power and wealth, the elaborateness of the style of life, all testify to this and call it forth. It is at the center that deference institutions function, and this gives an added focus and stimulus to deferential behavior. The center adds the vividness of a local deference system to the massive deference-evoking powers of centrality. Within each local or regional deference system, there are some persons who are more sensitive than others to the center, and they infuse into the local system some awareness of and sensitivity to the center.

There are occasions on which individuals whose preoccupations are mainly with the local deference systems—insofar as they are at all concerned with deference—place themselves on the macrosocial deference map. This self-location and the perception that others are also locating themselves is the precondition of a sense of affinity among those who place themselves macrosocially on approximately the same position in the distribution of deference. The placement of others is made of course on the basis of fragmentary evidence about occupational role, style of life, or elements of these, and the sense of affinity is loose, the self-location very vague, very inarticulated, and very approximate. In this way deference (or status) strata are constituted. They have no clear boundaries, and membership cannot be certified or specified. It is largely a matter of sensing one's membership and being regarded by others as a member. Those one "knows" are usually members, and beyond them the domain spreads out indefinitely and anonymously in accordance with vague cognitive stratification maps and an inchoate image of the "average man"; within each stratum an "average man" possesses the proper combination of positions on the distribution of significant deference entitlements.

Thus the formation of deference strata is a process of the mutual assimilation of local deference systems into a national deference system. It is through class consciousness that deference strata are formed.

In the course of its self-constitution a deference stratum also defines in a much vaguer way the other deference strata of its society. It draws boundary lines, but, except for those it draws about itself, the boundaries are matters of minor significance. Boundary lines are of importance only or mainly to those who are affected by the location of the boundary, i.e., those who live close to it on one side or the other. The location of a line of division in the distribution of deference is regarded as important primarily by those who fear that they themselves are in danger of expulsion or who are refused admission to the company of members of a stratum to whom they regard themselves as equal or to whom they wish to be equal and whose company they regard as more desirable than the one to which they would otherwise be confined. The members of any deference stratum are likely to be ignorant about the location of deference stratum boundaries which are remote from them, and if they are not ignorant, they are indifferent.

The various deference strata of local deference systems are in contact with each other through occasional face-to-face contacts. They are present in each others' imaginations and this deferential presence enters into all sorts of nondeferential actions of exchange, conflict, and authority.

In national deference systems too the different strata are in contact with each other, not very much through face-to-face contact but through their presence in each other's imagination. This presence carries with it the awareness of one's distance from the center, and it entails some acceptance of the centrality of the center and some acceptance of the greater dignity of the center. It is an implicit belief that the center embodies and enacts standards which are important in the assessment of oneself and one's own stratum.

In some sense, the center "is" the standard which is derived from the perception, correct or incorrect, of its conduct and bearing. These remote persons and strata which form the center might be deferred to, or condemned in speech, and the pattern of their conduct, bearing, outlook, etc., might be emulated or avoided. An "objective existence" is attributed to the rank ordering from centrality to peripherality of the other strata and within this rank ordering one's own stratum is located. The ontological, nonempirical reality which is attributed to position in the distribution of deference makes it different from "mere" evaluation and sometimes even antithetical to it.

On a much more earthly level, contacts between deference strata occur and in many forms—particularly through the division of labor and its coordination through the market and within corporate bodies and in the struggle for political power. This does not mean that the strata encounter each other in corporately organized forms or that, when there is contact between strata in the encounter of corporate bodies, the latter include all or most members of their respective strata. Much of this interstratum contact takes place through intermediaries who act as agents and who receive a deference which is a response both to their own deference-entitling properties and those of their principals. Those who act on behalf of these corporate bodies do so in a state of belief that they are "representing" the deference stratum to which they belong or feel akin.

Corporate organizations, membership in which is determined by a sense of affinity of deference positions and of positions in other distributions, seldom enlist the active membership of all the members of the stratum or even of all the adult male members of the stratum. Those who are not members of the corporate body are not, however, to be regarded as completely devoid of the sense of affinity with other members of their stratum. "Class consciousness" in this sense is very widespread but it is a long step from this type of "class consciousness" to the aggressively alienated class consciousness which Marxist doctrine predicted would spread throughout the class of manual workers in industry and which Marxist agitation has sought to cultivate.

A society can then have a deference system of relatively self-distinguishing and self-constituting deference strata, with the strata being in various kinds of relationship with each other. Such a situation is entirely compatible with the absence of the type of objective deference distribution which we rejected in the foregoing section. Each of the deference strata possesses in a vague form an image of a societywide deference distribution but these images cannot be correct in the sense of corresponding to an objective deference distribution, which might or might not actually exist.

Digression on Plural Societies

I have emphasized the importance of the self-constitutive character of the classes which make up a system of deference stratification. I have also emphasized the unreality of the construction of status distributions on which sociologists have expended so much effort, and at the same time I have also stressed the elements of integration of the deference strata into a single system focused on the center of society. Some writers contend that the deference system and the associated stratification systems of what are called plural societies are incompatible with this mode of analysis. By a plural society, they mean one in which various ethnic groups are so segregated from each other that they form societies separate and distinct from each other. Yet they do not go so far as to say that the various constituent societies are totally independent of each other; they acknowledge that they are integrated into a single economy and that they live under a single political authority. In that sense the constituent societies of a plural society are parts of a single society.

The problem which this poses for the study of deference systems is well worth consideration. What we find is that the ethnic entitlement is regarded in these societies, particularly by the more powerful section of the dominant ethnic group, as such a crucial criterion of deference that all other deference entitlements are of secondary importance. These other deference entitlements exist, and they do determine differences in the allocation of deference, but they are only capable of generating differences within each of the major ethnically determined deference strata. Each ethnically determined deference stratum is internally differentiated in accordance with the distribution of deference entitlements within it. Each approximates a completely self-contained deference system, but it does not become completely self-contained. It fails to do so because, despite its highly segregated pluralism, the society does have a center, and this center constitutes a focus of each of the partially separate deference systems. The latter bear some resemblance to the deference systems of whole societies because of the differentiation of occupational roles within each of the ethnic sectors, but the occupational structure of each sector is not the complete occupational structure of the total society. That total occupational structure is distributed between the ethnic sectors, and there is indeed some overlap between them. It is because of these points of overlap—between the bottom of the superordinate deference stratum and the peak of the subordinate deference stratum— that conflicts arise. These conflicts could only arise because the sectors or strata are parts of a peculiarly integrated single deference system.

Deference Systems and Stratification Systems

When it is not treated as an unreal, conceptually constructed amalgam of a number of positions on a variety of distributions, deference has often been treated as an epiphenomenon. It is often considered as having relatively little weight in the determination of conduct—apart from the choice of companions in conviviality or in the motivation of emulatory conduct. Yet it is deference which is responsible for the formation of strata or classes.

Deference, because it is the result of a generalization, is the crucial link in the stratification system. Without the intervention of considerations of deference position, the various very differentiated inequalities in the distribution of any particular facility or reward would not be grouped into a relatively small number of vaguely bounded strata. The very idea of an equivalence among positions in different distributions could not be realized if there were no generalization to cut across them.

By a stratification system, I mean a plurality of strata within a single society with some sense of their common identity, of their internal similarity and of their external differences vis-à-vis other strata. The stratification system is constituted by strata which are formed by persons who have approximately similar positions on a variety of separate distributions. This approximate similarity of positions is a precondition of the sense of affinity—because it strengthens the sense of identity of the self from which the sense of affinity of many selves is formed. If each person were randomly heterogeneous in his cluster of positions, the likelihood of a sense of identity and therewith of affinity would be much less than it is in fact.

The sense of identity is a vague perception of self and other, and it refers to some pervasive qualities of those so identified. These qualities by which strata identify themselves and others are frequently referred to by a shorthand terminology such as "wealth" or "poverty" or "rulers" or "people" or "workers" or "bosses." These terms refer to positions on particular distributions such as wealth and income, power and occupational role. Yet these terms have for those who use them a significance beyond the limited descriptive sense in which they are used. Each term stands for a position of each of a number of distributions and implies that positions in the various distributions are correlated and connected with each other. Those who are "workers" are also "poor" or in any case relatively low in wealth and income distributions. Those who are "bosses" are also "rich" or at least higher in the wealth and income distributions and they usually have more political power. Those who are "well off" have more education and more authority through their occupational roles and through political participation.

The connections between the positions of an individual on the different distributions are of two sorts. One is the connection through "life chances." Life chances are opportunities to enter into a higher position on any distribution from a lower position on that distribution or on several distributions. Life chances are determined by the power of income, by personal, civil and kinship relationships and by occupational role and level of education. Any one of these can have a determinative influence on the allocation of life chances, i.e., on the opportunity to ascend on that distribution or in others.

A life chance which arises from position on a particular distribution also affects chances for maintaining or acquiring life chances for positions on other distributions. Income permits education to be purchased; the acquisition of education increases the probability of higher deference and higher income; higher education increases the probability of greater political influence; increased political influences increase the likelihood. of a greater access to financial resources.

There is a widely experienced aspiration to bring positions on a series of distributions into an appropriate correspondence with each other. Each position provides resources for affecting positions on other distributions. Why should this be so? Why should there be thought to be an "appropriate" relationship among positions, an equilibrium which should be striven for? Why, when a person has much political power does he not use his political resources exclusively to enhance or maintain his political power instead of expending them on bringing his style of life or the education of his children "into line" with his political position? (Of course, one reply to this question is to say that it is generally believed that improving positions on the nonpolitical distributions is a necessary condition for maintenance or improvement of the position on the political distribution. But is not this very belief itself evidence of the belief in an appropriate pattern of positions which is thus a precondition for the more "costly" political support necessary for further improvement in political position? Another reply to the question is that most human beings, given the opportunity, will strive to enhance their position in any particular distribution and that being in a better position on one distribution provides resources for betterment on others. But although there is some truth in this assertion it does not confront the fact that there is a sense of an appropriate pattern of positions on different distributions.)

The belief that it is appropriate that the several positions on the various distributions should be consonant or harmonious with each other is attributable to the belief that they each express a common, essential quality. An "inappropriate" pattern of positions bears witness to the absence of the essential quality. There is something "unseemly" or "eccentric" or "perverse" or "unfortunate" about the individual or family whose positions are scattered at a variety of "unequal" points on the several distributions.

This common or essential quality is the charismatic quality which requires diffuse and pervasive expression in the various distributions. The cognitive element in an act of deference is the perception of the presence of this quality, and its generalization beyond any specific manifestation in action is an acknowledgment of the apparent possession of charismatic quality by the person deferred to. The demand for deference is the demand for a diffuse acknowledgment of the diffuse charisma which is possessed in some measure by the self and which is above all in its earthly form resident in the centers of society. Self-respect —deference to the self—is an acknowledgment of one's own charisma and of one's satisfactory proximity to the center in an essential respect.

The cognitive and evaluative map of a stratification system is a differential allocation of deference to a series of aggregates of persons— for the most part anonymous—in accordance with their proximity to the center and thus in accordance with the magnitude of their presumed charisma. The stratification system of a society is the product of imagination working on the hard facts of the unequal allocation of scarce resources and rewards. The charisma is putative but it has the effect of being "real" since it is so widely believed in as "real." Deference, which is basically a response to charisma, is only a matter of opinion, but it is an opinion with profound motivation and a response to profound needs in the grantor and in the recipient of deference.

III. The Mind at Work in Society

8

THE INTELLECTUALS
AND THE POWERS
SOME PERSPECTIVES FOR
COMPARATIVE ANALYSIS

In religion, in art, in all spheres of culture and politics, the mass of mankind in all hitherto known societies have not, except for transitory interludes, been preoccupied with the attainment of an immediate contact with the ultimate principles implicit in their beliefs and standards. The directly gratifying ends of particular actions, the exigencies of situations, considerations of individual and familial advantage, concrete moral maxims, concrete prescriptions and prohibitions, preponderate in the conduct of the majority of persons in most societies, large and small. The systematic coherence and the deeper and more general ground of beliefs and standards only intermittently hold their attention and touch on their passions. Ordinary life in every society is characterized by an unequal intensity of attachment to ultimate values, be they cognitive, moral, or aesthetic, and an unequal intensity of the need for coherence. Ordinary life shuns rigorous definition and consistent adherence to traditional or rational rules, and it has no need for continuous contact with the sacred. Ordinary life is slovenly, full of compromise and improvisation; it goes on in the "here and now."

In every society, however, there are some persons with an unusual sensitivity to the sacred, an uncommon reflectiveness about the nature of their universe and the rules which govern their society. There is in every society a minority of persons who, more than the ordinary run of their fellow men, are inquiring, and desirous of being in frequent communion with symbols which are more general than

Previously published in a slightly different form in *Comparative Studies in Society and History*, vol. 1, no. 1 (October 1958), pp. 5-22.

the immediate concrete situations of everyday life and remote in their reference in both time and space. In this minority, there is a need to externalize this quest in oral and written discourse, in poetic or plastic expression, in historical reminiscence or writing, in ritual performance and acts of worship. This interior need to penetrate beyond the screen of immediate concrete experience marks the existence of the intellectuals in every society.

The Tasks of Intellectuals

The personal need alone does not, however, create the body of intellectuals, nor does it determine its magnitude or its position within the structure of society. In every society, even among those sections of the population without the very pronounced sensitivity to remote symbols which characterizes the intellectuals, there is an intermittent need for contact with the sacred, and this gives rise to a demand for priests and theologians and to institutions or procedures for the education of these in the techniques and meanings of their functions. In every society, among those who cannot create images in the form of stories or pictures or statues or other works or art, there is still a considerable fraction which is receptive and indeed even demanding of the gratification provided by verbal images, colors, and forms. These persons provide the demand for art and literature, even though they themselves cannot create art or literature. Every society has a need for contact with its own past, and in more differentiated societies rulers seek to strengthen their claim to legitimacy by showing the continuity of their regimes with the great personalities of the past. Where this cannot be provided by the powers of individual memory within the kinship group, historical chroniclers and antiquarians are required. Correspondingly, ecclesiastical and proto-ecclesiastical bodies must likewise show the spiritual wealth of their antecedents and their living relevance; this gives rise to hagiography and the activity of the hagiographer. In societies on larger then tribal scale, with complex tasks and traditions, the education—at least of those who are expected to become rulers or the associates, counselors, and aides of rulers—is called for; this requires teachers and a system of educational institutions. In any society which transcends the scale of a kinship group, in which the organs of authority acquire a more or less continuous existence, there is a need for administrators capable of keeping records and issuing rules and decrees. These activities require a certain fairly high level of education, which in turn requires institutions with teaching staffs, whether they be palace schools or privately or state-conducted academies or universities. Members of every society, and above all those who exercise authority in it, need to have at least intermittently some sense of the stability, coherence, and orderliness of their society; they need therefore a body of symbols, such as songs, histories, poems, biographies, constitutions, etc., which diffuse a sense of affinity among the members of the society.

The intellectuals' activities and their situation in society are the products of a compromise and an articulation of the intellectual disposition and the needs of society for those actions which can be performed only by persons who of necessity, by virtue of the actions they perform, are intellectuals. The larger the society and the more complex the tasks its rulers undertake, the greater the need therefore for a body of religious and secular intellectuals.

All these needs would exist even if there were no especially sensitive, inquiring, curious, creative minds in the society. There would be intellectuals in society even if there were no intellectuals by disposition.[1]

The Functions of Intellectuals

The moral and intellectual unity of a society, which in the size of its population and its territory goes beyond what any one man can know from his average firsthand experience and which brings him into contact with persons outside his kinship group, depends on such intellectual institutions as schools, churches, newspapers, and similar structures. Through these, ordinary persons, in childhood, youth, or adulthood, enter into contact, however extensive, with those who are most familiar with the existing body of cultural values. By means of preaching, teaching, and writing, intellectuals infuse into sections of the population which are intellectual neither by inner vocation

1. The demand for intellectual services can sometimes exceed the supply of qualified persons; it will always exceed the supply of truly creative individuals. More frequently, however, modern societies have experienced an excess of the supply of technically qualified persons over the demand for their services.

nor by social role, a perceptiveness and an imagery which they would otherwise lack. By the provision of such techniques as reading and writing and calculation, they enable the laity to enter into a wider universe. The creation of nations out of tribes, in early modern times in Europe and in contemporary Asia and Africa, is the work of intellectuals, just as the formation of the American nation out of diverse ethnic groups is partly the work of teachers, clergymen, and journalists. The legitimation of the reigning authority is naturally a function of many factors, including the tendencies within a population towards submission to and rejection of authority, the effectiveness of the authority in maintaining order, showing strength, and dispensing a semblance of justice. The legitimacy of authority is, however, a function of what its subjects believe about it; beliefs about authority are far from resting entirely on firsthand experience, and much of what is believed beyond first-hand experience is the product of traditions and teachings which are the gradually accumulated and attenuated product of the activities of intellectuals.

Through their provision of models and standards, by the presentation of symbols to be appreciated, intellectuals elicit, guide, and form the expressive dispositions within a society. Not that the expressive life of a society is under the exclusive dominion of its intellectuals. Indeed the situation has never existed—and in fact could never exist—in which the expressive life of a society, its aesthetic tastes, its artistic creation, or the ultimately aesthetic grounds of its ethical judgments fell entirely within the traditions espoused by the intellectuals of the society. Societies vary in the extent to which the expressive actions and orientations are in accordance with what is taught and represented by the dominant intellectuals. With these variations much of the expressive life of a society, even what is most vulgar and tasteless, echoes some of the expressive elements in the central value system represented by the intellectuals.

The first two functions treated above show the intellectuals infusing into the laity attachments to more general symbols and providing for the laity a means of participation in the central value system. Intellectuals are not, however, concerned only to facilitate this wider participation in certain features of the central value system. They are above all concerned with its more intensive cultivation, with the elaboration and development of alternative potentialities. Where creativity and originality are emphatically acknowledged and prized, and where innovation is admitted and accepted, this is perceived as a primary obligation of intellectuals. However, even in systems where individual creativity is not seen as a positive value, the labor of powerful minds and irrepressible individualities working on what has been received from the past, modifies the heritage by systematization and rationalization and adapts it to new tasks and obstacles. In this process of elaboration, divergent potentialities of the system of cultural values are made explicit and conflicting positions are established. Each generation of intellectuals performs this elaborating function for its own and succeeding generations, and particularly for the next succeeding generation.

These specifically intellectual functions are performed not only for the intellectuals of a particular society but for the intellectuals of other societies as well. The intellectuals of different societies are ordered in a vague hierarchy, in which the lower learn from the higher. For Southeast Asia, the Indian intellectuals, in the Middle Ages and early modern times, performed this educative function. The intellectuals of republican and imperial Rome learned from Greek intellectuals. For Japan, for a time, Chinese intellectuals performed this function. In modern times, the British intellectuals, through Oxford, Cambridge, and the London School of Economics, have formed the intellectuals of India, Africa, and for a long time the United States. In the nineteenth century, German academic intellectuals provided a worldwide model, just as in the nineteenth and twentieth centuries French artistic and literary intellectuals have provided models of development for aesthetically sensitive intellectuals all over the civilized world. In the eighteenth century, the intellectuals of the French Enlightenment inspired their confreres in Spain, Italy, Prussia, and Russia. This function is performed for the intellectual community above all. The laity only comes to share in it at several removes and after a lapse of time.

The function of providing a model for intellectual activity, within and among societies, implies the acceptance of a general criterion of superior quality or achievement. The pattern of action of a certain group of intellectuals comes to be regarded as exemplary because it is thought to correspond more closely to certain ideal requirements of truth, beauty, or virtue. Such standards are never the objects of complete consensus, but they are often widely accepted over very extensive areas of the world at any given time.

The process of elaborating and developing further the potentialities inherent in a "system" of cultural values entails also the possibility of "rejection" of the inherited set of values in varying degrees of comprehensiveness. In all societies, even those in which the intellectuals are notable for their conservatism, the diverse paths of creativity, as well as an inevitable tendency toward negativism, impel a partial rejection of the prevailing system of cultural values. The very process of elaboration and development involves a measure of rejection. The range of rejection of the inherited varies greatly; it can never be complete and all-embracing. Even where the rejecting intellectuals allege that they are "nihilistic" with respect to everything that is inherited, complete rejection without physical self-annihilation is impossible.

It is practically given by the nature of the intellectuals' orientation that there should be some tension between the intellectuals and the value orientations embodied in the actual institutions of any society. This applies not only to the orientations of the ordinary members of society, i.e., the laity, but to the value orientations of those exercising authority in the society, since it is on them that the intellectuals' attention is most often focused, they being the custodians of the central institutional system. It is not this particular form of "rejection" or alienation which interests us most at the moment. Rather it is the rejection by intellectuals of the inherited and prevailing values of those intellectuals who are already incorporated in ongoing social institutions. This intra-intellectual alienation or dissensus is a crucial part of the intellectual heritage of any society. Furthermore it supplies the important function of molding and guiding the alternative tendencies which exist in any society. It provides an alternative pattern of integration for their own society, and for other societies the intellectuals of which come under their hegemony (e.g. the Fabian socialists in Britain and the Indian intellectuals, or the French and British constitutional liberals of the early nineteenth century and the intellectuals of many countries in Southeastern Europe, South America, Asia, etc.).

It is not only through the presentation of orientations toward general symbols which reaffirm, continue, modify, or reject the society's traditional inheritance of beliefs and standards that intellectuals leave their mark on society. The intellectuals do not exhaust their function through the establishment of a contact for the laity with the sacred values of their society. They fulfill authoritative, power-exercising functions over concrete actions as well. Intellectuals have played a great historical role on the higher levels of state administration, above all in China, in British and independent India, in the Ottoman Empire, and in modern Europe. Sovereigns have often considered a high standard of education, either humanistic or technical-legal, confirmed by diplomas and examinations, necessary for the satisfactory functioning of the state. The judiciary, too, has often been a domain of the intellectuals. In private economic organizations, the employment of intellectuals in administrative capacities has been uncommon to the point of rarity. Nor have intellectuals ever shown any inclination to become business enterprisers. It is only since the nineteenth century that business firms, first in Germany, then in America, and latterly in other industrialized countries, have taken to the large-scale employment of scientists in research departments and, to a much smaller extent, in executive capacities.

Equal in antiquity to the role of the highly educated in state administration is the role of the intellectual as personal agent, counselor, tutor, or friend to the sovereign. Plato's experience in Syracuse, Aristotle's relations with Alexander, Alcuin's with Charlemagne, Hobbes and Charles II prior to the Restoration, Milton and Cromwell, Lord Keynes and the Treasury, and the "Brains Trust" under President F. D. Roosevelt, represent only a few of numerous instances in ancient and modern states, oriental and occidental, in which intellectuals have been drawn into the entourage of rulers, their advice and aid sought, and their approval valued. Again, there are many states and periods in which this has not been so. The court of Wilhelm II, for example, drew relatively little on the educated classes of the time; important episodes of Chinese history are to be seen as a consequence of the intellectuals' reaction to the ruler's refusal to draw them into his most intimate and influential circle of counselors; American administrative and political history from the time of the Jacksonian revolution until the New Liberalism of Woodrow Wilson, was characterized by the separation of intellectuals from the higher administrative and the legislative branches of government. Intellectuals have emerged occasionally in monarchies at the highest pinnacles of authority, through sheer accident or at least through no deliberate process of selection. Asoka, Marcus Aurelius, Akhnaton, are only a few of the scattered coincidences of sovereignty and the concern with the highest truths. In the last century and a half under conditions of liberal-democratic party politics, Benjamin Disraeli, William Gladstone, F. M. Guizot, Woodrow Wilson, Jawaharlal Nehru, Thomas Masaryk, etc., have provided impressive instances of intellectuals who have been able, by their own efforts and a wide appreciation for their gifts of civil politics enriched by an intensity of intellectual interest and exertion, to play a notable role in the exercise of great political authority. This has not been accidental; liberal and constitutional politics in great modern states and liberal and "progressive" nationalist movements in subject territories have to a large extent been "intellectuals' politics."

Indeed, in modern times, first in the West and then, in the nineteenth and twentieth centuries, at the peripheries of Western civilization and the Orient, the major political vocation of the intellectuals has lain in the enunciation and pursuit of the ideal. Modern liberal and constitutional politics have largely been the creation of intellectuals with bourgeois affinities and sympathies, in societies dominated by landowning and military aristocracies. This has been one major form of the pursuit of the ideal. Another has been the cultivation of ideological politics, i.e., revolutionary politics working outside the circle of constitutional traditions. Prior to the origins of ideological politics (which came into the open with the European Reformation), conspiracies, putsches, and the subversion of the existing regime, although they often involved intellectuals, were not the objects of a particular affinity between intellectuals and revolutionary tendencies. In modern times, however, with the emergence of ideologically dominated political activities as a continuously constitutive part of public life, a genuine affinity has emerged.

Not by any means all intellectuals have been equally attracted by revolutionary politics. Moderates and partisans in civil politics, quiet apolitical concentration on their specialized intellectual preoccupations, cynical antipolitical passivity, and faithful acceptance and service of the existing order, are all to be found in substantial proportions among modern intellectuals, as among intellectuals in antiquity. Nonetheless, the function of modern intellectuals in furnishing the doctrine of revolutionary movements is to be considered as one of their most important accomplishments.

The Structure of the Intellectual Community

The performance of the functions enumerated above is possible only through a complex set of institutional arrangements. The institutional system in which intellectual objects are reproduced or created has varied markedly in history. Its variations have at least in part been affected by the nature of the intellectual tasks, the volume of the intellectual heritage, the material resources necessary and available for intellectual work, the modes of reproduction of intellectual achievements, and the scope of the audience.

The creation of imaginative works of literature and the production of works of analysis and meditation, at least since the end of the age of anonymity, has been a work of the individual creator, working under his own self-imposed discipline. As regards the actual work of creation, he has been free of the control imposed by corporate organization. Within the limits of what has been made available to him by his culture, he has chosen the tradition under which he was to work, the style, the attitude and the form. Considerations of flattering a prince or pleasing a patron or the reading public or a publisher have often entered extraneously—but not more than that—into the central process of creation; the process of creation itself has always been a process of free choice and adaptation. The avoidance of the strictures of the censor or the displeasure of a tyrant have also been only extraneous factors in a process of individual creation. For this reason the creation of literature has never been corporately organized. The literary man has always been a self-propelling entity. After the development of printing and the emergence of a large reading public, it became possible in the most advanced countries of the Western world for a small number of successful authors of both superior and inferior literature to earn substantial sums of money and for many to earn enough to maintain themselves. For this to happen required not only a large public, sufficiently well-educated, and relatively inexpensive means of large-scale mechanical reproduction, but a well-organized system of book and periodical distribution (publishers, booksellers, editors), a means of giving publicity to new publications (reviews, bibliographies, and literate convivial circles), and laws protecting rights to intellectual property (copyright laws). In the Western countries and in Japan, where the book trade is relatively well-organized, where there are many periodicals, and where there is a large reading public, there is room for thousands of freelance intellectuals; in other countries in Asia and Africa, the small size of the literate public and the ineffective machinery of publication and distribution, confines to rather a small figure the number of freelance intellectuals. But they exist there nonetheless and represent a genuine innovation in the cultural and social history of these countries.

Prior to these developments—which emerged only in the eighteenth century in Western Europe and later in other cultures—creative literary intellectuals were forced to depend on different sources of income. The minnesingers and troubadours who sought to sell their songs in return for hospitality, the Chinese philosopher-adventurers of the period of the Warring States who sought to enter the employment of princes as their counselors, poets in Moghul courts, the Brahmin pandits at the courts of the Peshwa, and the European humanists as stipendiaries of the ecclesiastical and secular princely courts at the beginning of the modern age, were approximations of the independent freelance intellectual whose wares were supplied for payment. They were not genuinely freelance since they were paid in pensions or stipends or in kind rather than through the sale of their products by contractual agreement. As intellectual clients rather than as autonomous agents, they constituted a patrimonial approximation to the freelance intellectual. The patronage of princes, great noblemen and courtiers, financiers and merchants, has contributed greatly to the support of the intellectual activities of those who inherited no wealth, at a time and in fields of intellectual activity in which the sale of intellectual products could not find a large and wealthy enough public of purchasers. The creation of sinecures in government for literary men has been one form of patronage which shades off into gainful employment in the career of the civil servant. This latter means of maintenance, which was known in China over several millennia, has found many practitioners in the nineteenth and twentieth centuries in the West, above all in Great Britain. Diplomacy, military service, employment in commerce and even industry, have provided the livelihood of many authors for whom literature has been an avocation. Thus, patronage, sinecures, and government service, together with the most favorable of all, the independent position of the aristocrat, gentry, and rentier-intellectual who lived from inherited wealth, provided almost the sole means of maintenance for those who aspired to do intellectual work. These were appropriate not only to literary creation but to philosophy, science, and scholarship. These were the ways in which the greatest poets and philosophers of antiquity lived—except for the Sophists, who were freelance intellectuals—as well as the great Chinese and Persian poets, the humanist scholars of the European Renaissance, and the leading scientists of early modern times.

Those intellectuals who took as their task the cultivation of the sacred symbols of religious life lived either in monasteries, endowed by wealthy patrons, or by begging for their daily needs and by occasional patronage. Merchants and bankers, tillers of the soil and handicraftsmen, and professional military men produced from their ranks very few intellectuals—the last, more than the first two groups. The secular and sacred officialdom and the legal profession nearly monopolized the capacity to read and write, and they attracted to their ranks—within the limits imposed by the opportunities afforded by the prevailing system of social selection—the intellectually disposed, and provided them with the leisure and facilities to perform intellectual work as a full-time vocation or as an auxiliary activity. The nature of the tasks which these intellectuals assumed, the relative quantitative meagerness of the intellectual heritage, the restricted size of their audience, and the small demand for intellectual services meant that intellectual activities required little corporate organization.

The development of the *modern* university—first in Germany, Holland, and Sweden, then in France, then in Great Britain, later in the United States, Russia and Japan, and more recently in Canada, Australia, India and other Commonwealth countries—has changed the structure of the intellectual community. Science, which was once the work of amateurs—rentiers, civil servants, and noblemen, for the most part—and scholarship, which was almost a monopoly of monks, secular officials, and rentiers, have now come into the almost exclusive jurisdiction of universities. The relationship between teacher and pupil through the laboratory, the research seminar, and the dissertation, has led to a great multiplication of the scientific and scholarly output and strengthened the continuity of intellectual development. In turn, the degree of specialization has been greatly increased as a result of the greater density of scientific and scholarly knowledge and the pursuit of the idol of originality. The independent intellectual, and the intellectual living on the income from the sale of his works and from patronage, still exist, and their creativity and productivity have not obviously diminished. The intellectual, however, who lives from a salary as a member of an institution devoted to the performance of intellectual work—teaching and scientific and scholarly research—has greatly increased in numbers, and his works make up a larger and larger proportion of the total intellectual product of every modern society.

The increased volume and complexity of the heritage of science and scholarship and the demand for continuity as well as the wider insistence on diplomatization, have aggrandized the student body. This stratum of the intellectuals, which in the nineteenth century already had acquired a special position in European public life, in the twentieth century has greatly expanded. In every country where national sensibilities are very tender, and which has been in a state of political, economic, or cultural dependency, the university (and high school) student body has taken on a special role in political life. It has become the bearer of the idea of nationality.

Concomitantly the absorption of intellectuals into executive positions—"staff and line" posts within large corporate organizations concerned not with intellectual matters but with the exercise of authority, the production and sale of material objects, i.e., consumption goods, capital equipment, weapons of war, etc.—has greatly increased. Science, which was a profound toy of amateurs until the nineteenth century, became by the end of that century a vital component of economic life. It has spread from the chemical industry into agriculture, into nearly every branch of industry, and into important sectors of commerce. In the first and second world wars, scientists, and increasingly pure scientists, were drawn into involvement with the armed forces. Scientists have become increasingly involved in research closely connected with agriculture, supported and conducted within institutions controlled by public and private bodies concerned with the improvement of plant and animal strains, with ecology, etc.

The spread of literacy, leisure, and material well-being, and the development of the mechanical means of reproduction and transmission of symbols in sounds and image, have also resulted in the creation of new corporate organizations in which intellectuals are employed. Whereas the creation of cultural objects for consumption by the educated was until nearly the end of the nineteenth century the work, at varying levels of quality, of the freelance intellectual, who sold his work to an enterpriser—a printer-bookseller—or whose work was commissioned by the latter, recent developments bring the intellectual producer of this kind of cultural object within the framework of a corporate organization, e.g. a film studio, a radio or television network.

The trend in the present century, therefore, in all countries of the world, liberal and totalitarian, has been toward an increasing incorporation of intellectuals into organized institutions. This represents a modification of the trend toward an increase in the proportion of institutionally independent intellectuals which had set in with the development of printing, and which in itself constituted—at least in numbers and in the quantity of intellectual products—a new phase in world history.

This diversity and specialization of intellectuals in the twentieth century raises a question concerning the extent to which they form a community, bound together by a sense of mutual affinity, by attachment to a common set of rules and common identifying symbols. They do not form such a community at present. There are, however, numerous subcommunities within the larger intellectual universe which do meet these criteria. The particular fields of the natural sciences and even science as a whole and scholarship as a whole do define actual communities bound together by the acceptance of a common body of standards—and this, even though there are controversy and disagreement within every field. These communities are only partially and very inadequately embodied in the professional and scientific societies. The literary and artistic worlds, too, form such communities with vague and indeterminate boundaries—even more vague and indeterminate than the boundaries of the scholarly and scientific communities.

These communities are not mere figures of speech. Their common standards are continually being applied by each member in his own work and in the institutions which assess and select works and persons for appreciation or condemnation. They operate like a common-law system without formal enactment of their rules but by the repeated and incessant application and clarification of the rules. The editors of learned scientific, scholarly, and literary journals, the readers of publishing houses, the reviewers of scientific, scholarly, and literary works, and the appointments committees which pass judgments on the candidates for posts in universities or scientific research institutes, are the central institutions of these communities. The training of the oncoming generations in colleges and universities in the rules of the respective intellectual communities specifies these rules by example and transmits them by the identification of the research student with his teacher, just as in ancient India the disciple sitting at the feet of his *guru* acquired not only a knowledge of the concrete subject matter but also the rules and the disposition for its interpretation and application. The award of prizes and distinctions such as the Nobel Prize or election to membership in the Royal Society or to a famous continental academy establishes models and affirms the rightness of certain patterns of thought. The most original scientists, the most profound thinkers, the most learned scholars, the greatest writers and artists provide the models, which embody the rules of the community, and teach by the example of their achievement.

The worldwide character of the community formed by mathematicians or physicists or other natural scientists approximates most closely to the ideal of a body, bound together by a universal devotion to a common set of standards derived from a common tradition and acknowledged by all who have passed through the discipline of scientific training. Even here however, specialization and considerations of military security impair the universality of the scientific community. In other fields of intellectual work, boundaries of language, national pride, and religious, political, and ethical beliefs engender reluctance to accept the claims of standards of intellectual communities to universal observance. Technical specialization, the reduction of the general humanistic component in secondary and higher education, and the intensification of the ideological factor in politics all resist the claims of the communities which in the modern world have nonetheless managed, despite enduring cleavages and intermittent crises, to command the allegiance of intellectuals.

Despite all impediments and counterclaims, the intellectual communities remain really effective systems of action. Whatever their distortions, they transmit the traditions of intellectual life and maintain its standards in various special fields and as a whole.

The Traditions of Intellectuals

Intellectual work is sustained by and transmits a complex tradition which persists through changes in the structure of the intellectual class. In these traditions, the most vital ones are the standards and rules in the light of which achievement is striven for and assessed and the substantive beliefs and symbols which constitute the heritage of valid achievement. It is by participation in these traditions of perception, appreciation, and expression, and by affirmation of the importance of performing in the modes accredited by these traditions, that the intellectual is defined. One could almost say that if these traditions did not confront the intellectual as an ineluctable inheritance, they could be created anew in each generation by the passionate disposition of the "natural" intellectual to be in contact, by perception, ratiocination, or expression, with symbols of general scope. They are traditions which are, so to speak, given by the nature of intellectual work. They are the immanent traditions of intellectual performance, the accepted body of rules of procedure, standards of judgment, criteria for the selection of subject matters and problems, modes of presentation, canons for the assessment of excellence, models of previous achievement and prospective emulation. Every field of intellectual performance, more than any other craft or profession possessing a long and acknowledged accumulation of achievements, has such a cultural tradition, always—though at varying rates—being added to and modified. What is called scientific method in each particular field of science or scholarship, and the techniques of literary creation and of work in the plastic and other arts, possess such a tradition, and without that tradition even the greatest and most creative geniuses who seek to discover and create in that domain could not be effective. Colleges and universities, scientific, scholarly, and artistic journals, museums, galleries—in short, the whole system of intellectual institutions—exist to select those who are qualified to work within these traditions and to train them in their appreciation, application, and development. Even the most creative and rapidly developing domains of intellectual performance could disregard them only with very great loss.

These traditions, though they make neither direct nor logically implicit reference to the position of their adherents in relation to the surrounding society and the authorities which rule it, seem from their very structure to entail a measure of tension between themselves and the laity. The very intensity and concentration of commitment to these values which are remote from the executive routines of daily life in family, firm, office, factory, church, and civil service, from the pleasures of the ordinary man and the obligations, compromises, and corruptions of those who exercise commanding authority in church, state, business, and army—entail an at least incipient sense, on each side, of the distance which separates these two trends of value orientation.

Intellectual work arose from religious preoccupations. In the early history of the human race, it tended, in its concern with the ultimate or at least with what lies beyond the immediate concrete experience, to operate with religious symbols. It continues to share with genuine religious experience the fascination with the sacred or the ultimate ground of thought and experience, and the aspiration to enter into intimate contact with it. In secular intellectual work, this involves the search for the truth, for the principles embedded in events and actions, or for the establishment of a relationship between the self and the essential, whether the relationship be cognitive, appreciative, or expressive. Intellectual action of an intense kind contains and continues the deeper religious attitude, the striving for contact with the most decisive and significant symbols and the realities underlying those symbols. It is therefore no stretching of the term to say that science and philosophy, even when they are not religious in a conventional sense, are as concerned with the sacred as religion itself. In consequence of this, in our enumeration of the traditions under which intellectual pursuits are carried on, we should say that the tradition of awesome respect and of serious striving for contact with the sacred is perhaps the first, the most comprehensive, and the most important of all traditions of the intellectuals. In the great religious cultures of Islam, Buddhism, Taoism, and Hinduism, prior to the emergence of a differentiated modern intellectual class, the care of the sacred through the mastery, interpretation, and exposition of sacred writings and the cultivation of the appropriate mental states or qualities were the first interests of the intellectuals. (In China, the development of a class of Confucian intellectual-civil servants produced its own tradition, more civil and aesthetic than religious in the conventional meaning.) In the West too, in antiquity, a substantial section of the philosophical intelligentsia bore this tradition, and, on the higher reaches, even those who cut themselves off from the tribal and territorial religions continued to be impelled by such considerations (Pythagoras, Euclid, Ptolemy, Aristotle, Plato, Socrates, Lucretius, Seneca). In modern times, although attracting a diminishing share of the creative capacities of the oncoming intellectual elite, religious orientations still remain a major preoccupation of a substantial fraction of the educated classes and not less of the most creative minds.

With this striving for contact with the ultimately important comes the self-esteem which always accompanies the performance of important activities. One who makes an effort to understand the traditions of the intellectuals and their relations with the authorities who rule the other sections of society at any given time, must bear in mind the crucial significance of the self-regard which comes from preoccupation and contact with the most vital facts of human and cosmic existence, and the implied attitude of derogation toward those who act in more mundane or more routine capacities.[2]

2. Naturally, this sentiment is not equally shared by all intellectuals. Not all are equally involved in these "vital facts"—and therefore not all have the same feeling of the dignity of their own activities. Intellectuals vary greatly in their sensitivity to their traditions—just as do the laity with respect to their traditions—but even in those who are relatively insensitive, there remains a considerable unwitting assimilation of many elements of these central traditions.

When intellectuals ceased to be solely bearers of religiosity, the very act of separation, however gradual and unwitting and undeliberate, set up a tension between the intellectuals and the religious authority of their society. Insofar as they were not merely civil servants and counselors to princes—itself an unsettling, tension-generating relationship—there was created a tension between the public authorities and the intellectuals. Ecclesiastical and exemplary religious authority became an object of the distrust of intellectuals, and insofar as the authority of the government of earthly affairs associated itself with the religious powers, it too shared in that skepticism. The attitude is by no means universal, nor need the distrust be aggressive. Confucian civil servants, disdainful toward Taoism or Buddhism, did not become rebels against their sovereigns as long as they themselves were treated respectfully. In the West, where the separation of religious and other intellectual activities has become most pronounced, a more general feeling of distance from authority has been engendered and has become one of the strongest of the traditions of the intellectuals. First in the West, and then in the past half-century in Africa and Asia among intellectuals who have come under the Western traditions, the tradition of distrust of secular and ecclesiastical authority—and in fact of tradition as such—has become the chief secondary tradition of the intellectuals. As such, it is nurtured by many of the subsidiary traditions such as scientism, revolutionism, progressivism, etc., which we shall treat below.

The tension between the intellectuals and the powers—their urge to submit to authority as the bearer of the highest good, whether it be order or progress or some other value, and to resist or condemn authority as a betrayer of the highest values—comes ultimately from the constitutive orientation of the intellectuals toward the sacred. Practically all the more concrete traditions in the light and shadows of which intellectuals have lived express this tension. We shall note, in brief, some of these traditions which, however diverse in their age and origins, have played a great part in forming the relations of the modern intellectuals to authority. They are (a) the tradition of scientism, (b) the romantic tradition, (c) the apocalyptic tradition, (d) the populistic tradition, and (e) the tradition of antiintellectual order.

All of these traditions are in conflict with other traditions of deference toward ecclesiastical and temporal authorities and the expectation of a career in their service. Even in those modern cultures where the traditions of the intellectuals' acceptance of authority are strongest, in modern Britain and modern Germany, they have by no means had the field to themselves. Similarly in modern Asia, where variants of the traditions of devotion to the religiously sacred values and the service of temporal authority have, in ancient as well as modern times, had a powerful hold, anti-authoritarian and anticivil traditions, diffused from the West and nurtured by related traditions derived from Taoism, Buddhism, and Hinduism, have found an eager and widespread reception.

The *tradition of scientism* is the tradition which denies the validity of tradition as such; it insists on the testing of everything which is received and on its rejection if it does not correspond with the "facts of experience." It is the tradition which demands the avoidance of every extraneous impediment to the precise perception of reality, regardless of whether that impediment comes from tradition, from institutional authority, or from internal passion or impulse. It is critical of the arbitrary and the irrational. In its emphasis on the indispensability of firsthand and direct experience, it sets itself in opposition to everything which comes between the mind of the knowing individual and "reality." It is easy to see how social convention and the traditional authority associated with institutions would fall prey to the ravages of this powerfully persuasive and corrosive tradition.

The *romantic tradition* appears at first sight to be in irreconcilable opposition to the tradition of scientism. At certain points, such as the estimation of the value of impulse and passion, there is a real and unbridgeable antagonism. In many important respects, however, they share fundamental features. Romanticism starts with the appreciation of the spontaneous manifestations of the essence of concrete individuality. Hence it values originality, i.e. the unique, that which is produced from the genius of the individual (or the folk), in contrast with the stereotyped and traditional actions of the philistine. Since ratiocination and detachment obstruct spontaneous expression, they are thought to be life-destroying. Institutions which have rules and which prescribe the conduct of the individual members by conventions and commands are likewise viewed as life-destroying. The bourgeois family, mercantile activity, the market, indeed civil society in general, with its curb on enthusiasm and its sober acceptance of obligation, are repugnant to the romantic tradition—all are the enemies of spontaneity and genuineness; they impose a role on the individual and do not permit him to be himself. They kill what is living in the folk. Civil society has no place for the intellectual, who is afflicted with a sense of his moral solitude within it. The affinities of the romantic tradition to the revolutionary criticism of the established order and to the bohemian refusal to have more part in it than is absolutely necessary are obvious. It too is one of the most explosively antiauthoritarian, and even anticivil, powers of modern intellectual life.

The *revolutionary tradition*, which has found so many of its leading recipients and exponents among intellectuals, draws much from scientism and romanticism, but essentially it rests on one much older, namely the *apocalyptic* or millenarian tradition. The belief that the evil world as we know it, so full of temptation and corruption, will come to an end one day and will be replaced by a purer and better world, originates in the apocalyptic outlook of the prophets of the Old Testament. It is promulgated in the Christian idea of the Kingdom of God, which the earlier Christians expected in their own time, and it lingers as a passionately turbulent stream, dammed up and hidden by the efforts of the Church, but recurrently appearing on the surface of history through the teaching and action of heretical sects. It received a powerful impetus from Manichaeanism. In the Donatists, in the Bogomils, in the Albigensians and Waldensians, in the Hussites and Lollards, in the Anabaptists and in the Fifth Monarchy Men, in the belief that the evil world, the world of the Children of Darkness, would be destroyed and supplanted by the world of the Children of Light after a decisive judgement by the Sovereign of the universe, this tradition has lived on. It has come down to our own times in a transmuted form. Although it still exists in its religious form among numerous Christian and quasi-Christian sects in Europe, America, and Africa, its true recipients are the modern revolutionary movements and above all the Marxian movements. Marxian writers of the early part of this century acknowledged the Anabaptists, the Fifth

Monarchy Men, the Levellers and the Diggers, as their forerunners, and although the Bolsheviks have been less willing to admit Russian sectarianism as an antecedent, there can be little doubt that the Russian sectarian image of the world and its cataclysmic history made it easier for the Marxian conception of society and its historical destiny to find acceptance in Russia. The disposition to distinguish sharply between good and evil and to refuse to admit the permissibility of any admixture, the insistence that justice be done though the heavens fall, the obstinate refusal to compromise or to tolerate compromise—all the features of doctrinaire politics, or the politics of the ideal, which are so common among the modern intellectuals, must be attributed in some measure at least to this tradition.

Another of the traditions which has everywhere in the world moved intellectuals in the last century and a half is the *populistic tradition.* Populism is a belief in the creativity and in the superior moral worth of the ordinary people, of the uneducated and unintellectual; it perceives their virtue in their actual qualities or in their potentialities. In the simplicity and wisdom of their ways, the populist tradition alleges that it has discerned virtues which are morally superior to those found in the educated and in the higher social classes. Even where, as in Marxism, the actual state of the lower classes is not esteemed, they are alleged to be by destiny fitted to become the salvationary nucleus of their society. Romanticism with its distrust of the rational and calculating elements in bourgeois society, revolutionism with its hatred of the upper classes as the agents of wicked authority, the apocalyptic attitude which sees the last coming first and which alleges that official learning (religious and secular) has falsified the truths which the Last Judgement and the leap into freedom will validate—all these manifest a populistic disposition. German historical and philological scholarship in the nineteenth century—imbued with the romantic hatred of the rational, the economic, the analytic spirit, which it castigated as the source and product of the whole revolutionary, rationalistic trend of Western European culture—discovered in the nameless masses, the folk, the fountain of linguistic and cultural creativity. French socialism went a step further, and Marxism elevated this essentially romantic outlook into a systematic "scientific" theory.

In all countries peripheral to the most creative centers of Western culture at the height of its hegemony over the modern mind, intellectuals were both fascinated and rendered uneasy by the culture of Western Europe. Not only in early nineteenth-century Germany, but in Russia of the fifties, in the twentieth-century middlewestern United States, in Brazil (in the doctrine of "Indianism"), in the resentful and embittered Weimar Republic, in India since the ascendancy of Gandhi and in the emerging intelligentsias of the new countries of Africa, populistic tendencies are massively at work. In all these countries the intellectuals have been educated either in foreign countries or in institutions within their own countries modeled on those at the center of the culture they sought or seek to emulate. In all these countries the intellectuals have developed anxiety about whether they have not allowed themselves to be currupted by excessive permeation with the admired foreign culture. To identify themselves with the people, to praise the culture of the ordinary people as richer, truer, wiser, and more relevant than the foreign culture in which they have themselves been educated, has been a way out of this distress. In most of these cases it is a protest against the "official" culture, the culture of the higher civil servants, of the universities, and of the culture—political, literary, and philosophical—which has come out of them. As such, it has fused easily with the other traditions of hostility to civil institutions and civil authority.

There is another tradition, closely connected with all of these and yet apparently their negation, which merits mention. This is the *antiintellectual tradition of order.* Best known in the West in the form of French positivism (Saint-Simon and Comte), it has its roots in antiquity and in the belief that excessive intellectual analysis and discussion can erode the foundations of order. Plato's attitude toward poets had its parallel in the burning of the books by the former Confucian, Li-Ssu, at the origin of the Ch'in Dynasty; Hobbes's analysis of the role of intellectuals in bringing about the English civil war, Taine's interpretation of the significance of the *philosophes* in bringing on the French Revolution of 1789, and the ideas of Joseph de Maistre, all testify to the ambivalence in the traditional antiauthoritarianism of intellectuals.

In Conclusion

Intellectuals are indispensable to any society, not just to industrial society, and the more complex the society, the more indispensable they are. An effective collaboration between intellectuals and the authorities which govern society is a requirement for order and continuity in public life and for the integration of the wider reaches of the laity into society. Yet, the original impetus to intellectual performance, and the traditions to which it has given rise and which are sustained by the institutions through which intellectual performance is made practicable, generate a tension between intellectuals and the laity, high and low. This tension can never be eliminated, either by a complete consensus between the laity and the intellectuals or by the complete ascendancy of the intellectuals over the laity.

Within these two extreme and impossible alternatives, a wide variety of forms of consensus and dissensus in the relations of the intellectuals and the ruling powers of society have existed. The discovery and the achievement of the optimum balance of civility and intellectual creativity are the tasks of the statesman and the responsible intellectual. The study of these diverse patterns of consensus and dissensus, their institutional and cultural concomitants, and the conditions under which they have emerged and waned are the first items on the agenda of the comparative study of the intellectuals and the powers.

9

IDEOLOGY

Ideology is one among the variety of comprehensive patterns of beliefs—cognitive and moral, about man, society, and the universe in relation to man and society—which exist in differentiated societies. These comprehensive patterns of belief comprise outlooks and creeds ("suboutlooks"), movements of thought, and programs, as well as ideologies.

These comprehensive patterns differ from each other in their degree of (a) explicitness and authoritativeness of formulation, (b) internal systemic integration, (c) acknowledged affinity with other contemporaneous patterns, (d) closure, (e) imperativeness of manifestation in conduct, (f) accompanying affect, (g) consensus demanded of exponents, and (h) association with a corporate collective form deliberately intended to realize the pattern of beliefs. Ideologies are characterized by a high degree of explicitness of formulation over a very wide range of the objects with which they deal; for their adherents there is an authoritative and explicit promulgation. They are relatively highly systematized or integrated around one or a few preeminent values (e.g., salvation, equality, or ethnic purity). They are more insistent on their distinctiveness from and unconnectedness with other outlooks or ideologies in their own society; they are more resistant against innovations in their beliefs and deny the existence or the significance of those which do occur.

Previously published in a slightly different form in the *International Encyclopaedia of the Social Sciences,* David L. Sills, editor. (New York: Macmillan Company and Free Press, 1968), vol. 7, pp. 66-76. Copyright © 1968 by Crowell Collier and Macmillan, Inc.

Their acceptance and promulgation have highly affective overtones. Complete subservience to the ideology is demanded of those who accept it, and it is regarded as essential and imperative that their conduct should be completely permeated by it. All adherents of the ideology are urgently expected to be in complete agreement with each other; corporate collective form is regarded as the appropriate mode of organization of adherents to maintain discipline over those already committed and to win over or dominate those not already committed to it.

Outlooks (and creeds) tend to lack one authoritative and explicit promulgation. They are pluralistic in their internal structure, not systematically integrated (creeds or "suboutlooks" have a greater likelihood of systematic integration when they are elaborated by a school of thought). Outlooks are inclusive rather than disjunctive in their relations with other patterns of thought. (Creeds or "suboutlooks" are less inclusive, but they too do not form sharp boundaries around themselves.) Outlooks contain within themselves a variety of creeds or "suboutlooks", which differ from each other by divergent emphasis on different elements in the outlook; they are often in conflict with each other on particular issues. The vagueness and diffuseness of outlooks and creeds is paralleled by the unevenness of the pressure for their observance in action. In expression, they are less affective. They are less demanding of consensus among their bearers. Outlooks and creeds, too, have their organizational counterparts.

Outlooks and creeds are the characteristic patterns of belief in those sections of the society which affirm or accept the existing order of society. One or another of the creeds is characteristically integrated into the central institutional system while the others are not remote from it. Creeds which become alienated from the central institutional system tend to acquire the properties of ideologies, over and above the element of alienation. Ideologies sometimes but do not normally dominate central institutional systems. Ideologies which dominate central institutional systems have a tendency to be transformed in the direction of creeds, and not merely with respect to their relationship to the central institutional system.

A movement of thought is a more or less explicit and systematic intellectual pattern, developed in the course of generally undirected collaboration and division of labor. It is elaborate and comprehensive. like ideologies, outlooks, and creeds. Insofar as it does not insist on total observance in behavior, a complete consensus among its adherents, and closure vis-a-vis other intellectual constructions, it does not become an ideology.

A program is a specification and narrowing of the focus of interest of an outlook, creed, or movement of thought onto a particular, limited objective. Depending on the pattern from which it originates, its relationship to more general cognitive and moral principles will be more or less elaborate and explicit. Since its major feature is the limited range of its objectives, in practice it is less likely to be immediately ideological in its origin or destination.

Movements of thought and programs tend to be dissensual towards contemporaneous outlooks and creeds and the practices through which these operate institutionally. Ideology differs from them, however, with respect to the intensity of the affect which accompanies its dissent, the completeness of its corporate self-separation, and of its intellectual closure, as well as in the range of its aspiration to encompass in cognition, evaluation, and practice all available objects and events.

Ideologies and those who espouse them allege to speak for a transcendent entity—a stratum, a society, a species, or an ideal value—which is broader than the membership of the corporate entity. Corporate carriers of ideologies, whatever their actual practice, claim to act on behalf of an "ideal," the beneficiaries of which always go beyond the members of the ideological group. The ideal always diverging from the existent, the ideology contends for the realization of a state of affairs which is alleged by its proponents either never to have existed previously or to have existed in the past but no longer to be in existence. (Karl Mannheim [*Ideology and Utopia*] designated the former ideals as utopias, the latter as ideologies. He also included under ideology sets of beliefs which affirm the existing order and which we designate as outlooks and suboutlooks, schools of thought and programs. Neither his terminology nor his classifications are adhered to in this paper.)

Ideology and Central Value Systems

Ideologies contend more strenuously than does the prevailing outlook or the constituent and overlapping creeds for a purer, fuller, or more ideal realization of particular cognitive and moral values than exists in the society in which the ideology obtains. Ideologies are more insistent on continuous contact with sacred symbols and with a fuller manifestation of the sacred in the existent. Whereas the outlooks and creeds connected with the central institutional system demand in their programmatic aspects segmental changes and changes which do not diverge profoundly from what already exists, ideologies impel their proponents to realize the ideal which is contained in the sacred through a "total transformation." They seek this completeness through total conquest or conversion or by total withdrawal from it so that the purer, ideal form of value can be cultivated in isolation from the contaminating influence of the environing society of the moment. Whereas the bearers of each of the several creeds of a prevailing outlook accept some measure of community with other creeds, the exponents of an ideology, being set against other ideologies and particularly against the dominant outlook (and creeds), stress the differences of their ideology vis-a-vis the other outlooks and ideologies within the society, and disavow the identities and affinities.

Nonetheless, every ideology, however great the originality of its creators, arises in the midst of an ongoing culture. However passionate its reaction against that culture, it cannot entirely divest itself of important elements of that culture. Ideologies are responses to insufficient regard for some particular element in the dominant outlooks and are attempts to place that neglected element in a more central position and to bring it into fulfillment. There are, therefore, always marked substantive affinities between the moral and cognitive orientations of any particular ideology and those of the outlooks and creeds which prevail in the environing society and which to greater or lesser degrees affirm or accept the central institutional and value systems.

In their formal structure, both the outlooks and the creeds which affirm or accept the central institutional and value system are constellations of very loosely integrated and ambiguous moral and cognitive propositions and attitudes toward a variety of particular, often quite concrete, objects and situations. In the minds of most of those who share them, they do not form consistent systems each concentrated on one central theme, principle, value, or symbol. An ideology is an intensification and generalization of certain of these propositions and attitudes, a reduced emphasis on others, and their subordination to one, or very few, which is, or are, raised to a position of predominance. An ideology differs therefore from a prevailing outlook and its creeds through *its greater explicitness*, its greater *internal integration* or *systematization*, the *comprehensiveness* of its scope, the *urgency* of its application, and the much higher *intensity of concentration* on certain central propositions or evaluations.

Because of these common structural properties, and despite their affinities with the dominant outlooks and creeds, ideologies, whether "progressive" or "traditionalistic," "revolutionary" or "reactionary," have certain common substantive features as well. They entail an aggressive alienation from the existing society; they recommend the transformation of the lives of their exponents in accordance with specific principles; they insist on consistency and thoroughgoingness in their exponents' application of principles; and they recommend the complete dominion over the societies in which they live or a total, self-protective withdrawal from them. (Even where the exponents of an ideology have been successful in attaining the key positions from which power is exercised in the central institutional system, the alienation of the exponents of the ideology from the outlook of the society and its creeds over which they exercise power still operates.)

Since ideologies are intellectual constructions, they passionately oppose the productions of the cultural institutions of the central institutional system. They claim that these have distorted the truth about "serious" things, and that they do so to maintain a system of injustice in the earthly order.

Ideologies insist on the primary value of the realization of principles in conduct; this is one of the reasons with which they accuse the central value and institutional systems of hypocrisy, the compromise of principles, and corruption by power. Corresponding to this rigorist attitude, ideologies and their exponents, whether out of power or in central positions of power over society, are relentlessly critical of the inconsistencies and shortcomings of conduct with respect to principles of right and justice in sectors of society over which they do not have complete control. Ideologies demand an intense and continuous observance of their imperatives in the conduct of their exponents; ideological groups tend to impose a stringent discipline on their members.

Some parts of these transindividual outlooks are more in the possession of some individuals and less in the possession of others; the latter might have a predilection for elements different from those espoused by the former. An ideology insists on a greater completeness of possession by each of those who are committed to sharing in it; there is less of a division of labor among the bearers of ideologies than there is among the bearers of a prevailing outlook or creed.

Ideological Politics

Ideologies are always concerned with authority, transcendent and earthly, and they cannot therefore avoid being political except by the extreme reaction of complete withdrawal from society. Even in ages which saw no public politics permitted, ideological groups forced themselves into the political arena. Since the seventeenth century, every ideology has had its views on politics; indeed, since the nineteenth century some ideologies have come apparently to have views about nothing but politics.

This appearance of thinking of nothing but politics is not the attitude of the professional politician, who lives for politics to the exclusion of everything else. Ideologies which concentrate on politics do so because for them politics subsumes everything else. The evaluation of authority is the center of the ideological outlook; it is around this evaluation that all other objects and their evaluations are integrated. Everything is political for ideological politics. No sphere has any intrinsic value of its own. There is no privacy, no autonomous spheres or art or religion or economic activity or science. Each, in this view, is to be understood politically. (This is true of Marxism as well, despite the fact that it is reputed to have made everything dependent on economic relationships. The relations of production were property relations, i.e., relationships of authority, supported by the power of the state!)

Ideology, whether nominally religious or antireligious, is concerned with the sacred. Ideology seeks to sacralize existence by bringing every part of it under the dominion of the ultimately right principles. The sacred and the sacrilegious reside in authority, the former in the authority acknowledged by ideology, the latter in that which prevails in the wicked world. Ordinary politics are the kingdom of darkness; ideological politics are the struggle of light against darkness.

Participation in the routine life of the civil political order is alien to the ideological spirit. In fact, there are many adulterations of this ideological purity, and purely ideological politics are marginal and exceptional. The need to build a machine strong enough to acquire power in the state, even by conspiracy and subversion, enforces compromises and concessions to the ongoing political order and to the less than complete ideological orientation of potential and desired supporters. Failure, too, damages the purity of ideological politics. The pressure of competition enforces alliances and the adoption of procedures which are alien to its nature. Nonetheless, ideological politics in splinters of rancorous purity or in attenuation often penetrates some way into civil politics.

Likewise among intellectuals there are many who have inherited an ideological tradition and to whom ideological politics appeal as the only right politics. Even where intellectuals often appear to be convinced of the inefficacy of ideological politics, the categories in which they view the world as it is, its techniques and its heroes, stir and master their imaginations.

The Bearers of Ideology

The disposition toward ideological construction is one of the fundamental properties of the human race, once it reaches a certain stage of intellectual development. It is, however, a disposition which is usually latent. It finds its fullest expression in a charismatic ideologist, a person with an overwhelmingly powerful drive to be in contact with the sacred and to promulgate that contact in comprehensive and coherent terms. The charismatic ideologist cannot, however, construct an ideology in isolation from a collectivity on behalf of which he speaks and with which it must be shared. An ideology-like intellectual construction produced in isolation from a political or religious sect would be no more than a system of religious, moral, social, and political philosophy. It becomes more than a rigorous system of moral, social, and political philosophy based on fundamental propositions about the cosmos and history when it is shared by a community constituted by the acceptance of that outlook.

The characteristic and primal bearer of an ideology is an *ideological primary group* (what Schmalenbach called a *Bund*). The bond which unites the members of the ideological primary group to each other is the attachment to each other as co-sharers of the ideological system of beliefs, the perception of the other as being in possession of or being possessed by the sacredness inherent in the acceptance of the ideology. In the ideological primary group, personal, primordial, and civil qualities are attenuated or suppressed in favor of the quality of "ideological possession." A comrade is a comrade by virtue of his beliefs, which are perceived as his most significant qualities. A fully developed ideological primary group is separated by sharply defined boundaries from the "world," from which it seeks to protect itself or over which it seeks to triumph. Stringent discipline over conduct and belief is a feature of ideological primary groups; intense solidarity and unwavering loyalty are demanded.

In reality, of course, the ideological quality never completely supplants all other qualities, and ideological primary groups are never completely realized. Ideological primary groups are subject therefore to recurrent strains not only because of the inherent strains within the ideology as an intellectual system but also because the other qualities become, in various measures, for many of the members of the group, significant qualities on the bases of which supplementary and often alternative and contradictory attachments are formed. Even the most disciplined ideological primary group is under the strain of divergent beliefs among members as well as the pull of their various attachments to the "world."

Ideologies are often espoused by more loosely integrated circles, particularly when the ideology itself has moved into a condition of disintegration. Ideologies have a self-reproductive power. Echoes and fragments of ideologies go on after their primal bearers have died or dissolved in defeat or disillusionment. They turn into movements borne by schools of thought. Fragments of ideology also become transformed into creeds and outlooks.

The Emergence of Ideologies

An ideology is the product of the need for an intellectually imposed order on the world. The need for an ideology is an intensification of the need for a cognitive and moral map of the universe, which in a less intense and more intermittent form is a fundamental, although unequally distributed, disposition of man.

Ideologies arise in conditions of crisis, in sectors of society to whom the hitherto prevailing outlook has become unacceptable. An ideology arises because there is a strongly felt need for an explanation of important experiences which the prevailing outlook does not explain, because there is a need for the firm guidance of conduct which, similarly, is not provided by the prevailing outlook, and because there is a need, likewise strongly felt, for a fundamental vindication of legitimation of the value and dignity of the persons in question. Mere rejection of the existing society and the prevailing outlook of the elites of that society is not sufficient. For an ideology to exist, there must also be an attendant vision of a positive alternative to the existing pattern of society and its culture and an intellectual capacity to articulate that vision as part of the cosmic order. Ideologies are the creations of charismatic persons with a powerful, expansive, and simplified vision, who also possess high intellectual and imaginative powers. An ideology, by placing at its very center certain cosmically, ethically fundamental propositions, brings to those who accept it the belief that they are in possession and in contact with what is ultimately right and true.

Some personalities are ideological by constitution. They feel continuously a need for a clearly ordered picture of the universe, and of their own place in it. They need clear and unambiguous criteria as to what is right and wrong in every situation. They must be able to explain whatever happens by a clear and readily applicable proposition, itself derived from a central proposition. Other persons become ideological in conditions of private and public crisis, which accentuate the need for meaningful moral and cognitive order. (When the crisis abates, the latter become less ideological.)

An ideology cannot come into existence without the prior existence of a general pattern of moral and cognitive judgments against which it is a reaction and of which it is a variant. It requires, in other words, a cultural tradition from which to deviate, and from which to draw the elements which it intensifies and raises to centrality. An intellectualized religion provides the precondition for the emergence of ideology since the former contains explicit propositions about the nature of the sacred and its cultivation, which is what ideologies are about. The fact that an ideology already exists serves both to form an ideological tradition and to provide a medium in which ideological dispositions can be precipitated by emulation and self-differentiation.

Ideologies and ideological orientations have existed in all high cultures. They have, however, been especially frequent in Western culture. The continuous working of the prophetic tradition of the Old Testament and the salvationary tradition of the mystery religions and of early Christianity have provided a set of cultural dispositions which have been recurrently activated in the course of the Christian era in the West. The secularization of the modern age has not changed this at all. The growth of literacy and of the educated classes and the "intellectualization" of politics have widened receptivity to ideological beliefs. The spread of Western ideas to Asia and Africa has been a spread among many other things of a culture full of ideological potentiality. (On the social origins of the bearers of ideology, little can be said. It was Max Weber's view that they came from the strata of traders and handicraftsmen, and from sections of society which are shaken by a disruption in their conventional mode of life. There is some plausibility in this hypothesis. They also appear to come from educated circles and from ethnic "outsiders," whose prior alienation makes them receptive to ideological beliefs.)

Endogenous and Exogenous Changes in Ideologies

Proponents of ideologies obdurately resist the explicit introduction of revision of their articles of belief. They aspire and pretend to systematic completeness. They do not appear to their proponents to be in need of improvement. Nonetheless, ideologies are never completely consistent or completely adequate to the facts of experience which they claim to interpret and dominate. Even the most systematically elaborated ideology, like all systems of belief, scientific and nonscientific, contains inconsistencies, ambiguities, and gaps. These render likely disputes among the adherents of the ideology who espouse divergent ways of filling the gaps and clarifying the ambiguities, each claiming that his way represents the "correct" interpretation of the unchanged and unchangeable fundamentals. Inconsistencies and ambiguities may be perceived on purely intellectual grounds, and the efforts to repair them may be motivated primarily by a concern for intellectual clarity and harmony. Such efforts are likely to arouse antagonism from the more orthodox exponents of the ideology, i.e., those who adhere to the previously dominant interpretation. In this way, either through the triumph of the innovators or the triumph of the orthodox, the previous formulation of the ideology undergoes a change.

In addition to these more intellectual sources of change in ideologies, endogenous changes occur in consequence of conflicts among the proponents of divergent policies which appear to be equally sanctioned by the ideology. As a result of the triumph of one of the contending groups over the other, new emphases and developments occur within the ideology. These very properties, which are sources of instability in ideologies and in the groups which support them, are also the condition of their further development to confront new situations and of their adaptation and compromise with the intractability of reality as an object of exhaustive cognition and control. It is through such internal changes that ideologies sometimes move back toward the prevailing outlook or contribute, by their reentry, to the modification of the prevailing outlook of the cultural value system.

Ideologies also change because of the pressure of external reality. The "world" does not easily accommodate itself to the requirements of ideologies. The "facts" of life do not fit their categories; those whose existence is among these facts do not yield to the exhortations and offensives of the ideologists. The proponents of ideologies are often defeated in their campaigns for total transformation. Defeat is a shock, a pressing occasion for revision of the ideology to make it fit the "facts" which have imposed themselves. Despite resistance, the ideology is retouched, at first superficially, later more deeply. Fissures among the ideologists, accompany this struggle to cope with the impregnability of the "world."

Another external factor which places a strain on ideology is the diminution of the crisis which gave rise to it and the consequent dissipation of ideological orientation. Those whom crisis had enflamed into an ideological state of mind either withdraw from or loosen their connections with the ideological primary group; if they are influential enough, they modify and adapt it to the demands of life in the environing society, to which they once more become assimilated. Under these conditions, the sharply defined boundaries become eroded. The members cease to define themselves exclusively by their ideological qualities. The specific modifications which the ideology introduced to differentiate it from the predominant outlook in the central institutional and value systems make the ideology less disjunctive, and its distinctive ideological elements fade into a ceremonially asserted formula. Quite frequently, the ideological accentuation returns to the prevailing, more widely shared outlook as an accentuation, as an intensification of those features of the prevailing outlook or creed which had previously been in a blurred and unemphasized state.

Quasi-ideological Phenomena

The potentialities of ideological orientations relatively seldom come to realization. Quite apart from the tenacious hold of the central institutional and value systems on many persons who are simultaneously ideologically disposed, ideological orientations often do not eventuate in fully developed ideologies or ideological primary groups because the ideological needs of those who come under their influence are not sufficiently intense, comprehensive, or persistent. Without a powerful ideological personality, powerful in intelligence and imagination, ideological propensities in the more ordinary human vessels of ideological needs do not attain fulfillment.

Furthermore, once an ideological primary group has fallen into dilapidation, the ideology persists in a somewhat disaggregated form among the late members of the group. In that form, too, it continues to find adherents who, without the discipline of an ideological primary group, select certain congenial elements of the ideology for application and development. They become an ideological tradition, which is available to subsequent ideologists and ideological primary groups.

Sometimes certain of these elements become a *program* of aggressive demands and criticism against the central institutional and value systems. Programs, like ideologies, also emerge from prevailing outlooks and suboutlooks, through "taking seriously" some particular element in the outlook and seeking to bring it to fulfillment within the existing order. A program accepts much of the prevailing institutional and value systems, although it fervently rejects one sector. Thus, a program stands midway between an ideology and a prevailing outlook or suboutlook. It can be reached from either direction (and testifies thereby to the affinities between ideologies and outlooks and creeds).

The programmatic forms of ideological orientation are sometimes concentrated on particular and segmented objects, e.g., the abolition of slavery or the rights of a particular sector of the population such as an ethnic group or a social stratum. They do not expand to the point where they embrace the whole society as the objects of the sought-for transformation. Attachment to the central institutional or value systems might be so strong that it survives an intense but segmental alienation with respect to particular institutional practices or particular beliefs. This is characteristic of certain modern "reform movements." These have focused their attention and efforts on a specific segment of the central institutional system, attacking it with a rigorism which insists on the conformity of conduct with moral principles, and which will neither yield nor compromise. The programs and the movements which are their structural counterparts do not insist on the complete transformation of the whole society but they are uncompromisingly insistent on the attainment of their particular restricted, ideally prescribed end.

Often these movements have, in such instances, been borne by a small circle of persons organized into a quasi-ideological primary group which to some extent draws boundaries around itself and regards itself as disjunctively separated from its enemies, who are not, however, as in more fully developed ideological primary groups, regarded as identical with the totality of the environing society.

A creed differs from an ideology, though it often shades off into one. Because creeds do not tend to take a sharply bounded corporate form and because they have very little orthodoxy compared with ideologies they cannot command the concerted intellectual power of ideologies. Subscription to them tends therefore to be partial, fragmentary, and occasional. Unless a creed is taken in hand by a school of thought it does not undergo systematic elaboration and its scope is not broadened to a point of universal comprehensiveness. Its founder or inspiring genius might have created a coherent system of moral, social, and political philosophy, which in its comprehensiveness, elaborateness, and explicitness might be equivalent to the intellectual core of an ideology, but if he forms neither a school of thought nor an ideological primary group, his influence, however great, will be carried by the winds. Each will take from it what he wants: it will become a pervasive influence but it will lose the unity and the force which it would have needed to be an ideology. If, furthermore, the great thinker is neither far-reachingly alienated from the central value and institutional systems of his society (and thus has no need for disjunction) nor unqualifiedly insistent on the complete realization of his doctrine in the conduct of his followers, there is little chance that an ideology will flow from his intellectual construction. At best, he will generate a creed or a school of thought.

Proto-ideological Phenomena

Another variant of ideological phenomena is to be seen in those collectivities which, although "sodality-like" in structure, such as adolescent gangs and military and paramilitary units, do not have the intellectual patterns which we call ideological. Alienated in outlook from the prevailing outlook associated with the central institutional and value systems, they draw sharply defined boundaries around themselves. They insist on a concentration of loyalty to the group and on stringent discipline to the standards of the group. They have simplistic criteria of partisanship and enmity. They do not, however, develop or espouse a coherent moral and intellectual doctrine. They have no well-developed, principled view of the contemporary society which surrounds them, and, no less important, they have no image of a comprehensive order to replace permanently the order from which they are alienated. The "world" is their enemy with which they are at war, but they have no interest in taking it over and refashioning it in the name of a cosmically significant principle. In this respect they approximate the "withdrawn" ideological primary groups, but unlike these they are aggressively at war with an enemy and they lack an intellectual culture.

The failure of proto-ideological primary groups to develop an ideology might be attributed to the insufficient intellectual endowment of their members and above all to the absence of a charismatic ideological personality, sufficiently educated or sufficiently creative intellectually to provide them with a more complex system of beliefs. They lack sufficient contact with both the central value system and the tradition of ideological orientation. They are "rebels without a cause." (The boys' gang cultures of the great cities of the Western world are typical of these proto-ideological formations, in contrast with the more ideological German youth groups of the last years of the nineteenth century to the coming of World War II.)

The Functions of Ideologies

Ideologies are often accepted by persons who by temperament or by culture are ideologically predisposed. Such persons might be inclined to express their views with aggressive affect, they might feel a strong need to distinguish between comrades and enemies, or they might have been raised in a salvationary, apocalyptic culture. There are, however, persons who are neither but who come under ideological influence fortuitously or through the strain of crisis when they need the support of an ideology. For such persons, ideologies—up to a point and for a limited time—can exert a powerful influence. By making them conceive of themselves as in contact with the ultimate powers of existence, their motivation to act will be greatly reinforced. They will gain courage from perceiving themselves as part of a cosmic scheme; actions which they would not dare to envisage before now will have the legitimacy which proximity to the sacred provides.

Ideologies intend either the disruption of the central institutional and value systems by conflict with them or the denial of their claims by withdrawal from them. They aim in the former case at "total" replacement. They do not succeed in this even where their bearers are successful in the acquisition of power in the larger society. Where an ideological primary group succeeds in overcoming existing elites and comes to rule over the society, it is incapable of completely and enduringly suppressing the previously predominant outlook. It is unsuccessful on a number of grounds, first of all because of the strength of attachments to the central value systems among the population at large and because, in view of this, the resources for their suppression available to the ideological elites are not adequate—too much remains outside the scope of their control or surveillance.

Then as time passes, some, although never all, of the previously prevailing outlook reasserts itself. This process is assisted by the fact that the members of the ideological primary group themselves, in the course of time, fall away from their zealous espousal of the ideology. When they fall away, many of them fall back toward one of the cultural outlooks from which the ideology sprang. Partial return occurs also because as the ideological primary group continues in power, the obstacles to the realization of their goals, the multiplicity of alternative paths of action, etc., cause some of the members of the group (especially newly recruited ones) to have recourse to ideas which fall outside the once-adhered-to, ideological system of thought.

Although ideological primary groups, whether or not they succeed in their aspiration to rule, inevitably fail in the fulfillment of their global aspirations, they often leave a profound impact on the "normal" pattern of value orientations which they have sought to overcome and which either persists or reasserts itself. They leave behind adherents who survive despite failure and in the face of restoration. Where routinization occurs, as in the case of an ideological elite which is not expelled from authority, the new routine is never the same as the one which it replaced, however much it diverges from the stringent demands of the ideology in the name of which it was originally established.

Once the ideological orientation comes to be passed on to the next generation by tradition as well as by systematic teaching, it encounters the resistances which are characteristic of intergenerational relationships, and these in their turn introduce modification in the direction of compromise and adaptation to primordial and personal needs as well as to civil exigencies. But there, too, the ideological orientation has not lived in vain. Those who appear to reject it or to have become more indifferent to it live under a tradition which has absorbed at least some of the heightened accents which the ideology has brought to the constellation of elements taken over from the prevailing outlook or suboutlooks.

Where an expansive ideological primary group does not succeed in attaining dominance, if it endures for a substantial period and has impinged on the awareness of the custodians of the central institutional and value system, it precipitates a partial reorientation of the previously dominant outlook, bringing about a new emphasis within the framework of the older outlook. It renews sensibilities, it heightens consciousness of the demands of moral and cognitive orientations which have slipped into a state of partial ineffectiveness. The old order against which it contended is never the same because the old order has adapted itself and assimilated into itself some of the emphases of the ideology.

Truth and Ideology

The question of the relationship between truth and ideology has been raised by the tradition of European thought which culminated in Marxism and in the sociology of knowledge developed by Karl Mannheim. According to this view, ideology was by its nature untruthful since it entailed a "masking" or "veiling" of unavowed and unperceived motives or "interests." These "interests" impelled the deception of antagonists and the transfiguration of narrow sectional ends and interests through their ostensible universalization. They distorted reality to the ideologists as well as to their antagonists. Ideology was a manifestation of a "false consciousness," and, given the position of the ideologists in the historical process and in the development of the spirit, it could not be otherwise.

Viewed from a more dispassionate standpoint, which is less involved in a particular historical metaphysic and less involved in proving everyone else wrong and itself incontestably and cosmically right, the question of the compatibility of scientific or scholarly truth with ideology does not admit of a single univocal answer. Ideologies, like all complex cognitive patterns, contain many propositions, and even though the ideologies strive and claim to possess systematic integration, this is seldom the case. Hence, true propositions can coexist with false ones. Ideologies hostile to the prevailing outlook and the central institutional system of that society have, not infrequently, contained truthful propositions about important particular features of the existing order, or they have pointed to particular variables, which were either not perceived or not acknowledged by scholars and thinkers who took a more affirmative or at least a less alienated attitude towards the existing order. On the other hand, they have no less frequently been in fundamental error about very important aspects of social structure, especially about the working of the central institutional system, about which they have had so many hostile fantasies.

With reference to the cognitive truthfulness of ideologies, it should be pointed out that no great ideology has ever regarded the disciplined pursuit of truth by the procedures and in the mood characteristic of modern science as part of its obligations. The very conception of an autonomous sphere and an autonomous tradition of disciplined intellectual activity is alien to the totalistic demands of the ideological orientation. Ideologies do not accredit the independent cognitive powers and strivings of man. This view is shared by the proposition that ideologies must necessarily be distortions of reality because they are impelled by considerations of prospective advantage or of interest. Like the ideological orientation, the view that asserts the inevitability of false consciousness assumes that cognitive motives and standards play little part in the determination of success or failure in the assessment of reality. It assumes that training in observation and discrimination, discipline in their exercise, rational criticism, and intellectual tradition are of little importance in the formation of propositions about reality. This is obviously incorrect in principle—even though, in reality, evaluative and therewith ideological orientations have often hampered the free exercise of the powers of reason, observation, and judgment. Its incorrectness must be acknowledged as such by those who assert that all knowledge is ideological and truth cannot be discerned because interests and passions interfere—at least if they believe in the truthfulness of their own assertion.

It is, of course, true that the ideological culture—in the sense described earlier—does in fact often interfere with the attainment of truth. To the extent that it does so, it is, however, a result of the closure of the ideological disposition to new evidence and its distrust of all who do not share the same ideological disposition. The chief source of tension between ideology and truth lies, therefore, in the demands of the exponents of ideologies for disciplined adherence on the part of their fellow believers, and their concurrent insistence on the unity of belief and conduct. Both these features of the ideological orientation make for dogmatic inflexibility and unwillingness to allow new experiences to contribute to the growth of truth. This applies particularly to the social sciences, the subject matter of which overlaps so considerably with that of ideology, and which is therefore so often the object of ideological and quasi-ideological judgments. The tension is less pronounced with respect to the natural sciences. There, too, however, since ideologies concern themselves with man's nature and the nature of the universe, and because they insist on the unity of knowledge, they inhibit the growth of understanding. Thus, however great the insight contained in some ideologies, the potentialities for the further development of understanding within the context of the ideology or by the efforts of the ideologists—especially where the proponents succeed in establishing control of the central institutional system, and above all of the central cultural institutional system—are hampered and deformed.

A related question, which has often been discussed, is whether all forms of scientific knowledge in the natural and social sciences are parts of ideologies. In the sense in which ideology has been defined and used in the foregoing analysis, this proposition must be rejected. The great advances in scientific knowledge have been influenced here and there by fragments of ideologies or quasi ideologies, just as they have been influenced by prevailing outlooks and suboutlooks. (The latter by virtue of their inherent pluralism allow more freedom for the uninhibited exercise of the cognitive powers of man.) But science is not and has never been an integral part of an ideological culture. The spirit in which science works is alien to ideology. Marxism is the only great ideology which has had a substantial scientific content, and the social sciences have in certain respects benefited from it. Nonetheless, the modern social sciences have not grown up in the context of ideologies, and their progress has carried with it an erosion of ideology. It is true that the social sciences have formed part of the prevailing outlook or suboutlooks of sectors of the educated classes of various modern societies. They have often been oppositional and critical toward various aspects of the existing social and cultural systems—but they have been so more as parts of some suboutlook rather than as part of an ideology. Strictly understood, they have absorbed and attenuated bits of ideologies but they themselves have not been either ideologies or parts of ideologies. They have not been ideological. Indeed, they have had a solvent effect on ideologies and in a sense are antiideological.

Insofar as the social sciences have been genuinely intellectual undertakings, with their own rules of observation and judgment, open to criticism and revision, they have not been ideological and are in fact antipathetic to ideology. The fact that they have come increasingly to contribute to the prevailing outlook of their respective societies is not and cannot be a judgment concerning their truthfulness.

All this is not intended to deny that scientific activities and outlooks, both in procedure and in substance, are parts of a general culture or in the sense used above, a prevailing outlook. But they are very loosely integrated parts of those cultures or outlooks—just as the various parts of science are not completely integrated among themselves. It is characteristic of prevailing outlooks to be loosely integrated, and no single element predominates exclusively over the others. In a great variety of ways the scientific and nonscientific parts of prevailing outlooks and suboutlooks influence each other, and at the same time each possesses considerable autonomy. It is likely that this relationship will become more intense in the future and that scientific knowledge, although never becoming exclusively dominant, will have an even greater influence on prevailing outlooks and suboutlooks than it has had hitherto. For all these reasons, assertions to the effect that "science is an ideology" or "the social sciences are as ideological as the ideologies they criticize" must be rejected.

The End of Ideology

In the 1950s, with the beginning of the "thaw" in the communist countries and the growing disillusionment about the realization of Marxist ideology in the advanced countries, reference was frequently made to an "end of ideology." The conception was originally intended by those who propounded it to refer to the then obtaining situation. Antagonists of the idea took it, however, to imply that ideologies in the sense used in this article could never again exist. They took it also to mean that ideals, ethical standards, general or comprehensive social views and policies, were no longer either relevant or possible in human society. This was a misunderstanding engendered to some extent by the failure of both proponents and critics of the concept of the "end of ideology" to distinguish between ideology and outlook. A better understanding of the distinction might have obviated much of the contention. It is still worthwhile to attempt to clarify some of the issues raised by the phrase.

In the first place, it is obvious that no society can exist without a cognitive, moral, and expressive culture. Standards of truth, beauty, goodness are inherent in the structure of human action. The culture which is generated from cognitive, moral, and expressive needs and which is transmitted and sustained by tradition is part of the very constitution of society. Thus every society, having a culture, will have a complex set of orientations toward man, society, and the universe in which ethical and metaphysical propositions, aesthetic judgments, and scientific knowledge will be present. These will form the outlooks and suboutlooks of the society. Thus there can never be an "end" of outlooks or suboutlooks. The contention arose from the failure to distinguish these and ideology in the sense here understood.

But the theoretical conception implicit in the idea of "the end of ideology" goes further than this. It asserts not only that the culture referred to is capable of being in a state of loose integration, with much autonomy of its different parts, but that in fact the ongoing cultures of societies of any considerable degree of differentiation are bound most of the time to be in that state, and that they cannot be completely supplanted by ideologies. This same implicit theory regards an ideological state of high integration of the elements of a culture to be a marginal state and a highly unstable one. The ideological state is one which is incapable of enduring extension to an entire society.

The exponents of the "end of ideology" were taking note of (a) the recession of the titanic attempts in Europe to extend the ideologies of fascism and communism to entire societies, and (b) the diminution of the belief among Western intellectuals that such extensions were enduringly possible and desirable.

Moreover, the exponents of the "end of ideology" did not assert or imply that the human race had reached a condition or a stage of development in and after which ideologies could no longer occur. The potentiality for ideology seems to be a permanent part of the human constitution. In conditions of crisis when hitherto prevailing elites fail and are discredited, when the central institutions and culture with which they associate themselves seem unable to find the right course of action, ideological propensities are heightened. The need for a direct contact with the sources or powers of creativity and legitimacy and for a comprehensive organization of life permeated by those powers is an intermittent and occasional need in most human beings and an overwhelming and continued need in a few. The confluence of the aroused need in the former with the presence of the latter generates and intensifies ideological orientations. As long as human societies are afflicted by crises, and as long as man has a need to be in direct contact with the sacred, ideologies will recur. The strongly ideological elements in the tradition contained in the modern Western outlook are almost a guarantee of the persistent potentiality. The idea of the "end of ideology" was only an assertion that the potentiality for ideology need not always be realized, and that the potentiality was receding in the West, in the fifties. It asserted that this was coming to be recognized and that both the facts and their recognition were desirable for the good ordering of society and man's well-being.

10

INTELLECTUALS AND THE CENTER OF SOCIETY IN THE UNITED STATES

I

The primary intellectual roles are constituted by: (1) the creation of patterns or symbols of general significance through the action of the imagination and the exercise of observational and rational powers and their precipitation into works, (2) the cultivation of the stocks of intellectual works, and (3) the transmission through interpretation of the traditions of intellectual works to those who have not yet experienced them. The secondary role is the performance of intellectual-practical (or intellectual-executive) actions in which intellectual works are intimately involved.

Each of these roles has a culture which may, for analytical purposes, be distinguished into a substantive culture, which consists of beliefs, categories of perception, and rules referring to the performance of the role, and a penumbral culture, which asserts beliefs about the value and dignity of the role and the works produced in it, and about the actual and proper relationship of the performers of intellectual roles and those who perform other roles in society.

Those who perform intellectual roles constitute the intellectual classes. The intellectual classes differ from society to society in composition and structure. They differ, for example, with respect to numbers or size; they differ in their distribution over the various types of intellectual roles and in the genres of works which they produce. They differ in their creative powers and in their knowledge of and attachment to the stocks and traditions of works; in their degree of internal differentiation and specialization. They differ too in the magnitude of their performance of secondary, intellectual-executive roles in their respective societies, in the degree of integration with other elites of their society, and in their influence on these elites and therewith on the working of their societies. The intellectual classes also differ in their penumbral intellectual culture, that is, their beliefs about intellectual actions and intellectual roles and about the proper place of intellectual actions and intellectuals in society.

Intellectuals exercise influence on their societies—on the predominantly nonintellectual institutions and elites of their own societies—through the works produced in their primary and the actions performed in their secondary roles. Their influence is a function of the attitudes of the nonintellectual elites—political, economic, military—toward intellectual works, intellectual institutions, and intellectuals; it is also a function of the reception of intellectual culture by the nonintellectual elites and of the establishment by the nonintellectual elites of secondary, intellectual-executive roles in the executive subsystems of society. The changes in the secondary roles of intellectuals in the United States and in their penumbral culture constitute the theme of what follows.

In most societies, prior to the present century, intellectuals exercised such influence as they did mainly through the creation of patterns of belief which permeated the outlook of the nonintellectual elites, usually very slowly and with long delay. They were enabled to do this by serving as tutors, courtiers, advisers and by their contribution to the creation of the intellectual ambience in which rulers moved. Through the preaching and exemplification of religious beliefs and precepts they also influenced the mass of the population more directly. When they performed intellectual-executive roles as civil servants or as ecclesiastical administrators, they acted in accordance with a code which was part of their secondary, penumbral traditions. Insofar as authority could be said to govern the working of their respective societies, they shared in this control. They were very seldom actually rulers, because ruling and the process of preparation for accession to ruling do not combine easily with the performance of the primary intellectual actions. (There have, however, been a few striking exceptions to this rule.)

The penumbral culture of intellectuals in the West, particularly in modern times, has included a marked distrust, and even abhorrence, of the nonintellectual elites in politics and in the economy. Institutions, established traditions, incumbents of positions of authority, and intellectuals who have accepted these have come in for severe criticism and rejection. This particular secondary, penumbral tradition has varied among western societies and in different epochs of each of these societies. Present-day American society is an instance of a society in which the intellectuals—literary, humanistic, and academic—for a century were alienated in sentiment and imagery from the nonintellectual elites, both national and local. They shared only slightly in the exercise of authority in American society, which reproduced itself and developed with minimal participation by its contemporary intellectuals. This structure changed in the second third of the twentieth century. The society became an increasingly "intellectual-based" and "knowledge-based" society. Education became an object of universal aspiration as a means to a better life and a higher social status. American society became a national society in which the distance between center and periphery was diminished through the formation of a common national identity, common foci of attention, and a common constellation of values. These major changes, which were not the only ones—nor were they by any means total and comprehensive in their extension into all sectors of American society—were accompanied by major changes in the structure and culture of the intellectual classes. Intellectual institutions proliferated, and the numbers of intellectuals grew correspondingly. As the number and proportion of intellectual-executive roles increased and with them the proportion of intellectuals formed in intellectual institutions and incumbent in such roles, the outlook of sectors of the nonintellectual elites absorbed many elements of the intellectuals' ethos.

The incorporation of intellectuals into the exercise of authority and influence in a society has usually been accompanied by their attachment to the central value system. The confluence of these two processes of incorporation into the central institutional system and of attachment to the central value system strengthened the former and secured internal peace, Naturally, it could not protect that society from all the vicissitudes of uncontrollable ecological and demographic changes, from the emergence of new centers of power outside itself and the inevitable ravages which are consequent on the limits of foresight, neglect, pride, rigidity of judgment, and un-adaptedness of conduct. In the United States, however, incorpora-tion, having had a strengthening effect for a third of a century, has generated in the latter part of the sixties a regressive effect. In consequence of their expanded numbers, their more frequent incumbency of authoritative roles, and the great permeation of their ethos resultant from the increased prominence and predominance of intellectual institutions, the developmental and integrative processes of American society have been obstructed. Authority has been weakened; the center of society has been placed in a moral shadow.

II

From the Jacksonian revolution until the administration of Franklin Roosevelt, intellectuals, particularly literary and humanistic-publicistic intellectuals in the United States, found much to distress them in the actions and culture of the ruling groups of their society. The long persistent, indeed, still lingeringly persistent, preoccupation of American intellectuals—especially literary men and humanistic publicists—with Europe was part of an attachment to a culture in which they thought intellectuals "counted." The preoccupation with Europe was dominated by the fact that Europe was, in literature, in science, in scholarship, and in art, the very center of creativity. They were also awed, though sometimes resentfully, by European power—that sheer economic and military might which was dominant, with only intermittent challenges, throughout Asia, Africa, and Latin America. In these three continents, paradoxically, the very success of the movement for independence corroborated the centrality of Europe. These features of cultural creativity and military and economic power of the European metropolis were very influential in the formation of the American intellectuals' image of Europe. They should not, however, obscure the utopian function of Europe for American intellectuals. Europe was, for American intellectuals a place where intellectuals were respected and taken seriously by those strata of society which exercised power.

When American intellectuals between the Civil War and the First World War looked at Europe, what did they see? In London, for much of the nineteenth century, politics and literature moved in overlapping circles. Disraeli, who was a famous novelist, had been a prime minister; other prime ministers, Gladstone for example, were classical scholars and students of theology. The British universities, above all Oxford, were the breeding grounds of famous politicians and the training schools for the highest class of the civil service both at home and in the empire.[1]

Dr. Maurice Dobb, the communist and economist of Trinity College, Cambridge, in a book published in Great Britain in 1928 ruefully compared Great Britain with the Continent, where revolutionary Marxism had found academic and otherwise learned proponents and expositors.[2] But to vaguely socialist American intellectuals of the time, the British condition at that time seemed almost paradisical. The Labour Party carried in its diadem such gems as Harold Laski, G. D. H. Cole, R. H. Tawney, and the Webbs—all intellectuals, some of them academic and all of them ostensibly influential. The Conservative Party, despite its serried ranks of "hard-faced businessmen who had made a good thing out of war," studiously maintained its Oxford connection. To many American intellectuals Oxford was as sustaining a pillar of conservatism and liberalism as the London School of Economics was of socialism— although socialism also had its Oxford adherents. Of France, it was known that Painlevé had been a mathematician and that Raymond Poincaré was the brother of a famous mathematician, that Jaurès had been a great historian, that Clemenceau had edited *l'Aurore*, that Anatole France, Henri Barbusse, and Romain Rolland were prized by Communist Party leaders. It was known that men of letters were honored by official distinctions and by banquets. It was known that in the Dreyfus affair a small circle of intellectuals had formed a party on behalf of the victim; the individual action of Emile

1. The American Rhodes scholars' image of Oxford in relation to British politics and the influence of this impression on American intellectuals' attitudes is a subject which deserves attention. Especially important in this regard are recollections of eminent British politicans coming to speak at the Oxford Union.

2. He cited "Labriola and Ferri in Italy . . . Kautsky, Bebel, Cunow and Luxemburg in Germany . . . Hilferding and Bauer in Austria . . . Struve and Plekhanov in Russia." Nor did Marxism "stir the waters of academic discussion in Oxford, Cambridge, and London, as it did in Berlin, Vienna, Rome, and Petersburg." (Dobb, *Russian Economic Development since the Revolution* [New York: E. P. Dutton & Co., 1928], p. 5).

Zola, one of the most important novelists of his time, undid a great injustice and delivered a staggering blow to the union of reactionaries who had wished, for various base considerations, to allow the earlier condemnation of Captain Dreyfus to stand.

The American intellectuals' image of Germany, vague though it was and very unevenly distributed, was much like their image of France. The academic intellectuals seemed to play a crucial role: the universities trained the higher civil service; the Verein für Sozialpolitik, crammed with professors, acted as if its declarations were respectfully listened to and seriously considered; learned lawyers sat in the Reichstag. Had not the Frankfurt parliament of 1848 been called the "professors' parliament"? Even the trade union movement was struggled over by intellectuals—a few of them university graduates and self-educated persons who vied with each other and other intellectuals in doctrinal disputes. Was not a great socialist intellectual, Lassalle, one of the fathers of the German trade union movement? Professors were sometimes nominated to be privy councillors (*Geheimräte*) and they were generally held in awe.

European artists too, despite their alienation in their respective societies, were regarded, from the obscurity in which American intellectuals thought they themselves were forced to live, as existing within the charismatic circle. European artists received commissions to adorn public buildings; there were officially maintained academies of art; modern art had its patrons among the wealthy and influential who were encouraged and educated by able dealers.

Even Russia, barbaric Russia, appeared to give a place to intellectuals which their American counterparts believed the United States did not provide. If it did not honor or patronize them, it at least persecuted them. Persecution was a form of attention. The greatest of all, Tolstoi, a count, which was not forgotten, criticized the czarist regime and Russian society for its moral degradation, and because he was so great and so famous internationally, the regime could do nothing to him. Dostoievsky had a halter put round his neck for having attended a meeting of the Petrashevsky circle, where Bielinsky's open letter denouncing Gogol's religious turn had been read. Turgenev, who had in the last part of the nineteenth century been regarded as second only to Tolstoi, was constrained to live abroad in exile. All this attention from czarist authority was regarded as a sort of honor.[3] Abroad, eminent intellectuals like Kropotkin and Vinogradoff denounced from visible positions the czarist autocracy. What was true of the Russians was true of other European countries: the revolutionaries were intellectuals. Engagement with the authorities, even subversive engagement, was at least a certain kind of intimacy. American intellectuals did not even have this gratification.

This in its roughest outlines was the map of the relations between intellectuals and the powers as it was perceived by many American intellectuals over the course of nearly a century, but particularly since the end of the Civil War. Looking around at their own situations, what did they find? Public life was a shambles, corruption rampant, mammon enthroned, and the muses rusticated, unregarded, disrespected, sometimes even, in spectacular cases, persecuted. The fate of *Leaves of Grass,* of Dreiser's early novels, the scandal of Maxim Gorki's "wife," the trial of Art Young, Max Eastman, and the editors of *The Masses* stood out as characteristic episodes. The trial of *Madame Bovary*, the humiliation and destruction of Oscar Wilde, the arrest of Bertrand Russell and his removal from his fellowship at Trinity College, the *Lex Arens*—these did not darken the American intellectuals' picture of the special relationship of European intellectuals and their powers.

American politicians appeared to their fellow countrymen to be very different from European politicians. Edmund Wilson epitomized a view which had been widely held when he wrote: "Our society has finally produced in its specialized professional politicians one of the most useless and obnoxious groups which has perhaps ever disgraced human history—a group that seems unique among the governing classes in having managed to be corrupt, uncultivated and incompetent all at once.[4]

3. This masochistic yearning is still not dead. Only a few years ago, Miss McCarthy wrote in *The New York Review of Books* that the persecution of Siniavsky and Daniel by the Soviet government was evidence that literature was taken seriously by the Soviet government. She contrasted this with the example of the unworthy United States government, which demonstrated its indifference to letters by abstention from interference with the freedom of writers.

4. "An Appeal to Progressives" *The New Republic* 14th Jan. 1931, reprinted in *The Shores of Light: A Literary Chronicle of the Twenties and Thirties.* (London: W. H. Allen, 1952) p. 529.

The businessmen were of a piece. Among literary men, especially those who made the running from the Civil War onward, business-men had a very bad press. There were very few like Dreiser who admired power so much that a figure like Cowperwood, the hero of *The Financier,* could be made acceptable by sheer force of character. The army offered no respectable career; the church was hopeless: the Roman Catholic hierarchy was the epitome of benightedness, and the Protestants ranging from the despicable stuffiness and sycophancy of the Espiscopalians and the Presbyterians in the presence of the mighty to the innumerable sects of ranters and Bible-pounders who had fallen out of the bottom of the Baptists and Methodists were no better. The civil service had never been an object of aspiration to American intellectuals:[5] here and there one of them was ingloriously employed in it, Melville as a minor official in the customs service, Whitman a clerk in the attorney-general's office, some sound scientists in the Department of Agriculture. The diplo-matic and consular services, despite the xenotropism of the intellec-tuals, were tarred with the brush of government and politics. Few intellectuals sought their place in them—there were a few major exceptions, mainly from New England—and in any case the selection of ambassadors through political patronage gave intellectuals little opportunity.

The society at large appalled them. For the most part, American scholarly and literary intellectuals lived in a world they never made and for which they took no responsibility. But they were not immune to the claims of the primordial ties. They suffered from their membership in a society to which they were bound by an unexpungible identity and which at the same time revolted them. They were perverted patriots bound to a country from which they could not release themselves and which they could not love. The self-exiled Americans in Paris lived among other Americans. Few were able to denationalize themselves even by long residence abroad.

---

5. One of the major public actions of American intellectuals between the Civil War and the Spanish-American War was the campaign to reform the civil service. This would have entailed replacing the power which politicians exercised in the form of patronage by appointment on the basis of educational qualifications and performance in examinations.

III

American intellectuals were pained by their membership in a society, the rulers of which seemed to have no need for them. This was partly a misunderstanding. They could not have come into existence in the United States had the government and the society been totally antiintellectual. Universities were maintained with increasing munificence after about 1880; periodicals with quite large audiences and of a respectable intellectual level existed, giving intellectuals, literary men and publicists places for the publication of their shorter and some of their longer works. There were publishing firms which produced their works and sold them to an American audience. It is true that there prevailed a puritanical attitude in the cultural and intellectual institutions, and these were not wholly sympathetic with the "advanced" views of the new European realism—which for that matter was encountering difficulties in Europe too.

There was a demand for intellectual services in the United States in the latter part of the nineteenth and the early part of the twentieth centuries. The federal government, despite the antiintellectualism of many politicians and the low estimate in which officials were held, probably employed more intellectuals than most European governments. Many intellectuals were hidden away in the Surgeon-General's Office, in the Geological Survey, in the Bureau of Indian Affairs, in the Patent Office, and latterly in the Department of Agriculture, which in time became a leading intellectual institution in agricultural economics and statistics. They were, however, obscure and they did not move in the circles of the powerful. They worked peacefully and quietly and they were unknown to the great world. They were specialists, and the literary and humanistic intellectuals had little sense of affinity with them. The country was huge and there were many colleges and universities; the literary and humanistic intellectuals did not usually pass through the same institutions as the scientific civil service. But even if a sense of affinity had existed, it would not have overcome the feeling of exclusion. The scientific civil servants were servants. They were not masters; they did not make major policies or associate with those who did. Although progressive politicians in the Northwest and in Wisconsin brought academic social scientists into their councils, the same did not happen on the federal level to any extent which the intellectuals cared to remark.

It was from the great world that the intellectuals felt excluded. It was in the great world—the center of society where it appeared that decisions were made and where the regalia reposed—that the intellectuals felt the cold wind of indifference and perhaps contempt.

And they were largely correct in this.

The political elite felt no need for the support or the collaboration of the literary and humanistic intellectuals and it did not seek their company.[6] For the most part, the political elite in the United States had come up through long service in the political machines, where in the rough and tumble of the ill-educated, they had learned the arts of compromise and combination and even more unsavory things. The American political elite was by and large the product of a populistic polity and had not, by origin or by association, acquired the refinements of European political elites drawn from the aristocracy and gentry and the professional classes.[7] The American political elite by and large, and least of all at the municipal and state levels where political apprenticeships had to be served and support had to be elicited, did not think that they needed the company and still less the services of literary and humanistic intellectuals. Scientists were regarded by politicians as all right—in their place, which was not in the political arena. Nor did the intellectuals seek to enter politics: the hurly-burly of low company was not to their taste and without a capacity to stand such company, the chances of a political career were slight. What a contrast between this and the occasional British practice of patronizing a well-connected young man, freshly down from Oxford, and granting him an opportunity to stand for a parliamentary constituency! The American system was not judged favorably with respect to this difference.

Nor did the big businessmen think they needed university graduates, even scientists, in their firms. Only the chemical industry employed university graduates in large numbers; the chemists were

6. Theodore Roosevelt was far more friendly with Rudyard Kipling than he was with any American literary men of comparable quality.

7. American intellectuals, particularly the humanistic intellectuals and some of the non-bohemian literary men, had for a long time a belief in the superiority of the genteel and the well-born. This lasted until well into the 1920s and it faded only with the Great Depression. This naturally nurtured a prejudice against the uncouth politician in his "long-johns," his galluses, his string necktie, and his chewing tobacco. Long after the respect for gentility has disappeared and the backwoodsman among legislators has become rare, the stereotype persists.

kept in research and in production but they rose in management only after they had lightened their burden of scientific curiosity. Agriculture too made use of scientists in the state agricultural research stations. They had a significant part in the advance of American agriculture and they were respected by farmers. The agricultural scientists were, however, specialists. They were local and not national notables and they regarded themselves as scientists and not as part of a larger class of intellectuals. Iron and steel, coal mining, and the railways, on the other hand—the great industries of the industrial expansion of the half-century between the Civil War and the First World War were the industries in which the great free-booting capitalists operated—had no use for intellectuals. The technological and managerial innovations which gave these industries their central place in the American economy and which enabled the American economy to come to the forefront of the world, arose from within the industries themselves. They were not the products of research done by university-trained scientists and engineers. The great capitalists who patronized art patronized either long-dead painters or society painters, disesteemed by the intellectuals, who regarded themselves as custodians of the more advanced "European" culture. Even those plutocrats who were generous patrons of academic learning associated very little with scholars if they were not also university presidents; they did not associate even that much with literary men.

Banking progressed without economists; the federal government likewise eschewed the knowledge and wisdom of economists, although Wisconsin and a few other progressive states drew on such knowledge as they possessed. Such social work as there was, was done by local politicians and by amateurs of the prosperous classes, some of whom were strong personalities and outstanding intelligences who became important humanitarian reformers. Only in the press, in the churches, and in the reformist politics of certain states of the Midwest and Northwest did a certain kind of intellectual hold his own among the incumbents of the central institutions. In the press, where the reportorial function was regarded as a proper training for a young man aspiring to become a naturalistic novelist, a certain robust class of intellectuals was to be found; in the editorial rooms were to be found intellectuals who felt no kinship either with

European intellectual trends or with those Americans who did feel that kinship. Still, the interchange between the press and the literary and the humanistic intellectuals between 1890 and 1910 was more pronounced, above all in the muck-raking era, than that between the intellectuals and any other sector of the elite. In fact it was through the press that American intellectuals reentered the center of society—but they did so as an active counter-elite, depicting the degradations of corrupting plutocrats and corrupt politicians. Some of them stayed on to play a part in the reform politics of Theodore Roosevelt and Woodrow Wilson. By the 1920s much of this participation had disappeared, and it was recalled, by the generation of intellectuals which came to prominence after the First World War, as a failure. All that remained was the reinforcement of an anti-political, anticivil tradition. At the periphery of the Protestant churches, a certain kind of active, social-reforming, Christian intellectual was to be found, but, on the whole, literary and humanistic intellectuals had no affectionate connections with these circles. Theologians and ecclesiastical dignitaries, insofar as they had intellectual roles, were regarded as alien to the valid intellectual tradition. Those who had close connections with the plutocracy and the leading politicians were regarded by literary and humanistic intellectuals as traitors to the true cause of the intellect.

Thus, American society, although it was nurturing a vigorous and creative body of intellectuals of many diverse interests and talents, can scarcely be said to have been structurally dependent on their cooperation, and insofar as it actually was dependent, in agriculture, in the chemical industry and in the scientific civil service, these functions were invisible to those members of the intellectual classes—the literary and humanistic intellectuals—who designated themselves as "the intellectuals" and who had grievances against American society for its neglect of intellectual things. Through much of this period, many of the most accomplished literary and humanistic intellectuals were hostile toward the "practical" elites. They censured the indifference of these other sectors toward intellectual things and, by implication, toward intellectuals. They disapproved of American society because intellectuals were not actually incorporated into its symbolic ornamentation. They thought that a good society, quite apart from any merits it might have in the relations between rulers and ruled or among fellow citizens or in the conduct of parents and children or in the accomplishments of the practitioners of crafts and professions, must, in justice, accord a high status to intellectuals in the circle of rulers. As a result, many intellectuals lived in an "inner exile" and some lived in actual, voluntary exile.

Politicians and businessmen were well aware of this mainly silent, but sometimes harshly expressed, hostility. They paid the intellectuals back in their own coin. They despised them as effete and unmanly, as Anglophile and snobbish. They usually ignored their existence. When American universities began to bestir themselves intellectually from the 1890s onward until the 1930s, academics, mainly in the social sciences, were sporadically harassed, threatened, and dismissed from their posts for criticism of existing economic and political institutions and those who exercised authority in them.[8]

Yet American society prospered, this withdrawal of intellectuals notwithstanding. It was a rough and, in many respects, a callow society but it performed great things. It settled the open country, coped powerfully with nature, and drew great rewards; it attracted vast populations from among the wretched of the earth, assimilated them to a new way of life which prized individual exertion and accomplishment. Its conflicts—except for the Civil War—were not often deep or long-lasting, although they were frequently violent. New tasks were undertaken continuously, and very many were handled with considerable success. Government, despite a long period of pervasive corruption, was brought into increasing responsiveness to popular desires. A common culture was formed out of heterogeneous elements; an inclusive educational system was developed which not only diffused the common culture but also provided the early stages of what later became a prodigious scientific and scholarly creativity. A lively democratic political life was developed, with many glaring defects but generally democratic and competitive withal.

All of this was accomplished with a relatively marginal and

8. Cf. my: "Limitations on the Freedom and Research and Teaching in the Social Sciences," chap. 15, this volume.

diffuse participation of the contemporaneous or recently-living highly educated or the intellectually most creative in the processes through which the society was maintained and developed. Technological innovation was the work of inventors rather than of scientifically educated scientists; the managers of business enterprises drew relatively little from the higher culture of society. The army likewise made little use of the academically trained intellectuals until the Second World War. The growth of the powers of the federal government owed much to the exertions of very strong personalities among legislators, mainly middle western and northwestern populists—usually men of no great culture but intelligent and of strong character, guided in two significant periods by presidents who were professional politicians of outstanding intellectual propensities—one of them Woodrow Wilson, being formerly a professor of political science and a university president as well. Business enterprisers, farmers, professional politicians, journalists, amateur social workers and religious and social reformers, labor leaders, civil servants, school administrators, and judges were the main architects of the growth of American society. The growth of American society was its transformation into an urban and industrial society, liberal and democratic generally in its political institutions and increasingly drawing its heterogeneous, newly entered ethnic segments into a national society and a common culture. Only the rural Negroes in the South as a relatively massive minority and a few small pockets of Red Indians in their reservations were omitted from this contraction of the space between center and periphery. The leading agents of this transformation included only a few intellectuals in crucial and prominent roles. Men like Theodore Roosevelt and Woodrow Wilson, Herbert Croly and Louis Brandeis, John Dewey and Alfred Mahan were very influential in guiding of policies and providing the ideas which led American society into its new form, but they did not affect the image of the antiintellectual character of American society which dominated the thought of American humanistic intellectuals.[9]

9. Again the persistence of this view is manifested in Professor Richard Hofstadter's *Anti-Intellectualism in American Life.* Despite Professor Hofstadter's thorough and scholarly mastery of the facts, his important book permits it to be believed that the antiintellectual Yahoos have had the upper hand at all times.

IV

The coming and conduct of the Second World War greatly widened and complicated the reincorporation of the intellectuals into the center of American society which had begun in the progressive era. The curve which had swung upward in the period of the New Liberalism relapsed, following the First World War, into a trough as deep as any in the nineteenth century. Then in the 1930s at a time when the Great Depression was transforming American society in so many significant respects, the intellectuals reentered the center. The damage to the puritanical ethos which was previously unchallenged, in principle, except for a very small number of reformers and bohemians; the assimilation of Jews into the center; the raising of expectations concerning the creative capacities of governmental action, were among the major effects of the Great Depression. All of these involved the intellectuals, touched on their interests, gave them new opportunities to assert themselves.

Ordinarily, a crisis like the Great Depression disintegrates a society and discredits its elite. In part this is what happened in the United States. The business elite was discredited and so was the incumbent Republican administration. The clergy, associated with the reigning economic and political elites, saw their authority diminished at the top although, at the level of parish and congregation, their devotion and solicitude was a compensation for the diminution of prestige of the higher ecclesiastical authority. The decentralized character of Protestant ecclesiastical organization in the United States helped to save the status of the religious elite. Municipal and state political elites on the other hand would have suffered a further diminution of their already not very high prestige had the new national administration under Franklin Roosevelt not acceded to power. As a result of the indomitable personality of President Roosevelt in the face of every vicissitude and every failure, and the appearance and, to some extent, the reality of effective action by his administration, the legitimacy of the authority of the state governments was saved—undeservedly.

But the chief beneficiaries among the elites of the policies of the Roosevelt administration were the central political elites themselves and the intellectuals. The numerous reforms instituted by or credited to the federal government—first, and most symbolically, the

National Recovery Act itself—the reforms in agriculture which halted and reversed the course of the disasters suffered by the entire rural population, the enactment and implementation of the new social security arrangements, the guarantee of bank deposits, the encouragement and protection given to trade unions of the semi-skilled workers, the various public work schemes, the salvaging of youth through the Civilian Conservation Corps and the National Youth Administration—all of these contributed to the restabilization of American society in a new structure after the disaggregation which had been going on since the end of 1929. The vital personality of President Roosevelt, his moving eloquence and patient compassion, his confident castigation of the failed elites and his imaginative deployment of the constitutional powers and the financial resources available to him offset the previously rising and still very strong current of real deprivations being suffered by most sections of the population.

The traditional structure of recruitment to the higher civil service and the great expansion of governmental activities permitted and necessitated a very large-scale recruitment of civil servants from outside the existing cadres. In a very short time and in a way they did not expect or demand, the aspirations of the civil service reformers of the last quarter of the nineteenth century were brought into reality. The British and German practice of recruitment of the administrative elite from the universities—so much admired for so many years by American intellectuals with civic concerns—was given an approximate American counterpart.

The "Brains Trust" of the presidential campaign of 1932, which drew primarily on Columbia University social scientists, was a foreshadowing of the role which intellectuals were to play throughout the remainder of the Roosevelt administration. President Roosevelt was a loyal Harvard graduate, and he was always ready to permit himself to be identified with the universities. From the very beginning of his term of office, academic intellectuals, primarily professors from the law faculties of the major universities, economists and political scientists as well, were called to the highest offices in practically every new administrative agency. Professors and historians were sent abroad as ambassadors; the National Planning Board, although its chairman was the president's uncle, was replete with academics. The National Academy of Sciences began to move into the role from which it has never since receded. There had never been anything like it in the history of American universities, never anything like it in the history of the American intellectual classes since the formation of the Republic and the drafting and promulgation of the constitution.

Some of these intellectuals were given major administrative responsibilities; on the whole, however, they did not become administrators. Many who were appointed as legal counsel to departments and agencies were assigned the tasks of devising substantive policies to be espoused by the president and to be enacted into legislation by Congress. Even where they had administrative posts, their tasks were to think about policy on behalf of the president. They formed an extended, informal personal cabinet around the president, superseding the actual cabinet.

The outbreak of the war in Europe was followed by a gradual movement toward American participation. The "lend-lease" legislation brought in more academic lawyers and some economists. The entry of America into the war produced a vast proliferation of new organizations. The greatest of these was the Manhattan Project, which drew scientists of many sorts and of the highest quality into government service on a scale never undertaken before in any country or in any epoch. There were many other major scientific projects. Other new organizations which drew on intellectuals to fill their ranks were the Office of Strategic Services, the War Production Board, the Board of Economic Warfare, the Office of Price Administration, and the Office of War Information. Older departments expanded their activities; the Department of State, the Department of Justice, and others added new functions, provided places for intellectuals: university teachers of law, economics, history, geography, and even political science and sociology. Anthropologists and linguists, even teachers of French, German, and English literature and practically every other discipline of the human sciences served in minor policy-making and in important intelligence and administrative capacities in civilian and military organizations. The physical and biological scientists were absorbed to a probably greater extent— there were more of them and there was more precedent and basis for their services. Mathematicians and statisticians were heavily drawn upon. For the most part, these academics were glad of the vacation from teaching and they enjoyed the excitement of proximity to great events and to great authority as well as the occasional exercise of power on their own.

The war was in part a contest of industrial strength and skill. Industry and agriculture in the two decades preceding the war had become much more "science-based." From chemistry and agriculture, science extended its dominion into the communications industry and its industrial supplements. Engineering in its various branches was becoming more and more scientific and therewith more intellectual. Statistics began to be more widely used in many branches of economic life and in government; the Roosevelt administration greatly increased the scale of statistical services of the federal government, although the Hoover administration had already shown the way forward from the stimulus given to it by Hoover himself when he was secretary of commerce in the Coolidge administration.

Nonetheless, it was war production itself which extended so much the domain of the "science-based" industry. The war therefore became a contest of mobilized intellect working through or on the basis of research.

The combination of opportunities to carry on work which was a continuation of their peacetime activities with immeasurably greater resources and in contexts which excited by their proximity to power together with their affirmation of the general purpose of the war, brought American intellectuals into solidarity with the political and even the business and military elites of the country. Many who had been fellow travelers of the Communist Party in the 1930s rallied to the government after the period of embarrassment which lasted from the signing of the Ribbentrop-Molotov agreement in September 1938 to the German invasion of Russia in June 1941. It is true that those with firm Stalinist attachments gave only a conditional affirmation to the government, but they too shared even if only superficially and hypocritically in the general consensus of the intellectuals. In contrast with the First World War, when many Americans had expressed reservations about America's engagement in the war, there were few pacifists or conscientious objectors.

Isolationism among intellectuals—which had been slight enough in any case—almost disappeared during the war.[10] Those who were pro-German or pro-Japanese or pro-Italian were infinitesimal in number, and those who served the enemy directly, as did Ezra Pound abroad or George Sylvester Viereck at home, had no audience among American intellectuals in their traitorous activities.

V

When the Second World War ended, the unanimity of intellectuals was broken by the reemergence of the Stalinists and their fellow travelers maneuvering for protective cover behind Henry Wallace and by small circles of Trotskyites and miscellaneous non-Stalinist sects. There remained a very comprehensive consensus. Most of the leading intellectuals in the natural and social sciences and the humanities who had been in governmental and military service, returned to academic life, but they did not give up their sense of being at the center. Many of them retained an active relationship with the government, either with the Department of Defense or with other governmental or quasi-governmental bodies, which wished to retain the connection with intellectuals formed during the war, with such happy results. New research institutions were established, living mainly from government research contracts, and some of them were able to attract natural and social scientists of a very high quality. This too maintained a sense of affinity with the center.

The end of the war saw the emergence into public light of a new phenomenon in the United States: pressure groups of scientists seeking to influence governmental policy through public agitation, representations to legislators and to the highest levels of executive branch. The Szilard-Einstein letter to President Roosevelt was the first step in this process. The atomic scientists' movement, of which the *Bulletin of Atomic Scientists* and the Pugwash meetings are the

10. Stalinists, prosperous German-American businessmen, congressmen who remembered the inquiries into the munitions industry, and some Irish-Americans were the main opponents of America's aid to Britain after the fall of France. Robert Hutchins and Charles Beard, who stuck to their isolationism until the very declaration of war, did not have many sympathizers among intellectuals.

monuments, was a remarkable expression of civility in a sector of the American intellectual classes, which except for a slight rash of Stalinism in the 1930s, had never concerned itself much with politics.

The expansion of the universities greatly increased the opportunities for teaching and research appointments and salaries increased. There were more graduate students to work with, and libraries improved. For many university teachers, especially those who had completed their studies early in the Great Depression and who had, despite the niggardliness of those times, survived, the situation seemed beyond the dreams of avarice. Carrying out scientific and scholarly research did not seem incompatible with serving the government; there seemed to be an identity of interests. It did not seem anomalous that the government should support these activities. Its goodwill towards intellectuals—despite McCarthyism—appeared to be self-evident. Through an elaborate system of federal government support, scientists at their universities did research in which the military was sufficiently interested to provide financial support—although it should be emphasized that much of this research had only the most tenuous connection with military practice. The profusion of opportunities and resources turned many heads and bred a state of mind in which all things seemed possible because the reign of scarcity appeared to have ended.

Industry and commerce had learned from the wartime experience of the government and from the conduct of the war and they too sought the services of the intellectuals—mainly chemists, physicists, mathematicians, statisticians, and economists. The tremendous expansion of television and advertising absorbed many literary and artistic intellectuals or provided supplementary income for them. The affluence of the country enabled literary men to benefit from the prodigality of private foundations; grants for young and established writers became common, and the shift of emphasis at the undergraduate level of the universities to expression rather than learning and to presentness rather than pastness gave literary men an entrée to the universities such as had been previously unknown.

American intellectuals were now honored in their own country. They felt honored. Even literary intellectuals who had not enjoyed the enormous prosperity of the academic intellectuals felt their tradition of alienation being eroded.[11] Some tried to remind themselves that it was not their calling to affirm the principles embodied in the practices of their society, Others were well aware of the dilemma created by their new functions and the larger intellectual consensus in confrontation with the traditions in which they had grown up. The general revulsion against Stalinism as practiced in the Soviet Union and the "people's democracies" and by the Communist Party of the United States made it easier for intellectuals who had in the past been uncompromisingly anti-capitalist to reconcile themselves to postwar America.[12]

By the end of the 1940s, America had become the center of the world. The increasing number of American intellectuals—academic

11. The two symposia conducted by the *Partisan Review* were expressive of what was happening among the chief heirs of the tradition of alienation among literary and humanistic intellectuals. Cf. Arvin, Newton, et al., *America and the Intellectuals,* PR Series no. 4 (New York, 1953), (originally published as "Our Country and Our Culture." *Partisan Review,* 1952). Cf. also Agee, James, et al., *Religion and the Intellectuals.* PR series no. 3 (New York, 1950).

12. By the end of the 1950s, the truth about the Stalinist purges had been accepted by most intellectuals in the United States. Khrushchev's revelations of February 1956 at the 22nd Congress of the Communist Party of the Soviet Union was only a final and authoritative confirmation of what had already been generally recognized. Attachment to the center of American society included awareness of the moral value of material well-being, individual freedom, and a pluralistic structure of society. None of these had been attained in the communist countries, where the two latter had been deliberately suppressed on the ground that their suppression was a necessary condition for the attainment of the former, which had nonetheless remained unattained. The issues raised by the Soviet Union dominated the international perspective of American intellectuals after the war, in part because in fact the communists had mounted a very vociferous intellectual campaign before the war which had touched the conscience and influenced the cognitive maps of many American intellectuals. In any case, the evident superiority of the United States to the Soviet Union in the very categories which communists insisted should be applied to the assessment of the merits of societies, and the disillusionment about the Soviet Union among those who had once been enthusiasts, made for readiness to appreciate American society.

There was one rift in the lute. This was the first McCarthyism which disturbed the atmosphere of the decade after the war, harrying fellow travelers, doing considerable damage in a small number of instances, intimidating communists and quasi-communists, and discrediting American society in the minds of men who would have wished to reaffirm their connection with it. Much more lastingly damaging was the impediment which it formed to the healing of the breach between American literary and publicistic intellectuals who had grown up in a tradition of alienation and American politicians at a time when so many other factors tended to erode this tradition. McCarthyism reinforced it.

and literary—who went abroad, thanks to the largesse of their government and the private philanthropic foundations, were made aware of this. The bitterness of the anti-Americanism among foreign intellectuals only testified to their preoccupation with America; not only were foreign societies being "Coco-Colonized" but their intellectuals could not resist the fascination of America. American intellectuals were even less able to resist the attractive power of the centrality of the United States. From the condition of being peripheral in a society which they believed was culturally provincial, American intellectuals came to see themselves as effective members of the center of an intellectual metropolis. Their earlier feelings of provinciality had not been experienced as a happy condition. They embraced with enthusiasm the escape from peripherality in a province to centrality in a metropolis.

The gratification over incorporation into the center probably derives some of its impetus from the fact that many of the intellectuals of the generation which came into prominence from the 1930s onward were of Jewish, mainly Eastern European Jewish, origin. They were the first generation of the offspring of the immigrants who came to the United States in such great numbers between the mid-1880s and about 1912. Intellectual aptitude and intellectual passion were coupled with social ambition. The white Anglo-Saxon protestant ascendancy was still publicly unchallenged, and to move in their company was regarded by many Jewish intellectuals, however radical some of them were, as a good thing. The attainment of that ideal, in association with and through intellectual accomplishment, could be a cause of self-congratulation.

But at the root of this affirmation was the reality of a strong state. Although the dominant, most visible tradition of American intellectuals of almost all kinds has been that of distrust toward the regnant political and economic powers, it has ever since the 1880s at least, been associated with a tradition which asserts that the ills of society can be cured by a strong and virtuous authority. Long before American intellectuals became socialists, Stalinists, Trotskyists or whatever, they believed that "the state should do it." When the idea of planning, very simplistically conceived, came upon the scene, it was seized upon as the right solution. It was no wonder that at a time when the mythology of planning was most flourishing, so many intellectuals came under Stalinist influence. They were, however, only sharers in the common intellectual culture. A strong state was their ideal. The strong and active state of the long administration of President Roosevelt gratified this desire.

VI

Education has always been regarded as a good thing in America. The state universities and the land grant colleges as well as the universality of public education without fees and the late school-leaving age were evidence of this. Science, too, had been spoken of in terms of awe and in anticipation of benefits. But pure science, abstract thought and the life of letters tended to be treated with levity and disparagement. In the period after the Second World War, higher education, scientific, technological, and, to a lesser extent, humanistic research and belles lettres, were all elevated—although not uniformly. In this period what had been esteemed became more esteemed; what had been disparaged or taken lightly was treated more seriously and in good earnest. The munificent support of higher education and research in private and state universities by federal and state governments and the readiness of businessmen to support higher education and research in private universities, both bespoke the widespread conviction of the nonintellectual elites of the value, practical and glorious, of the intellectuals. The intellectuals were of the same view. It appeared as if an old dream had come true.

Through the length and breadth of the academic and non-academic intellectual classes, particularly in the natural and social sciences, this self-serving view was espoused. Grants and subsidies for study and research were available, and even those who were in principle opposed to the government and "the system" were able to avail themselves of such benefits and were eager to do so.[13]

There was little dissent by the intellectuals from the obligation laid upon the universities to educate and train persons who could fill all the various roles in the higher level of government and business administration and technology thought to be needed for the further development of the American economy. It was taken for granted by

13. It is against this background that the one original contribution of the "student revolution," the expectation of a state-subsidized "revolution," is to be understood.

the critics of the "organization man" no less than by others that the universities should do this and that the government and businessmen should provide the money for it. The doctrine of the "multiversity" was only a precipitation of what was already general policy and belief.

This had in fact been done by the American universities in earlier decades, but it was done on a much grander scale in the two decades immediately following the Second World War. Those responsible for the institutions were delighted to have their services so tangibly appreciated. University teachers were equally pleased—the expansion provided more students to train in research and for teaching careers. It also represented an approximation toward the ideal of equal access to higher education, thus meeting one of the standing grievances of the populistic and radical wing of the alienated intellectuals against the universities, namely that they were for the offspring of the rich.

There were many new roles for intellectuals which had scarcely existed before the war: scientists in the Department of Defense and in the national laboratories of the A.E.C., economists in the Council of Economic Advisors, a scientist as chief scientific advisor to the president,[14] the entire apparatus of the National Science Foundation. In the Policy Planning Board of the Department of State were academics and historians and political scientists, together with such distinguished professional diplomat-intellectuals as George Kennan and, at a somewhat lower level of the intellectual hierarchy, Paul Nitze, Charles Bohlen, and Louis Halle; in the Department of Defense, which became more science-based than any other part of the government or part of any government, a series of eminent scientists occupied the office of assistant secretary with responsibility for guiding the immense research activity of the armed services; an academic economist became the dominant spirit in the reorganization of the procurement policy of the Department of Defense. Private organizations like the Rand Corporation performed research on contract for the air force on matters at the very center

14. The agitational, critical role of the scientists in the first years following the war shriveled as scientists became advisors, members of grant-awarding panels, etc. The high point was reached when the American section of Pugwash was nearly assimilated into the Disarmament Agency.

of military policy. There were many roles filled by intellectuals in the two decades after 1945 which had not as much as existed previously.

Old roles became more influential. In the Federal Reserve system, which had become more important than ever before in the maintenance of the economy in its state of stability and growth, academically trained economists retaining intimate relations with the academic economic professions were more numerous, more prominent, and more influential than previously. Professors of law outside the government played an important part in the selection of their best students to serve as clerks to justices of the Supreme Court. Congressional committees invited intellectuals to testify before them with higher frequency than before, and several staff directors of certain important committees such as the Senate Foreign Affairs Committee have been intellectuals of reasonable stature—an unprecedented development. At numerous points where policies were made, intellectuals shared in varying degrees in the process of decision making. High officials turned repeatedly and frequently to the universities for assistance, enlightenment, counsel, guidance, and personnel. This structure of collaboration between the government and the intellectuals was the achievement of the Democratic administrations—and the intellectuals had always had, at least since the Wilson administration, a penchant toward the Democratic Party as the relatively antiplutocratic party and the party of the ethnic outcasts and therewith a party closer to an alienated outlook. The practice was not, however, notably reduced by the Republican administration of President Eisenhower.[15]

The Kennedy administration continued the collaboration, begun under President Roosevelt, in a more spectacular way and reached out more energetically toward the literary and artistic intellectuals as well.[16] The White House court became a nest of singing birds, although they sometimes sang, as almost all nonscientist intellectuals

15. The great weapon in the verbal armory of the New Left—"industrial-military complex"—was given to the nation as a parting gift by President Eisenhower, but he in his turn had it entrusted to him by one of his court intellectuals, an academic social scientist.

16. Despite the elevation of Robert Frost to an equivalent of poet laureate, no literary intellectuals attained the intimate and influential position which had been held by Robert Sherwood in his relations with President Roosevelt.

do nowadays, the songs of social science. With varying external fortunes, the Johnson and the Nixon administrations continued the dependence. Although the alienation in sentiment of American intellectuals in the two latter administrations has been in many respects more vehement and acrimonious than it has been since the 1920s and perhaps than it has ever been before, the number of complainers being greater and the language more rancorous than ever before, Patrick Moynihan and Henry Kissinger, President Nixon's two chief advisors—both with cabinet rank—in domestic and foreign affairs are among the most distinguished intellectuals in the country. Professor Milton Friedman's ideas have probably had more direct influence in the Nixon administration than those of any economist in any major country since John Maynard Keynes. The list is indefinitely extensible.

So much for the incorporation of the intellectuals into roles of authority and influence in American society.

VII

It would require more space than I can take here and more knowledge than I have at my ready command at the moment to trace in detail the consequences of the enlarged and more central roles filled by intellectuals in every sphere of the life of American society in the twenty years following the end of the Second World War. It was certainly large, very ramified, and very pervasive; the United States became to an unprecedented extent an "intellectual-based" country. It was a major change for a society which intellectuals had asserted was the society most uncongenial to the life of the spirit of any great society known in history.

Let us take the major changes and attempt to estimate the part intellectuals played in them. First of all: the relatively easy transition from war to peace, the demobilization, then the continuing growth and stability of the economy; then the remarkable integration of American society—twenty years of internal peace, of the moderation of political conflict, of strikes without violence; the continuous improvement in the condition of the Negro; after the end of McCarthyism and of the persecution of the shriveled remnant of the Communist Party, a greatly broadened tolerance of political dissent, a greater freedom of individual action, particularly in the private sphere, the further attenuation of puritanism; a reduction in ethnic hostility except in the southern states,[17] a reduction in the traditional animosity among Roman Catholics, Protestant, and Jews.

To some extent, these accomplishments were the fruit of older ideas—the Keynesian economists of the 1930s, the liberal ideas of equal justice before the law and of equality of opportunity, the idea of the moral equality of all human beings drawn from certain strands of Protestant Christianity and from the Enlightenment. The main general feature of all these changes was the narrowing of the distance between center and periphery through a reduction of the moral ascendancy of the center. In large measures this was made possible by the extraordinary productivity of American agriculture and industry, which was in some considerable measure the result of the work of the agricultural research stations connected with the land grant colleges, and of the scientific and technological research in chemistry, metallurgy, food processing, electronics, industrial management, etc. The affluence of American society helped to change the self-image of the mass of the population in the working classes and the lower middle classes by permitting their standard of living to improve, by permitting them to receive more education and to live in a more "appropriate" style which was an adaptation of a middle-class style. The development of the technology of mass communications contributed to the creation of a single national society with a common focus of attention and to some extent, a common culture. The direct agents of this common culture were literary and artistic intellectuals—just as its indirect ones were scientific and technological; sometimes the former were of outstanding quality, although more frequently they were mediocre and derivative.[18]

17. The "backlash" among whites has amounted to very little outside the south. The growth of antiwhite sentiment among Negroes is largely a phenomenon of the last half-decade following the period to which I refer above.

18. The "intellectualization" of the mass media was evinced in the weekly periodicals of mass circulation. *The Saturday Evening Post* and *Colliers* among the deceased, and *Life* and *Time* among the still surviving, all became more and more "intellectual" in their most recent phase. Works of great art and superior literary and culture became a large part of their stock-in-trade. Even the ocean of triviality and meretriciousness which constitutes much of this common culture is the product of intellectuals—many of them intellectuals *manqués* who resent their self-exclusion from intellectual grace.

The economic growth and stability of the period undoubtedly owed something not only to the scientific and technological research to which I have already referred, but to the vigorous empirical research and elaborate theoretical analyses of economists inside the government and outside it. The improvement in the condition of the Negroes—much of which was a function of their urbanization and northward movement in response to the growth in the employment opportunities in industry—was certainly affected by the change in opinion to which judicial decisions and a more humane public opinion contributed; these in turn were affected by the research done by sociologists on the situation of the Negro—epitomized and summarized just at the end of the Second World War by Gunnar Myrdal's *American Dilemma.* Even the villainous McCarthyism, although it continued an older tradition of nativism and populist antiintellectualism, certainly owed something to the evidence of ex-communist intellectual turncoats like Whittaker Chambers, J. B. Mathews, et al. It should also not be forgotten that McCarthyism in the broadest sense owed something to the fact that intellectuals like the late Henry Dexter White and others, who had risen to high positions in the federal government, had apparently become involved in communist espionage.[19]

The attenuation of puritanism had been moving apace with the urbanization of American society, but its models and legitimators who had fought for it a long time were literary and humanistic intellectuals. If the whole country has been turned into a macrocosm of what used to be found only in Greenwich Village and among the bohemians of Chicago and San Francisco, the model provided by one sector of the intellectuals has certainly played a part. (To this should be added the shattering blow given to puritanism by the "pill," which was the product of elaborate research by biochemists and physiologists.)

The general culture of impulse owes much of course to the weakness of authority in the family and in society. This certainly cannot be accounted for without reference to the long intellectual

19. McCarthyism was itself a response to the greatly increased prominence of intellectuals in government service. Its greatest accomplishment was the elaborate degradation of Robert Oppenheimer. The antiintellectuals had never before had such a grand intellectual in government service to persecute.

tradition of the restriction of the legitimacy of authority from the seventeenth century onward. The popularization of psychoanalysis through Margaret Mead, Erich Fromm, Karen Horney and many others less gifted, the research of Arnold Gesell, and the educational doctrine of John Dewey, all led to Dr. Spock's famous handbook of child rearing. It is not by accident that humanitarian and liberal attitudes toward children and their rights began and is still most widespread in families in which the parents are more highly educated. Assertions about the power and influence of intellectuals should not disregard this.

VIII

The affirmation of American society and culture and participation in its direction and orientation at the center and in numerous subcenters did not absorb all American intellectuals—nor was the affirmation unqualified in those who were engaged in it. Alongside of and intertwined with the acts of affirmation in practice and in statement was a continuous denial. The alienation of American intellectuals had always been strongest among literary and artistic intellectuals, and it never died out, even in the period of the greatest measure of affirmation. There was an illustrious and honorable line of direct descent from the aesthetic alienation of Edgar Allan Poe and Henry James, the moral alienation of Herman Melville and Theodore Dreiser, the patrician alienation of Henry Adams, the bohemian alienation of Floyd Dell and Art Young, the socialist alienation of Jack London, Upton Sinclair, and John Dos Passos. In the 1920s these different currents of alienation crossed each other, and there were partial fusions. H. L. Mencken, Ernest Hemingway, Sherwood Anderson, Eugene O'Neill, Edmund Wilson, and many others continued this line through the 1920s and into the 1930s.

The Communist Party and its agents who conducted the *New Masses* attempted to amalgamate these various kinds of alienation and to exploit them by giving them the status which Dante gave to Virgil, namely that of annunciations of the comprehensive alienation of Marxism-Leninism. They were, however, hampered by their guilefulness and their need for political purposes to appear to be something which they were not. The *Partisan Review,* following its removal shortly after its birth from the control of the fellow travelers and agents of the Communist Party, was a more genuine heir and representative of some of the diverse traditions of the alienated American intellectuals.

The Communists lost their hegemony during the war. Having renounced their identity in the larger cause of the Soviet alliance with the Western powers, they could not recover significantly after the alliance ended. Their line was blurred by internal conflicts, then by a new form of popular front tactics, and their organizations further enfeebled by the persecutions to which they were subjected by congressional investigative committees and the prosecutions under the Smith Act. The alienation of those who had traveled with the communists went out of sight under the pressure of intimidation by congressional committees and the Department of Justice and unpopularity among the large majority of intellectuals. Their confidence was shattered by the latter as much as by the two former, whereas before the war they had bullied, censored, and defamed the characters of their critics and acted generally as self-confident cocks of the walk. In publishing and literary circles they were shunned after the war. Their friends took cover. But while the communists and their friends took cover or changed their external guise, a more honest alienation was expressed in the *Partisan Review* and in *Politics.* The *Partisan Review* became the organ of a miscellaneous bundle of alienations and it could not withstand the delights of being at the center. Its Trotskyist anti-Stalinism tended to fade into American anticommunism. Alienation and reluctant affirmation mingled in its pages. *Politics,* on the other hand, was for the pure in heart; in a more humorless and a more self-righteous way, it continued in the traditions of the *Masses* and the *Liberator.*

The main criticism of American society of the alienated intellectuals of the late 1940s and most of the 1950s—the critique of mass culture—had its seat there. The self-destructive tendencies of capitalism and the baseness of the politicians yielded their place of honor in the alienated intellectuals' image of American society to the vulgarity of American culture and to the damage which this mass culture did to the high culture. This critique, which had a multiple ancestry in patrician disdain, aesthetic revulsion, puritanical disapprobation and a high-brow Marxism, did not have a wide adherence. Literary publicists and a handful of sociologists under the influence of German *Edelmarxismus* were its chief carriers. It was probably shared in a fairly inert manner by the academic humanists whose preconceptions were directed by the older tradition of aesthetic alienation and the abhorrence of the genteel classes for money-grubbing and the baser pleasures.

The critique of mass society and of mass culture did not have a long life. It was swept away by a new current. Many of its proponents, eager to swim in a new, more turbulent stream, jettisoned it for something stronger and more fashionable.[20] Others forgot it as they withdrew to higher ground.

IX

Since the middle of the 1960s a pronounced change in the relations of American intellectuals to the center of their society has occurred. The tiny rivulets of twenty years earlier have turned into a broad and shallow river which seems to have no banks and which has inundated nearly all the reclaimed intellectual terrain, turning it into a muddy marshland. The change set in shortly after the accession to power of President Lyndon Johnson. The first triumphs of the Negro civil rights movement had raised hopes and these led to frustrations. The "poor" were discovered—not the working classes, who remained written off as the brutish enjoyers of mass culture and who were now regarded as gross, unthinking supports of the existing order— but the *Lumpenproletariat*, who had never enjoyed such a good press as in the past five years. The flowery rhetoric and ill-natured bearing of President Johnson reawakened the dormant animosities of the American intellectuals toward the plebeian professional politician. The failure of the military leadership of the country to bring the war in Viet Nam to a successful conclusion broke the attachment to authority which had grown up among American intellectuals when American power appeared supreme in the world.

The withdrawal from the center was symbolized by the agitated euphoria of certain circles of literary and publicistic intellectuals in refusing the invitation of President Johnson to attend a series of

20. One could not go on inveighing against "mass culture" while praising a new radicalism which includes hipsterism, the Beatles, pot and acid rock, and being covered with buttons like a "Pearly."

ceremonial festivities at the White House in 1965. Under President Kennedy, when such festivities had been inaugurated, the invitation to the company of the mighty of the earth was the final seal on the union of power and intellect. The seal was a very fragile one and of very brief duration. The affirmative attitude which had been so common in the period just preceding was not solely a product of the perception in American society of values—moral, aesthetic and political—which were part of the intellectuals' internal traditions. It had also been the result of the attraction of strong and effective power which has always been characteristic of intellectuals. At a time when America was only a province of the great European world and when the political and economic elites were indifferent and even sometimes hostile toward literary and humanistic intellectuals, American intellectuals saw no merit in those who ruled American society. When, however, they were taken to the bosom of those who exercised power and when the latter seemed to be the most powerful elite the world had known, American intellectuals found much to be pleased with in their situation and in the situation of their country. Once the power began to falter, however, to be not merely unsuccessful in action but perplexed and lacking in decisiveness and self-confidence, large numbers of intellectuals—literary publicistic, scientific, and humanistic—decided that the American political elites were no longer worthy of their affection. No condemnation could be strong enough. It was not simply the older accusations of vulgarity and venality and indifference to "life's finer things." The accusations were more bitter. The accusation of "genocide" became the coin of the intellectuals' realm—"genocide" at home and abroad. In its more extreme forms, in the view of Noam Chomsky for example, any performance of a governmental service was culpable.

What was striking about the hyperbolically acrimonious and embittered criticism of the post-1965 alienation was its relationship to the older traditions of intellectual alienation. The first initiators of the new alienation had been either socialists of the tradition who had abstained from the incorporation into and affirmation of the center—*Dissent* and Michael Harrington—or Stalinoids like Paul Sweezy, the late Leo Huberman, and I. F. Stone, who had survived the hard times of the late 1940s and the 1960s. The new alienation in contrast, once it was in full spate, found many of its main bearers among those who had little connection with the older tradition of alienation. No less striking was the durability and toughness of the non-Marxist tradition of alienation which came back into a strength fuller than ever after a period of attrition which had lasted for more than a quarter of a century.[21]

Bohemianism has long been associated with revolution. The recent advance of aesthetic sensibility has greatly extended and modified the social sources of affiliation to the movement of alienation. Jazz commentators, mod. journalists, television comedians, packagers of fun goods, specialists in pornography, cartoonists, interior decorators, "young people" in publishing, advertising executives—all these so responsive to fluctuations in style— are new recruits to alienation. To these are joined the "new class" of college and university teachers, clergymen, black intellectuals, liberating women, and the university and college students—the very vanguard of the whole thing.

The clergy in the United States, leaving out the self-designated preachers in store-front churches and those who bash the Bible and froth at the mouth in berating the Devil, form an important component in the present-day disorder of the intellectuals. Having with the aid of Deweyan naturalism, "demythologization" and existentialism, disposed of their deity or at least placed him in a weak position, Protestant clergymen in the United States have been suffering from the intellectual equivalent of technological unemployment. Superior in attitude toward their benighted flocks, displaced by atheism and psychiatry from the cure of souls, they were for a long time at loose ends. The tradition of "social Christianity" did not arouse their enthusiasm. With the Negro civil rights movement, however, they found something to do; with the war in Viet Nam they found much else to do. Reinforced by restless Roman Catholic priests from whom the hand of authority had been lifted and by a rabbinate of doubting piety—all fearful of not being in tune with the

21. It is true that there has been a small revival of Marxism, but that has come in a roundabout way rather than through the direct filiation of tradition. It is in part a consequence of revival to half-life of the Communist Party which has made the writings of Marx and Engels available through its publishing house and partly as a result of the diversity and intellectual randomness of the younger left. It is also a product of the elevation to fame of Professor Marcuse, whose sexual doctrines seem more attractive than his Marxism.

times—the clergy has reentered the public life of the intellectual classes. They have not been a steadying element.

Negro intellectuals for the first time in American history have gained the attention of the white intellectuals. In the past, worthy Negro intellectuals knocked in vain at the doors of American intellectual life but, outside socialist and communist circles, few attended to them. Then in a short time a handful of Negro intellectuals—a few of them of some genuine talent, most of them of little talent and the beneficiaries of a forced levy—appeared on the scene. Their passionate abuse of American society could not have come at a luckier time; without the audience of white intellectuals they could not have been so encouraged.

Finally, the students in higher educational institutions should be mentioned. In an age which praises youthfulness with fewer qualifications than devout Marxists used to praise the working classes, and in a situation in which intellectuals had become convinced of their indispensability, university and college students got whatever benefits there were in being both youthful and intellectuals. The students' hostility against authority—characteristic of adolescence, and in America adolescence is prolonged—was reinforced by their elders' chorus of denunciation of authority, including their own, and by the supineness of authority, academic and governmental.

When one looks over the various kinds of radical activists, one finds that many of them share one major characteristic of the amateur politician pointed out by Max Weber, namely, they are "wirtschaftlich abkömmlich."[22] Many are not employed at all, or employed irregularly. They have no fixed hours of work in general; they come and go as they please. They are more prosperous than the lawyers without briefs and physicians without patients whom Marx saw as the supporters of his rivals. They have much leisure and much flexibility in their work schedules, where they work at all. They belong to the free as over against the workaday sector of society. From this comes some of their sense of affinity with the *Lumpenproletariat.* It also renders them easily available for their characteristic political techniques, the demonstration and the mass meeting.

22. Weber, *Politik als Beruf,* 2d edition (Munich and Leipzig: Duncker and Humblot, 1926), p. 16.

The consequence of all this is a spiral of mutually reinforcing animosity against their own society, combining withdrawal and aggressiveness.

These new recruits to the espousal of the intellectuals' traditions of alienation, diverse and novel though they might be, have only a loose connection with the intellectually substantial parts of that tradition. Bohemianism never had much intellectual substance, and that is the part of the tradition to which many of the new recruits give their allegiance. The very looseness of their connection with a definitive and elaborate doctrine such as Marxism is part of the larger paradox of their outlook. Despite their hostility toward the intellectuals who were in the forefront during the period of incorporation and affirmation, the new recruits to the movement of alienation continue some of the culture of those they revile.

The period of incorporation and affirmation generated two convictions among the intellectuals who participated in it. The first of these—bred by experience and propaganda—was that intellectuals were indispensable to America's functioning. The second, based on this, was that intellectuals were in a crucial position because in a variety of ways the authorities of society were dependent on them. From having felt unwanted and unused, intellectuals moved to the opposite extreme of a conviction of indispensability. The conviction of indispensability has been fully compatible with hostility toward those who seem to deny the rights which come with indispensability.

X

The movement from a sense of nullity in making decisions to a sense of weightiness has not been undone by the movement from denial to affirmation and back to denial. Civility has made progress even though its name is momentarily darkened. For one thing, a great many intellectuals have not made the return journey to denial; many have remained in the positions of authority in decision making at or connected with the institutional centers of American society. Economists and scientific advisers are firmly entrenched and they cannot be done away with. They are, however, simply continuations of positions and outlooks consolidated during the years between 1933 and 1965.

The persistence of the civil attitude is also evident in its deformation. The denial of the legitimacy of authority shows traces of the period of civility through which it has passed in the last third of a century. Those who hate authority and deny its legitimacy now think that it is plausible to require that authority should yield to their demands. The new relationship of the deniers to the authority which they deny includes their giving orders to it which they think they can force it to implement and which it should implement. The passionate deniers think that they should be part of the existing central institutional system. This is unique in the history of the critique of authority. Furthermore, the expectations of the deniers are rendered plausible by the fact that they have in fact benefited by some partial success in establishing their own view of the matter at the center where the authority is exercised.[23]

An "intellectualization" of public life has taken place in the United States. Some of the values of the alienated intellectuals have become established in the circles of authority. The centuries-long process of the "civilization" of authority, which entailed authority's becoming modest in its self-legitimation, restrained in its public declaration of its claims, responsive in its sensibility to the demands of those it ruled, has now gone a step further. Elites now quail before the charges of "elitism." The exercise of authority and the management of affairs are now disguised as "decision making." The maintenance of law and order and the eforcement of law which political and administrative elites have always in the past taken as their first charge, and which are indeed inseparable from the maintenance of society and the protection of its members, have become matters about which those who rule have become shame-faced. The prevention of riots or their restraint, suppression, and dispersal when they do occur, have become thought of as inadmiss-ible—although in practice they remain drastic and sometimes harsh. Judges and publicists acknowledge a right of violent demonstration as part of the freedom of expression and as a legitimate procedure when constitutionally provided procedures are unsatisfactory or not immediately effective. In principle—and to a great extent, in fact—the legitimacy of dissent, derived from the freedom of expression, is

23. I cite at random the recent opinion of Judge Wyzanski on conscien-tious objection and the numerous pronouncements of Mr. Justice W. O. Douglas.

granted even where it involves coercive action and the disruption of institutions.

The penetration of the aggrieved intellectuals' outlook occurs in a twofold process. The first, the recruitment of intellectuals of alienated outlook, is part of the general process of the increased recruitment into intellectual-executive roles. Since the alienated anti-authoritarian outlook is so widespread among the younger generation of intellectuals and those in humanistic and social sciences from which the recruits were drawn, it is only to be expected that in the mass communications, in the universities, and in government too, despite the persistence of the practice of "security clearance," the new recruits bear with them some influence of the alienated outlook. Through their influence as speech writers and as "idea men," as research workers and as staff members of special investigative commissions, authority has come often to speak—if not equally often to act—in accordance with the voice of the aggrieved intellectual.

But the penetration goes further than the incumbency of the bearers of the outlook in the roles of greater functional importance and of greater numbers. There has also been a penetration into the outlook of incumbents of traditionally authoritative roles who themselves are not intellectuals or who, even if intellectuals, have up until recently espoused outlooks conventional to those in authority, the crucial element of which is the belief in the legitimacy of their own authority. For one thing, the sociological sciences have come since the 1950s to dominate this idiom of discourse on public events, not only the terminology but the conceptions of causation and motivation as well as the implicit political outlook of workers in these fields. In addition to this, intellectuals in the United States have become demonstrators, not by rational argument, but by standing in public places, by covering themselves in buttons and badges, by signing petitions and public declarations. They have come to fill the air and the press. Politicians have been in some measure responsive to this clamor. They have been increasingly deferential to intellectuals ever since the end of the war and the atomic scientists' movement. It was noticeable ever since the Second World War in the deference accorded scientists when they testified before congressional committees—the McCarthy procedures were rearguard actions in this respect. Social scientists have now slipped into place alongside scientists. The American politicians' attribution of greater importance to clamorous demand than to reasoned argument and the quiet preferences of the mass of the population, the fear of the politicians of being out of step with the view which they think to be prevalent, gives resonance to the demands of the aggrieved intellectuals.

Since the alienated intellectuals, like ideologists and radicals everywhere, cannot be completely alienated, their claims take the form of the intensification and underscoring of certain elements already present in the central value system of American society. The values of substantive equality are intensified at the expense of the value of an equivalence between reward and exertion. The value of majority rule has long been transformed, by a clamorous insistence, into the supremacy of the uncriticizably virtuous "people" (meaning, in the vocabulary of those who clamor, a number of Negroes, Puerto Ricans, discontented females, and rebellious university students).[24] The value of individuality has been intensified into the value of the immediate gratification of spontaneous impulse.

Because of this affinity between the central value system and the ideologically exacerbated interpretation of certain elements of this system, the political and publicistic elites who are often not very subtle, and who are sometimes easily disoriented, regard these claims as plausible and consistent with what they believed before.

There is more to it than this. Many politicians—omitting the cavemen—feel inferior to intellectuals. They might behave rudely toward them as President Johnson often did, but the same President

24. "The people," those bearers of virtue and touchstones of policy according to the principle of populistic democracy, have yielded place to "people." This disappearance of the definite article is not just a linguistic quirk characteristic of a generation which has been brought up to express its sentiments but which has lost contact with the traditions of English speech. There is more to it than that. "The people" used to mean the mass of the population: the majority. But the majority are now in bad odor among aggrieved intellectuals. The majority are now the industrial working classes, truck drivers, office workers, etc., lawyers and doctors, government employees, conservative, complacent, hedonistic, looking after their own pleasures and comforts. The majority are now the "scissorbills," sunk in the morass of bourgeois society. "People" on the other hand are any minority of outcasts who are impoverished, unemployed, on relief rolls, and in need of support by the welfare services of the state. They are also those who make demands on their behalf.

Johnson following his retirement said that he had not felt qualified to lead the country effectively because he had not gone to one of the major universities. He implied that because of this he could not command the respect of those who had done so.

The mass communications show a similar success for their intellectuals. Although aggrieved radicals in all countries in the twentieth century have criticized the conduct of the media of communication—whether privately or governmentally owned—where they have had the freedom to express their views, the situation nowadays is much different from what it was before the Second World War. Although there is still much criticism of the privately owned press in the United States, there is also a very strong representation of aggrieved intellectuals within the institutions of public opinion. In television there is a similar situation. The professional tradition of muckraking, the tradition of reportorial vigor, the tradition of sensationalism and of the maxim that "good news is no news" all mean that disorder, failure, catastrophe are given the greatest prominence. Delight in disorder, occasional sympathy with its perpetrators and the cause which it purportedly serves, cause the disorder to be much attended to in the mass media.[25]

In book publishing, which is centered mainly in New York, practically all publishers and editors and other intellectuals who are members of the industry are permeated by the aggrieved outlook either from conviction or from the desire to be stylish or because of the belief that that is what the spirit of the age requires. The far-reaching relaxation of censorship and the inclusion of sexual polymorphousness and publicity as part of the culture of the new strata of the alienated intellectuals as well as some of their older outriders and followers, give the intellectuals in the publishing industry a commercial interest as well as a cultural one in being

25. It is in the nature of the present movement of hostility against the center of society that it is driven by hunger for publicity. Its violence is in part propaganda of the deed: its main political actions are extra-institutional as well as anti-institutional. The brief civility of the organizations for Senator Robert Kennedy and Eugene McCarthy quickly exhausted their resources. Demonstrative politics, intended to gain attention rather than to modify institutions, have replaced it.

"with it."[26] Many are reluctant to publish any book which is critical of the aggrieved view of American society, again out of conviction or out of fear of being out of fashion.[27]

The universities, as has been indicated, have become the scene and seedbed of the intellectual life in the United States. Not only do they carry on the traditional functions of the universities of training for the learned, practical-intellectual professions and conducting pure research, but they have accepted the burdens of applied research for government, trained for numerous not so learned occupations, performed numerous tasks which governments should properly have performed themselves, provided the support for little magazines and for other activities which in the past were in the sphere of bohemia. All these miscellaneous actions, encouraged and applauded on the outside, led to and fed on a form of *Grössenwahn* among university authorities. All this expansion should, one might have thought, been the work of strong characters. Nothing could have been more erroneous. Many of the great university and college administrators who presided over the vast expansion of universities in the indiscriminate service of American society have turned out to be characterless weathervanes facing whichever way the wind blew.

The release of animosity against authority, beginning with the murder of John F. Kennedy, first manifested itself on a trivial issue at the University of California in Berkeley. The University of California, after its recovery from the ravages of the loyalty oath controversy, had been one of the major pillars of the new structure of cooperation of authority and the intellectuals. Its administrators and teachers were full of pride, justified pride over their accomplishments. Yet, with the first onslaught it fell into disorder. The teachers fell out with each other, the presidents and deans were thrown into

26. The Grove Press combines the culture of the literary avant-garde with the heritage of Mr. Girodias' Olympia Press. It is also the agent of Fanonist and other phantasms of a morally purifying destructiveness.

27. Professor Mathew Hodgart's Swiftian parable of the events at Cornell University in 1969 was refused by twelve American publishers before it was finally accepted. The book had already been accepted for publication in Great Britain. Professor Hodgart is a very reputable scholar, but his letter to the *Times* (London) describing and passing reasoned judgment on the Cornell events aroused the disapprobation of the *bien pensant* aggrieved intellectuals in the American publishing industry. This is not the only instance.

confusion. The "rightfulness" of the students' cause called forth much support, and those who denied it could not bring the university back to where it was. Similar events occurred with increasing frequency over the ensuing half-decade. Finally, even Harvard, which had rebuffed McCarthy, fell before its students. It was only to be expected that the universities which had helped to generate so much of the new culture should be so riddled by it. Presidents, deans, professors, from conviction or cowardice, fell for obviously nonsensical arguments. No authorities under attack had ever gone so far in flattering and beslavering their insatiable antagonists and attempting to placate them.

XI

The new renunciation of civil collaboration by the American intellectuals began even before the failure of effective power in Viet Nam, although much of the weakening of belief in the effectiveness of the American political and military elites is attributable to that. The civility of the American intellectual would have had a hard row to hoe even if things had gone more favorably for the United States in Viet Nam and if President Kennedy had not been assassinated, both of which events showed the vulnerability of power.

American intellectuals, even more than most intellectuals in most other countries, have inherited an antipolitical tradition. What they have received from their intellectual forebears and what they themselves teach and believe outside scientific research fosters an antipolitical, anticivil outlook. The very favorable structural circumstances of three decades—indulgence by the center, occupational opportunities at the center, and centrality in the world—had put this tradition into the margins of the mind. The first and the third of these circumstances were modified by the deterioration of President Johnson's demeanor in consequence of the resultlessness of the war in Viet Nam. The tradition reasserted itself when the major politician of the country was rude in tone and ineffective in action. But whereas the older tradition was one of antipolitical withdrawal, the new disposition, while remaining antipolitical, has been far more active. One variant of it resembled, after the outburst of civil political energy on behalf of Robert Kennedy and then Eugene McCarthy, the new politics of the intellectuals under Franklin Roosevelt. The politics of the intellectuals under the New Deal were not electoral or party politics but rather political activity carried on in advisory and counseling capacities under the auspices of a powerful political personage. Political activists among intellectuals do not now seek electoral office any more now than they did then. They seek programs and grants paid for by the public treasury to work against the government.[28] This paradoxical antipolitical civility is a novelty, although it has superficial resemblances to the communist technique of "boring from within."

Another variant of the new antipolitical politics is part of an older tradition: namely demonstration. The technique of demonstration was not an intellectual's device until the intellectuals and the communists came together under the auspices of Willi Münzenberg. Demonstrations have now been given up by the working classes since they have trade unions to represent their interests; demonstrations have become once more part of the technique of those who regard themselves as outside the central institutional system in which interests are represented and compromised.

The activist element is at its most extreme in violent, disruptive demonstrations, where the aim is to prevent an institution, usually a defenseless one like a university or a church, from functioning in a normal manner. Although there is much talk of power in intellectual circles, the new politics of the intellectuals do not seem to aim to accede to positions of authority in the existing system or in a new revolutionarily established system. Hating it and denying its legitimacy as they do, they still seem to acquiesce to its factuality. They seem to count on its continued existence and they anticipate its responsiveness to abusive influence, rather than to influence within consensus. In that sense, the new revolutionary intellectuals—there are some exceptions of course—seem themselves to be the victims of the tentacular powers of the center.

XII

Can a modern society maintain a stable and orderly structure when the political elites and those other sectors of the elite who share power with them have lost their self-confidence and are dominated

28. Compare the role of the most brilliant young graduates of the major law schools nowadays with those of the period of the New Deal and its successors!

by a clamorous hostility against that society and those who rule it? An elite which wavers and abdicates the responsibility which is inherent in the roles which it fills becomes uncertain of its entitlement to legitimacy. If it cannot claim legitimacy for the actions it undertakes, its actions will be ineffective. Ineffectiveness on the part of an elite breeds disrespect and the refusal of legitimacy. No society, least of all one as complicated as present-day American society, and so difficult to govern under the best of circumstances, can survive in its ongoing form, nor can it develop peacefully from that form if its central institutional system has lost its legitimacy. American society is a noisy and a violent society, even in good times. In bad times like the present, it strains the capacities of even the best of governments.

The containment of conflict in a culture so consecrated to the gratification of demands has always been difficult. The institutionalization of class conflict—a by no means perfect institutionalization—was one of the great accomplishments of the Roosevelt and subsequent administrations. Its continuation depends on the continued legitimacy of authority in government, business enterprises, and trade unions. The evaporation of legitimacy renders the continued institutionalization more problematic than it has been for about a third of a century. Inflation and the demonstration-effect of the successful pursuit of expanded demands places the machinery of collaboration of classes under a heavy burden. The sight of successfully affronted authority is a great stimulant to antinomian impulses.

The ineptitude of governmental institutions in the face of ethnic conflicts—an ineptitude arising from serious disagreements within the government on the merits of the claims and how to treat them, diminished self-confidence in dealing with violence, particularly violence by some thousands of university students and by a section of the Negro population, the legitimate moral claims of which have been usurped and exaggerated by a small, violently inclined group— has further eroded legitimacy.

The inconclusiveness of the war in Viet Nam has damaged the legitimacy of the federal government more than any other factor. The Russian czarist government, incompetent and ineffective though it was in a time of peace, was shaken by revolution (in 1905) only after military defeat at the hands of the Japanese. It was finally overthrown following its disasters on the battlefield in the first two and a half years of the First World War. The agitations and the terroristic activities of a small group of conspiratorial intellectuals from 1825 onward would undoubtedly have come to nothing had the czarist government not experienced those two shattering military defeats in little more than a decade. The Habsburg monarchy was a ramshackle political system but it decomposed only after defeat in the First World War. The Hohenzollern regime in Germany was one of the most stable in the world until its defeat by the Allies in the First World War. The German revolutionaries were feeble indeed—witness the weakness of their creation, the Weimar Republic—but the ancien régime had lost its legitimacy. Similarly the legitimacy of the National Socialist regime, which had been so firm in 1943, began to falter when the German armies suffered their first great reverses at Stalingrad· and in North Africa. Thereafter, as defeat followed defeat, the Nazi regime which had exterminated or paralyzed all opposition began to crumble within, and, when it was totally defeated in 1945, it lost practically all domestic support. In short, governments which lose wars are governments which have undertaken to do more than they can. A war is an undertaking which involves national identity and, as such, it touches on the deepest roots of the acknowledgment of legitimacy. The loss of a war endangers the real and the symbolic existences of the entire national community and it thereby weakens the readiness to acknowledge the right to rule of those who have taken to themselves the care of the name and safety of that national community. Among those whose inclination to acknowledge the legitimacy of rulers is—for all sorts of reasons and motives—already weak, such failure is a further ground for denial.

The situation of the American government is different. It has not lost the war. It has, however, not won it, and that is almost as bad in some respects because it has dragged on and brought with it an inflation which injures most classes of the population and above all those who are otherwise the most faithful devotees of the legitimacy of government. It also exacerbated class conflict through the continuous demand for higher wages, resulting in strikes and the disruption of services. All this has weakened the legitimacy of government by further revealing and emphasizing its ineffectiveness.

In this situation of weakened legitimacy, the alienation of the now pervasive intellectual classes is of consequence. Had intellectuals continued to be as marginal as they were forty years ago both in their functional roles and in their symbolic prominence and appreciation, their alienation would not concern any one by themselves and students of their attitudes. As it is, however, the question merits further scrutiny.

The first thing to be said is that the alienation in question here is not universal among intellectuals. Large sections of the intellectual classes do not share in it. Those in the practical-intellectual professions are less alienated than those in the primarily intellectual professions. Those in the scientific and technological professions are less alienated than those in the social science, literary, and humanistic professions. Even in the latter professions, among the social scientists, for example, the economists and the political scientists are less alienated than the sociologists (and anthropologists); in the humanistic subjects it is those concerned with English and American literary studies who are most alienated. Certain Negro intellectuals are among the most vociferous, but there are many who do not receive publicity and who are less alienated although no less critical of the traditional treatment and position of the Negro in American society. The younger generations, especially students in higher educational institutions, are more alienated than the older generations, although there is a wide spread of opinion among them also. In each of these sectors of the intellectual classes, the tide of aggressive alienation seems to have ebbed, and the more aggressive are separating themselves from the rest.

The diminution of the volume of echo which white intellectuals give to the most radical Negroes is likely to diminish, partly because those who do the echoing are creatures of fashion and do not sustain any fashion for long. If this occurs, the more radical Negro intellectuals will have less resonance, and their pressure on the more moderate ones will decrease. Their isolation will have the same effect on the whites that the isolation of the white extremist intellectuals will have on their Negro counterparts. They will shrink into conspiratorial circles and will be subject not to the laws of movement of intellectual opinion but to those of the security services. These developments depend in part on the capacity of the political and administrative elites to regain control of their nerves and to discriminate between destructive actions and reasonable demands for improvement. They depend on the avoidance of exciting rhetoric. They depend most of all on the restoration of effectiveness and on the image of effectiveness on the part of the government. They depend very much on bringing the war in Viet Nam to an end, and in managing this without generating in sectors of the political elite and in the society at large a "stab-in-the-back" legend.

The intellectuals, sensitive as they are to power, would respond by a renewal of their sense of affinity, as they did under Franklin Roosevelt, even though there is a strong prejudice against any Republican administration. In addition to this it should be pointed out that at present, in the ranks of the alienated intellectuals, the most alienated are primarily concentrated in the functionally most marginal roles. Economists and engineers are more important to society than students and teachers and research workers in sociology and English and American literature. Their danger to social stability arises more from their role in the mass communications than from any "direct action" they can take from the inside as incumbents of executive roles or from the outside as demonstrators and bomb throwers. Nonetheless, in the present period when intellectuals possess so much prestige and many politicians are inclined to listen to them so deferentially, the most vociferous and most demonstrative, especially in the Negro-white collaboration—are capable of making demands and accusations which rattle the established political and administrative elites and cause them either to lose self-confidence or to react in an extremely aggressive and repressive manner. Either of these responses threatens to weaken the legitimacy of the established elite among those intellectuals who are inclined to give it the benefit of the doubt; it neutralizes them, weakens their civility, or makes them more sympathetic with the more extremely alienated.

Yet, the fact remains that the American economy—despite the burden of inflation—continues to operate with a most impressive effectiveness. The business elite, despite concessions here and there to the mounting lunacy, is more archaic in its sentiment and ethos. The leaders of the trade unions continue with an unruffled "business as usual" demeanor. It comes down therefore to the question whether the political elites in the federal government and in the big cities can reequilibrate themselves, regain their equanimity, reassert themselves by placing confidence in those sections of the population which support them, show initiative in bringing about some noticeable improvement, and in so doing, resume a steady course.

It is a far from easy task. It is encumbered on one side by an alliance with politicians of an irreconcilable outlook, particularly regarding ethnic questions; it is encumbered on the other by many within its own ranks who have been overrun by extremely alienated intellectuals—not as extremely alienated as the bomb throwers but extremely alienated nonetheless—who claim to speak on behalf of "people." What is called for is the reestablishment of a sovereignty deriving ultimately and through representative institutions from "the people" and the reduction of the direct ascendancy of "people," i.e. the "plebiscitary" democracy of a small minority. But that sovereignty cannot be reasserted unless it is done by those who have accepted the rewards and responsibilities of leadership in representative institutions.

XIII

The growth to prominence of the intellectual classes in American society has been a function of changes in the function of the political and administrative elites and the changes in the character of physical and social technology from empirical to "scientific." Intellectuals became more prominent in the minds of the nonintellectual sectors of the elite as the technological procedures in American society came to require systematic study for their practice and development. In consequence, the number of intellectual roles in the society increased greatly, the number of intellectual institutions for training incumbents for those roles increased, and the number of persons filling the roles—practical-intellectual and intellectual—involved in the practice of the technology and training for it grew disproportionately.

The political, administrative, economic, and military elites, who had in the past not been notably appreciative of intellectual works and intellectuals, thus came to take an active part in the promotion of the institutions where such intellectuals were to be trained and in the recruitment of intellectuals so trained into their own institutions.

In the past the distance which the nonintellectual elites had maintained with respect to intellectuals was reciprocated. American intellectuals, particularly those concerned with the production and cultivation of literary and humanistic works, were hostile toward those in positions of authority in American society. They believed themselves to be disesteemed by them and they avoided entry into roles which entailed service and close association with the authoritative elites of their society. The intellectuals developed a penumbral tradition, which is seldom far from the surface of intellectual activities in general and was perhaps even stronger in the United States than in any other advanced country of the nineteenth century. This penumbral tradition prescribed distance from and disparagement of those in authoritative roles. Although the tradition was not developed in an equally extreme form among scientific and technological intellectuals in the nineteenth century, of whom there were not so many, they too shared in it. The intellectuals in the last two-thirds of the nineteenth century had practically no positive influence in American society. Even if their sense of alienation was caused in part by this exclusion from influence and authority, their hostility made little difference because of their lack of influence.

The transformation of American society in which authoritative roles came to be linked more intimately with intellectual roles had two major consequences: it brought about the partial suspension of the hostility of the intellectual elites toward the nonintellectual or authority-exercising elites, i.e. toward the executive elites in the broadest sense of the term. It also brought about the incorporation of the intellectuals into a closer, more collaborative relationship with the executive elites. In the course of this, intellectuals came in a variety of ways to have great influence on American culture and social structure.

The incorporation of the intellectuals into the central institutional system is now integral to the structure of American society. The penumbral traditions of the intellectuals have, however, retained their vitality despite their several decades of submergence, and in the recent troubles of the political, administrative, and military elites, the tradition of alienation has been reactivated. This time, however, as a result of the structural incorporation of the intellectuals into the center of American society, their cultural influence has been great. As a result, the legitimacy of the executive elites—a cultural phenomenon—has been impaired, and the effectiveness of these elites has been further damaged with a resultant further deterioration of their legitimacy.

The stability of American society has thus come to depend upon a sector of the society which lives in a tradition of alienation, part of which, in its extreme form, is historically contingent and part of which is almost self-generating in the primary culture of the intellectual role. At the same time, it should be observed that the primary culture of the intellectuals is increasingly generated in academic institutions, where there is a delicately poised and not always equally stable balance between, on the one hand, a discipline which acknowledges at least the authority of its own traditions and of the institutions which sustain them and, on the other, a more antinomian and expressive culture. The latter has a long and deep tradition, which developed before it came within academic confines. The stability of the larger society depends, therefore, on the maintenance, within the culture and the institutional system of the intellectuals, of the predominance of that element which accepts an objective discipline and the integration of academic institutions into the central institutional system of American society.

IV. The Self-Contemplation of Society

11

TRADITION, ECOLOGY, AND INSTITUTION IN THE HISTORY OF SOCIOLOGY

Sociology at present is a heterogeneous aggregate of topics, related to each other by a common name, by more or less common techniques, by a community of key words and conceptions, by a more or less commonly held aggregate of major interpretative ideas and schemes. It is held together too by a more or less common tradition—a heterogeneous one in which certain currents stand out—linked to common monuments or classical figures and works. It is also held together by the knowledge which its practitioners possess that they have in common—their location in universities, a common set of journals, and a group of publishers who produce their works.

The tradition, more or less commonly shared, lives in a self-image which links those now calling themselves sociologists with a sequence of famous authors running back into the nineteenth century. Although in fact the lines of the main ideas which live on in contemporary sociology have a much older history, sociologists do not generally see themselves as having an ancestry originating any earlier than the nineteenth century. All see themselves immersed in much shorter traditions, but they are recurrently reminded of the longer past.

Most of sociology is not scientific in the sense in which this term is used in English-speaking countries. It contains little of generality of scope and little of fundamental importance which is rigorously demonstrated by commonly accepted procedures for making relatively reproducible observations of important things. Its theories are not

This is a revised version of an essay that originally appeared in *Daedalus*. Reprinted by permission from *Daedalus,* Journal of the American Academy of Arts and Sciences, Boston, Mass., vol. 99, no. 4 (Fall 1970).

ineluctably bound to its observations. The standards of proof are not stringent. Despite valiant efforts, its main concepts are not precisely defined; its most interesting interpretative propositions are not unambiguously articulated.

There are differences, of course, among the various substantive fields of sociology, some being more scientific in certain respects than others, but on the whole the standard of scientific accomplishment is low. This does not mean that in those parts which are not very scientific there is not some very substantial learning or that there is not an accumulated wisdom which merits regard and consideration. Nor does it mean that some of it even in its present intellectual state is incapable of contributing, if it were taken to heart, to the improvement of policy, administration, and to civility in a broad sense. It only means what it says, namely, that much of contemporary social science is not very scientific in the sense in which the term has come to be understood.

Nonetheless, sociology does exist. It has a large institutional embodiment in departments of sociology in universities and in many research institutions, some affiliated to universities and some independent. It has a history which present-day sociologists regard as their history—although of course the image of this history varies somewhat from country to country and among sociologists within particular countries. It has a contemporaneous existence constituted by its vast and rapidly expanding stock of works, a large and also rapidly expanding personnel working in and forming academic institutions given over to sociological research, teaching, training and consultation; these include governmental institutions for sociological research and consultation and private, nongovernmental, nonacademic institutions in which sociologists perform some of the same activities as they perform when they are employed in governmental institutions. The stock of works, heterogeneous though it is in its particular subject-matters, in its techniques of observation and analysis, and in its particular interpretations is also characterized by a few widely pervasive major ideas or beliefs about society, by a few major concepts or delineations of significant variables. It is characterized above all by the sociological approach which believes that human actions and, at least in part, social actions are affected in varying degrees by the social setting in which they are carried on. The sociological approach is as simple as that; it is an approach of far-reaching implications. It is the faith of sociologists and it gives them their self-confidence.

Its characteristic concepts include those of social system, of society and its constituent institutions, of primary groups, of social stratification and social mobility, of power and legitimate authority, of elites and ruling classes, of law and freedom, of social status, of occupational roles, of bureaucracy and corporate organization, of kinship and local community, of history and tradition, of intellectuals and ideology, of consensus and conflict, of solidarity and alienation, conformity and deviance, charisma and routine, of reverence before the sacred and rebellion against institutions. These various concepts have been grouped into a conception of modern society or *Gesellschaft* (and its variant of mass society) which is further defined by contrast with a conceptual construction variously designated as folk society, traditional society, or *Gemeinschaft*.

How has all this come about? Why has the intellectual stock of sociology come to be what it is and why has it taken that form in particular places? Why have certain ideas which are now thought to be constitutive of sociology come to dominate the subject?

One of the older answers was that sociology could not emerge until men were capable of sufficient detachment from involvement in their own affairs and in their beliefs about these affairs; a corollary of this was that sociology could arise only when authority had lost some of its sanctity, when traditional beliefs became somewhat discredited, and when a secularized attitude had come to prevail in the educated parts of society. This view has been put forward by a number of writers, most notably Durkheim and Sombart. There is something in this view—but not enough. The heavens belonged to the gods and religious beliefs and to those who took those beliefs in their charge on behalf of the gods, but that did not prevent the emergence of astronomy. It might have impeded the emergence of astronomy but it did not prevent it. Man's body in the West was God's creation, but that too did not prevent the study of anatomy or the understanding of the circulation of the blood. In Greece and in Rome and in medieval Islam, in the writings of Aristotle, Polybius, Thucydides, and Ibn Khaldun ideas were put forth which have reappeared in modern sociology, but the subject never became precipitated in the way in which physics or mathematics became established in the seventeenth and eighteenth centuries. Ancient Greece and Rome and medieval Islam were not secularized societies, they were not traditionless societies in which authority and custom had receded from earlier strength. So the hypothesis that sociology requires for its existence a secularized society is not quite satisfactory. There is however something in the hypothesis that sociology requires a cultural matrix or setting which is not so exigent in its demands on substantive belief that it stifles detachment. There is something in the hypothesis that sociology requires a loosening of the belief that divine or magical powers intervene at will in human affairs. It is also true that sociology as a body of generalized knowledge about society requires freedom from a jealous and pervasive ecclesiastical or secular authority which is apprehensive about the potential dangers of the formation of beliefs which are not necessarily identical with those it holds about itself and its society. These conditions, however, are the conditions of any intellectual activity which is not wholly committed in advance to agreement with the views held by ecclesiastical and earthly authorities in matters which those authorities believe are vital.

What I wish to say here is that the recession of earthly and ecclesiastical authority, and a loosening of the grip of traditional beliefs which consecrate that authority, are only very general preconditions. They tell very little about the intellectual direction and the territorial location of the growth of sociology.

Sociology, even if it is not very scientific, is, in its better manifestations, an intellectual accomplishment. The practice of sociology—i.e., sociological teaching, sociological investigation, and sociological reflection—is an intellectual activity. As an intellectual activity, it operates within the pattern of thought contained in intellectual traditions; each sociological action takes place within the framework of the traditions which it in turn affects and, in some important instances, modifies markedly. The traditions of sociology are even now not rigorously coherent and authoritative in their presentation and they were less so in their earlier states in the nineteenth and twentieth centuries. These traditions have offered to their recipients a variety of possibilities. There has been a process of selection by individuals confronting the traditions. The selection has been limited by intellectual givenness or self-evidentness (which is characteristic of any tradition), and opportunity for exposure of individuals to particular streams of tradition; this exposure is disciplined when it takes place through institutions which both consciously and unthinkingly determine which constituents of the traditional stock should be presented to the individuals who expose themselves. Institutions have not created sociology; it has been created by individual sociologists exercising their powers of observation and analysis on social situations apprehended within the focusing framework of sociological traditions. Observation includes second- and third-hand observation through informants, documents, and printed works which report observations by others. Each of these sources is a precipitate of observations made within the framework of traditions. It is the task of the sociologist to interpret these precipitates of other traditions in the light of his own sociological traditions. These sociological traditions can be acquired by individuals who seek them out in the books and persons in which they are embodied. Institutions reduce the task of seeking; they make it easier and they reduce the freedom of a somewhat more random, autodidactic search. Institutions concentrate attention on particular elements of a tradition; they reinforce certain selected ways of perceiving and interpreting experience. Institutions foster the production of works, and the works, with what they contain in the way of interpretation of social reality, become part of the focusing tradition. Institutions present a resonant and echoing intellectual environment to those within them and they make what is produced under their influence more visible in the public realm outside the institution. The sociological ideas which undergo institutionalization are thereby given a greater weight in the competition of interpretations of social reality.

Institutionalization

By institutionalization of an intellectual activity I mean the relatively dense interaction of persons who conduct that activity within a social arrangement which has boundaries, endurance, and a name. The interaction has a structure. The more intense the interaction, the more its structure makes place for authority which makes decisions regarding assessment, admission, promotion, allocation; the authority also sets the criteria for the selection of those particular traditions which are to be cultivated in teaching and inquiry. There need not be a formal stipulation of the criteria; they can and usually are simply embodied in the practice of the authorities—in this case, those who are most imposing intellectually. The high degree of institutionalization of an intellectual activity entails its teaching and investigation within the regulated, scheduled, and systematically administered organization. The organization regulates access through a scrutiny of qualification, and it provides for the organized assessment of performance; it allocates facilities, opportunities, and rewards for performance, e.g., study, teaching, investigation, publication, appointment, etc. It also entails the acquisition of the resources—monetary or material—needed to support the activity from outside the particular institutions. It entails too, provision for the diffusion of the results of the activity beyond the boundaries of the institution through publication in the most general sense of making the results available to the public, lay or specialized, outside the boundaries of the particular institution. (Marginal exceptions exist with regard to this last feature: an institution for the cultivation of a hermetic science or philosophy, or an institution doing "secret" research with the results of the research being transmitted to the privileged "user.") An intellectual activity need not be equally institutionalized in all the indicated respects. It should also be remembered that an intellectual activity can be carried on fruitfully with only a very rudimentary degree of institutionalization. Indeed, some of the greatest periods of intellectual production in the sciences and philosophy have been marked by relatively rudimentary institutional organization. There must be some institutional organization for the acquisition of elementary instruction and for the transmission of the results of inquiry in printed or manuscript form. Institutional organization is not necessarily good. All I contend here is that its presence and form make a difference to the fate of traditions.

Sociology is more institutionalized where it can be studied in a university than where it has to be the object of private study; where it can be studied in a university as a major subject than where it can only be studied as an adjunct subject; and where it has a specialized teaching staff of its own rather than teachers who do it only as a marginal obligation while their main obligation is the teaching of economics or philosophy. Sociology is more institutionalized where there are opportunities for the publication of sociological works in specifically sociological journals rather than in journals devoted primarily to other subjects; where there is financial, administrative, and logistic provision for sociological investigation through established institutions rather than from the private resources of the investigator; where there are established and remunerated opportunities for the practice of sociology in teaching and research; and where there is a "demand" for the results of sociological research.

Sociology today is a relatively highly institutionalized branch of study in the countries of Western Europe and of North America—more recently in the former than in the latter. The social sciences became established as academic subjects later than most of the other major academic disciplines, e.g., mathematics, physics, chemistry, zoology, botany, classics, oriental studies, the national language and literature, which are now to be found in university courses of study. Sociology was the last of the social sciences to attain this status. The social sciences have, however, now made up the distance. Degrees, undergraduate and postgraduate, are now awarded for the completion of organized courses of study in these subjects; research training under qualified teachers is provided, often in research teams whose work is organized by the teachers, supervised, and reported preliminarily in seminars where the work is criticized. Journals with professionally and academically qualified referees and often supported by learned societies and sometimes by commercial publishers are available for the publication of the results of research in each field and often for quite specialized subfields. In addition to more routine and periodic meetings of learned societies, there is, for practitioners and apprentices in each field and in many subfields and even in the informally circumscribed domain of a problem, an elaborate network of communication through the circulation of offprints, memoranda, and preliminary versions of research reports. Practically all of these activities are firmly incorporated into the structure of universities and professional societies which have a momentum of their own.

In the first half of the nineteenth century, sociology did not exist as an academic subject anywhere, although of course it had academic forerunners in the *Staatswissenschaften,* in the juridical sciences, in the occasional teaching of economics, especially historical economics, and in moral philosophy. Its academic establishment which began slowly and unevenly in the last years of the nineteenth century was however made possible by a loosely articulated set of intellectual traditions of study which extend back of Western antiquity and which acquired focus and delineation in the course of the nineteenth century. The successful intellectual development of economics in England and its relative failure in Germany show that institutionalization is neither a necessary nor sufficient condition of intellectual achievement. Economics was only very faintly institutionalized in the former and it was quite well institutionalized in Germany. To be well institutionalized is in a certain sense to be a success, but this is not the same as intellectual success.

The chief figures of the tradition of economic analysis in Great Britain were not generally university teachers; often they were not even university graduates. Indeed, not even in economics which became an intellectually orderly discipline—relatively speaking—much earlier than sociology and political science did the academic element have the field to itself. Adam Smith stands out as the first great important academic contributor to the subject, although political economy was only one of the four subjects for which he was responsible within his rather short tenure as professor, first of logic and then of moral philosophy. He had been out of academic life for thirteen years when *The Wealth of Nations* was published in 1776. Ricardo was never an academic, nor was James Mill, and the Reverend William Paley's teaching at Haileybury could not be regarded as strictly academic since that body was closer to a secondary school than a university. The synthesist of economic theory of the middle of the century, John Stuart Mill, had only the most marginal academic connections; he was rector of St. Andrews, a wholly honorific position and a very transient one; he never attended a university or taught at one. Cairnes, Senior, Fawcett, Sidgwick, and Jevons were university teachers, and beginning no later than with Alfred Marshall's first academic steps, serious students could obtain at a few places in Great Britain disciplined training in economic analysis. Empirical economic research was another matter, being largely in the hands of government officials, private amateurs, and voluntary bodies; it was largely avocational and minimally institutionalized. Even in this field, however, the possibility of acquiring guidance in the techniques of research existed within the academic frame. Thorold Rogers as professor at Oxford and Archdeacon Cunningham at Cambridge and King's College, London, could help a young man to learn to do economic research with a quantitative accent. If we compare the situation with that prevailing in France where economics was taught seriously only in the Conservatoire des arts et métiers, at the École des ponts et chaussées, and at other technical institutions where young men were being prepared for technological careers, or at the Collège de France where there were no students in economics, or at the Faculté de droit in Paris where economics was established in the 1870s and was suffocated under the legal lumber, we see one of the reasons why British economics led the world in the nineteenth and early twentieth centuries. British economics first established a sound intellectual tradition and became institutionalized only after it had done so.

It must be repeatedly emphasized that reference to institutionalization does not by any means wholly account for the great ascendancy of British economic analysis in this period. The British economists had a better idea of the problems to be studied, and this was partly a function of the high level of the organs of public opinion in Great Britain; the contacts of economists with the worldly affairs of parliament, investigative commissions, governmental departments, and leading politicians and businessmen also gave them experience on which they could exercise their analytical powers. The British economists had a more fruitful point of departure because they analyzed the equilibrium of an economic system and not the budgetary economic necessities of govenments. It was preoccupation with the latter which held back the development of economics in the German universities since it obstructed the understanding of the autonomy of the market. The discovery of the market was not a function of the academic institutionalization of economics; but once the discovery was made institutionalization did help to clarify, correct, and differentiate the original insight and to make it more widely available.

Sociology is little different in age from economics, and its institutional establishment in universities in the United States follows the institutional establishment of economics by only a few decades. Economics, however, had two clearly defined traditions—British economic theory and German historical economics—and it had one great figure who presided over the institutional establishment of economics in Great Britain; this was Alfred Marshall. Sociology had no such distinguished figure who was present at its academic establishment, and this caused the subject to lead a motley intellectual life, even up to the present.

Sociology had several important figures who established the name of the subject—itself a significant step—and who studied its subject-matter. Auguste Comte and Herbert Spencer were the greatest of these forerunners.

Each had many admirers and critics who regarded themselves as sociologists. When sociology was being established in universities both of them had fallen from the height of their reputations and there was no authoritative body of knowledge and theory to replace their doctrines. Tocqueville and Marx can certainly be regarded with legitimacy as forerunners of sociology but they were not recognized as sociologists at the beginning of the present century; it is only recently that they have been nominated for retroactive membership in the tradition. They were neither more nor less academic than Comte or Spencer, they had no students, no assistants, no monographic series or seminars; no dissertations were written under them to work out their ideas and to apply them to situations with which they had not dealt.[1] Comte and Spencer installed themselves at the beginning of the tradition by giving a name and a vague set of boundaries to the subject still to be born. But when the time came for sociology to be admitted into universities, they became part of the unused tradition.

Other originators, German historians and British and French statisticians, who in effect generated and impelled forward the tradition from which sociology as we know it emerged, have also not been equally acknowledged as the forerunners of sociology. The techniques which these scholars used and the subject-matters which they chose left an enduring imprint on the sociology which developed, but the substance of their ideas was not equally regarded. They merely added to the heterogeneity of sociology as it moved towards institutional establishment.

The European Founders: Academic Cultivation without Institutionalized Establishment

The distance between the universities and sociology during the first three-quarters of the nineteenth century was reduced when founders

1. Spencer's *Descriptive Sociology* played no part whatsoever in his entry into the tradition of sociology—which in substance departed very far from his ideas and has only recently showed a partial turn towards them.

replaced forerunners. Sociologists taught in the universities but sociology could not be studied. The five European founders who stand between the forerunners and the academically established generations of the present century were all academics. Only one of them, however, was academically responsible for teaching and training in sociology. Ferdinand Tönnies was *Privatdozent* in philosophy and later for several years professor of economics and statistics; he taught sociology only after his retirement. Vilfredo Pareto never taught sociology; he was a professor of economics for about five years in his late forties. Max Weber during his short academic career was professor of economics; he apparently taught sociology only after his brief return to university teaching in 1918. Georg Simmel taught philosophy as *Privatdozent* and *ausserordentlicher Professor* for most of his career—he occasionally lectured on sociological topics—and became *ordentlicher Professor* (but not for sociology) only a few years before his death. Emile Durkheim was the only one of the generation of founders who made a full academic career with an official responsibility for sociology. He was professor of sociology and education at Bordeaux from 1887 to 1902 and from then until his death in 1917 professor of the same subjects under various titles at the Sorbonne.

France. Of all the founders of sociology, only Durkheim was successful in establishing his subject during his lifetime. Only he had pupils and collaborators, regularly, over a long period. Sociology acquired an academic institutional form only around Durkheim and that was less through provision by the university than from Durkheim's own organizational initiative and skill in the formation of the *Année sociologique*.

Durkheim followed the German pattern: the professor of the subject covered the whole field himself, trained younger collaborators through intensive discussions, and published the results of their individual and joint work in the organ of the institute which was reserved primarily for contributors from his personal circle. One difference was that in Germany the university provided funds for the "institute" which was attached to the chair; in France there was no such provision for university professors. Another important difference between Germany and France was that in German universities those who worked with a professor in his institute were specializing in his discipline, were writing dissertations on it, and would depend on his sponsorship for *Habilitation* and subsequent academic appointment. There was provision for training in research at an advanced level in Germany from the early part of the century; in France it was only when the École pratique des hautes études was founded in 1868 that there was provision for training in research. But neither in Germany nor in France were these opportunities available to sociologists at the beginning of the twentieth century. Sociology as part of the "human sciences" came into the EPHE only when the *sixième section* was formed after the Second World War. There were furthermore few opportunities under the French educational and administrative systems for persons who had experience in sociological research. Those who studied sociology did it because they were genuinely interested rather than because they expected to make a career out of it, since very few could. This meant that Durkheim's entourage consisted of intellectually deeply interested persons whose professional possibilities and aspirations lay outside sociology. While they were active members of his circle they produced important sociological works, but once they became active in their own careers, which entailed research and teaching in specialized fields such as sinology, ethnography, comparative religion, and philosophy, they produced little which belonged to the core of sociology. Their reproductive capacity as sociologists was slight since very few of them became teachers of sociologists. They became sinologists, linguists, administrators, etc. They did not train sociologists because there were very few students of sociology; there were very few students of sociology because there were practically no posts in sociology to which they could hope to be appointed later in their careers.

In France, therefore, the institutionalization and the resultant expansion and continuity of production was generated almost entirely by the personal force of the individual professor. He was helped, of course, by the existence of the EPHE and the section on *sciences réligieuses,* which was not dominated by professors.[2]

The sociological ideas of Durkheim largely died away in France not

2. Because the EPHE was not dominated by professors, it was possible for Durkheim to attract to his circle young men who were preparing to enter other disciplines. This would have been impossible in Germany. A professor would not hold commerce with a research student who did not give promise of becoming a disciple, and a student would not dare to risk his career by serving a professor outside his own subject, the subject in which he wished to make his career. French professors were jealous and students depended on them for

very long after Durkheim himself died, as far as their application to modern society was concerned. Davy, who published an important Durkheimian treatise in the early 1920s, taught in a provincial university, entered educational administration first in a provincial university and then in the government, and became a professor of sociology only in 1944. Bouglé too became an administrator and ceased to concern himself primarily with sociology. Simiand worked as a government official and only later in his life became a professor—of labor history. Granet continued to be a faithful and creative Durkheimian and a great sociologist but his teaching was entirely sinological and he had no students of sociology. Mauss became professor of "primitive religion" early on and later became director of the Institut d'ethnologie at the Sorbonne as well as professor at the Collège de France; in none of these capacities did he have students of sociology, understood either as a general theory of society or as the study of modern societies. The *Année sociologique* came upon hard times and appeared with increasing infrequency during the 1920s; no other French sociological journal replaced it.

Durkheim left behind a wonderful band of disciples in specialized fields which were at the periphery of sociology; but since sociology was not institutionalized at the center, their accomplishments remained dispersed. There was no consolidation and no sociological succession. Only Maurice Halbwachs continued the Durkheimian tradition as a sociologist studying modern societies, but, aside from his own work, there was little extension. Halbwachs was a man of exceptional intellectual power and great erudition and he was also a very productive author. He was faithful to Durkheim's tradition but he was not paralyzed by it; he approached new topics and he had original ideas. Yet he was unable to reestablish the school by extending and deepening the traditions flowing from Durkheim. His work and that from which it drew the main lines of its outlook was not taken up by younger French sociologists and did not enter into the course of the sociological development.

A tentative explanation does not seem too difficult. Halbwachs was

---

patronage. Nonetheless, Durkheim did attract young men who could not make a career in sociology and who would ultimately have to make a career in some other academic discipline. Perhaps this is to be accounted for by the power of Durkheim's intellectual personality and by the fact that in the fields from which Durkheim drew his adherents there were so few opportunities that even subservience to the incumbent professor was usually professionally fruitless.

a professor at Strasbourg, a distinguished university, but not one to which the best students flocked from all over France. It had recently been converted from being a German university. At Strasbourg, Halbwachs as a sociologist was alone. He did not, as far as I know, supervise dissertations, this privilege being reserved by convention and prudence for Parisian professors. He had no younger colleagues to associate themselves with him. Thus, this powerfully and sensitively intelligent man who carried forward the Durkheimian tradition, but in no uncritically submissive way, had no juniors of sufficient quality and in sufficient numbers on whom to leave a mark. The intellectual population around him was not dense enough; the necessary complement of institutions—specializing students, postgraduate training, research projects, and research assistants and journals—were not available to him.

Durkheim's ideas were of course available in a "free-floating" form, as Max Weber's were in Germany in the 1920s. Not all intellectual filiations need to be transmitted by an apostolic succession within the framework of a corporate body. Influences certainly need not be transmitted only through institutional establishment and impressed by reenactment in research and publication under supervision and in collaboration. This situation requires the existence of a lay public interested in the subject and ready to support it financially and intellectually. This was lacking in France. The heart had gone out of the quest for a new secular morality which was one of the driving forces of Durkheim's sociology. The teaching of sociology in the lycées which was intended to realize this goal did not compensate for its evaporation.[3] It is sometimes said that the death in battle of some of the most distinguished of the younger collaborators of the Année sociologique was the cause of the cessation of the Durkheimian outlook in French sociology, and there is some truth in this. More important, however, was the fact that the institutional structure built by Durkheim rested only on him and was not integrated into the institu-

3. The one form in which Durkheimian tradition was institutionalized in France after his death was in the teaching and the textbooks of civic morals used in the lycées. But rather than recruit sociologists, it alienated persons who might have become sociologists. Raymond Aron was one of those who was alienated from Durkheim's tradition by this mode of presentation. He was recovered only by encountering Max Weber when he went to Germany at the beginning of the 1930s.

tional structure of the French academic system or into the opportunities for professional careers outside the universities.

Germany. The fate of sociology in Germany supports this interpretation. Since the three great founders of sociology in Germany were not professors of the subject, they had no research institutes such as German professors ordinarily had for their subjects. They had no ongoing seminars for training students in research and for bringing their dissertations to the point where they could be published as monographs. Also there was no place for them to go as professional sociologists once they finished their training—had such training been available in Germany. There were before the First World War no professorships of sociology in universities, in technical or teacher-training colleges. There were no junior posts in sociology in the universities, just as there were no senior posts. There was practically no employment for sociologists as sociologists outside universities.

Max Weber was located in Heidelberg from 1896 to 1918. It was in Heidelberg that he developed his most significant sociological ideas. He did not teach during most of this time, and his audience was confined to personal friends and his "circle"; not many of them did much to develop his ideas further. There was no established academic except Ernst Troeltsch who worked out any of Max Weber's ideas. Ernst Troeltsch was professor in Heidelberg from 1894 to 1914 and it was while he was professor there that he published his *Die Bedeutung des Protestantismus für die Entstehung der modernen Welt* and *Die Soziallehren der christlichen Kirchen und Sekten*, which Max Weber in his turn helped to amplify and more widely distribute.

Weber had close relations with Heinrich Rickert and Karl Jaspers in Heidelberg but they were only marginally interested in sociological work. Eberhard Gothein was a little closer to Max Weber's sociological interests. Among younger scholars Georg Lukàcs and Paul Honigsheim were the closest to sociology; the former became a Marxist during the war, then a communist, and spent the rest of his life as a Marxist literary critic and philosopher with little understanding for sociology; Honigsheim never succeeded in making an academic career in Germany. There was no chair of sociology in Heidelberg and hence no seriously interested students. The *Archiv für Sozialwissenschaft und Sozialpolitik* covered all the social sciences and could not give sociology the dignity which a journal of equal quality concentrated on the subject could confer. Weber shared the editorship of the *Archiv* with other distinguished scholars whose interests were not primarily in sociology. His intellectual-convivial life was spent in a diverse company which included philosophers, jurists, and literary critics, and Weber neither gave it a sociological focus nor shaped its output in the manner in which Durkheim had done with his entourage.

In the next generation, Alexander von Schelting and Karl Mannheim were Weber's main sociological continuators. Alexander von Schelting understood Max Weber's methodological ideas with a precision and elaborateness which was unique. He was not, however, *habilitated* until after the end of the Weimar republic. He went into exile and taught briefly at Columbia before the renaissance created by Merton and Lazarsfeld. Then after years of severe poverty in Switzerland he died without influence and with the sociological part of his study of the Russian intelligentsia unfinished. His *Max Weber's Wissenschaftslehre* remains the most thorough analysis of the subject. It was drawn on by Parsons in his analysis of Max Weber's methodological ideas but it remained without influence in Germany.

Mannheim was in Heidelberg through the 1920s. He was a protégé and devotee of Alfred Weber; from him he adopted the idea of *freischwebende Intelligenz*. He attended Marianne Weber's colloquia. Max Weber's ideas were a living presence but only a very general one at Heidelberg at that time. Except for Mannheim, none of the numerous professors and *Privatdozenten* who professed sympathy and admiration for Max Weber's ideas undertook to apply them. It was Max Weber's ideas on bureaucracy which Mannheim absorbed and which he tried to elaborate in his essay on *Erfolgsstreben;* Max Weber's ideas about rationalization were at the bases of *Mensch und Gesellschaft im Zeitalter des Umbaus,* which he wrote and published while in exile. It was also an idea of Max Weber, the idea of a charismatic revolutionary directly inspired by a believed contact with ultimate things, which Mannheim adapted in his essay on the utopian mentality in *Ideologie und Utopie* and which he took up again towards the end of his life in his development of the notion of "paradigmatic experiences" in the *The Diagnosis of Our Time.*

Mannheim's relations with Max Weber's ideas were affected by the fact that he came to Heidelberg only after Weber had died, and his mind was confused by his subjection to certain fundamental categories of Marxism at the same time that he was aware of its untenability; he was also affected by working in Heidelberg in a situation in which there was no systematic analysis or discriminating application of Weber's substantive sociological ideas. It should also be said that the failure of the imprint of Weber's ideas was fostered not just by the absence of any sustaining intellectual-institutional structure around Mannheim, but also by Mannheim's hidden and ambivalent struggle to establish a distinctive line of his own different from Scheler's, different from Marx's, and different from that of German idealism.

When Mannheim went to Frankfurt, he replaced Franz Oppenheimer, who had been a *Privatdozent* and finally a professor after nearly twenty years in private medical practice and whose immense eight-volume treatise, written in the service of his ideas on the monopoly of landed property-owners, had no intellectual afterlife at all. Mannheim brought Max Weber's ideas to Frankfurt. He was an attractive teacher and had enthusiastic students but his tenure was too brief and there were few opportunities for employment for those who took their degrees under him. In any case, they were soon scattered by exile or silenced by National Socialism. This was the end of Mannheim's influence in Germany. It was also the end of such influence as Max Weber's ideas had had through Mannheim's interpretation of them.

During the Weimar republic there were many professors of sociology or of sociology and a related discipline. They were poorly equiped to do research in the light of their own ideas and they were not disposed towards the acceptance of Weber's ideas either. Some of the work on white-collar employees owed something to the stimulus of Weber's writing on bureaucracy, although I think that only Hans Speier's work is clear-cut in this respect. The professors of sociology in Germany in the Weimar period—Vierkandt, Rumpf, von Wiese, Geiger, Freyer, Meusel, Walther, Dunckmann, et al.—were proper German professors in the sense that each one wanted to have a system of his own which he wanted his students to carry on. Most of them wrote books of "principles" which were largely variations on the theme of *Gemeinschaft* and *Gesellschaft*. They had few ideas of their own; they had little interest in research which would do other than reiterate some part of their conceptual scheme. They certainly had no interest in Max Weber's substantive sociology. They were, however, unlike the classical type of German professor in that they created nothing important of their own and they trained no *Nachwuchs*. Albert Salomon, who was a professor in a normal school for training teachers, was a devotee of Max Weber but he had no products and no heirs. Hans Speier, who was a pupil of Mannheim and a protégé of Emil Lederer, was one of the very few who did interesting research on social stratification much influenced by Max Weber's ideas.

In any case, it all ended with the virtual obliteration of sociology by the Nazi regime.

Max Weber faded out of German sociology in the decade when a number of professorships in sociology were created in universities and technical and pedagogical colleges. It was an outsider to Heidelberg and Germany who did more for the animation of Max Weber's sociological ideas than anyone else. Talcott Parsons came to Heidelberg in the middle of the 1920s. He did more to bring Max Weber's sociological ideas into the heart of the subject than anyone else. But that is another chapter.

Until the 1920s, when the *Kölner Vierteljahreshefte für Soziologie* was founded, German sociologists had no journal of their own in which they could publish their works and thereby define their identity as sociologists. In consequence of this, there was no concentration of minds on the ideas of great potentiality which came from the three or four great German figures to whom the sociological world now looks back as founders. The ideas of Max Weber, Georg Simmel, and Ferdinand Tönnies—and possibly Max Scheler—did not undergo the process of reinterpretation, partial assimilation, and elaboration which is the characteristic course of development of intellectual products. The failure to do this reinforced the causes of the failure. At the University of Cologne there was, it is true, one active professor of philosophy and sociology, and one professor of sociology. Leopold von Wiese was the professor of sociology; he had students, a research institute, and a journal, those three important constituents of the institutionalization of an academic subject. Unfortunately for German sociology, von Wiese's ideas were incapable of development. He was concerned primarily with nomenclature and taxonomy and led his students to no other tasks. Institutionalization could only have consolidated intellectual sterility.[4] Max Scheler, who was professor of philosophy and sociology, was an extremely fertile scholar who worked in the area between philosophy and sociology. He was full of interesting ideas and for a time gathered about himself a number of younger scholars but he left the field after five years and returned to philosophy.

Great Britain. Another "founder" of sociology was L. T. Hobhouse, who was professor of sociology at the London School of Economics from 1907 until 1929. Hobhouse had a widely ranging comparative interest. The breadth of his knowledge and his interest in the trends of social changes were in some ways comparable to Weber's, and he organized one major piece of research which was unique until recently for its use of quantitative methods in comparative study. In his time, he was the only professor of sociology in the United Kingdom devoting all his time to his subject. The subject was not taught in other universities. There was no employment for graduates in sociology, no undergraduate specialization in sociology, and very few postgraduate students. The one sociological journal, *The Sociological Review*, in Hobhouse's lifetime was under the dominion of geographers and amateur followers of Le Play. *The New Survey of London Life and Labour* seems to have been planned and executed without Hobhouse's participation. He lacked an interest in the concrete details of modern societies. His power of inspiration was not great enough to offset the institutional obstacles. Today Hobhouse is almost entirely disregarded by sociologists.[5] Part of the explanation for the oblivion into which Hobhouse has fallen lies partly in the fact that

4. Von Wiese's pupils did do a small amount of fieldwork (see *Das Dorf als soziales Gebilde* [*Kölner Vierteljahreshefte für Soziologie*, Beiheft I, 1928]). The result was simply the discovery of illustrations of the concepts of *allgemeine Beziehungslehre*. Dr. Willy Gierlichs, a pupil of von Wiese, taught in a police training college; again this first step in the institutionalization of sociology in an applied form led to nothing because von Wiese chose the most sterile part of Simmel's sociology to try to develop. Neither the conceptions of formal sociology nor of *Zu- und Auseinander* were very fertile points of departure and von Wiese did not have the imaginative powers to draw out of them what little they contained.

5. In the index of the *International Encyclopaedia of the Social Sciences*, there are two references to Hobhouse, fifty-eight to Durkheim, and sixty-four to Max Weber.

his interpretation of modern society was not vivid enough to arouse the interest of the students of the London School of Economics so that they would risk their careers in order to benefit from his guidance. This was a major difference between him and Durkheim. Hobhouse had a colleague, Edward Westermarck,[6] who taught part of each session; they were the sole incumbents of professorial chairs of sociology in the United Kingdom. Furthermore, despite the sympathetic support of R. H. Tawney, there was no informal consensus among the more esteemed academic personalities regarding the value of the sociological approach to social matters. (Such a consensus began to appear only after the Second World War.)

The great tradition of empirical sociological inquiry in Great Britain which had developed independently of the universities remained so until well after the First World War; it had been the work of government officials and public-spirited private citizens of means without the help of the universities. Officially, the situation was not too different from that in France, but the strength of Durkheim's personality, the persuasiveness of his convictions, and the superior prestige of the Sorbonne in the French university system—which the London School of Economics did not at that time possess—made a great difference. More important than the relatively low prestige of the London School of Economics in British academic life during Hobhouse's career there from 1907 to 1929 was that the type of young collaborators available to Durkheim at the Sorbonne were not available to Hobhouse at the London School of Economics. Whereas Durkheim was able to draw to himself young scholars who were specialists in folklore, oriental studies, and linguistics, these subjects did not exist at the London School of Economics. Such studies were pursued at University College, London, and at the School of Oriental and African Studies, where they had practically no contact with sociology. There were few postgraduate students and young lecturers at these other institutions and they had to make their careers by meeting the specialized requirements of their own departments. Young Oxford and Cambridge dons in classics and oriental studies in the first quarter of the present century were unlikely to be drawn to a professor at the London

6. Westermarck, whose own work was in the tradition of German *Völkerkunde*, had one pupil who transformed his subject; that was Malinowski, and what he did was for a long time coterminous with social anthropology.

School of Economics. The fact that the latter was not an imperious personality like Durkheim and lacked his organizing enterprise and the fact that evolutionism, even of the more cautious type espoused by Hobhouse, enjoyed little intellectual esteem at the time in British academic circles, tightened the limitations on any influence which Hobhouse might have exerted. Hobhouse's one distinguished protégés was Professor Morris Ginsberg, who succeeded him, but Ginsberg was a shy and self-critical person and not a vigorous organizer like Durkheim. The result was that the French sociology of Durkheim's circle left behind a massive deposit. British academic sociology—Hobhouse's variant of sociological evolutionism—left behind only the one work on the material culture of simpler peoples.[7]

The eugenics movement, which was not academically institutionalized, came in a roundabout way to have a more powerful impact on British sociology. It did so through its connection with the development of sophisticated statistical techniques by Galton, Pearson, and Fisher and through the short-lived Department of Social Biology at the London School of Economics under the leadership of Lancelot Hogben in the 1930s and the Population Investigation Committee, which has had a longer life. Important British studies in social selection and mobility belong to this tradition rather than to Hobhouse's. The greatest British survey was *The Life and Labour of the People of London* in seventeen volumes. This work was a culmination of a tradition of the *Reports* of the poor law commissioners and of the work of the great officials interested in public health, housing,

---

7. Professor Talcott Parsons spent one year at the London School of Economics before going to Heidelberg where he also spent a year. Hobhouse, whose seminar he attended, made no intellectual impact on him—all he could say of it years later was, quoting Crane Brinton, "Who now reads Herbert Spencer?" Weber, who had been dead for about five years when Parsons came to Heidelberg, made a profound impression of lifelong duration. Here again it is obvious that institutionalization is not the only factor which determines intellectual impact—in both Germany and in England, in their different ways, sociology was very slightly institutionalized academically. The power of their intellectual penetration, the pregnancy of the problem, the scope of its ramifications, the persuasiveness of the argument (insight, logic, evidence), and the magnetism of the rhetoric and the responsiveness and intellectual power of the student are surely of the first importance. Yet, the fact that Weber had no impact in Germany despite his greatness and his ubiquitous fame shows that the factor of institutionalization is an independent variable of some importance.

and "sanitary conditions." Practically none of this work was done under academic auspices. The surveys of the middle of the century were done by government officials. Mayhew's *London Labour and the London Poor* was the work of a journalist; Booth was a wealthy shipping merchant who financed and directed his survey as a private inquiry. Rowntree, who conducted the survey of York called *Poverty: A Study of Town Life* at the beginning of the century, was also a wealthy businessman without university connections.

When in the 1920s a *New Survey of London Life and Labour* was undertaken, it was directed from the London School of Economics, but it had no connection with the Department of Sociology at the school. Furthermore, it was a transient enterprise. When the survey was finished, the organization through which it had been conducted was disbanded. While the Population Investigation Committee functioned at the London School of Economics and produced important works in demography and social selection, it worked wholly independently of the department of sociology. It did not serve to train and recruit professional sociologists, except for Professor David Glass who was at that time a geographer and who came into the department of sociology only after the end of the Second World War. A department of research techniques was created after the war; it was also entirely separate from the department of sociology but it at least represented the institutionalization of social research. By this time, opportunities for employment in social research had begun to increase as a result of the use of survey techniques by government and private business.

American Founders: The Beginnings of Institutional Establishment in the Universities

Sociology had a different fate in the American universities. It became institutionalized earlier in the United States than anywhere else in the world; it became institutionalized earlier at the University of Chicago than elsewhere. Provision for teaching sociology at Columbia and Yale universities also occurred at about the time it did at Chicago, but by the turn of the century provision for training and research began at Chicago—hesitantly but encouragingly. There was not much to show at first. Research was occasional and discontinuous. In its first decade Chicago had little to show apart from very minor and scattered pieces of research. The University of Pennsylvania, which sponsored W. E. B. Du Bois' *The Negro in Philadelphia,* and Columbia University, where James Mickel Williams did a pioneering community study, *An American Town,* as his doctoral dissertation, did not lag markedly behind Chicago at this time. The youth of the latter, the first president's determination to make it into a university in which research was as important as teaching—Gilman had already taken the lead in this direction at Johns Hopkins University—the large number of vigorous young professors wishing to install in Chicago the research-centered seminars which they had known in German universities, created a propitious atmosphere for research from the very start. Furthermore all the departments being new, there was no "old guard" to hamper the immediate establishment of a department of sociology. There was also a "demand" for sociology in the city of Chicago. Movements to improve the condition of the poor and to improve the quality of public institutions were also very active and from the first they drew to themselves the professors of the new university, above all Professors G. R. Henderson and G. H. Mead. It was perhaps the first time that academic sociologists as a class were welcomed by reformers with much practical experience. There were so many propitious signs.

Nonetheless, the movement of sociology was slow and there was little to show for it. Albion Small was steeped in German historical scholarship; indeed, it was there that he had found the origins of sociology. But scholar and idealist that he was, his confidence in the future of the subject with which he had been entrusted by the president of the university rested on its capacity for direct, firsthand observation of the contemporary scene.

Small believed in what later came to be called "empirical research"; he believed in seminars and postgraduate studies where such research would be treated. But for the time being, there were none. Henderson, who was primarily concerned with urban welfare problems, also appreciated the desirability of descriptions and analyses of urban life, particularly the life of the poor, the immigrants, the working classes, etc., but he did not do research either. He also believed that it should be done, that it should be based on firsthand observation, and that its results would be helpful in the improvement of society. The Germanic respect for learning, intellectual curiosity, a belief that what had been inherited was not enough and that the welfare of society had need of it, all made for the conviction that a new type of research was needed. It did not come straightaway. Even W. I. Thomas, who received the third Ph.D. granted by the Department of Sociology and who became in a sense the first American sociologist of the new dispensation continued to work at first from printed scientific literature in physical anthropology and from the published literature of ethnography.[8] Participant-observational studies and the use of human documents came forward only gradually.

W. I. Thomas was more than any other person responsible for this development. He developed further a new type of study which had been created in Germany—the *Volkskunde* of living German rural society, based on field observation and interviewing—but which had never found a place in German university studies in the social sciences.[9] Thomas' readiness to observe directly, to collect the "human documents" of living persons was welcomed by Small and Henderson. They did not think that it was undignified for a professor or for the professor's pupils to wander about the streets or to interest themselves in "low life." This was very different from the German academic situation where even those senior academic figures who were members of the *Verein für Sozialpolitik* and thus very concerned about the condition of the working classes thought that information about them had to be obtained through *Sachverständige,* i.e., from middle-class persons who in a professional capacity—as magistrates, clergymen, municipal administrators, physicians, etc.—were in contact with the lower classes. Even Max Weber in his studies of the East Elban agricultural workers used that device.

This accomplishment of the Chicago Department of Sociology in the first decades of the century hardly seems to be a great intellectual accomplishment. Yet it marked the beginning of a specific and vital feature of modern sociology. It was a change from the concern with

8. As did William Graham Sumner at Yale. Sumner never went beyond this, and since his students were in the vast majority undergraduates who had no interest in pursuing sociology further Yale did not become an important center of sociology.

9. Thomas spent the academic session of 1888–89 at the universities of Berlin and Göttingen. This was before he enrolled as a Ph.D. student at the University of Chicago which was, in fact, nonexistent during Thomas' German years.

abstractly formulated laws, from cut-and-dried pronouncements about statistical regularities; it was an introduction of vividness and immediacy. It linked sociology with journalism and literature. It opened it to a wider audience. It gave it a new strength and added another weakness. This distinctive development went further when, at the beginning of the second decade of the century, W. I. Thomas, succeeded in persuading Robert Park, who until then had led a somewhat errant existence as a newspaperman, an organizer of the American Congo Society, a student in Germany, an assistant in philosophy at Harvard, an amanuensis to Booker T. Washington at Tuskegee Institute, and a man of omnivorous intellectual curiosity and of a capacious and variegated learning, to join the Department of Sociology at Chicago. Park brought with him several things which were already present at Chicago but which he reinforced to the point where they made a great difference. As a newspaperman interested in urban life and as a detached observer of the humanitarian and civic movements, he was already acquainted with the surveys by which civically concerned bodies and individuals had attempted to arouse public opinion regarding the condition of the poor in the great cities. These surveys were an intellectual inheritance from the American promoters of social improvement of the second half of the nineteenth century and the muckrakers at the turn of the century; they were of course greatly influenced by the British surveys of the preceding century.[10]

The surveys which attracted Park's attention had been conceived and carried out without benefit of academic sociology and without any connection with universities; when they were finished, the organization which had been created to carry them out disbanded. There was no provision for training a new generation of "surveyors" or for studious criticism of the techniques with a view to their improvement. The Chicago Department of Sociology changed this. Although the department itself never conducted surveys of the types conducted in Pittsburgh, Cleveland, and Springfield, it assimilated their techniques of direct observation and interviewing and the quantitative treatment—albeit elementary—of results into the training of postgraduate students. It pondered the technique of field study, reflected

10. See Abrams, Philip, *Origins of British Sociology* (Chicago: University of Chicago Press, 1968).

on interviewing, on the dangers of bias, and on the need to combine detachment and intimate understanding. I do not know whether Park had reflected much on these technical matters before he came to Chicago but he certainly thought a lot about them once he settled down to become a professional socioiogist.

Park also brought to Chicago a fresh and vivid sense of the essential themes of German analytical sociology. Park had attended Simmel's lectures at Berlin, he read his works, and he absorbed his views about certain features of modern society,[11] such as the limited character and impersonality of relationships and the rationalizing, calculating attitude. He brought too an awareness of American society outside the large cities of the North and the small towns of the Middle West; Africa, Asia, and Europe were already on his mind. The movements of peoples and the mixing and conflicts of ethnic groups, the restless expansiveness of nationality and the integration of societies through the flow of information were among his interests; they were not identical with Thomas' interests but they were close enough for the two men to precipitate an enduring sociological outlook. They were together only for less than a decade but during that short period each one reinforced the other. Without collaboration on any particular piece of research, they developed a basic consensus. Thomas alone, standing somewhat apart from the piety, humanitarianism, and civic agitation of the other members of the department, might not have had the impact on sociology in the 1920s which he did in fact have. Park, for his part, had never before been constrained by the presence of a powerful intellectual equal in close daily contact. Thomas' presence imposed some discipline on the intellectually wilful Park; and Park tried to formulate some general themes in a more orderly way than he had done before. His essentially ruminative mind was forced into a greater orderliness by the conventions of academic discourse. The combination of Park and Thomas and the intellectual virtues each evoked in the other showed the value of the American departmental mode of organization. The German chair placed the professor in a

11. He undoubtedly encountered the ideas of Tönnies about *Gemeinschaft* and *Gesellschaft,* but there is no reference to Tönnies in his dissertation, *Masse und Publikum,* or in his autobiographical reminiscences. He did reproduce a section from Tönnies *Die Sitte* (1913) in the *Introduction to the Science of Sociology* (Chicago: The University of Chicago Press, 1921), pp. 103–5.

position of a supreme being whom only professors of the same subject in other universities could criticize—often acrimoniously. Colleagueship is the heart of the department as an institution; it brought valuable results to sociology.

This combination came to fruition just after the end of the First World War—just as Thomas was forced to leave the University of Chicago. Privately financed, nonacademic bodies concerned with the relations of ethnic groups provided *debouchés* for sociologists. Among these were the Carnegie Corporation's studies of "Americanization" which enlisted the collaboration of Park and Thomas and a number of former students at Chicago; the report on *The Negro in Chicago* supported by the Commission on Race Relations, guided by Park, and conducted by Charles Johnson, then a graduate student in the Department of Sociology; and the Chicago Crime Commission, which employed John Landesco. Civic and municipal organizations concerned with juvenile delinquency likewise provided support and employment opportunities as well as willingness to open their records to sociologists. The establishment of the Institute of Juvenile Research provided employment for a number of graduate students, some of whom later became quite eminent sociologists. The institutional framework for a department of sociology which had been provided by Harper, Small, and Henderson before there was an intellectual content to put into it had such a content put into it by Thomas and Park. Without that framework, the content might not even been as well precipitated as it was; certainly this was so in the case of Park. The presence of Thomas, and then, after the latter's departure, the presence of energetic graduate students put Park on his mettle but it also kept him in the discipline of attempting to work out his ideas through teaching and guiding research.

The decade of the 1920s was the time when sociology became well-established institutionally. The teaching of sociology centered on "Park and Burgess," which promulgated the main principles of analysis. Ernest Burgess, whom Park chose as a collaborator, was a younger colleague; he carried on the tradition after Park withdrew. This tradition entailed undergraduate courses, postgraduate courses of lectures, seminars, examinations, individual supervision of small pieces of field research to be submitted as course and seminar papers and dissertations done under close supervision fitting into the scheme of analysis developed by Thomas, Park, and Burgess. It was sustained by the publication of some of the best dissertations in the Chicago Sociological Series published by the University of Chicago Press, which was also the publisher of other works by Chicago social scientists, and by the transformation of the *American Journal of Sociology* from an organ of aspirations and programs into an organ for the publication of the best research being done in the country. It was a means for keeping the graduates who had gone out to teach sociology in other universities and colleges within the intellectual community which had its most intense form in the department. It was reinforced by public authorities and civic groups which offered sponsorship and access to the records needed for research and by financial support from the university and from the Rockefeller Foundation. It was fortified by the proximity of the Department of Political Science in which Charles Merriam, Harold Lasswell, Leonard White, and Harold Gosnell complemented the work of the Department of Sociology. Merriam had a stock of knowledge on Chicago which was as intense and intimate as Park's, Thomas', and Burgess'.[12] The Local Community Research Committee which he initiated, with funds supplied by the Laura Spelman Rockefeller Memorial fund, brought together all those interested in working on Chicago. Lasswell, who was much younger, had interests as wide as the world; he spent many hours with Park, acknowledging a "long-standing indebtedness" to the older man for "his sagacious insight" and expressing admiration for Park's "creative interplay between hours of high abstraction and days of patient contact with humble detail."[13] Leonard White studied *The Prestige Value of Public Employment in Chicago*[14] and Gosnell studied voting and abstention from voting, and Negro political leaders in Chicago.[15]

12. Charles E. Merriam, *Chicago: A More Intimate View of Urban Politics* (New York: Macmillan, 1929), and Charles E. Merriam and Harold F. Gosnell, *Non-voting: Causes and Methods of Control* (Chicago: The University of Chicago Press, 1924).

13. Harold D. Lasswell, *World Politics and Personal Insecurity* (New York and London: McGraw-Hill, 1935), pp. v–vi.

14. Chicago: The University of Chicago Press, 1929.

15. *Getting Out the Vote* (Chicago: The University of Chicago Press, 1924), and *Negro Politicians* (Chicago: The University of Chicago Press, 1935).

An International Illustration of the Difference Made by
Institutionalization: The Diverse Fates of Horkheimer and
Mannheim

The significance of the institutional setting of sociology even in the
limited measure in which it was possible in sociology in Germany in
the 1920s and the early 1930s may be seen in the divergent destinies of
the ideas of Karl Mannheim on the one side and of Max Horkheimer
on the other. The differences in impact of the ideas of Mannheim and
Horkheimer after they left Germany also attest to the consequences of
the differences between Great Britain and the United States with
respect to the institutionalization of sociology.

Mannheim was the more original and many-sided of the two. He
had a richer theoretical imagination, a more differentiated perception
of contemporary society, a more vivid grasp of particular details than
Horkheimer and at least the same breadth of interest in macro-
sociological anaylsis. His knowledge of contemporary empirical research was greater than Horkheimer's and some of his ideas could
more easily have been translated into concrete research problems
than Horkheimer's. He wrote more and on more particular topics than
Horkheimer. Mannheim raised important problems; he dealt with
many issues of which only a few may be mentioned for illustrative
purposes: the conditions of political detachment and partisanship
among intellectuals, the patterns and functions of beliefs in society,
the conditions of different forms of conflict and consensus
among generations, the influence of different types of political
partisanship on conceptions of historical time. He touched on important epistemological questions and had vivid insight. His
problems involved matters of great contemporary interest, and some
of them were capable of being empirically investigated in the current
sociological style. Yet Mannheim has had little influence, and Horkheimer is in certain respects one of the most influential of modern
intellectuals. Mannheim was, according to some of his former students, a scintillating teacher, but in Germany he was a professor for
only four years before he was forced into exile. Although several very
interesting dissertations[16] and other works were produced under his

16. Hans Gerth, *Die sozialgeschichtliche Lage der bürgerlichen Intelligenz*
in Deutschland um die Wende des 18ten Jahrhunderts; Wilhelm Carlé, *Wel-*

inspiration, the output of his pupils during his Frankfurt period was neither massive nor concentrated enough to provide a focus of attention and to create a far-reaching consensus as to what ought to be done and how to go about it; several of them had in fact to be submitted after the Nazis had come to power and their authors were scattered over the earth. In 1933, Mannheim left Germany and went to the London School of Economics where, as in the time of Hobhouse and Westermarck, there were still very few postgraduate students of sociology, where there was little institutional provision for the organization, support, and supervision of research in sociology, where there was no organ of publication, and where there were no opportunities for the employment of those who had been trained in the subject. The years of the depression blocked numerous potential academic careers in Britain in well-established subjects while the labor market for students of a fledgling subject like sociology remained at a standstill. The war years brought further attrition of what was already meager. Mannheim left the London School of Economics in the middle forties and became professor of the sociology of education at the Institute of Education in London. He died in January 1947. He had, it is true, succeeded in establishing the International Library of Sociology and Social Reconstruction, an eclectic series which became a popular organ of sociological ideas after his death, although few of the works published in the series developed Mannheim's own line of thought.

The fortunes of Horkheimer's ideas were very different. Horkheimer's ideas themselves were relatively simple: all thought is embedded in the historical-social context in which it is conceived; modern society has become increasingly destructive of individuality as authority has become more concentrated and as organization has become more inclusive and more impersonal; man has become a pawn manipulated by the powerful; the capacity for and the use of reason have declined. They were the basic ideas of the "theory of mass society."

---

tanschauung und Presse; Jakob Katz, *Die Entstehung der Judenassimilation in Deutschland und deren Ideologie.* (These three works were printed only as dissertations.) Norbert Elias, *Uber den Prozess der Zivilisation,* 2 vols. (Basel: Vorlag zum Falken, 1938); Hans Weil, *Die Entstehung des dentichen Bildungsprinzips* (Bonn: F. C. Cohen, 1930), E. Kohn Bramstedt, *Aristocracy and Middle Classes in German Literature in the Nineteenth Century* (London: P. S. King, 1937).

In many respects Horkheimer's ideas were like Mannheim's although they were simpler and exhibited a slighter intimacy with the facts of contemporary societies. Horkheimer became in the course of several decades one of the most influential sociological writers of his time. He has certainly had a much greater impact on sociological work than Mannheim. Why was this so?

Horkheimer had the advantage of taking over the professorship of Professor Carl Grünberg, a historian of the emancipation of the peasantry in Central Europe and of the labor and socialist movements. Since before the First World War, Grünberg had produced an admirable scholarly journal, the *Archiv für die Geschichte des Sozialismus und der Arbeiterbewegung*. In the middle 1920s Grünberg began to publish a series of *Beihefte* which contained monographs on the subjects which came within the terms of reference of his chair—terms of reference which were becoming broader throughout the 1920s. An institute of social research was under Grünberg's direction. The same wealthy patrons who supported Grünberg's activities took over the responsibilities for the activities associated with the chair when Horkheimer succeeded to it. When Horkheimer was appointed to succeed Grünberg, the title of the chair was changed from "the history of socialism" to "social philosophy"; the *Archiv für die Geschichte des Sozialismus* was wound up and it was replaced by the *Zeitschrift für Sozialforschung*. The *Zeitschrift für Sozialforschung* and the Institut für Sozialforschung provided Horkheimer with two important institutional conditions for the expansion of his influence. Friedrich Pollock was the editor of the *Zeitschrift* but Horkheimer was obviously the leading spirit intellectually in the determination of editorial policy. The Institute already had to its credit a number of large monographic publications, one of which was a major work of sinological scholarship by the then Marxist scholar, K. A. Wittfogel (*Wirtschaft und Gesellschaft Chinas*), and another, under commission, was a Marxist study of European thought by Franz Borkenau (*Der Übergang von feudalen zum burgerlichen Weltbild*). No additional volumes of the series appeared during the remainder of Horkheimer's direction of the Institute in Germany. The journal was changed in content from the history of socialism and the labor movement to Marxist macrosociology and social psychology which combined Marxism and psychoanalysis. Only a few issues appeared before the

Nazis forced the Institute to cease its activities in Germany and to emigrate. It went first to Paris, where it was given transient hospitality at the Centre de documentation sociale which Charles Bouglé had created and attached to the École normale supérieure. In Paris, the *Zeitschrift* was taken up again and the large collaborative work on *Autorität und Familie* was published. This volume which combined psychoanalysis and Marxism—called "critical philosophy" by Horkheimer and his colleagues—was an impressive undertaking. It brought together the work of numerous collaborators and it testified to Horkheimer's outstanding skill as an organizer.

Since his patrons apparently had much of their wealth abroad, it was possible for Horkheimer to emigrate to the United States, together with his most devoted collaborators, and reassemble the group once he got here. Thanks to Horkheimer's enterprise, the Institute became affiliated to Columbia University. Horkheimer was granted a special status as a member of the staff of Columbia University and close ties were cultivated with certain members of the university. A collective institutional life was maintained and the journal was again produced, this time under the title of *Studies in Philosophy and Social Science*. When the United States entered the war, several of its members found employment in the Office of Strategic Services. Meanwhile, other members were making their way as authors and as scholars. As the war came towards its end, Horkheimer became research director of the American Jewish Committee which granted him a sum of money, which for that time was very large, to conduct a widely ranging study of anti-Semitism. This afforded financial support for a number of the stipendaries and associates of the Institute and it also brought the Institute into closer connection with American academics who were qualified in these techniques of social-psychological research. On the intellectual side, this arrangement permitted the Institute to fuse its "critical" point of view—an amalgam of Marxism, psychoanalysis, and patrician contempt for "mass society," i.e., American society—with the techniques of American social psychology and with the idiom then prevailing in American sociology. The outcome was a weighty, quite technical work on *The Authoritarian Personality* and a number of monographs on anti-Semitism and ethnic prejudices. The former work aroused a great deal of attention and has had a considerable influence on subsequent research. Franz Neumann and Otto Kircheimer, who did not belong to the inner nucleus of the Institute, after their service in the Office of Strategic Services became members of the Department of Government of Columbia University in the postwar expansion of the social sciences. They exercised much influence over younger staff members and postgraduate students. Both were notable scholars in their own right. Leo Löwenthal became professor at the University of California in Berkeley in the School of Speech and in the Department of Sociology. He became a leading writer on "mass culture" and on the sociology of literature. Herbert Marcuse, after having worked in the Office of Strategic Services and having then played a minor role as a "Sovietologist" at the Columbia University Institute of Russian Studies, became a professor at Brandeis and then in California and by the cunning of history, if not of reason, became an intellectual idol of the "new left." After establishing his reputation by warning against the dangers of freedom, Erich Fromm became the apostle of a society to be constituted by love and the sage of "socialist humanism." Karl Wittfogel became a leading anti-Communist student of Chinese history, after having been a crude and aggressive Communist polemicist as a young man in Weimar Germany. He became an eminent member of the University of Washington in Seattle.

The Institute then returned to Germany, carrying with it what it had learned of American sociological and social psychological techniques, and its own "critical philosophy" and its theory of mass society. It began at once a monograph series—not at all like the historical-sociological studies of the pre-Nazi period, but based to some extent on fieldwork, on interviews, sample surveys, group discussions, etc. Horkheimer and Adorno came to rank with the leading intellectual figures of the German Federal Republic.

In Germany, Jürgen Habermas, the leading protégé of Horkheimer and Adorno, became the main exponent of "critical sociology" and for a time one of the main intellectual inspirations of the Sozialistsche Deutsche Studentenbund. One of its younger associates, Ludwig von Friedenburg, became minister of education in the government of Hesse in which capacity he promoted the "emancipationist" doctrine of the Institute in the reform of primary and secondary education until he was forced to resign.

But the history of the Institut für Sozialforschung in Weimar Germany, the United States, and the Federal German Republic is not just the story of the cat which landed on its feet. It is a testimonial to the skill of a shrewd academic administrator, who by good luck and foresight inherited a favorable institutional situation and developed its connections within the various universities in which it was located, maintained its internal structure, and extended its external connections outside the university. As a result it became the mechanism by which some of the most influential ideas of present-day sociology developed. The doctrine of "mass society," which asserts the dehumanizing effects of subjugation by authority and which analyzes "mass culture" as a result of this dehumanization owes a great deal to the Institut für Sozialforschung. The allegations about the potentialities for fascism in liberal-democratic societies, and the delineation of the "power elite" are likewise in debt to the Institute. It has not only provided current ideas of the "new left," it has influenced and called forth a large amount of research among sociologists who had no direct connection with that political belief. In contrast with this, Karl Mannheim, who lacked the institutional setting which might have helped to create an orderly following, has found none since his death, despite the repeated calls for a sociology of knowledge.

This digression about the Institut für Sozialforschung has been intended only to show the significance of institutional establishment for the propagation of a set of ideas. Institutionalization is not a guarantee of truthfulness: it only renders more probable the consolidation, elaboration, and diffusion of the set of ideas which possess an appropriate institutional counterpart. It is not the sole determinant of the acceptance of diffusion of ideas. Intellectual persuasiveness, appropriateness to "interesting" problems, affinity with certain prior dispositions and patterns of thought of the potential recipient are also very significant. Institutionalization serves however to make the ideas so affected more available to potential recipients, it increases attention to them and renders concentration of effort on them more likely. In so far as it offers the possibility of a professional career in the cultivation of the particular intellectual activity, it both makes more likely the continuity and concentration and it adds a further motive for further exertion on their behalf. The existence of practical-intellectual professions which require the study of a particular body of knowledge as a qualification and as a constituent of professional practice provides a student body and teaching opportunities—and therewith research opportunities which develop in the interstices of teaching. In these ways, institutional establishment has made a difference in determining which currents of the heterogeneous tradition of sociology have become dominant.

The Institution of Sociology and Academic Systems

The practice of sociology may be seen as a constellation of centers and a set of overlapping and concentric circles formed by institutions and individuals. In Durkheim's case we saw the creation by an outstanding individual of a rudimentary institution of sociological work, which did not attain, however, an elaborated corporate structure in the production of the works themselves. Durkheim did not conduct seminars; he held informal discussions with his protégés. A corporate form was achieved in the organization and production of the *Année sociologique* and the *Travaux de l'Année sociologique*. The circle which Durkheim formed was a rudimentary institutionalization. It had various *ad hoc* connections with other institutions, e.g., the École pratique des hautes études, the École des langues orientales, etc., where the informally adherent members of the circle had their employment, and with Félix Alcan, the publisher of their works. Durkheim himself held a professorship at the Sorbonne and he himself therefore was an incorporated member of an academic institution: it was not, however, in that capacity that he organized the work of his circle. He created a protoinstitution with only peripheral and fragmentary institutional connections.

Max Weber's activity as a sociologist was much less institutionalized. He was not a professor of the subject; he supervised for a limited period several research projects for the Verein für Sozialpolitik, he tried—and failed—to institutionalize two research projects on the press and on voluntary associations through the Deutsche Gesellschaft für Soziologie; he wrote *Wirtschaft und Gesellschaft* as one section of a comprehensive series of handbooks on economics, organized by the publisher Siebeck; he edited a great journal of social science and social policy, very little of which was devoted to sociology. The connections of his sociological activities with institutions were peripheral, fragmentary, and transient.

Thomas and Park were more institutionalized in their practice of sociology—they taught the subject regularly within the framework of a systematic course of study, organized toward the granting of an undergraduate degree; they taught courses, conducted seminars, and supervised the research of students who were working towards postgraduate degrees. They themselves conducted organized research projects, employing assistants or collaborators, supported by university or externally granted funds. Many of the students whom they trained went on towards sociological careers as teachers and research workers. They occupied a constitutionally provided position in the structure of the university. They were linked relatively densely with civic, municipal, and private bodies which were interested in the results of their research and which encouraged them by their interest and occasionally by their financial support as well as by accommodating research workers in their midst or under their auspices. In the 1920s, private philanthropic foundations established the grant of funds for sociology, the Social Science Research Council established predoctoral and, later, postdoctoral fellowships for the promotion of sociology; some of these fellowships were granted for study in Chicago. In the decade of the depression, Chicago sociologists found employment as social statisticians in a number of governmental departments and agencies. Thus Chicago sociology, i.e., the sociology of Thomas and Park, was institutionally established at its center and in a fairly dense network of connected institutions removed at various degrees from their main activities in education and research.

The primary institutional system of sociology is thus affected by its linkages with the environing institutional context—the university itself, foundations, civic bodies, government, occupational careers, publishing enterprises, etc. The availability of the external institutions was of some consequence for the internal, primary institutional establishment of sociology, by the provision of legitimacy through the sponsorship of established institutions and through the provision of resources and opportunities for employment of students who had been awarded degrees in the subject.

The study of the establishment and diffusion of sociology and the influence of this process of institutionalization on the substantive composition of the sociological traditions cannot be confined to the study of primary institutionalization. It is necessary to ask why sociology was able to become institutionalized at a particular time in the United States when it did not become equally institutionalized in Europe, although at the same time the intellectual accomplishments of European sociology were greater in certain respects than those of American sociology.

To account for this we must go beyond the tradition of sociology and beyond the primary institutionalization of sociology. We must consider the wider social structures which permitted it, or inhibited it, or fostered it. The academic systems first of all: In Germany the creation of a new chair depended on the consensual decision of other professors in the same faculty (rivals for resources and prestige), of the university senate, and of the state minister of education. A new subject might be created by a *Privatdozent* but it could not by virtue of that become established in the university. An old university had an established allocation of resources, the beneficiaries of which would not readily allow it to be changed in favor of a subject lacking the legitimacy of age and accomplishment. New universities were more likely to allow new subjects to be taught than longer-established universities—thus sociology was first given the dignity of a professorial chair in Cologne which was founded—for the second time—in 1919 and in the University of Frankfurt which was founded as a private university in 1914. It became established as a teaching subject more easily in technical colleges than in universities. It was more sympathetically viewed by ministers of culture after the republican regime was established at the end of the First World War.

In France as in Germany, universities were rigid. The oligarchy of established professors of a faculty and the high degree of centralization of the control over the total university system in the hands of the national ministry of education hindered the creation of new chairs for new subjects. In British universities, although a chair was created at the London School of Economics in 1902—on a private endowment—no additional chair was created until after the Second World War.[17] At Oxford and Cambridge, the matter was not even canvassed until after the Second World War and then the democratic oligarchy of the representatives of established subjects in those universities prevented the diversion of resources to a subject of questionable legitimacy.

17. Westermarck's chair was occupied only during the Easter term of each year from 1907 to 1930.

In the United States, in contrast with the academic systems of Europe, the universities were independent of central control and professors of established subjects did not rule the universities. Sociology first became institutionalized in the era of the autocratic university president. Such a president could create a new department if he desired to do so and if he could persuade the board of trustees to agree and raise the financial resources to pay for it. The availability of private financial support and the practice of its active solicitation gave a flexibility to university budgets which the European universities did not have. This too helped.

It was not, however, only the structure of government of the universities which facilitated the earlier academic establishment of sociology in the United States. There were in the middle-western American culture of the period of the establishment of sociology a number of features which made a notable difference. It was in the Middle West that sociology first became academically established—in Chicago, Wisconsin, and Michigan primarily but also in Indiana, Iowa, Nebraska, and Illinois. The intellectual leaders of the universities of the Middle West were in a relationship of rivalry with the hegemony of the older Eastern universities; they were distrustful of what they thought was the excessive respect for the past of those universities. They thought that knowledge was not degraded by being about contemporary and practical things. There was, in short, no hard, thick incrustation of genteel, traditional, humanistic, Christian, patrician culture such as prevailed in the older universities in the East. The hierarchy of deference was weaker in the Middle West, there was more egalitarianism and a greater sympathy with the common life, more understanding for ordinary people and therefore more readiness to be intellectually and socially concerned about them.

Among middle-western intellectuals—publicistic and academic social science intellectuals—there was a more critical attitude towards the activities of the business class—industrialists, railway magnates, and bankers of the Eastern seaboard—and a greater skepticism about the adequacy of the classical economic theory which was adduced to explain their actions. It was in the Middle West that "institutional economics" was developed, most notably by John R. Commons, who emphasized that there was more to society than what was accounted for by classical economic theory.[18] Sociological jurisprudence was part of the same atmosphere; in the United States it was largely the work of Roscoe Pound from Nebraska and Brandeis, an outsider by origin to the dominant culture of the educated classes of the northeastern part of the country. Pound, despite his sociological interest, did not succeed in having a department of sociology established at Harvard University. At the University of Chicago, the most eminent professor of law, Ernst Freund, collaborated with sociologists and political scientists in numerous civic enterprises.

Quite apart from the cultural relations of the Middle West and the Eastern seaboard, it should be pointed out that the middle-western universities, even those which were founded before the Civil War, became intellectually expansive at that time. Harvard, Princeton, Columbia, Yale, Pennsylvania had developed strong cultures of their own before the Civil War and they were, therefore, somewhat more resistant to the German academic culture which was being brought back into the United States by an increasing number of young men with scientific and scholarly ambitions in the post–Civil War period. German historicism, which was one of the main sources of sociology, and the conception of the university as a scene of teaching and research were more readily received in the Middle West—at Chicago, Wisconsin, and Michigan especially, than in the older universities of the East. Johns Hopkins University, which was only a little older than the University of Chicago and which was the first university in the country to receive and adapt the German model of research and research training, did not establish a department of sociology for many years.

Sociology and the Larger Intellectual Tradition

In Great Britain the empirical tradition of sociology grew up in a

18. Walton Hamilton, prior to going to Amherst where his pupils included Talcott Parsons, was at the University of Texas—away from the pressure of conventional economics. It should however be acknowledged that Johns Hopkins University in Baltimore played an early part in this introduction of German historicism into the United States. But Johns Hopkins was the new university of the country until the University of Chicago was founded. (Simon N. Patten was an exception who does not fit into this picture; his most eminent pupil was Rexford Tugwell, who did not take any interest in sociology.)

setting of a tradition of the discussion of the control of authority. Authority was to be scrutinized and held to account; it had to justify itself by its actions. From Bacon to Bentham, there developed also a related tradition of belief which asserted that systematically gathered empirical knowledge—scientific knowledge—could be an instrument for the improvement of man's estate. The great civil servants who encouraged the system of social reporting which accompanied the legislation enacted under Benthamite inspiration were themselves the heirs of this tradition. Knowledge acquired through field surveys, the acquisition of information from experts and experienced persons through questionnaires and through depositions before commissions of inquiry were intended to be assimilated into the process of enacting laws and verifying their efficacy. The ancient English universities and the Scottish universities did not share this attitude towards knowledge, and public opinion outside the universities did not share it sufficiently to pervade the universities and cause them to change their minds. This belief was confined to limited circles of politicians, publicists, businessmen, and administrators.

The situation was otherwise in the United States. There was a fairly widespread belief in the superior value of a life illuminated by knowledge of nature and of man. There was also a widespread belief in the value of knowledge as an integral part of ameliorative action. The federal establishment of the land grant colleges and the generous support by middle western state legislatures was impelled by this belief which was best realized in the state of Wisconsin. There, academic social scientists, perhaps earlier than anywhere else, were summoned by politicians to aid them in the drafting and execution of legislation. Even sociologists like Robert Park, who was not very sanguine about the efficacy of movements for reform, thought that the results of social research would enter into public opinion and thus affect the state of society. There is no evidence that Park ever read the writings of Jeremy Bentham, but he believed that social surveys which disclosed an existing condition of society enlightened public opinion and brought moral judgment into play and were therefore integral to the movement of society. In his analysis of ''collective behavior'' he used to point to the role of the ''survey movement'' as a stage in the mobilization of belief about what had to be done to improve social conditions. The view of the matter held by sociologists was shared by many other persons in civic organizations, in business, and in the learned professions. However censorious traditional historians, economic theorists, and physicists within the universities might have been about the capacities of sociology, there were at the same time other quite estimable persons who had higher hopes for what sociological knowledge could offer to what they thought was a rational program of the improvement of society. The willingness of wealthy individuals and organizations to support sociological research gave this research a ground for self-respect at a time when its intellectual achievements were still insufficient for that purpose.

This is not to say that the intellectual content of the sociology which was taking form within the support of this extra-academic attitude was determined by it. It does mean, however, that the prevailing culture outside the universities contributed to the institutional establishment of sociology in the United States. The particular subject-matters of sociology in the United States—and in Great Britain—were also in part selected by the direction of interest of its sympathizers, admirers, and patrons. The principles of interpretation—the intellectual substance of the central tradition—derived, however, from more strictly intellectual sources, and increasingly so as the years passed.

The Ecology of Sociology

An intellectual field or discipline has an ecological pattern as well as an institutional structure. Intellectual activities have, of course, a spatial location but ecology is not just about position in space; it is also about hierarchy, about domination and subordination, and about the movements to and fro, upward and downward. Institutional establishment occurs within a bounded space. Ecological processes are about the relationships between the institutions within their bounded spaces. To illustrate: we would say that sociology became institutionally established at Chicago, Wisconsin, and Columbia; the positions of Chicago, Wisconsin, and Columbia in the cosmos of American sociology would fall into what I call here the ecological sphere. Institutionalization and ecological position are closely related to each other; there is no clear definitional boundary between them—at least thus far—but they can nonetheless be distinguished from one another, as they are in this paper.

The construction of a relatively new idea in a tradition always occurs in space, and so does its acceptance. A successful idea is one which is true and which finds acceptance by someone other than its creator. This always involves some movements in space. Obviously the rational pervasiveness of an idea is one of the major determinants of the extent of its movement, but it is not the only one. Institutionalization is one of the factors which affects the directions of the spatial movement of an intellectual activity and its substantive results, just as it is a mechanism of elaboration, promotion, or utilization of ideas. Ideas are likely to move with more momentum if they are institutionalized at their place of origin; just as they are more likely to be taken up, elaborated and "used"—at least up to a certain point—the more institutionalized they are at their place of reception.[19]

The movements are both national and international.

International

From Germany. Before the First World War Max Weber seems to have been quite unknown in the rest of Europe and in the United States despite his journey to the exposition in St. Louis and the publication of one paper in English in the proceedings of the conference held there. Hugo Munsterberg, a German philosopher and psychologist then teaching at Harvard University, arranged for Weber's invitation to the exposition but he did nothing else which made Weber's ideas known in America. No American sociologist referred to Max Weber before the First World War. Even Albion Small, who knew a lot of German sociological literature, did not refer to him in his writings; there is no evidence that he dealt with him in his teaching. Troeltsch's *Die Bedeutung des Protestantismus,* with

19. Science in the heroic age might be reexamined in the light of the approach taken in this paper. Aside from the genius of its main actors, it owes some of its growth to its informal organization as a society of correspondence among individual scientists who worked in relatively dense centers of scientific activity. It is plausible to say that before the existence of scientific periodicals a more important role was filled by communication directly addressed to particular scientists. This gave individual scientists more control over where their ideas went in their own lifetime. Nonetheless, the directly addressed audience of known persons remains an important feature of contemporary science. The publication of books and papers apparently addressed to an almost entirely anonymous audience does not mean that their contents move in all directions randomly and indifferently to their authors' intentions.

numerous references to Weber, was translated into English in the Crown Theological Library, yet this too passed unnoticed by American sociologists.

After the First World War, the situation did not change much. Frank Knight of Chicago, who was always interested in the limits of neoclassical, analytical economic theory, while himself being one of the most eminent economic theorists of the interbellum period, translated the *Wirtschaftsgeschichte,* the book made up from the lectures which Weber delivered at Munich in the last year of his life. It was not noticed by sociologists. The appearance of Parsons' translation of the first part of the *Religionssoziologie* likewise made no stir among sociologists. Theodore Abel's doctoral dissertation at Columbia, W. J. Warner's doctoral dissertation at the London School of Economics, Heinrich Maurer's writings in the *American Journal of Sociology,* Parsons' Heidelberg dissertation on Weber and Sombart, and L. J. Benniou's dissertation on Weber's methodology were the first writings by American sociologists in the 1920s to deal with Weber. It is interesting that three of them were done as doctoral dissertations outside the United States; only one of them was done in a leading department of sociology.

There was more attention to Max Weber in the United States in the 1930s. The Graduate Faculty of Social and Political Science at the New School of Social Research presented Weber's ideas in their courses and in their journal, *Social Research.* Knight gave a seminar on *Wirtschaft und Gesellschaft* at Chicago in 1935; von Schelting lectured and held seminars on Weber at Columbia in the second half of the 1930s; the appearance in 1936 of the English translation of Mannheim's *Ideologie und Utopie* brought some of Weber's ideas before a wider audience. Taylor Cole's dissertation at Harvard on the Swiss civil service was part of the thickening atmosphere of awareness of Weber's ideas. The most decisive event however was the publication in 1937 of Talcott Parsons' *The Structure of Social Action.* It was a work of fundamental theoretical importance in its own right; it was a clarification, elaboration, and extension of some of Weber's own fundamental ideas and it was also a rich restatement of certain principal themes of Weber's work. It was a memorable movement in the ecology of sociology.

In France Weber seems to have caused not even a ripple. Durkheim reviewed Marianne Weber's book on the legal status of women—rather slightingly—but he did not discuss Max Weber. I do not know of any reference to Max Weber in France before the First World War aside from those contained in the French translation of Sombart's *Der Bourgeois*. The two leading Germanists in France at this time were Charles Andler and Lucien Herr. Neither of them seems to have paid any attention to Weber. In the numerous denunciations of German professors by French professors during the war, Max Weber's existence and his criticism of imperial policy passed unnoticed.

The situation did not change significantly after the end of the war. French sociology itself was in a process of dissolution after the death of Durkheim. Only Maurice Halbwachs, at Strasbourg in that period, knew of Weber and in fact wrote in an obscure Strasbourg journal one of the most understanding of any of the secondary treatments of Weber's ideas on the Protestant ethic and the growth of capitalism and then, in 1929, a more comprehensive essay on Weber in the *Annales de l'histoire économique et sociale*. Then there was silence until Raymond Aron wrote a well-rounded, thoroughly informed chapter on Weber in his little book on *Sociologie française contemporaine*. Then there was silence again until after the Second World War, when under Aron's auspices translations of some of Weber's work began to appear in French and Aron himself lectured at the Sorbonne on him and then published a full treatment of Weber's ideas in *les Étapes de la pensée sociologique*. Since that time, Max Weber's ideas, although not absorbed, have been present in France as much as those of any serious foreign writer of the present century.

In Italy too, Weber was unknown.[20] Pareto never referred to him, nor did Mondolfo or Antonio Labriola. Only his protégé, Roberto Michels, who in 1907 had become a *Privatdozent* (*libero docento*) in Turin, referred to his writings steadily; but there was no echo. The situation did not change significantly until after the Second World War and the end of the Fascist regime. Then many books began to treat Weber's ideas, e.g., those of Carlo Antoni, Paolo Rossi, and Franco Ferrarotti. *Wirtschaft und Gesellschaft* was translated into Italian.

20. It appears that his "Agrarverhältnisse im Altertum," and *Zur Geschichte der Handelsgesellschaften im Mittelalter* were unknown to Italian classical historians and medievalists of his time.

There were a number of references to Max Weber in British publications before the First World War. The translation of Troeltsch's *Die Bedeutung des Protestantismus* in English under the title of *Protestantism and Progress* was the first appearance of Weber's name in Great Britain. Not long after that an essay by an Anglican clergyman, H. G. Wood, in an anthology on the rights and duties of the owners of property referred again to the Protestant ethic. By the 1920s there were many references to Weber in the British literature; George O'Brien's *The Economic Effects of the Reformation* and, above all, R. H. Tawney's *Religion and the Rise of Capitalism* brought the "Weber-thesis" to public attention. It became sufficiently known for John Clapham at Cambridge to prompt his pupil H. M. Robertson to write a doctoral dissertation which denied Weber's argument; it was published under the name of *The Rise of Economic Individualism*. In sociology proper, Morris Ginsberg was quite well acquainted with Max Weber's writings but did not regard them sympathetically.

The situation changed in 1933 with the coming of Karl Mannheim and a considerable number of refugees, one of whom, Franz Neumann, was for a time a postgraduate student at the London School of Economics. Mannheim presented Weber's ideas in his teaching and by references in his writings. T. H. Marshall and Morris Ginsberg did the same. This was a time when, despite the limited existence of sociology in Great Britain, Max Weber's ideas became accepted as part of the subject—and not just as an ingenious thesis bearing on a much-discussed problem of economic history. I think that this was to a large extent a result of Mannheim's propaganda for his own kind of sociology, which included much that was derived from Weber's ideas.

After the Second World War, partly as a result of the assimilation of Max Weber into American sociology, Weber became more or less naturalized in British sociology. His writings became as much a part of the British academic syllabus in sociology as they were of the academic syllabus in the United States.

At the beginning of the century Simmel was better known abroad than Max Weber. In France the *Année sociologique* published a translation of one of his works. Durkheim's early approval changed markedly: both *Soziologie* and *Die Philosophie des Geldes* were censured by Durkheim, and that was the end of Simmel as far as French sociology was concerned. In the United States various essays of Simmel appeared in English translation in the *American Journal of Sociology;* translations were published before the appearance in Chicago of Robert Park. It was undoubtedly Small who was responsible, but there was no trace of Simmel's ideas in Small's work. Only when Robert Park came to Chicago did Simmel's ideas take up residence in Chicago sociological research. Simmel's influence received its definitive expression in Louis Wirth's "Urbanism as a Way of Life," whence it became a common possession of American sociology, but this took place very much later.

Simmel was also taken up in the United States by Arthur Bentley, who attended Simmel's lectures in Berlin in the academic session of 1893–94. Simmel's ideas about groups overlapping in membership and the common ground of parties in antagonism appeared in Bentley's writings. But Bentley was not a university teacher, he was a journalist and then a private scholar and it was only after many years that his ideas began to exercise influence in political science through their assimilation in an already existing interest in "pressure groups." As far as sociology is concerned, Bentley seems to have had little influence although he taught for one year as a "docent" in the department of sociology at the University of Chicago. Despite the intellectual congeniality of Albion Small, who shared Bentley's interest in Simmel and Gumplowicz, Bentley departed for journalism and farming without leaving a mark on sociology.

Tönnies, despite his sojourn in Great Britain, his major contribution to Hobbesian studies, his close affinity to Henry Sumner Maine, and his great emphasis on quantitative work, found no response in British sociology. Durkheim knew *Gemeinschaft und Gesellschaft* but despite a certain community of outlook, criticized it sharply, and his adherents made no use of Tönnies' ideas. In the United States on the other hand, these ideas were resonant in Park's writing and teaching. Tönnies' main categories and theories, like those of Simmel, entered into American sociology through Robert Park's and Robert MacIver's writings.

The Austrian sociologists whose names were once famous may be mentioned here. They are Gustav Ratzenhofer and Ludwig Gumplowicz. The former was a professional soldier whose sociological work was avocational; the latter was professor of law at the University of Graz, and his sociology too was avocational. Their works were widely read in Europe but their effective contribution to sociology came about as a result of their being read by Albion Small. Unlike German sociologists of his time, Small was in a position in which what he read and accepted could make a difference to the generation which followed him. There have been writers of great influence whose work was not carried on and diffused in the setting of institutional establishment: Charles Darwin was the greatest of these but many other instances could be given. Nonetheless, under modern conditions, when so much of intellectual activity is institutionally established, those authors whose work is not produced and diffused in such a setting are handicapped. Both Gumplowicz and Ratzenhofer were victims of this situation. Only the intervention of Small into the path of their writings permitted them to have a longer afterlife in sociology. This seems to have come about in obscure and indirect ways. I do not know whether Small encountered their writings while he was studying in Germany or whether he encountered them by reading reviews and following up clues given by other writers. He did however give their ideas a prominent place in his own sociological theory. W. I. Thomas, who was less interested in the theories of other sociologists, must have found the views of the two men congruent with his own interests in the conflicts of national groups in German Poland. They were certainly attractive to Robert Park. Park did not show much interest in Gumplowicz and Ratzenhofer before he came to Chicago and he did not cite them frequently in the 1920s or after. But I have the impression that during the First World War, when he was attempting to develop his conception of the four processes of competition, conflict, accommodation, and assimilation, he was rather affected by their view about the conflicts of ethnic and national groups. Thus although their names are no longer seriously considered when the forerunners and founders of sociology are enumerated, they have anonymously entered into the substantive tradition of sociology. They have been enabled to do so because their ideas were taken up by scholars in an academic institution and were incorporated there into a widely used textbook and into the syllabus of instruction.

From France. For founding ideas to travel across national boundaries in subjects which have no universally intelligible symbolism such as that provided by mathematics, language barriers must be absent or there must be many translations. There must also be, as in the case of the Weber-Parsons relationship, a strong intellectual personality who has immersed himself deeply in the founding ideas and who can sustain the newly acquired ideas either with the aid of institutions in the new setting or through sheer force of intellectual character.

Durkheim's ideas traveled little out of France because there was no one to carry them. Ziya Gökalp took them to Turkey, but that was a dead end because Gökalp, although he taught sociology at Salonika and became professor of the subject in Istanbul, was not a strong intellectual personality: he was more interested in legitimating Turkish nationalism and secularism than in sociological theory and research. Nor did he have research students. One of the reasons why he had none was that there would have been no careers for them. There was nothing in British sociology of the period before the Second World War which bore marks of Durkheim's influence. *Les formes elémentaires de la vie réligieuse* was first translated and published in Great Britain in 1912. It did not create much of an impression, certainly not in the very restricted circles which were interested in sociology. Although students of religion such as Clement Webb—who was negative—and anthropologists like Radcliffe-Brown—who was positive—were interested, it did not gain the serious consideration of Hobhouse or Westermarck. Durkheim visited England once, at the beginning of the century, and delivered a lecture before the Sociological Society justifying the existence of sociology. The brevity of the visit, the inconsequentiality of the subject, and the absence of receiving institutions formed no bridge over which Durkheim's ideas could travel. Sociology did not yet exist as a university subject in England at the time of Durkheim's visit. Sociology was a subject of the laity which was interested in eugenics, in evolution, and in the condition of the poor. There was nothing in Durkheim which made an immediate sympathetic connection with any of these.[21]

Germans took no interest in those ideas of Durkheim which were available in the original, in German translation, or in the surveys of

21. Durkheim did exert through Radcliffe-Brown a marked influence on British social anthropology, but until very recently the social anthropology deriving from Radcliffe-Brown and Malinowski had very little connection with British sociology.

the sociological theories of Squillace and Sorokin and in the dissertation of a Roumanian named Georges Marica. There was an extended
treatment of Durkheim and his followers in *Philosophische
Strömungen der Gegenwart im Frankreich*, a work written in German
by a Swiss, Isaac Benrubi. I cannot recall its having ever been cited
by a German sociologist nor do I recall Durkheim ever being mentioned in the 1920s by Ernst Robert Curtius, who was the chief German connoiseur of French intellectual life.

Max Weber never referred to Durkheim. Tönnies had some interest
in Durkheim but his views were not affected by him. Max Scheler was
the only important sociologist who took seriously some of Durkheim's
ideas as they bore on his own effort to construct a sociology of knowledge. Franz Jerusalem was also aware that Durkheim had something
to say about that subject. Karl Mannheim studiously avoided reference to Durkheim in his essay on the sociology of knowledge in the
Handwörterbuch der Soziologie. The other German sociologists who
were interested primarily in classificatory schemes had no occasion to
bring Durkheim into their work.

Durkheim fared only a little better in his first contacts with American sociology. In the United States before 1914, sociology was either
under the inspiration of Germanic ethnographic erudition, e.g., William Graham Sumner, or it was conscientiously making its first contacts with the poor of the big cities—an effort unprecedented in
academic life but carrying on a civic tradition which had been cultivated by philanthropists and administrators in France, Great Britain,
and the United States over about three-quarters of a century.
Theoretically, it was struggling with the idea of "social forces" and
the facts of social conflict, disorder, and change. It too was critical of
the inherited evolutionary theory of Herbert Spencer but it did not
quite find an acceptable answer in *De la Division du travail social*.
Perhaps American sociologists thought that their intellectual guidance
could best come from Germany. Durkheim's existence was certainly
known to Small but he did not assimilate any of his ideas into his own
writings or teachings. There were only two American sociologists
who had the theoretical sensibility to learn from Durkheim before the
First World War, because they were both deep and learned enough to
have been able to accommodate his ideas. One was William I.
Thomas, whose study of the European sociological literature ceased

as he immersed himself in his great inquiry into the Polish immigrant in America.[22] As far as I know, Thomas was quite ignorant of Durkheim; he certainly did not regard him as a source of his ideas, although as a matter of fact his views in many matters were very close to Durkheim's.[23]

The other was Robert Park, who had studied in Strasbourg, Heidelberg, and Berlin with Windelband and Simmel, but whose knowledge of Durkheim—and of Max Weber for that matter—was slight but appreciative. Park was pleased to have Durkheim's idea of *représentations collectives* since that fitted so harmoniously into his own ideas about the mechanisms of public opinion and collective behavior. Later in his life, he was much drawn to the idea of anomie as a description of certain aspects of urban society, but I have the impression that it was his reading of Elton Mayo more than his reading of Durkheim which commended it to him.[24]

Charles Gehlke, who later became professor of sociology at Ohio State University, wrote a doctoral dissertation at Columbia University on Durkheim. It was nominally about Durkheim's "contribution to sociological theory" but it was in the main about his definition of a social fact. Gehlke apparently never wrote anything in subsequent years in which Durkheim's ideas were applied. Nonetheless, Park did read the dissertation, and some of his knowledge of *représentations collectives* came from it.

At Chicago, under the inspiration of Park and Burgess, Mrs. Ruth

22. It may be noted in passing that not many years earlier Max Weber had studied the German side of the same problem—the impact of the immigration of Polish agricultural laborers into the East Elban landed estates—while Thomas was studying the consequences for the Polish immigrants of their movement into the United States. There is no evidence that Thomas was aware of Max Weber's work on the subject.

23. Thomas' *Source Book for Social Origins* contains nothing written by Durkheim and there are only two references to articles by Durkheim in a bibliography of forty-two pages.

24. I knew him well in the period just after his retirement from the University of Chicago and used often to talk with him, or rather listen to him, but he never mentioned Durkheim or Weber, even though he knew I was more or less conversant with European sociology. I attended his last lectures at the University of Chicago in the spring of 1934, and, although Bagehot, Tarde, and Sighele and all sorts of books including Theodore Geiger's *Die Masse und ihre Aktion* were mentioned, Durkheim was passed over without a word. There were, however, two excerpts from Durkheim in *An Introduction to the Science of Sociology*.

Shonle Cavan wrote a book, *Suicide*, in which Durkheim was not more than mentioned. Ellsworth Faris never did more than refer to the "exteriority of the social fact." The important research in *Mental Disorder in Urban Areas* by Robert Faris and Warren Dunham—a very "Durkheimian" problem—also did not consider Durkheim's ideas about social and personal disorganization. Herbert Blumer at the beginning of the 1930s knew the writings of Durkheim and his followers and heirs very well, but I do not think that he ever wrote anything about it. His various critical essays about certain trends in American sociology were made from an anti-individualistic, anti-psychologistic standpoint which showed the influence of his Durkheimian studies. Durkheim had been given a bad name by Alexander Goldenweiser in 1916 and it took a long time for his reputation in the United States to recover.

The implantation of Durkheim's ideas in the United States was largely the work of Elton Mayo and Talcott Parsons. I am not certain how Elton Mayo came to be interested in Durkheim. Perhaps it was through Radcliffe-Brown. Nonetheless it was through Mayo that the idea of anomie, which he applied in the interpretation of the results of the studies of the Western Electric plant at Hawthorne, Illinois, became better known to American sociologists. Professor Parsons' interest in Durkheim grew in the atmosphere generated by Elton Mayo and Lawrence Henderson in the late 1920s and early 1930s. At a time when there was little interest in Durkheim in France, and not much more in the United States, it was Professor Parsons whose imaginative reinterpretation of Durkheim placed him into a position in sociological thought which he scarcely occupied even in his own lifetime in France. As a result of the prominence conferred by Parsons' treatment in *The Structure of Social Action* and the subsequent translation or republication of the old translations of Durkheim's books, American sociologists began to study Durkheim seriously for the first time. Parsons' assimilation of Durkheim to Weber's themes and categories helped in this, as did the facts that *Suicide* was a statistical study and *De la Division du travail social* was so systematically and even schematically formulated that it seemed to lend itself to the construction of scientific hypotheses. Robert Merton, who first studied Durkheim under Parsons and Sorokin, and Lloyd Warner, who was guided by Elton Mayo, also gave strong impetus to the installation of Durkheim in American sociology. Merton's systematic reformulation of the concept of anomie made it into a common possession of sociologists. It has entered from his essay on the subject, reproduced in *Social Theory and Social Structure,* into the studies of criminality and delinquency and of what is now called "deviancy," poverty, rebellion, and "counter-culture." It has given new life to the older study of "social disorganization" and "social pathology." Lloyd Warner's success was smaller, but, for his invocation of Durkheim in the last volume of his voluminous work on "Yankee City," Warner must be given some of the credit for the growth of appreciation of Durkheim among social anthropologists and hence for the establishment of many bridges between sociology and social anthropology which is one of the overdue accomplishments of recent years.

From Great Britain. The relatively uninstitutionalized structure of British sociology up to 1914 permitted a great miscellany of sociological tendencies to have an erratic existence. Some of them, such as the interest in genetics and eugenics, came subsequently to have a very great impact on American sociology and then on sociology all over the world through the development of refined statistical measures of general application and of less weighty but still considerable influence on the study of social mobility. Francis Galton was in both cases the great progenitor. Sorokin's *Social Mobility,* which summarized the great body of this literature, was a significant transmitter of this influence. Taussig and Joslyn's *American Business Leaders,* Bendix and Lipset's *Social Mobility in Industrial Society,* Blau and Duncan's *Occupational Mobility in the United States,* to mention a few of the high points, owe much to the stimulus and techniques which arose from this current of British sociology. (Two important intermediaries of this influence were Hogben's *Political Arithmetic* and Glass' *Social Mobility in Britain.*)

No less important was the related field of the social survey of the condition of the urban working classes. This is one of the oldest traditions of British sociology, and the surveys in London and York at the turn of the century had a marked influence on American urban sociology. Robert Park assimilated their lessons and adapted them to the financial position of doctoral research at the University of Chicago. The study of *Middletown* was the first major American survey of an entire community, and it too bears the marks of the British influence—although it was much influenced by the original work of Galpin and his colleagues and the social anthropology being developed by Franz Boas at Columbia. The technique received a tremendous impetus from the development of sample surveys of opinion which began to flourish in the 1930s.

The evolutionary sociology deriving in part from Spencer did not find much response in the United States, except marginally in the work of Sumner, in the early works of Thomas, and in the unimportant textbooks now rightly forgotten.

These great influences on sociology in the United States and elsewhere came mainly from those parts of British sociology which were not institutionally established. The institutionalized parts of British sociology were for the most part rather incapable of expansion beyond the classroom or the seminar—although these are, under the appropriate circumstances, the very heart of institutional establishment of a field of intellectual activity. L. T. Hobhouse had no influence outside other than that exercised by *The Material Culture and Social Institutions of the Simpler Peoples* on Lloyd Warner's *The Social System of a Modern Community*. Family studies, which in the United States were mainly the study of family disorganization, were not influenced by Westermarck. In so far as they were subjected to influences from Great Britain they derived rather from the British social survey tradition with its interest in the conditions of life of the poor. (They were also to some extent influenced by the German studies of standards of living which had been initiated by Le Play and Engel and applied in the United States by Carroll D. Wright, the commissioner of the Bureau of Labor Statistics.) Morris Ginsberg's several studies of social mobility were assimilated into American work in that field but his theoretical concerns were without issue. Carr-Saunders and Wilson's study of the professions became a standard work referred to by American sociologists more perhaps than any single investigation, even though American studies used quite different techniques. T. H. Marshall's *Citizenship and Social Class* has entered as an ingredient into much recent work on social stratification and the development of the welfare state. The interchange between British and American sociology has become very active. British sociological journals are the most read by American sociologists after their own, and British sociological works are frequently published in the United States as well as in Great Britain. Since the British output is very much smaller than the American sociological output, except for the case of Marshall's ideas on the development of citizenship, it tends to be assimilated without a significantly identifiable influence.

From the United States. American sociology had practically no echo in Europe before the Second World War. A few American sociological works were translated into European languages. The translation of Charles Ellwood's textbook into French is hard to account for because even though Ellwood was once considered a sociologist of note, not even at the height of his fame was he regarded as a scholar of the first rank. It is possible that René Worms found his ideas about instincts attractive; in any case there is no evidence that Ellwood's writing ever influenced sociological theory or research in France. Durkheim was utterly uninterested in American sociology (although he did make considerable use of British ethnography in *Les Formes élémentaires de la religion*). Halbwachs, who visited the University of Chicago in the late 1920s, wrote an extremely intelligent and well-informed paper on urban sociology in Chicago in the *Annales de l'histoire économique et sociale*. This occurred while he was working on "social morphology," and he saw an affinity between what he was doing and what the urban sociologists were doing. It did not however go much further than that. Except through Halbwachs, American sociology in France was nearly unknown in the 1930s. While the *Nouvelle encyclopédie scientifique*, which was published by Alcan, did include the solid little book by Raymond Aron on German sociology and a quite good one by Bouglé on *Sociologie française contemporaine*, there was never even the announcement of any parallel title on American sociology. It probably would have been difficult to find anyone who could have written it except perhaps Halbwachs.

In Germany, nearly complete ignorance of American sociology existed before the First World War. Simmel never indicated the slightest awareness of American sociology but he must have had some inkling of its existence. He did after all agree to serve as a member of the editorial board of the *American Journal of Sociology* when it was founded and he probably gave his permission for the translation of parts of *Soziologie* for publication in that journal. Max Weber on his visit to the United States came to Chicago and would appear to have gone out to the University of Chicago, but there is no record of his having met any of the teaching staff. He never referred to any American sociological work although there is an obscure passage in *Wissenschaft als Beruf* where he refers to "the Americans having developed technical sociological concepts" to describe the success of the second or third candidates in a contest over the originally favored candidates. No names were mentioned. He met W. E. B. Du Bois and invited him to contribute to the *Archiv für Sozialwissenschaft und Sozialpolitik,* which he did; Small attended the exposition in St. Louis at which Weber delivered a paper but there is no record of their contact. In any case, Max Weber carried nothing of American sociology away from his visit. He read a goodly amount of American religious history and he was much interested in American politics, but American sociology did not attract his attention.

Tönnies was a little more informed. He was appreciative of Walter Lippmann's *Public Opinion* and he reviewed a few American sociological works. Nonetheless, his views were formed long before he ever read any American sociology and they were not affected by the little that he read.

With von Wiese, we come to a different condition. He definitely was attracted by E. A. Ross' *Principles of Sociology* and it was translated into German under his aegis. He did in fact regard himself as a mediator between American and German sociology. Perhaps because of his liberalism and perhaps too because he had an American disciple—Howard Becker, who was translating the *System der allgemeinen Soziologie* and adapting it by adding American material to it—he had a sense of affinity with American sociologists. He was also in touch with Louis Wirth, who had begun to translate the *Beziehungslehre* independently of Becker and who renounced the task once he learned of Becker's undertaking. When the Nazis seized power in German, von Wiese came for a time to the University of Wisconsin and Harvard University and furthered his knowledge of American sociology. This appeared more fully represented—to the extent that this could be done in a tiny volume of the *Sammlung Goschen*—in a postwar edition of *Soziologie, Geschichte und Hauptprobleme.*

Max Scheler was acquainted with Ross' sociological work and with a few other writers who were less interesting than Ross.

There was one general book on American sociology written by

Andreas Walther of Hamburg at the end of the 1920s. It was a poor book since the author, not knowing enough to discriminate the better from the poorer work, treated it all indiscriminately. In the style of much of German sociology of that time, it dealt with definitions of groups, instincts, attitudes, processes and relatively little with the results of sociological study. Nonetheless it did indicate a greater openness to American sociology than was present in other countries at that time, where indifference or disdain were common among the few who knew of its existence.

A change was presaged when Louis Wirth visited Mannheim in Frankfurt in 1931 or 1932. Mannheim was much more open to American sociology than any other German sociologist had ever been. On Wirth's recommendation, he read Thomas and Znaniecki's *The Polish Peasant in Europe and America*. By arrangement with Wirth, he wrote a long review of the "casebook" entitled *Methods in Social Sciences* which had been edited by Stuart Rice on behalf of the Social Science Research Council; it appeared in the *American Journal of Sociology* in 1932, not long before Mannheim went into exile. His response was not too different from the conventional defense of "theory" against "empiricism," of large perspectives—of what would now be called macrosociology—against small, precisely defined investigations. Still it left an imprint when in the following year Mannheim published a plan for the organization of sociological teaching in Germany; the reading of Rice's "casebook" and of some American sociological literature was evident.

After going into exile, Mannheim's interest in American sociological literature increased steadily. The shift in attention from the sociology of knowledge to the study of social structure was not attributable to this interest but the shift did make it easier for him to assimilate a certain amount of American material in so far as it fitted into his desire to show the feasibility and desirability of democratic planning. In his years in Britain, he was surely the sociologist most interested in learning about the achievements, such as they were, of American sociology.

Shifting Centers and Peripheries

After the passing of Comte and Spencer from dominance over what was called sociology in the second half of the nineteenth century, the subject became much more national. Comte and Spencer receded even in their own countries; they certainly lost their international dominance. In so far as they were still treated it was to refute their views, not to affirm them. Durkheim used Spencer as a foil, Scheler used Comte for the same purpose. As the literature of sociology increased in volume and diversity in each country, so each country increasingly lived from its own sociological products. The spread of sociology into the Netherlands and the Scandanavian countries accentuated this tendency which never came to complete fulfillment. When Spencer and Comte were dethroned, French sociology became nearly self-sufficient.[25] So did German sociology; Dutch sociology too moved in the same direction as did Swedish sociology (which was very sparse); Polish sociology seemed to move in a similar fashion. American sociology which almost from the beginning became better established institutionally than the sociology of other countries soon built up a large body of literature and its own distinct concerns. But it also kept to the path which it had laid out for itself when it first became committed to the ideas about urban society which it drew from Germany as well as from its own experience. Nonetheless, through the interwar period American sociology in its most productive centers was also becoming self-sufficient. It was only the belated appreciation of Weber's and Durkheim's ideas which created an anachronistic dependence of certain creative centers of American sociology on centers which had in fact disappeared. German sociology and French sociology of the time of the resurrection of Weber and Durkheim in the United States had declined to a rather low point.

The Second World War in so far as it did not suspend the practice of sociology in universities accentuated the self-sufficiency of the various "national sociologies." It was really only in the United States that sociology continued to be practiced throughout the years of the war. Many sociologists were taken into governmental service as sociologists, but more remained in universities, even though there were very few students. American sociology also had the advantage that the United

25. Although Durkheim disregarded foreign writers who called themselves sociologists, just as he disregarded French *soi-disant* sociologists, he did make much use of ethnographic work from Germany and Great Britain and, to some extent, the United States. Spencer and Gillen's writings on Australia provided much of the factual foundation of *Les Formes élémentaires de la religion*.

States became engaged in the war more than two years later than France, Great Britain, and Germany. (I omit the Soviet Union, which also entered the war considerably later than the Western European states, because sociology had virtually ceased to exist there since the 1920s.)

The far greater degree of institutionalization of sociology in the United States, the large scale of its output before the war, the continued activity in American sociology throughout the war, the postwar ascent of the United States to a condition of academic centrality in many subjects (as well as the greater power and prominence of the United States outside the intellectual sphere), and the formation, to some extent, of an international sociological culture all contributed to change the direction of the ecological process. The United States became the chief center of sociology and Europe and the rest of the world went to sociological school there.

This process has been much aided by the increased institutionalization of sociology in teaching and research in Europe. It has also been aided by the increase in institutional and individual communication in sociology across national boundaries. Institutionalization increases receptive power just as it increases radiative power between countries as well as within countries. Institutional establishment reduces random movement and it also reduces the freedom of the individual sociologist to do whatever he wishes. If syllabuses and reading lists prescribe more American sociological literature, the European student's freedom is restricted. The sheer quantity of American sociological literature and its interestingness imposed itself on Europe after the long sociological drought in that part of the world.

The greatly increased facility in the reading of English in almost all sections of the population in the European continent, institutions like the Salzburg Seminar, and the availability of grants and stipends for study in American universities affected many subjects and sociology not least. The opportunities offered by institutions would not have been sought had not American sociology become so attractive. The preponderance of the American center diminished after several decades. European sociologists became more numerous and more productive than they had ever been before. They created new journals, new monographic series; new publishing houses embraced sociology, new universities offered more appointments to sociologists, and more students chose to study sociology. This has been happening in every

Western European country. From having been largely peripheral for about a decade European sociology began to take the form of a network of national sub-centers: American sociology still continued in its central position but the distance between center and periphery has been greatly diminished.

After the Second World War, sociology in Germany had almost to begin again. Practically no sociologists had been trained in the twelve years of the National Socialist regime. A few very old sociologists such as Alfred Weber and Leopold von Wiese were called back into service. The refugees Horkheimer and Adorno returned from the United States. Von Wiese in a more appreciative way, Horkheimer and Adorno more grudgingly brought American sociological literature into their syllabuses. At first, there was too little German sociological literature for pedagogical purposes. American literature had to be turned to. Not long after the war, I encountered German students who had read Max Weber only in English because they could not obtain German editions.

As the demand for sociology in the universities increased, the demand for books also increased. The result was a rapid growth in the publication of sociological books.

The expansion of sociological publication in Germany has been accompanied by the publication of translations of American sociological works on an unprecedented scale. The teaching of sociology in German universities has been extended with many more chairs, assistant professorships, and assistantships. Sociological research has not had a similar institutional expansion. Survey research institutes are independent of universities, and as a result the proportion of empirical research in the total body of academic sociological publications is fairly small. For several decades the very considerable German knowledge of American research and theory and the frequency of citation from the published literature contrasted sharply with the small amount of research done in Germany. This has begun to change. German sociological monographic series, e.g., Göttinger Abhandlungen zur Soziologie, Frankfurter Beiträge, Bonner Beiträge zur Soziologie, Soziologische Gegenwartsfragen, increasingly give place to reports on field research although there still remains the practice of publishing summaries and assessments of the work of leading theorists.

Similarly, although the proportion of papers devoted to research in the *Volnische Zeitschrift für Soziologie* is very much greater than it was when the journal was first revived and than it was in its earlier form, reviews of the literature and general papers still predominate. The new *Zeitschrift für Soziologie* has moved further away from the older tradition.

The academic establishment of sociology has increased in France as it has in Germany; there are many new universities and many chairs of sociology as well as numerous posts of lower rank. France too has moved towards the reassertion of an autonomous production, although not perhaps to an autonomous tradition. New periodicals accord a large proportion of their space to reports of the results of research. The deficiencies of the French universities with respect to their provision for research and advanced training are compensated institutionally—to some extent at least—by the generous policies of the Conseil national de la recherche scientifique (CNRS). The establishment of the Maison des sciences de l'homme, of the sixth section of the École pratique des hautes études, and of the Centre européenne de la recherche sociologique at the initiative of Raymond Aron have greatly enhanced the institutional provision for the conduct of, and training in, research. In France, however, as well as in Germany, the point of reference is still largely the American literature of theory and research.

The situation is not greatly different in Britain. There too the increased number of universities and the increased interest in and appreciation of sociology have led to a pronounced increase in the number of students of sociology and of teachers of sociology in universities, institutes of education, and technical colleges. The creation of the Social Science Research Council has increased the funds available for sociological research. There are now three journals of sociology devoted to publication of papers by professional sociologists, in contrast with one journal before the war that had relatively few papers contributed by professionally qualified sociologists. The market for sociological books among the laity has increased. The traditional British study of social stratification has persisted, the study of the poor has persisted; professional sociology has shown recognizable continuity with amateur or avocational sociology. British sociology is more continuous with its past than German or French sociology. Nonetheless there too the presence of American sociology has become very tangible; it is perhaps most acknowledged where it is most criticized.

Thus the international ecological pattern of sociology has changed and changed again since the beginning of the present century. There have been concurrent changes within national societies and nowhere more than in the United States.

Ecology: Within National Sociological Communities

I shall confine my observations on the ecology of sociology within a national society to the United States and more particularly to the relations between dominance and institutionalization. From about the outbreak of the First World War to the end of the Second, the Department of Sociology of the University of Chicago was the center par excellence of sociological studies in the United States and in the world, although in the last decade of its dominance it was living from the momentum of the preceding two decades. As the leading institution for postgraduate studies in sociology, it had continuously present a group of mature and concentrated students, each of whom was engaged in a piece of research—almost always field research—under the inspiration and often the direction of two men who were in a close and assymetrical consensus—Professors Park and Burgess. What they taught had been in principle codified—rather primitively by present-day standards—in "Park and Burgess," their *Introduction to the Science of Sociology*. Intensive instruction was amply provided in seminars and informal lectures as well as in numerous individual consultations between teachers and students. The teachers lived near the university and were in their offices much of the time; the students had ready access to them. "Term papers" and the "seminar papers" were obligatory, and they had to be based on research in the library and in the field. Each student accepted it as an ineluctable obligation to produce such a paper, and the teachers regarded it as theirs to supervise their production and scrutinize their results. The good relations which the Department of Sociology had built up with civic, local, and manicipal groups in the first twenty years of the existence of the department made it easier for the students to gain entry into the field for direct observation, interviewing, and the collection and examination of documents. There were certain adjunct institutions to which students could be attached for their research (and sometimes employment) such as the Institute for Juvenile Research, the Chicago Crime Commission, the Juvenile Protective Association, etc. For the most successful there were the rewards of publication in the journal conducted by the department, the *American Journal of Sociology* or, even higher, inclusion of a finished work in the Chicago Sociological Series. The journal, although owned by the University of Chicago and edited by the Department of Sociology of the university, was the official organ of the American Sociological Society and it was the only important national journal on the subject. Relatively few students attained the dignity of publication in the *Journal,* but its existence near at hand made them aware that publication is the end which any scholar should seek. The existence of the Chicago Sociological Series exemplified the standards of the department in visible form and it added to the awareness of membership in an institution at the center of the world of sociological activities. For many years the seat of the American Sociological Society was at the University of Chicago. In nearly every important state university of the Middle and Far West, sociology was taught by graduates of the department. Even in famous universities like the University of Michigan, much older than the University of Chicago and with at least one sociologist as distinguished as those at Chicago, there were Chicago graduates. Departments of sociology at state universities like those of Washington, Iowa, and Illinois were headed by Chicago graduates. It was to Chicago that they turned most frequently for new members and it was to Chicago that they sent their best graduates for further study. There were other departments of sociology in the country, most notably at Columbia, Michigan, North Carolina, Brown, Pennsylvania, Yale; each had its distinctions and each had its small areas of hegemony to which its graduates were appointed. There were eminent sociologists at some of these institutions. Ward had spent his last years at Brown, Sumner had been professor at Yale, Odum at North Carolina, Ogburn, Lynd, and MacIver had at one time or another taught at Columbia, Cooley at Michigan; and valuable monographs based on dissertations were produced. But all these lesser centers were different from Chicago. None had the common standpoint of Chicago's sociologists, its continuity of effort, or the liveliness and intensity of its intellectual community.

It succeeded in rising to ascendancy not only because of the intellectual power of some of its staff members, but because, in addition to that intellectual power, it was more institutionalized; it produced more work with a common stamp, and the quantity as well as the quality aroused attention and respect. This in turn enabled it to draw outstanding graduate students whom it trained and then sent out to maintain the dominance of Chicago's sociology and sociology department.

Although the sociology which Chicago practiced was embedded in a more ramified corporate network, one important feature of its institutional establishment was like that of Durkheim's school. It depended very much on one major intellectual personality at a time. For a while, between about 1912 and 1919, there were two, but when Thomas' academic career came to an inglorious end there was only one. When Robert Park withdrew from Chicago towards the end of his life, preferring to spend his last years at Fisk University with his old pupil, Charles Johnson, then president of the university, Chicago sociology began to falter. None of the other members of the department had such wide interests and concerned himself so much with every aspect of the subject as Park had done. A spurious conflict between quantitative methods represented by Ogburn and Stouffer and some other method represented by Blumer and Wirth, and later Hughes, infected the department. Students came to think that they had to be partisans. Members of the department began to think that the central administration was hostile to their subject. The early years of the depression also produced a feeling of despondency. The work of the department lost its focus on urban and ethnic studies; new persons, changes of interest, and a diminution of intellectual authority within the institution in consequence of intellectual and then personal disagreements all contributed to weaken the sense of centrality in the subject.

Perhaps more important was the fact that the fundamental ideas of Chicago sociology were coming to a standstill and were not being extended and deepened. With Park's departure, the analysis of ecological processes diminished and so did the use of the "ecological technique." Park's going coincided with the appearance of the sample survey. The use of the survey of samples of individuals permitted correlations of the characteristics of individuals instead of the characteristics of aggregates such as census tracts. "Spot-maps" lost their heuristic value. As a result, the spatial aspect of social events became less visible; the ecological problems of the causal and symbolic significance of spatial position and of the relationship between spatial and social positions faded away. The problems had never been sharply or systematically formulated—that was not Park's way—and when they lost the immediacy which cartographic representation gave them, they practically disappeared. The studies of small and local communities also declined so that there was no development of the concepts which would have permitted more refined studies of the type which had once been so productive. Burgess' predictive studies of the adjustment of engaged and married couples, Ogburn's statistical time series of various social phenomena, Stouffer's subtle studies of internal migration were all outstanding intellectual accomplishments. But they all seemed to be separate from each other. None of them had the perspective which Park's unlimited curiosity and his incessant movement between microcosm and macrocosm conferred on even the narrowest and most specialized study. The radiative and attractive power of Chicago as a center was reduced. Ogburn's interest in the quantitative description of long-term trends and his simplistic and undifferentiated concept of "cultural-lag" were never articulated with microsociological analyses of situations which could be studied by methods of participant-observation. The inchoate, global, macrosociological interests of Park found no steady, persistent, and compelling formulation. The individual who best represented Park's view of society was Everett Hughes, but in the situation in which he found himself in the department he could not take over the intellectual leadership. There had always been a heterogeneity of interests and talents in the department at Chicago but they had also been congenial to each other. This ceased to be the case.

There was no successor to Park at Chicago strong and expansive enough intellectually and temperamentally to continue the Chicago tradition and to assimilate into it the new problems and modes of thought and inquiry which began to emerge in the years just before the outbreak of World War II. No one at Chicago at that time was ready to move onto the problem of the integration of the national society, which in a very fragmentary and disordered way was emerging as the main problem after the war. Not that other departments were successful in grappling with the problem, but the department at Chicago did not undertake to do it. Under Burgess' and Ogburn's chairmanships, Blumer and Stouffer departed for California and Harvard respectively. Wirth's death and Faris' retirement weakened the current of the older tradition. The loss of a center within the department accompanied the loss of centrality in the national sociological system. The relationship was a circular one.

It was not only internal developments which reduced the centrality of Chicago. New centers were emerging at universities in the East which had never been subcenters of Chicago. Columbia and Harvard came forward into prominence.

Columbia by the early 1950s markedly surpassed Chicago as a center. There were several major factors. One of the most obvious is that Columbia possessed two major intellectual personalities, Robert Merton and Paul Lazarsfeld, who combined what was most "needed" in sociology: ingeniously contrived techniques of survey research with interesting, quite specific substantive hypotheses. The second factor, closely connected with the first, was the formation of a superior form of institutionalization at Columbia in the Bureau of Applied Social Research. The scale of operation, the interests of Lazarsfeld, who was its moving spirit, and the stage of development of sociology at the time required and permitted a higher degree of formalization of procedures—intellectual and organizational—than temperament, capacity, the more primitive state of the subject, and the small scale of operations had fostered at Chicago in earlier decades. The routinization of training facilitated the routinization of research organization and research procedures, at the very moment when new techniques of observation—sample surveys of opinion—and new techniques of analyzing data were brought into sociology from market research and statistics. The research for which Columbia graduate students were trained could be done without personal inspiration; it was made easily capable of reproduction and multiplication. This brought the Columbia center to a relatively high level of technical competence and diffused its procedures and mode of thought into many nonacademic institutions that had not been penetrated by sociology before. It also made Columbia sociology into a national and international center.

Another reason for the emergence of Columbia as a center was the intellectual style of Robert Merton. A product of Harvard, where he had studied under Parsons and Sorokin, Merton had a very wide sociological culture. Unlike Parsons, who possessed a profound vision of sociey which he struggled unceasingly to articulate in a systematic manner, Merton's view of society was less comprehensive or less unitary but it was more adequately articulated and it had the expository advantage of being less abstract. Merton's espousal of "middle range theories" was perhaps less profound than Parson's efforts at a "general theory," but they were easier to apprehend and therefore more effectively taught. Easier to formulate in a testable way, they seemed to involve no *weltanschauliche* commitment, and they were more congenial to institutionalized routines. Merton himself became directly interested in the improvement of the techniques of research and this rendered easier his collaboration with Lazarsfeld. All these factors together resulted in a larger production of works bearing a common stamp and of persons capable of producing more such works in the future. This led to a wide diffusion of Columbia sociology and it generated—more on the level of procedure than of substance—a mode of work in sociology which was capable of endurance.

Harvard before 1945 in Comparison with Chicago

The development of sociology at Harvard University suggests some instructive observations on the significance of institutional arrangements and of the traditions which are fostered by them.

The teaching of sociology began at Harvard University at about the same time that it began at the University of Chicago. In 1893, Edward Cummings began to teach Economics 3 as an assistant professor. This course covered more or less the same subjects as the sociological teaching of Charles Henderson at Chicago. It was centered on "the social problem," i.e., the conditions of the urban poor. It treated housing conditions, child labor, women's labor, sweatshops, desertion and divorce, orphans, the organization of charities, and similar topics. Like Henderson, Cummings desired his students to observe the phenomena at first hand, and he arranged for them to visit institutions. He was also interested in objective, scientifically disciplined methods of investigation. Like Henderson, he believed that the knowledge which could be provided by scientific social investigation was a necessary condition for ameliorative action. Admission to the course was restricted to undergraduates.

Cummings like Henderson was a clergyman; unlike Henderson, he had not studied in Germany. Also unlike Henderson, he seems to have known about contemporary European sociological interests. All in all, in their individual intellectual qualifications the two men matched each other fairly closely. Yet Henderson, in a diffuse way, was rather influential in the development of sociology at Chicago while Cummings left no mark at Harvard.

At the beginning of the twentieth century, Cummings' appointment was discontinued. He was replaced by Thomas Nixon Carver in 1901; Carver taught theoretical sociology mainly along the lines laid down by Herbert Spencer. He had little interest in empirical investigation nor did he follow the more recent development of sociological works by Durkheim, Tarde, and others as Cummings had done. Alongside of Carver, William Z. Ripley gave a course on "labor problems," and he wrote a large book on the races of Europe. Edward Cummings' brother, John, taught "statistics in relation to social investigation" and wrote critically on physical anthropology in relation to society.

These were, then, the rudiments of a potential development of sociology at Harvard; yet nothing came of them. The most important reason for this failure was that the sociologists were neither independent nor enabled to concentrate their activities on being sociologists or thinking of themselves as sociologists.

Teaching of a rather similar sort was offered in the Divinity School at Harvard by Professor Francis Greenwood Peabody. From 1883 on, he had taught a course on "ethics and theology and moral reform" in which he dealt with temperance, charity, labor, prison discipline, and divorce. From 1906 onward, this course became Social Ethics 2. (It too was confined to undergraduates.) Peabody himself was less interested in scientific investigation than Cummings but much of the course dealt with particular social conditions. Undergraduates used to refer to Peabody's course as, "Peabo on drains, drunkenness, and divorce." In 1906, as the result of a gift of $50,000 by Alfred Treadway White, a department of social ethics was created and was assured of space in the newly built Emerson Hall, one floor of which was to be devoted by the terms of the gift to the new department. Two subsequent gifts of $100,000 each from the same source assured the position of the Department of Social Ethics. Within the department, a course on "practical problems of charities, public aid and correction" was taught, as well as one on "criminology and penology." The training of social workers was provided for in conjunction with Simmons College. After Peabody's retirement in 1913, his professorship was left vacant until 1920 when Richard Clarke Cabot, then professor of clinical medicine at Harvard Medical School, was appointed. Cabot had little interest in empirical social investigation and none in sociological theory. A variety of younger colleagues who later became moderately well known as sociologists at other universities were members of the department.

This was the position at Harvard just after the First World War. By this time there had been an independent Department of Sociology at Chicago for more than a quarter of a century. Its head, although he had written little of substance in sociology, was a tireless champion of its possibilities. He was eclectic in his ideas about sociology, he knew the large body of sociological literature and was sympathetic with a variety of possibilities. He had moreover the German ideal of *Wissenschaftlichkeit;* he wanted sociology to become an intellectual discipline and his position and influence in the University of Chicago enabled him to keep this ideal alive while waiting for the time when it could be realized. His second in command did no sociological research of his own but he helped to focus the minds of the students on the life of the lower classes in the city of Chicago. The department had graduate students, which was another advantage over Harvard; one of the graduate students of the Department of Sociology in the University of Chicago was W. I. Thomas. Thomas developed slowly as a sociologist and began to produce significant sociological works only after being a member of the department for more than ten years. Park had joined the department in a marginal capacity before the First World War and taught about one course per year. Like Small, Park was well educated in the literature of sociology; unlike Small, he was also acquainted at first hand with urban life and the world in general. He had also studied the empirical research done by British and American sociologists. He was ready to do the kind of work which later defined the character of sociology. The availability of graduate students to receive his ideas and to carry them out in their doctoral dissertations was decisive; he himself did little research of a sustained sort but he could give direction and inspiration to others to do research. Graduate students had for more than ten years increasingly been coming to take advanced degrees and were being set on problems of empirical investigation conducted mainly within the city of Chicago. Here again Chicago's departmental organization of sociology gave it an advantage over Harvard. Chicago had still another advantage over Harvard. This was the *American Journal of Sociology;* there was not yet anything like enough solid material to publish in such a journal but its existence helped to consolidate the goal of a professional, scholarly sociology producing works of intellectual substance like any other dignified academic discipline. There were other advantages. There was a large number of well-established and reputable persons in the city of Chicago who looked to the Department of Sociology for investigations of "social problems" and for cooperation in the guidance of reforming activities. Finally, the city of Chicago itself was the most rapidly and energetically growing city in the United States. It pressed on the attention of socially sensitive academics problems which startled and horrified persons of conventional middle-class experience; the mind could not be averted from them. Boston too had problems which were not wholly dissimilar but Boston was not growing so rapidly, and Harvard had in a sense surrendered Boston to the immigrants and their politicians. The University of Chicago had no such self-enclosed culture as Harvard with its long history and traditions possessed at this time; it was more exposed to the outside community. Although it was located in an outlying area, Hyde Park itself was not as self-contained vis-à-vis Chicago as Cambridge was vis-à-vis Boston.

The representation of sociology in the Departments of Social Ethics and of Economics at Harvard by no means exhausts the sociology which existed at Harvard in the 1920s. Indeed, the activities of those two departments gives very little sense of what important things began to go on there from the middle of that decade onward. For one thing, there was Lawrence J. Henderson, whose enthusiasm had been aroused by Pareto's *Trattato di sociologia generale* (Henderson probably read it in the French translation). Disregarding the sociology which was going on elsewhere at Harvard and the sociology being done elsewhere in the United States, Henderson became a passionate partisan of sociology as he understood it from his reading of the *Trattato*. In the early thirties he organized a seminar which had a large attendance of senior and junior members of the university, including such eminent scholars as A. D. Nock and such promising younger ones as Crane Brinton. There was also Talcott Parsons, who, having returned from Heidelberg in 1927, had been appointed to an instructorship in the economics department, where presumably he taught economics with a sociological bent.

By 1927 there was growing discontent at Harvard about the standing of sociology as a subject for studies and research. In that year a Committee on Sociology and Social Ethics was appointed under the chairmanship of Ralph Barton Perry which recommended that something more fully corresponding to sociology as generally known at the time should be established at Harvard.

At the same time, under the inspiring pressure of Henderson, there had been established an industrial fatigue laboratory for studying the physiological factors affecting the productivity of industrial workers. Elton Mayo was in charge of this and was working under the guidance—or domination—of Henderson. The work was proving to be less fruitful than anticipated. In order to explain differences in the output of individual workers, Mayo and Henderson began to consider "larger systems." Mayo had studied Radcliffe-Brown and Durkheim and was moving closer and closer to a sociological interpretation of industrial productivity. He gathered around himself Dickson and Roethlisberger, T. N. Whitehead, and finally Lloyd Warner. The latter was encouraged to undertake a study of an entire "larger system," namely, the town of Newburyport. Also in the 1930s, George Homans, an unemployed graduate from a well-connected Harvard family, came under the influence of Henderson and was persuaded that he should become a sociologist in the Paretian manner. Homans wrote a small book on Pareto with George Curtis. Then he began an investigation into English history following the instruction of Henderson, who ordered him to immerse himself in the facts of some particular subject. Homans, having studied Anglo-Saxon as an undergraduate in English at Harvard, began to work on English medieval economic history and, having read Seebohm's book on the English rural community, began the investigation which led to his *English Villagers in the Thirteenth Century*.

Meanwhile the Committee on Sociology and Social Ethics had moved to recommend the establishment of a full department of sociology. The university invited Pitirim Sorokin to become the professor of sociology and chairman of the department. The department of social ethics was pushed to the wall and ceased to function, although officially it was to be incorporated into the Department of Sociology. Sorokin brought with him Carle Zimmermann, a rural sociologist from the University of Minnesota, where Sorokin had been professor after he came to the United States as a refugee from the Russian Revolution.

By the middle of the 1930s, then, the department consisted of Sorokin, Zimmermann, and Parsons. It had acquired, largely in response to Parsons' teaching, an outstanding group of graduate students, the most eminent of whom were Robert Merton, Kingsley Davis, Logan Wilson, and Robin Williams. Henderson continued to teach and promote his own brand of sociology. Towards the end of the 1930s he gave his Sociology 23, which was attended by a number of young men later to become eminent sociologists; Homans was put to work by Henderson on the "wirebank" experiment at the Western Electric plant. In short, sociology at Harvard was launched. With outstanding teachers, outstanding students, and an independent department, the work in sociology began to produce some important results. In 1937 *The Structure of Social Action* appeared. Robert Merton's doctoral dissertation on seventeenth-century science, which showed the influence of both Parsons and Sorokin, was produced towards the end of the decade.

Harvard after 1945

Harvard's later centrality, based on traditions transplanted from Heidelberg (Max Weber), and Vienna (Freud), was attributable to a new pattern of institutionalization which emerged in the second half of the 1940s. At Harvard, under the leadership of Talcott Parsons, Henry Murray, and Clyde Kluckhohn, a deliberate attempt was made to integrate the theories of social structure, culture, and personality. The teaching program was adapted to this conception of the subject, but the research training program did not keep up with it. The Laboratory of Social Relations never became the intellectual factory and drill ground which the Bureau of Applied Social Research became shortly after the end of the Second World War. It became the administrative sponsor and the home of a variety of investigations which, to a greater extent than at Columbia, were small-scale projects which required neither an intricate division of labor nor a thoroughgoing routinization and stereotyping of procedure. It never became the solidary collectivity with an identity of its own which the Columbia bureau succeeded in becoming and, even before the death of the gifted Samuel Stouffer who had come there from Chicago via the War Department, it became more of an administrative name and rather less of a corporate intellectual reality. Although valiant efforts were made to create it, Harvard lacked the high degree of consensus among its central personalities which was possessed to such a degree at Columbia. As long as the center at Harvard was a triumvirate with an outward appearance of unity, it presented a powerful force to the outer world of sociology. Nonetheless, it was in fact a center consisting internally of several relatively noncommunicating segments—and this reduced its capacity to impose itself effectively on the subject as a whole. Each of the major segments was a powerful intellectual personality—Parsons, Murray, Kluckhohn, Bruner, Stouffer, and Homans, each of them was in one way or another a forceful generator of ideas and works, but there was no fundamental agreement among them. It did not have what Chicago possessed at its height, namely, a pervasive agreement underlying a wide diversity of substantive interests. A higher degree of consensus among them might have swept the field. (They did very well as it was!) It also lacked what Chicago in the 1920s and early 1930s possessed, namely, its own distinctive organs of publication and stable extra-academic institutional links with the local community for research and training purposes.

On the other hand, it had in Professor Parsons a motive force of great power; his continuous and pervasive productivity spread his influence over the country into the by this time numerous subcenters with highly institutionalized training provision for postgraduate students. The role of one particular publishing enterprise—the Free Press—which became the main source of sociological nutriment for the growing number of graduate students and young teachers from the end of the Second World War until about 1960—provided Professor Parsons with a surrogate for a journal of his own. His numerous, widely scattered essays were concentrated into a few easily available volumes. These essays enabled a new generation to acquire the underlying disposition of Parsons' theory as it was manifested in confrontation with a wide variety of particular problems. The enhancement of the prestige of Harvard University as a whole coincided chronologically with the prestige of the department of social relations which was largely the prestige of Talcott Parsons—although not exclusively so. This attracted to Harvard a succession of gifted students.

Other centers

The sociology department of the University of California in Berkeley also should be mentioned in these observations about the emergence of new centers in American sociology. The University of California in Berkeley was the last great American university to establish a department of sociology. It came into existence after Chicago, Harvard, and Columbia were well-established with dominant traditions of their own. Berkeley could not recruit its staff from within except at the level of its youngest members; it had to recruit its staff from other universities, e.g., Lipset trained at Columbia under Merton and Lazarsfeld, Blumer under Mead and Faris at Chicago, Bendix under Wirth at Chicago, Selznick at Columbia, Kornhauser at Chicago, Kingsley Davis at Harvard, Löwenthal at Frankfurt. The size of the staff of the department and the size of the student body as well as the amplitude of resources all made for centrifugality. The high degree of institutionalization coexisted with a diversity of standpoints so that, despite the eminence of the department as an aggregation of outstanding and productive sociologists whose works drew the attention of the country and the world, it lacked the coherence which Durkheim, Park, and Parsons gave to their respective circles of colleagues, collaborators, and pupils.

Sociology at the University of Michigan had been gently influential through the writings of Charles Cooley ever since the turn of the century. Both Thomas and Park had assimilated Cooley's ideas about the primary group into their own dominant traditions. There had not, however, been an independent department of sociology at Michigan until 1930, when Roderick McKenzie, a Chicago product and a close collaborator of Park, came there from the University of Washington. The Department of Sociology at the University of Michigan became one of the major departments of the country, partly through the extension of ecological studies and partly through the establishment of the Survey Research Center there. The latter was an important step in the institutionalization of training and research at Michigan; in its ecological and related studies, Michigan continued and developed the Chicago tradition with the aid of many recruits from Chicago.

From Chicago in its earlier years and from Harvard and Columbia in the several decades after the end of the Second World War, we know how effective is a unitary center created by one dominant or two strong consensual figures. A pluralistic assemblage of eminent figures is not likely to be equally effective. Berkeley did not show a capacity to create a *Nachwuchs* which could renew the department while unifying it or to produce a body of graduates who would diffuse its "line" more widely in the United States.

The functions of a center are performed, nationally and internationally, through the channels of communication which are integral to institutionalization; namely, learned journals, monograph series, and books. But one essential organ of institutionalization is the face-to-face encounter of teachers with students. It is through these encounters that the *Nachwuchs* is formed and that ideas are generated, tried out, and selected from among a variety of alternatives.

The absence of a systematically trained *Nachwuchs* does not mean that an intellectual subject cannot develop: it did so in the heroic age of science prior to the formation of the modern university. The absence of a systematically trained *Nachwuchs* means that the pressure of tradition is lightened. The development of an intellectual subject under such circumstances is more a matter of individual genius than it has become since the transformation of universities into institutions of research and training.

The questions which then follow are: would the proliferation of centers damage the subject intellectually, would it disorder sociology by making its work less coherent and more scrappy? Is a unified center possible under present circumstances in the world of learning?

The proliferation of sociologists and of sociological works in the past quarter of a century has resulted in great specialization; in a subject still as deficient in fundamental theory as is sociology this might mean that it will disintegrate, losing whatever coherence it has gained over the preceding three-quarters of a century. Sociology might break up into the specialisms like those which exist now in the physical and biological sciences, without being able to draw on a basic or fundamental science like physics, chemistry, or genetics.

The constituent elements of the traditions of present-day sociology have been in a process of selection and coalescence through the work of Weber, Durkheim, Parsons, et al. This coalescence is still very imperfect. (It can never be perfect, and, if it did become perfect, the subject would come to a complete halt.) Greater coalescence than it possesses at present is, however, a necessary condition not just for aesthetic or architectonic reasons, but because, until there is such a coalescence, the interrelations of the different phenomena in society will be too poorly understood. The multiplication of sociological persons and works and the high degree of specialization might render more difficult the ascendancy of a more complex and comprehensive theory because it would render more difficult the ascendancy of a theorist whose mastery of the results of specialized study would be great enough to call forth the respect and adherence of the practitioners of the diverse and numerous specialisms.

Sociological Traditions: Selection, Rejection, Coalescence

If one takes up the compendious work by Sorokin, *Contemporary Sociological Theories,* which presented the stock of sociology of the fifty years which lay across the turn of the century, one is struck with how few of the names which are cited are known today by any but sociological antiquarians. Weber, Durkheim, Pareto, Park, and Thomas are there, so are Floyd Allport, Otto Ammon, Emory Bogardus, Stuart Chapin, Filipo Carli, E. de Roberty, Charles Ellwood, Franklin Giddings, Maxim Kovalevsky, E. A. Ross, Gabriel Tarde, William Graham Sumner, Alfred Vierkandt, Leopold von Wiese, L. Winiarsky, and Sorokin himself, who is cited more than any other two authors. What has become of these authors and of the ideas they espoused? They have fallen by the wayside.

Some of them were weak intellectually, and their ideas did not recommend themselves to critical contemporaries. Some of them were in the wrong places, their books were the only ways in which they spoke to their contemporaries, they had no students or no students who had the ability, received the inspiration, and learned how to press further with what they had received. They might have been in the "wrong" countries and written in the "wrong" language. Some of them were known and respected figures, contemporary with Durkheim, Weber, and Park, but the world turned away from them.

There were many ideas floating about in sociology in the latter part of the nineteenth century. Practically all of them were influenced in one way or another by Hegel, Comte, and Darwin. Evolutionary and biological ideas were common. The major idea was one of historical stages of human society from simple to differentiated, from traditional to rational, from unenlightened to enlightened, from societies with tool-based technology to societies with a machine-based technology using artificially generated power, from loosely integrated societies to closely integrated societies. The Darwinian evolutionary viewpoint fitted into and rendered more plausible this theory of stages of development; the prestige of Darwinism also activated a tendency to analyze social structures and their functions in society in the categories appropriate to the study of biological organisms. (This type of sociological analysis was submerged rather early and left little trace.) The Darwinian influence was also present among those sociologists who, impressed by the competition of species, stressed the importance of the competition and the conflict of races as a central phenomenon in society. Others, also impressed by the idea of natural selection, were concerned with social selection and hence with the social origins and the presumed biological heredity of the members of various strata, above all, the leading strata in contemporary Western societies. Many studies were intended to demonstrate the biological transmission of socially relevant characteristics. Much of the substance of these traditions no longer has any place in the currently effective traditions of sociology. Certain variables in this set of beliefs have survived, for example the study of the social origins of elites and the social origins of particular professions, but the matrix of propositions has fallen away. And what has survived has not been comfortably assimilated into the traditions of sociology now prevailing.[26]

A few words should be said at this point about Marxian sociology which has so many self-alleged proponents at present. "Marxian sociology," such as it is, is an amalgam of Hegelian evolutionism into which has been inserted a conception of conflict drawn from Darwinism[27] and from the studies of the "poor." It includes also a con-

26. I refer here to the awkwardness of present "elite studies" which are sometimes legitimated by associating them with the study of power and authority—very unconvincingly—at other times with the "circulation of elites" which likewise has not found a comfortable home in contemporary sociology.

27. One variant of the Darwinian tradition elaborated by Ratzenhofer and Gumplowicz had an enduring afterlife via Albion Small, W. I. Thomas, and Robert Park. The affinity of this conception of conflict to competition in the animal and plant worlds had a powerful effect on Chicago sociology. It also had a pronounced influence on Arthur Bentley and through him on American political sociology.

ception of "interest" which has been generalized from the conservative conception of the "landed interest" which was developed in the
seventeenth and eighteenth centuries in England. This results in
something different from the mere substitution of "class" for ethnic,
national, and territorial "groups," which had been stressed by Ratzenhofer and Gumplowicz, and it is also something different from that
type of conflict which arises from contention for the possession of
scarce objects. The prevailing conception of society derived from
Weber and Durkheim allows, despite the assertions of the critics of
the "consensus-model,"[28] ample place for conflict but it can make no
place for "real" interests which are independent of what is desired by
actual human beings in situations of scarcity. This historical
metaphysics of "real" interests could obviously not find a place in a
tradition which received one of its possible promulgations in *Towards
a General Theory of Action*. The same may be said about the distinction between the superstructure and the substructure and about the
causal primacy of the latter. The distinction derives from a conception
of human action which is alien to the more realistic, synthetic tradition which is contained in much of contemporary sociology.

Thus a considerable amount of the Darwinian or biologistic and the
metaphysical evolutionary conceptions could not be fused with the
traditions which prevail in contemporary sociology. They have either
become extinct or they lead a restless, uncomfortable existence recur-
ring intermittently at the margins of sociological culture, functioning
to criticize but incapable of positive development in a culture which is
committed to empirical research—however theoretical.

Of the Comtean and the Hegelian concepts of social evolution,
certain very important elements have survived. The conception of
society as a moral order in which discrete individuals are bound together in collective actions of various sorts by common images of
themselves as parts of that order and by common beliefs defining
themselves and their obligations to the collectivity is one of the chief
precipitates of the coalescence of the various intellectual traditions of
the eighteenth and nineteenth centuries. From Rousseau's conception
of the collective will, from Hegel and the German theorists of the

28. A characteristic allegation of this sort appears in an essay by Professor
Ralf Dahrendorf: "Out of Utopia," *American Journal of Sociology* 64, no. 2
(1958).

Volksgeist, from Comte's portrayal of the morally disintegrated condition of the then contemporary society in its "critical," skeptical state, and from Marx's conception of the dissolution of the moral bonds in modern bourgeois society emerged a variety of conceptions of the significance of beliefs (about the ultimately valuable) in the regulation of individual conduct and in the determination of the degree of integration of society. Max Weber's typology of legitimate authority was developed from the presupposition of the significance of beliefs and of a consensus of beliefs about ultimate things; the moral state of society which engaged Durkheim's interest, the conception of *Gemeinschaft* and *Gesellschaft* in Tönnies, the conception of the moral order in Park—all these beliefs about the scale and significance of a consensus of moral beliefs in the working of society have been the products of a confluence of traditions to which Hobbes, Rousseau, Hegel, Marx, Lazarus, Steinthal, and H. S. Maine have contributed. The Marxian concept of bourgeois society unbridgeably divided into competing and conflicting classes; the Simmelian conception of urban society, differentiated by division of labor, sectional interests, and individuation; Tönnies' conception of modern bourgeois society—*Gesellschaft*—which resembled Hobbes' picture of the state of nature where a relationship of *homo homini lupus* prevailed; all implied a great concern with the extent and the significance of a consensus of moral beliefs. The problem was: to what extent do individual men act on the basis of conceptions of themselves, their rights and obligations, in ways which minimize or aggravate the conflicts between themselves as individuals and as members of groups, with other individuals and groups. Consensus became the main variable of analytical or theoretical sociology. Even those authors who claimed that modern societies were atomized had their point of departure in an image of a consensual society: they regarded the dissensual character of modern societies as the phenomenon to be accounted for. The very definition of modern society involved placing the variable of consensus in the center of attention.

The struggle for existence which was one variable of the sociological Darwinism and the basic theorem of the sociological theory of the *Rassenkampf* could be assimilated into the emerging sociological tradition because it constantly raised the problem of "defective consensus." In Ratzenhofer and Gumplowicz, the conflict of races was given; it was not problematic. In the analytical sociology which became ascendant in the work of the European and American founders, conflict was not a given; it became a variable to be accounted for. Its converse—consensus—was likewise not given. It too had to be explained. Research on the adjustment of immigrants or on family disorganization, on ethnic conflict, on segregation, suicide, anomie, on the formation of sects, on the role of charismatic authority and of rational-legal authority were all attempts to cope with this fundamental problem. Features of other ideas which could not be assimilated were discarded.

Certain other important ideas of contemporary sociology were possible only within the context of a concern about the moral beliefs of a society. The idea of the charismatic or the sacred was an extension of this conception. The delineation of the properties of bureaucratic authority and the assessment of the role of bureaucracy in modern societies were elaborations of the conceptions of *Gesellschaft* in Tönnies and of capitalistic society in Marx. The same obtains for the conceptions of "mass society," "modernization," and "organizations" which assumed such prominence in subsequent sociological studies; they were developed out of the fundamental conceptions of the sociology formed by the continental founders of the subject.

Even before it became anywhere nearly as institutionalized as it had been for the past thirty years, this tradition was in the process of gaining ascendancy. It was, as Talcott Parsons pointed out in *The Structure of Social Action,* contained implicitly in the three main European traditions of idealism, positivism, and utilitarianism and it was elicited from potentiality by the powerful intelligences of the major European theorists. The American theorists of the founding generation were not of equally powerful theoretical intelligence, but they too—Thomas and Park—came upon the essential. In neither the case of Thomas nor of Park did they ever succeed—nor did they try in any large-scale effort—in discarding the elements of incompatible traditions. In Park's case, fragments of Darwinism remained in his ecological ideas. Thomas, indeed, after his exclusion from the University of Chicago, turned away not only from his sociological work but also from the framework which he had developed in it and which brought him near to Weber and Durkheim; he was attracted by an eclectic behavioristic psychology which was alien to what he had believed previously. (There is some reason to believe however that, after this digression, he began to find his way back again, but no published work ever announced his arrival.)

Somehow, despite its very scanty institutionalization in Germany, despite its submergence in France, despite its numerous competitors in Great Britain, the now dominant tradition grew and ramified. With institutionalization and the emergence of new centers in which a more stringent formulation of the tradition was presented, it finally triumphed over competitors—not totally—in the United States. Once the United States became the center, however, the reinterpreted and modified tradition then spread back to Europe, where, despite resistances, it established itself in all the main European countries in a way in which it had never done before when Europe was itself the center from which the tradition emanated.

To what extent is its wide diffusion and dominance attributable to institutionalization?[29]

The turning of direction of a tradition, the amalgamation of elements of several traditions, is a creative action. It is not an institutional action. It is the work of an individual mind and it can and has been done under conditions of very rudimentary institutionalization. As a matter of fact it might even be said that institutionalization, as important as it is for consolidation, multiplication, and diffusion, can be something of a hindrance to the turning and amalgamation of traditions. Max Weber had the advantage of an uninstitutionalized sociology in his time. He had studied law and economics, he came on the study of religion without institutional supervision. Durkheim had not

29. It must be remembered that what is institutionalized is an intellectual process and that an account of the process is not exhausted by an account of the institutional setting in which it occurs. There is the sheer power of intelligence in confrontation with problems. The problems can be perceived through a number of mechanisms. They can be contained in the intellectual works which a searching, questing intelligence has discovered—either by its own curiosity or by moving along paths which it has made for itself in only very lightly charted territory. Intellectual works themselves are linked with other intellectual works contained in them by references to other books and authors. Even without the aid of the contemporary institutional elaboration of teaching, of bibliographical services, libraries, learned societies, a seeking intelligence with the sensitivity of an Indian tracker could find like-minded persons across the stretches of a relatively unorganized Europe. Nonetheless, the task was more difficult before institutionalization through universities and learned journals.

studied sociology as an academic subject. Park studied it under conditions of very scanty institutionalization and Thomas studied it in Chicago when the subject still scarcely existed intellectually, although an institutional structure had been created for it.

A tradition can give birth to a product at one stage of its existence which it could not produce at an earlier time. Its potentialities might be presumed to have an inherent sequentiality and it is quite possible that this stage had been reached at the end of the nineteenth century so that, in a number of countries, persons who had assimilated positivism, utilitarianism, and idealism began to produce results which had marked affinities with each other. Those who produced these results entered into practically no contact with each other. It was for the next generation of those born after the beginning of the new century, with Parsons in the forefront, to draw together into a more explicit and coherent pattern these separately generated approximations to a tradition. The subsequent history of the consolidation and diffusion of the tradition is very much a history in which the institutional system of sociology has played a crucial role.

Endogenous Traditions, Exogenous Traditions, and Exogenous Stimuli

An intellectual discipline exists when a number of persons believe themselves to possess an identity defined by the common subject of their intellectual activity, when many or all of the problems which they study are raised by or derived from the tradition, i.e., the body of literature and oral interpretation produced by those who regard themselves as practitioners of the discipline. An intellectual discipline is an academic discipline when it is taught, discussed, and investigated in academic institutions which bear the name of the discipline or something akin to it, and when its members publish works in organs bearing the name of the discipline. A discipline has an intellectual and social structure.

In the early years of sociology, while its proponents were still struggling to establish their intellectual and academic dignity, a relatively common activity of sociologists in Germany, France, Great Britain, and the United States was the delineation of the field of sociology, its demarcation from other already existing academic disciplines, and the laying out of its internal subdivisions. Sociologists at that time had no social structure for their discipline in most instances and so they sought to define it by its intellectual properties. This was extremely difficult to do since the ancestry to which they laid claim was not universally acknowledged by nonsociologists and because there was little intellectual substance which they could invoke in self-legitimation. This was why they argued in principle and made claims for the future. This activity has now practically ceased, mainly because most sociologists have come to accept a vaguely delineated body of problems, ideas, and procedures as sociological, despite the unclarity of boundaries and the heterogeneity of subject matters, problems, and "approaches." The large body of literature which contains these problems, ideas, and procedures, which appears in sociological journals, which is reviewed there, and which is produced by persons called sociologists, fortifies this sense of sociological identity. Sociology is also now recognized as a subject by the educated public inside and outside the universities, and this too helps to define the boundaries of the subject and of the profession which cultivates it or at least to allay apprehensions about its legitimacy.

The definition of sociology by the social structure of sociology and by its corpus of works has a retroactive effect on the construction of the sociological tradition. While traditions work forward in time, the construction of a legitimatory, inspirational tradition is a movement through time in the reverse direction. Tradition is not, however, a mythological construction, although it has some of the functions of mythology. The works and ideas which have been admitted to a tradition, i.e., which are regarded as part of it, help to set the problems. They can set problems in a situation in which the ostensibly valid part of the tradition is the work which has most recently been published, although the problems of the recently published works were set earlier by a major work which might have been written many years in the past. Alternatively—although it is not so different—current work might constantly refer explicitly to a major work done many years earlier. Sociology is at present a mixture of these two relationships to "its own past." The significant fact is that sociology now has a number of less dominant traditions. Some of these less dominant traditions are in a sense "counter-traditions." These counter-traditions are mainly polemical rather than substantive. Behaviorism as exemplified in the work of George Lundberg was one of these; the self-designated ''critical sociology''—an evasive name for highbrow Marxism—is another. Both of these counter-traditions, when their adherents produce substantive works, turn out to have little nutritive value intellectually; their adherents are in fact dominated by the prevailing central tradition in their selection of problems and in their selection of the major variables with which they operate. Even allowing for the ambiguity and lack of rigor of practically all sociological work and the large degree of freedom of interpretation permitted by the poor data and the disjunctiveness of detailed empirical research, even the interpretations offered by adherents of the counter-traditions turn out to be little different from the interpretations offered by the adherents of the dominant tradition.

Some of the less dominant traditions are subsidiary traditions which are not polemical. They have a more positive relationship to the dominant traditions. They are viewed sympathetically by adherents of the dominant traditions. They have become tributaries which flow into the dominant traditions even though they arose outside them. Comparative religious studies are of this sort. Thanks to the work of Weber and Durkheim, the results of comparative studies in religion have found a place in the dominant traditions, although comparative religious studies still constitute an autonomous field of work with a great central tradition of its own, with a vast literature and many very distinguished contributers. Modern economic analysis is another. At one time, in the writings of the European founders, economics up to the time of Mill and Senior found its way into sociology. Talcott Parsons succeeded in bringing in Marshallian economics too (his later efforts to assimilate the Keynesian development from neoclassical economics has apparently been less successful). More recently economists like Becker, Arrow, Nerlove, and Schultz have applied economic analysis to subjects like the family, ethnic relations, and education, ordinarily treated by sociologists, and the results of these enquiries are likely to be assimilated into sociology.

Animal and plant ecology and the economic theory of location also coalesced with the central sociological traditions as Chicago was emerging into dominance, but they fell away as the center shifted from Chicago. Since these subsidiary traditions were never persuasively and explicitly integrated in an authoritative work by Park or his associates and protégés, they became submerged or disassociated as far as sociology was concerned.

The psychoanalytic theory of personality is another tradition which partly coalesced with the central sociological tradition. The particular propositions of psychoanalysis might not be true; the mechanism of the Oedipus complex might not be as psychoanalysis has described it; the same can be said about the genesis and mechanisms of aggression, conscience, anxiety, repression, etc. Nonetheless, these variables in the coherent pattern which psychoanalysis set forth have been assimilated into the sociological tradition. The naming and description of these phenomena has made sociologists more aware of them, more realistic in their perception of them, in the assessment of their magnitude, and in the estimate of the probability of their occurrence under determinate conditions.

The traditions of social anthropology are similarly subsidiary traditions with respect to the main traditions of sociology. Social anthropology developed quite independently of sociology. There was a time when they were both independently established within the same academic department, but even then they were separate. They each had a distinctive subject matter; one studied modern Western urban societies, the other studied "primitive" agrarian societies in Asia, Africa, and the Americas. They used techniques of research which were quite different from each other. They sometimes overlapped when sociologists studied illiterate peasants or aboriginals within their own societies, as they did in South Eastern Europe or when social anthropologists studied the urbanization of African tribesmen in East or South Africa. By and large however each kept to its own jurisdiction and cultivated its own theories. When Radcliffe-Brown drew on Durkheim, a step was taken towards the fusion of the two sets of traditions by the adduction of a strand of tradition which was common to both. Robert Redfield's adaptation of Park's ideas to the study of villages in Mexico and Guatemala was another such step. Still another step was taken when Lloyd Warner, who had studied Australian aborigines, undertook to study sectors of contemporary American society. Bit by bit, the two traditions began to come closer to each other. When after the Second World War, anthropologists, sociologists, political scientists began to study the problems of the new states of Asia and Africa, the sociologists among them had to read the literature of social anthropology, even though they were studying institutions of a type which had not existed earlier in the societies studied by social anthropologists. Thus the two traditions came closer to each other. The two subjects are not amalgamated; they remain institutionally separate from each other albeit within the same universities. Nonetheless, in certain respects, the subsidiary tradition of social anthropology is becoming incorporated into the sociological tradition; the same is true in reverse. Each remains an integral and distinctive tradition but each has incorporated a considerable amount of the substance of the other.

There have been other coalescences of the sociological traditions and the intellectual traditions external to sociology. Traditions from various currents of philosophy, e.g., from phenomenology, from legal studies, from literary and linguistic studies, have flowed into the sociological traditions, sometimes becoming conceptually well integrated, sometimes less so.

Sometimes the traditions which reach towards sociology are contemporaneously active. Sometimes they have been relatively dormant outside of sociology for a long time. The most striking instance of the latter is the revival of Tocqueville's ideas about the consequences of equality and the delineation of the structure of an equalitarian society. The revival of Tocqueville occurred first in political science after the Second World War and it moved into sociology with the increased attention to the structure of "mass society." The account of Tocqueville as a sociologist in Raymond Aron's *Etapes de la pensée sociologique* has now made Tocqueville's ideas retroactively into a constitutive element in the contemporaneously effective traditions of sociology.

Sociology and comparative religious studies, sociology and economics, sociology and ecology, sociology and psychoanalysis, sociology and social anthropology, sociology and cybernetics, sociology and the theory of administration—all these coalescences with their simultaneous modifications of the content of sociology today and of the image which sociologists have of their own past are coalescences of substantive traditions, of traditions which have grown out of the sociological tradition endogenously and of intellectual traditions which have developed outside of sociology. But they are all substantive traditions. Sociology is not merely a body of substantive assertions: it purports to be a science, and as such it exists within the more broadly embracing tradition of discourse which requires systematic confirmation of its assertions. In consequence of this sense of intellectual obligation, the substantive traditions of sociology have increasingly, although unequally, become affiliated to traditions of observational, analytical, and statistical techniques. The entire conception of sociology as a science is of this character.

There is a long and many-streamed tradition of sociological procedure which has become more and more coalescent, in practice and in retrospect, with the substantive traditions. Albion Small looked back to Niebuhr and Savigny; Paul Lazarsfeld drew a retrospective map which went back to William Petty and the English demographers of the seventeenth century. Later, he established Quetelet as a precursor. Philip Abrams more recently presented a coherent account of the course of the ''statistical'' tradition and Keith Baker has reinstated Condorcet as a precursor of the science of society. Every new step in sociology towards a more rigorous procedure of empirical research adds a new set of ancestral deities to the pantheon of the sociological tradition. These in turn add their force to the movement of coalescence. These newly acknowledged traditions are not fictions. It is true that, in some instances, they were not effective until they were proclaimed to be traditions. The fact that Park and Thomas and Durkheim and Weber did not incorporate Tocqueville into their work does not deny that, for later generations, he has become a part of their effective tradition.

The initiatives for the coalescence of endogenous and exogenous intellectual traditions have in most cases come from within sociology. In that sense sociology has been a realm of its own with its own center of gravity, its own discriminatory powers. This has been tantamount to a continuing expansion of sociology in its subject-matters, in the differentiation of its analytical schemes and its corresponding interpretative hypotheses; it has entailed the increasing stringency of its procedural standards.

The tradition which is regarded as sociological is heterogeneous; it is really more proper to speak of sociological traditions within a sociological tradition. It is heterogeneous because of the imperfections in the assimilation or integration of the many coalescent subsidiary or tributary traditions, and it is heterogeneous because very few sociologists accept or even know all of it. The various strands of the sociological tradition are not shared equally by all sociologists. Not only are there the limitations imposed by the specialization of knowledge, but there are also differences in interest and esteem which mean that any particular sociologist will be more sympathetic to one strand or family of traditions and more hostile towards certain others.

Sociology does not however live from an intellectual inheritance alone. Its exertions are not confined to the refinement and enrichment of that inheritance by the study of the problems which that inheritance offers and by the incorporation of new elements from exogenous intellectual traditions. Sociology does not just live within its primary institutional system however dense and absorbing that is. It also belongs to the larger world. Its subject-matter is that larger world. Those who profess it are parts of the larger world. Sociologists are members of social classes, nationalities, ethnic groups, religious communities, political organizations, and they share to some extent the culture of these parts of society. They belong to their society and their generation and they share to some extent in the cognitive beliefs and evaluative attitudes of their society and generation. Sociologists are citizens in their own societies and they respond to the problems of their societies. The institutional establishment of sociology proceeded partly on an assumption that sociological knowledge would be "used" to improve societies; it has entailed training students for roles in their societies. The institutionalization itself has been greatly furthered by the belief of those in positions of authority and influence in that larger world that sociology "has something to contribute" beyond its contribution to the intellectual improvement of the sociological tradition. Part of the institutionalization of sociology in recent decades has involved both the financial support—by grants and contracts—of research by university research workers on particular subjects designated by the patron and the conduct of research within the corporate framework of public or private bodies concerned in a practical way with certain problems which sociological knowledge would presumably help to solve.

It has been claimed that sociology often chooses its problems and its subject-matters according to criteria of value-relevance and not just in terms of the pattern of problems presented by the intellectual tradition. For example, the study of the Negro, as developed by the

Chicago sociologists, has been asserted to be a "response" to the problems of urbanization and migration. It was that but it was at least as importantly a study of the processes of competition, conflict, accommodation, and assimilation and of the conditions of their increase and decrease. These categories had been developed by Park from his study of Simmel, Kistiakowski, and Gumplowicz, from his study of the work of Warming, and from his own observations, both direct and historical, in the United States and in other countries. These seem to me to be still more or less the right categories in which to study the relations between groups, including those between whites and blacks in the United States. Before the Second World War, the study of the Negro in America was further enriched by the introduction of certain variables of psychoanalytic origin, and a number of valuable monographs were produced along these lines. There was nothing in the world of practical affairs which "required" this reaching out from sociology towards psychoanalysis. It simply appeared to John Dollard, who was a collaborator of Ogburn and connected with Lasswell, to be reasonable to interpret certain actions and attitudes in psychoanalytic terms. But at a time when the Negro question was not less urgent than it had been before, and for no good reason other than the fact that the newly emergent sociological theory did not deal with ethnic groups and their relations with each other as a particular concrete subject-matter, the Negro receded as an object of sociological study in the United States. This occurred very little after the time when Myrdal's vast synthesis of American, to a large extent Chicago, research appeared. Why? Had the analytical problems involving competition, conflict, accommodation, and assimilation been so exhaustively solved that the subject no longer had anything interesting to offer? Or did the Negroes themselves cease to be a "value-problem" in the United States? Neither of these answers is acceptable.

The decline in intellectual interest in the Negroes in the United States was a result of several factors. The first is that the new centers of sociological study—Harvard and Columbia in particular—had their own substantive intellectual traditions which did not include in substance the study of the Negro. In Max Weber, primordial things received little explicit attention—in *Wirtschaft und Gesellschaft* only one small chapter eleven pages in length is given to "ethnische Gemeinschaften," and in the writings of Talcott Parsons they received no attention until the 1960s, when the Negro problem became very urgent in the United States. I think that until relatively recently not more than two Harvard Ph.D. dissertations were written on Negroes. At Columbia, where several interesting dissertations had been written on Negroes, e.g., Kiser's *Sea Island to City,* in the 1930s, the period in which Paul Lazarsfeld and Robert Merton ruled, the subject nearly disappeared. It did not recommend itself theoretically and there was little interest in supporting research on it. The eclectic analytical outlook of Professor Merton could certainly have been accommodated to almost any subject matter and the technical virtuosity of Professor Lazarsfeld was likewise as applicable to the study of race relations and to the study of Negro society as it was to mass communications, housing estates, etc. Yet practically no work was done at Columbia on the Negro, although the Negro quarter of New York was immediately adjacent to Columbia University. In Chicago, in the disorientation referred to earlier and under the impact of the Harvard and Columbia styles of sociological theory and research, the interest in the Negro was allowed to lapse. The old center lost its confidence in its own substantive tradition.

In the 1960s, when the "Negro problem" came to the forefront of American political and public opinion with an unprecedented urgency, the study of the Negro was revived, but within a rather narrower framework and in any case a different one from that which guided the earlier studies. New methods of measurement of occupational discrimination, of the share of the Negro population in the national income, etc., have been undertaken, but the social structure of Negro communities and of Negro-white relationships as developed in the tradition of W. I. Thomas, Park, and Burgess by Charles Johnson, Franklin Frazier, Bertram Doyle, Harold Gosnell, Edward Thompson, and Everett Hughes has not been taken up again. The "Negro subject-matter" of sociology might have survived the period from 1940 to 1960 if the Chicago tradition had received an authoritative theoretical formulation capable of demanding explicit incorporation into a new analytical scheme equal in attractiveness to that which was developing at Harvard. Since, however, it had not gone beyond fragmentary, only implicitly coherent statements, its competitive power was not sufficient. Thus, despite the analytical affinity of the Chicago tradition with the newer developments in the sociological tradition, its idiom was submerged and, with that, its particular subject-matter. Had its idiom survived in the new analytical scheme, its associated subject-matter would likewise have survived.

The vicissitudes of the study of the Negro in the United States would indicate that the substantive analytical or theoretical tradition is not primarily a product of exogenous, nonintellectual occurrences. The change in the tradition of studying a particular subject-matter was, in my view, to a large extent a result of the adhesion of particular subject-matters to particular analytical traditions and of changes in the institutional system of sociology (e.g., the relocation of the center from Chicago). It was not wholly so; the absence of patronage for research on Negroes was probably another factor as was the fact that in the 1950s many white sociologists were giving their attention to other problems of American life such as "McCarthyism," "mass culture," "underdeveloped countries," etc. The reemergence of the Negro as a subject-matter of sociological research has indeed been a consequence of exogenous events, which occur outside of the intellectual sphere as well as outside sociology. The migration of Negroes to northern cities in response to opportunities for employment and the greater measure of freedom, and the determination of the federal government to assure the civil rights of the Negroes, were events which might be called demographic, economic, and political. They belonged to a category of things different from sociology but they drew the attention of sociologists and induced the sociologists to study these events. But the scheme of analysis was not much affected by these demographic, economic, and political events. Rather it remained very much a product of the sociological tradition; in its emphasis on the anomic element in the black section of American society it drew more and more on the Durkheimian element of the sociological tradition, mediated by Merton's reformulation.

The study of "popular" or "mass culture" is another illustration of the interplay of endogenous and exogenous intellectual traditions and exogenous nonintellectual events. Tönnies, Simmel, and Weber created the tradition, but it was the sociologists'—especially Mannheim's and Horkheimer's—response to the National Socialist movement and its triumph in Germany and the great expansion of the study of the content of and "exposure" to mass communications which led to the expansion of attention to "mass society" in American sociology in the 1950s. Changes in the outlook of certain literary and publicistic intellectuals in the United States—I think particularly of their disillusionment with Marxism attendant on the identification of Marxism and Stalinism and the simultaneous disillusionment with the "working classes" for their failure to act as agents of revolution and as the "heirs of German classical philosophy"—made for the animation of certain elements already contained in the central tradition of sociology. The nonintellectual events—the successes of the National Socialists and the increased prominence of "mass culture"—did not divert the tradition of sociology. The tradition of sociology elaborated what it already contained in order to treat these events.

The career of industrial sociology and the sociology of work is another instance of a subject which was developed in the framework of the central tradition of sociology—much influenced by Durkheim's ideas about anomie and Max Weber's ideas about bureaucracy—and supported by private business management. In the United States, after about twenty-five years of fairly fruitful work by Mayo, Whyte, and Hughes, the subject lost its glamour—although obviously not its intellectual or practical significance. American sociologists left the subject.[30]

They went on to organizational analyses—under the inspiration of Chester Barnard, Max Weber, and Herbert Simon—and on to studies of the professions of medicine, law, and science. The theoretical or analytical scheme remains what is offered by the older tradition, enriched and differentiated by the new data. The change in particular subject-matters is perhaps more a product of the availability of financial support for the study of these subjects, the much greater prominence in public opinion of the learned professions and especially of the scientific profession, and the decline among intellectuals of the prestige of the working classes. Following this, sociologists in the United States returned to the lower classes—not so much to the employed "respectable" proletariat as to the unemployed, the "poor," or what was called by Marx the *Lumpenproletariat*. This

30. During the years of the depression of the 1930s, interesting investigations were made into the effects of unemployment on individual morale, family life, etc. Such studies were dropped from the agenda of sociological research when nearly full employment replaced massive unemployment.

change is partly a function of changes in the focus of attention in public opinion and in intellectual circles and of the opportunities afforded by the availability of financial support for such research. The relocation of subject-matter interest is relatively recent but thus far there is no evidence that it has affected the intellectual pattern of the central tradition.

These successions of subject-matters are never disjunctive. When a subject-matter ceases to be cultivated at a center, the cessation does not simultaneously occur at the peripheries or at secondary centers. A subject-matter tends to persist longer at the periphery than at the center. Indeed sometimes an institution in the periphery or a sub-center may persist in dealing with a certain subject-matter over a long period during which a center can pass through several fashions in subject-matter.

In Great Britain, a large proportion of the much increased volume of sociological research in the quarter of a century following the war was concerned with the working classes and the poor. This showed the strength of the British intellectual tradition—largely pre-academic—deriving from the statistical surveys of poverty of the nineteenth and early twentieth centuries, as well as of the availability of financial support for inquiries into such subject-matters. The power of this tradition in Great Britain has been so great that the analytical tradition such as has been preponderant on the Continent and in the United States has not made its way easily. The chief analytical achievement of British sociology, T. H. Marshall's *Citizenship and Social Class,* is very much an elaboration of the British tradition, formulated in more general terms than ever before. Yet this tradition has been brought into fusion with the American and Continental variants of the sociological tradition in the work of Michael Young. W. G. Runciman, and David Lockwood.

What we see from these few sketchily presented illustrations is that exogenous nonintellectual conditions or situations have indeed played a significant part in bringing subject-matters into the center of attention of sociological research. This happens because sociologists are citizens of their societies and are concerned with what they think are its practical problems; it also happens because governments and philanthropic bodies are more inclined to support sociological research when it deals with a "practical problem," i.e., studies a condition with which government and public opinion are concerned, than they are to support research which does not appear to be practical. Nonetheless, these variations in the choice of subject-matters do not impose parallel variations in the analytical framework of sociology which is contained in the central tradition. This traditional framework of sociology has extraordinary continuity and stability. At the same time, this framework remains vague and ambiguous in its major categories; this gives it flexibility and assimilative capacity. That is why it has been able to incorporate into itself certain exogenous intellectual traditions. These exogenous traditions when they are incorporated sometimes only involve making more explicit elements in the central tradition itself, as in the case of the incorporation of some elements of the "science of religion" into sociology. In other instances, as in the case of the elaboration of the "theory of culture," they are compelling the jettisoning of the Darwinian, Deweyan-Freudian tradition that cultural works are the products of the efforts of the individual organism to survive in a dangerous environment.

The Form of a Sociological Work

The strength of a dominant tradition of sociology vis-à-vis exogenous intellectual traditions and practical situations is evident also in the character of its influence on contemporary research.

A tradition can be influential in an academic discipline in several ways. In one way, the most recent period's output of works provides the immediate point of departure for the next stage of research; the works produced in that most recent period were produced from a point of departure constituted by a body of works produced still earlier. The works of the relatively remote past—the past of the middle distance—are influential either through having served in their own time as a point of departure for the step which followed or through the constitution of a framework of concepts or variables and fundamental problems within which the works which constitute a sequence of successive points of departure are produced. The latter are the monuments of the subject, not merely honorific monuments, but effective ones. It is conceivable that these monuments are unknown by name to those who work within the framework to which the monuments have contributed. There is nothing especially damaging about this except for the shamefulness of ignorance and disregard of intellectual ancestry and indebtedness. It is often said that what is relevant for the development of knowledge in a given field is after all contained in the latest stage of the tradition, that is, in the detailed research or the detailed analytical paper which provides the immediate point of departure for the next stage of the subject. But nutriment is also to be obtained from constant recourse to the monument.

There are thus two patterns in the relationship of present work in a field to the tradition of that field. These two patterns correspond to the patterns prevailing in the natural sciences and in sociology respectively.

The most common form of scientific work is the short journal article which states the problem, which formulates and locates the hypothesis in relation to what has been established and what has been left open by previous research, which describes the arrangements of research or experimental procedure, reports the observations or experimental results, and proposes the modification of previous hypotheses or beliefs required by the results of the reported investigation. There are also synthetic, compendious summaries of existing theoretical and experimental work which intend not to establish new knowledge but to consolidate and order what is known in a broad field. These might be monographs with an element of originality of interpretation of what has been demonstrated by research or they might be textbooks which summarize what students and research workers at a certain level of their scientific development are expected to know.

In sociology, parallel to the differences in the procedures and intellectual structure of the subject in comparison with the sciences, works tend to take the following forms: monographic treatises describing a particular subject-matter, e.g., a territorially delineated sector of society, a group or a stratum or a profession. They sometimes take the physical form of the monograph of twenty thousand words or more frequently a full-length book of one hundred thousand words. (The latter is often only an expansion of the former.) They contain much descriptive data with analytical remarks and usually, at the end, a general interpretation of the phenomenon in relation to its larger setting. These monographs or monographs-within-books are usually directed at a problem—relationships between variables—although their ostensible point of departure is a particular subject-matter, e.g., the medical profession in a given city or country, or a particular process, e.g., social mobility within a given country. There are also monographs which seek to deal with problems: these begin with an attempt to explain a major phenomenon, e.g., specifically capitalistic acquisitive behavior as in Max Weber's *Protestant Ethic*, the causes of various kinds of suicide as in Durkheim's *Suicide*, the effect of political campaigns on voting choice as in Lazarsfeld's *The People's Choice*, or the influence on the educational accomplishment of school children of the intellectual composition of their school class as in Coleman's *Equality of Educational Opportunity*.

There is also the journal article—corresponding to the scientific paper—which summarizes the existing state of knowledge on a particular problem, formulates a hypothesis, presents the data which report observations made by the author or by others—and then attempts to harmonize the resultant interpretation of the data with previous interpretations.

There are also essays which clarify, refine, and differentiate particular ideas—concepts, categories, processes, variables, etc.— without close reference to observations except for illustrative purposes, and which put forward hypotheses about the relationships among variables only incidentally or illustratively.

There are also comprehensive theoretical treatises which present "all" the major concepts or variables which the author believes relevant to sociology as a whole as well as some hypotheses about the behavior of these variables under different conditions. One might mention here works as various as Weber's *Wirtschaft und Gesellschaft*, Parsons' *The Social System*, and Homan's *Social Behavior*.

These theoretical treatises verge at their lower levels into textbooks which cover all the concepts of variables and present illustrative data and some hypotheses. Such works as Kingsley Davis and Wilbert Moore's *Society: An Analysis*, H. M. Johnson's *Sociology*, or Park and Burgess' *Introduction to the Science of Sociology* are representative. Sociological textbooks usually contain much descriptive material from monographs and articles but very little rigorously established, widely accepted knowledge—unlike textbooks in the natural sciences.

Finally, there are collections of essays of single authors; this form has become relatively widespread since the end of the Second World War. Indeed collections of essays by Parsons and Merton have been among the most influential books of the past two decades. The essays have usually been analyses of concepts, elaborations of themes, rather than scientific papers.[31] Such collections are also found in the sciences, but for the most part they are monumental in intention, being the works of very distinguished figures, living or dead, and many of the papers published in these collections have already played a great part in the development of these subjects and have outlived their immediate usefulness. They have a different function from the collection of papers in sociology because of the longer life of the sociological paper.

The function of the books composed of sociological essays discloses a major difference between the characteristic patterns of the growth of the knowledge in sociology and in the sciences. In the latter, the most important means of speedy, non-oral communication are journal papers and, more recently, preprints. The journal paper in its original form is important in the production of scientific research; when reprinted in book form, it is likely only to have historical interest. The "preprint" in science is the very opposite of the reprinting of sociological essays in book form. The scientific "preprint" is a product of the speed with which the tradition of a scientific field is being modified or supplemented; the reprint of a sociological essay is a function of the continued dominance of the tradition, particularly the dominance of the monuments.

The essay can be reprinted in a sociological book because it has a long life, whereas a scientific paper must perform its function within a relatively short time after its moment of publication.[32] The difference

31. The collection of essays is different from the "reader" which in sociology is a more "scientific" type of textbook than the conventional compendium of discursive expositions of concepts and illustrative data. The "reader" as a textbook is usually a collection of research reports which have appeared as articles in journals. The editors, unlike the authors of textbooks in scientific subjects, do not consolidate existing knowledge as it bears on particular problems; they simply present the sources—journal articles—from which in scientific textbooks interpretative consolidation is made.

32. The tendency, now widespread among social scientists, to distribute their writings in mimeographed, dittoed, or xeroxed form before publication is

might be accounted for by the much sharper focus of research in the sciences, by the more consensual perception and interpretation of the results of any particular piece of research, and by the more immediate response in the form of further investigation of the problems which that particular piece of research raises.

The completion of a piece of research in science entails its publication. Scientific knowledge is a collective possession; the results of research become accredited as scientific knowledge when they are affirmed by other qualified scientists. Discovery, therefore, integrally entails publication. To launch on a campaign of discovery is to launch on a course which requires publication as the temporary end-state of the act of discovery. A work of research which does not contribute to the pool of knowledge is a wasted effort and failure to publish results which might be right is as much of a waste as wrong results. If the delay in publication is long, then the results of research will usually be rendered out-of-date. They will have been superseded by the results of the research of someone else. This high probability of supersession is a function of the greater precision of the formulation of problems in the sciences and of the greater specificity of formulation and the greater concentration of effort on particular problems in the natural sciences.

There are relatively few instances of the very specific articulation of successive research papers in sociology in comparison with any field of comparable scope in the natural sciences. This is partly a function of the much lower degree of specialization and the much less differentiated division of labor in sociology than in the sciences. The less differentiated division of labor in sociology is in turn a function of the much greater quantity of literature produced in any field of the sciences and of the closely related phenomenon, the larger number of

---

not an effort to inform the rest of the social science community of results achieved and verified, but rather the opposite. The distributed paper is a preliminary version, and the distribution is an effort to elicit criticisms; it is an acknowledgment of the tentative and uncertain status of what is presented in the paper circulated. It is also a product of the affluence of university departments and of the generosity of research grants which could offer the financial means for such reproduction and distribution of preliminary results. There is little fear in sociology of "anticipation" by other workers engaged in research on similar problems; this is one of the considerations underlying the production and circulation of "preprints" in the natural sciences.

persons working in any special field in the sciences. But without the specificity of focus and the greater consensus about the crucial problem which is characteristic of the natural sciences, the number of workers and the volume of literature on a given problem would not be decisive in abbreviating the life span of a scientific paper.

This greater concentration of minds on particular, specifically delineated problems results in a more rapid obsolescence of works in the natural sciences than in sociology. That is why the book made up of essays published over a period of twenty years can be an esteemed sociological work, as it has been in the case of the collections of Parsons' and Merton's essays, while its counterpart would make rather little sense in the natural sciences.

It would be wrong to describe the movement of any specialized branch of the natural sciences as linear. Nonetheless, movement in those fields is more linear than it is in sociology. In sociology, the function of a classic is not to be assimilated, surpassed, and rendered out-of-date as in the natural sciences, but to be elaborated, adapted, put into a new idiom, applied to a new situation. The results of research support an illustration and confirm the plausibility of a general theme; there are very few instances of a demonstration or confirmation of a general proposition. There is little linear movement in sociology: there is an intensification of intimacy. That is why the monuments, the classic works of sociology, continue to intrigue sociologists. I do not know whether it must necessarily be so for all times in the future. That, however, is the way it has been.

There are many reasons for this persisting value of the classics of sociology. In the first place, the greatest sociologists are plainly much better than most sociologists. Sociologists, despite the disparagement to whch they are often subjected, do have a sense of quality and they appreciate broad perspective and the deeply penetrating insight. This is not the whole story. These broad perspectives and penetrating insights are into social situations which interest sociologists. They are directed towards relatively contemporary situations. After all, sociological theory has mainly been about modern Western society; other societies have been treated for purposes of a clearer delineation of the features of modern society, and modern Western society despite marked changes over the course of the past century still has sufficient identity with what it was a century or three-quarters of a century ago for observations made then to be pertinent to the understanding of present-day society. Furthermore, because of the disjunctiveness of particular investigations, the results of any single investigation, not being articulated with other investigations, the same subjects have no coercive influence over theoretical interpretation. Sociological theory has been relatively free from domination by the results of research. Theory has not been rendered out-of-date by research because research is not consulted by theory, partly because of the discreteness of many investigations into the same subject-matters.

Indeed it is because of the chaos of the results of research that the famous theorists are clung to; they are sources of intellectual order in the midst of intellectual disorder. Such sense as can be made of the variegated results of so many disjunctive inquiries can only be made with the aid of the leading theorists. Their ideas, however they might be judged *sub specie aeternitatis,* are the best ideas available to sociologists and they are in fact often very helpful for the task to which they are summoned. The movement is not circular. Theory might help in the interpretation of the results of particular investigations or in synthesizing those results, but the theory is not correspondingly enriched or made more precise. The continuing independence of theory from research or at least the very loose relations between them explains to some extent why the classics of sociological theory do not become absolute in the way in which great works of natural science do.

The Profession of Sociology

Whereas at the turn of the century there were very few persons who called themselves sociologists anywhere in the world and even fewer who made a livelihood from it, there are now many thousands who teach what is called sociology in lists of courses offered in universities and thousands who are employed by governmental bodies, independent research institutions, market research organizations, public opinion surveying organizations, industrial firms, hospitals, military organizations, to do research which is generally classified as sociological. Most of the colleges and universities in the Western world now provide teaching in sociology and so do many in Latin America, the Far East, South Asia, and Africa south of the Sahara. Most of them permit sociology to serve alone or in one combination or another as a qualification for a degree. There are at least twenty-five journals in the major languages which have the word "sociology" or "sociological" in their titles or subtitles. There are about thirty national professional sociological societies, and in some countries there are also more specialized professional associations which regard themselves as covering a section of sociology. There is an international association with affiliated societies in every continent. Sociology has become a subject of a profession formed around a rather loosely delineated body of learning and a more or less common intellectual interest.

One consequence of the formation of this profession is a movement towards homogeneity. National differences still exist among the dominant types of sociology—differences in theoretical inclinations, preferred subjects of research, favored techniques, etc.—but there has also formed a large common sociological culture—just as there is such a culture, despite specialization, within each country with many sociologists.

This common culture is the result of the fusion of productions of major writers from different countries into a common pool and of the ascendancy of the sociologists of a particular country—in the last three decades, those of the United States. It is true that sociology written in the English language enjoys the advantages of an assymetrically greater accessibility. Sociologists everywhere read what is written by sociologists in English, but sociologists in the English-speaking world read less of what is written in most other countries. Efforts are made to overcome this by publication in English, e.g., the *Acta Sociologica* of the Scandinavian countries and *Sociologica Nederlandica* which brings representative works of Dutch sociologists before those sociologists who cannot read Dutch. It is probably true that on average the sociologists of the English-speaking world are less capable of reading French and German than their predecessors were seventy-five years ago. Nonetheless they probably have more of European sociology more easily available to them through translations and personal meetings than did their predecessors.

The professional cultivation of sociology has not made sociology self-sufficient. It has continued to draw upon other intellectual traditions, both academic and nonacademic. In each country sociology has also found an audience outside of professional sociologists. Before sociology became institutionally established, the audience of sociological writings was inevitably lay to a very large extent. Comte and Spencer wrote for all educated and earnest persons. In the early years of sociology at Chicago, the intended audience was both lay and professional, although not always in the same writings. This bifurcation became more pronounced through the 1920s. *Middletown* was written for both lay and professional audiences; so were the books in the Carnegie Corporation's series on "Americanization" by Park, Thomas, and others. Nonetheless, most writings by sociologists were intended for study by other sociologists. In the 1930s *Recent Social Trends* was intended for the two audiences simultaneously; so was *The American Dilemma* which although written by a Swede was very much an American sociological work. While more and more sociology was being written exclusively for a professional audience, books like *The Lonely Crowd* were obviously intended as much for a lay as a professional audience. The writings of Horkheimer, Adorno, Habermas, Schelsky, and Dahrendorf in Germany certainly have not been intended only for a professional audience. Much of the work of Raymond Aron is likewise intended for an audience wider than students of sociology and their teachers.

Despite the fact that sociology in the English language has shown a potentiality of isolating itself through its ponderous and inexact language and stylistic barbarism the isolation has not in fact occurred. The curiosity of the educated classes outside of sociology has grown as their stylistic intolerance has diminished. Perhaps they no longer know any better, perhaps they do not mind—the rest of the academic profession now writes in a style not too different from that of sociology at its worst. In any case, sociology has not been rendered inaccessible to nonsociologists by reason of its astonishing literary qualities. It is not even likely that the mathematization of sociology which is in prospect—in some measure at least—will isolate sociology from the increasingly mathematically educated classes. As the years pass, with the proportion of the population which has attended university still increasing, the proportion which has studied some sociology at university is still increasing. This creates a lay audience with a smattering of the knowledge possessed by professional sociologists.

The earlier generations of sociologists in the present century were for the most part a fairly optimistic lot of men. Max Weber was rather exceptional. They assumed that knowledge itself was a good, they assumed that sociology was on the right path towards the development of a better knowledge of society, and they thought that society would be correspondingly improved as it guided itself through taking into consideration knowledge created and provided by sociologists. The institutional establishment of sociology was intended to further the realization of all three of these desirable ends. Institutional establishment has certainly occurred in nearly all its aspects and probably beyond the capacities of the sociologists attracted to the profession and hence beyond the knowledge which they have been able to create.

There are dangers to a society the expectations of which are greater than its resources, economic and cognitive. Truths are expected of sociology which sociology has not yet produced and which it might not produce in the near future. A society places itself at risk when it entrusts itself—even if only in small measure—to lightly attained opinions which pass as knowledge. Institutional establishment only strengthens the position of such opinions; it does not necessarily correct them.

The Dominance of Tradition and the Growth of Sociology

As sociology has become more institutionalized, it has become more prolific. The institutionalization of training has produced a human product with a mastery of some techniques of research, a modicum of a sociological culture, and an ethos which prizes research. The institutionalization of research—the institutional provision of opportunities, funds, and employment, of facilities for research and publication, the standardization of research procedures, and the general approbation of research within intellectual institutions and the larger society all contribute to an increased volume of research. This is true in the United States above all but it is also true of numerous countries where the contemporary type of research is a much newer growth, whether it is either a new implantation or a renewed practice of an older tradition.

This change has taken place under the auspices of "science." Sociologists increasingly believe that their work falls under the tradition of science and that it is one member of the family of sciences. The old discussions regarding the differences between the natural and the social sciences have evaporated with the arguments which demonstrated that sociology had a rightful place in "the classification of the sciences." The discussion as to whether sociology is a "natural science" is cold mutton. Part of the conception which sociologists have of themselves is expressed in their preferred form of publication, namely, the paper published in a professional journal. The bibliography of sociology is increasingly made up of papers in journals in which the state of the problem and its literature are reviewed, a hypothesis formulated, data presented, and an interpretation made. With the multiplication of the literature, the size of the subcommunity of sociologists becoming larger in almost every subfield of sociology, a sociologist can now spend most of his sociological career as a specialist on juvenile delinquents, military organization, the aged, the mass media, penal institutions, urbanization, the police, narcotics addicts, etc. Many of the specialized fields acquire and establish an identity of their own with their own elites and counter-elites, their own culture, sometimes their own journals. The literature of the other specialized fields becomes more and more remote from them. As sociologists become "professionals," as so many proudly aver, specialization is accepted, sometimes with the melancholy resignation counseled in *Wissenschaft als Beruf,* sometimes with an air of self-congratulation. The new professionals of sociology are a tough-minded lot, they shun armchairs, they speak of questionnaires as "instruments," they speak of "research technology," they are conversant with the language of computers, they are condescending towards "grand theory," negotiations for grants for research projects are frequently on their minds and lips. They are doggedly optimistic about building a science of sociology and, as a science under present-day conditions, it must in their view be specialized and it must be cumulative.

There are limits to specialization in sociology as there are in the natural sciences; as a result of these limits, specialization which is necessary is not likely to be injurious. The limits are not those which would arise from the sterility of an uninhibited narrowing of the focus of attention—of "knowing more and more about less and less." They are limits engendered by the institutionalization which has made specialization possible within sociology. This specialization is not likely to disintegrate the community of sociologists.

There has formed within each country—and increasingly between countries—an intellectual community, the members of which read each other's works, some of them even before publication. To some extent they read more or less the same body of literature; they exist within departments which are diverse in the specialized interests of their members, but as teachers jointly responsible for the students' education in sociology they have to look beyond their own specialized research.

It is of course true that the large number of sociologists within a large national sociological community, and internationally, does permit the formation of relatively self-centered subcommunities of specialists in such fields as educational sociology, gerontological sociology, etc.

These specialized fields do not however wholly isolate their members from those of other specialized fields. No field fails to impinge on another equally specialized field. Thus, for example, a sociologist studying the aged cannot avoid the necessity for studying the literature on the family, on urbanization and demography, on geriatric medicine and medical sociology, etc.; and the same holds for every other field of sociological specialization. As a result, the consensus as regards techniques of research, findings, and lines of interpretation extends beyond the boundaries of any subcommunity of specialists into adjacent subcommunities of specialists. In this way a series of overlaps links the entire profession of sociology. Specialization of sociology has not yet progressed to the point, nor is it likely to do so in the foreseeable future, where one field cuts itself off entirely from its intellectual neighbors or from the sociological family as a whole.

There are, furthermore, limits in specialization imposed by the dominance within the institutional system of the tradition which is constantly reexhibited in the sociological essay, which is common, and in the less frequent sociological treatise. After all, the institutionalization has occurred in universities, and in universities abstract ideas have a pride of place, however hard pressed they are by the demands of specialization. If a postgraduate student has done sociology as an undergraduate, he has acquired a sociological culture which is common to sociologists; even if he has done a different subject as an undergraduate and begins his sociological studies in a situation committed to specialized research, he must nonetheless absorb a certain amount of the common sociological culture which is made up of the dominant traditions and some of the subsidiary traditions.

Sociological training is much less specialized than sociological research. A student must cover a much wider body of literature than that directly pertinent to the field in which he will do his research. Sociology now being an academic subject, the leading research workers are also teachers of sociology: and this means that they have often to teach subjects which are somewhat outside their specialized field of research. This, too, has a unifying effect, although it does not create or maintain a completely common sociological culture. The fact that sociology is no longer the work of amateurs but is taught and largely practiced within universities in which "theory" has prestige despite the criticism directed against particular theories, means that the prestige-conferring "classics" are taught in practically all universities. For better or for worse, there is a *tronc commun* from which sociologists derive some of their intellectual dignity. Durkheim, Weber, Parsons, Merton, and lesser lights are repeatedly quoted and invoked over a very wide range of specialized fields of research.

These famous sociologists are so generally recurred to, not just because those who have recourse to them wish to avoid the appearance of being no better than intellectual hewers of wood and drawers of water. They are brought in because there is a deeply felt need among sociologists to be part of an ongoing intellectual tradition which has among its other merits that of helping to explain one's particular findings in the light of certain major variables, such as solidarity and conflict, equality and inequality, deference and presumption, authority and rejection, charisma and rational and traditional routine, bureaucracy, etc., and the vague, unarticulated interpretations which are associated with them. Contemporary sociologists are less the creators of their tradition than they are its beneficiaries and prisoners.[33] They cannot escape from their traditions. This might hold sociology back from making marked scientific progress but at the same time it enables

33. One of the difficulties is that we cannot imagine anything beyond variations on the themes set by the great figures of nineteenth- and twentieth-century sociology. The fact that the conception of "postindustrial society" is an amalgam of what St. Simon, Comte, Tocqueville, and Weber furnished to our imaginations is evidence that we are confined to an ambiguously defined circle which is more impermeable than it ought to be.

it to cope with otherwise bewildering results of empirical research and from the loss of perspective which specialization would otherwise engender.

It might be said that the unifying classics of sociology are so important to its contemporary practitioners because sociology is not at present a real science. If sociology were a science, its masterworks would have become so assimilated into the flow of sociological work that their accomplishment would have been taken for granted. The classics of sociology remain important because sociological analysis is so much devoted to the elucidation of certain major themes which continue to dominate the attention of sociologists, partly because the great figures drew attention to them, and partly because experience and the concern which they have molded have shown them to be the proper subjects of study.

An effective intellectual tradition is not merely a timeless gallery of works nor is it merely a sequence in time of works arranged by later scholars. An effective intellectual tradition is a linkage of works through influence exercised over time. This is the kind of tradition which obtains in the real sciences and it also obtains in sociology. In the real sciences, intellectual influence is usually fairly immediate—there are exceptions—and the works which are enduringly constitutive of tradition function through entering anonymously into the continuing flow; they lose their identity in so doing. Such tradition-setting works provide a framework of concepts which sets research tasks—and they provide the next stage of research, particular hypotheses to be revised, rejected, or confirmed, and observations which may be accepted as given or which require reinterpretation. In sociology the situation is both similar and different.

It is similar in the sense that major works provide a framework of concepts which set tasks for research. It is different in that particular investigations are only loosely and vaguely linked with their guiding and legitimating ideas and are also only very loosely linked with other particular investigations of the same subject-matter which have gone just before.

Sociological theory does not quite stand still, but such progress as it makes is not the result of revisions in the light of accumulated observations, rigorously conducted and analyzed.

Many years ago I wrote about the "discontinuity" of sociological development; I had in mind among other things the flightiness of sociologists who take up a subject, cultivate it for a time, and then drop it before the subject has been brought to intellectual fruition. I had in mind as instances the study of human ecology and of primary groups. I also had in mind the more specific unconnectedness of exact investigations of ostensibly identical subject-matters or problems. This latter type of discontinuity between specialized investigations of what are alleged to be the same variables persists relatively undiminished, despite the greatly increased "scientificness" of sociology.

It is at just this point that one of the chief difficulties of present-day sociology lies. To take up where one predecessor left off entails the acceptance of the delineation of the variables studied by the predecessor in exactly the form in which they were put by the predecessor. The point of leaving off in sociology is difficult to locate because of the vagueness in the definition of variables and the vagueness of interpretations of data. The categories involved in interpretation, i.e., the theoretical categories, are always broader and vaguer than the categories in which the data were collected or the observations made. The latter vary much from one investigator to another, even though they believe themselves to be working on the same problem. When, for good reasons or for poor ones, each subsequent investigator "improves" on his predecessor's working delineation of the relevant variables, by asking different questions or using different indicators, then articulation, comparison, and accumulation become difficult. What does in fact happen is that a somewhat different variable replaces the one previously studied; they are both presumed to represent the same thing when such is not actually the case; careful attempts to collate them and to make the results coherent are often frustrated. There are many other causes for this disarticulation: different populations studied; different criteria of classification, etc. One additional source of this difficulty lies in the "great ideas" of sociology; they obviously refer to very important things—otherwise they would not hold the attention of sociologists as they have for so many decades—but they are extremely ambiguous and they are resistant to authoritative clarification.

The unity which transcends the passage of time and the growing specialization in sociology rests on this common preoccupation with a relatively small number of "key words." The "key words" and the ideas which they evoke have become indelibly imprinted on the sociological tradition—so much so that they can never be merely an honorific decoration. They have become constitutive of sociological analysis. They have formed the sociological mind. Theory is recognized as such by the presence of those "key words" in all their misty and simple grandeur. Their adduction in dealing with the results of empirical investigations into particular contemporary situations is an essential phase of interpretation.

It would be better if sociology had a much more differentiated set of categories, a much more differentiated set of names for distinguishable things. It would be better if it could name many more things and name them in agreed and recognizable ways. Above all, it would be a great improvement if the general terms of theories could become more intimately and more rigorously linked with the particular things which are observed. But this will involve moving from research to theory as well as from theory to research and from theory to theory.

There is no necessary reason why this should be impossible. It is simply difficult. It has not been done before and the deficiencies of institutional establishment cannot be adduced to explain the failure. For a time, at the height of their collaboration, Merton and Lazarsfeld at Columbia seemed to be moving in the right direction. But this moment has passed and the prospect seems less bright than it was.

Now this does not mean that all sociology is prattle or that even if it never becomes truly scientific that it is not a very worthy activity as an understanding, intimate type of history. Its theories are not superfluous just because they have not been scientifically confirmed. Some of them—or at least parts of them—do render events more intelligible, they do illuminate the associations which research discovers among particular facts. They are not arbitrary; sometimes they contain exceptionally wise insight into human affairs. Some of the theories make more sense out of the diversity of events than others, but even then much is left in a blurred condition.

Institutional establishment has not been able to overcome this difficulty although it has provided conditions for the amelioration of a situation which was once worse in this respect than it is at present.

The benefits of institutional establishment are real but there are vices which it cannot cure and errors which it cannot prevent. It cannot make wise men and women out of fools; it has not been able to prevent the outcropping of antinomian ideology which puts itself forward as serious sociology. Just as fruitful theoretical interpretation requires good judgment and much learning so does institutional establishment. Without persons committed to the traditional ethos of learning, institutional establishment is powerless. At its best, institutional establishment can foster the mutual criticism which is needed for the improvement of the present situation: it can by its support of continuous teaching and research keep the challenge and demand alive. It can keep the stage set for the closer approximation to what now appears to be the desirable next steps. But these steps cannot be set in motion by the design or the by-products of institutions. For that, imagination on the order of genius is required, proceeding from the tradition which we now have. This tradition might be an encumbrance but it must also be the point of departure for the next steps which are urgently needed for the improvement of sociology.